BROADCASTING PLURALISM AND DIVERSITY

Broadcasting Pluralism and Diversity is a study of the policy and regulatory measures relating to the promotion of media diversity in three jurisdictions: the United Kingdom, the United States, and Australia. A central focus of the book is regulation of media ownership and control, and, taking an historical approach, the book argues that early policy and regulatory decisions continue to have a significant influence on current reforms. Whilst policy and reform debates focus on ownership and control measures, the book also argues that such measures cannot be considered in isolation from other regulatory instruments, and that a holistic regulatory approach is required. As such content regulation and competition regulation are also considered. Underlying the study is the contention that much of the policy informing pluralism and diversity regulation, although making reference to the importance of the media's role in the democratic process, has also been skewed by a futile focus on the different regulatory treatment of the press and broadcasting, which is adversely influencing current policy debates. The book argues that a different approach, using the public sphere concept, needs to be adopted and used as a measure against which regulatory reform in the changing media environment can be assessed.

Broadcasting Pluralism and Diversity

A Comparative Study of Policy and Regulation

Lesley Hitchens

·HART·
PUBLISHING

OXFORD AND PORTLAND, OREGON
2006

Published in North America (US and Canada) by
Hart Publishing
c/o International Specialized Book Services
920 NE 58th Avenue, Suite 300
Portland, OR 97213-3786
USA
Tel: +1 503 287 3093 or toll-free: (1) 800 944 6190
Fax: +1 503 280 8832
E-mail: orders@isbs.com
Website: www.isbs.com

Hart Publishing, 16C Worcester Place, Oxford, OX1 2JW
Telephone: +44 (0)1865 517530 Fax: +44 (0)1865 510710
E-mail: mail@hartpub.co.uk
Website: http://www.hartpub.co.uk

British Library Cataloguing in Publication Data
Data Available
ISBN-13: 978–1–84113–214–3 (hardback)
ISBN-10: 1–84113–214–4 (hardback)

Typeset by Hope Services, Abingdon
Printed and bound in Great Britain by
Biddles Ltd, king's Lynn, Norfolk

PREFACE

This book is a comparative study of media pluralism and diversity. In writing this book, one of the dilemmas has been the title, because, although a major focus of the book is regulation and reform of ownership and control of media, particularly broadcasting, it would have been misleading to have used the term 'ownership and control' in the title. For diversity, we can not rely simply on ownership and control regulation. This is why the book also examines other broadcasting regulatory measures. Indeed, it is argued that a combination of regulatory measures, which must be considered in relation to one another, is necessary for the protection of pluralism and diversity. Thus, but at the risk of opacity, the title focuses on the policy outcomes sought by these various aspects of broadcasting regulation. The terms 'pluralism' and 'diversity' are more common in the United Kingdom, whilst 'diversity' alone is more commonly used in the United States and Australia – hence another dilemma for the title – but the terms and the sense in which they are used in this book are described in Chapter One.

Two such dilemmas might be considered sufficient for one title, but a third presented itself as well – whether to refer to 'media' or 'broadcasting'. Although the book's focus is broadcasting, other media are clearly relevant, but the term 'media' might have conveyed a much broader subject matter. It is not possible to discuss broadcasting ownership and control regulation without also referring to the press – the three jurisdictions examined here all regulate cross-media interests – but the book does not otherwise examine the press. Another difficulty with using the term 'broadcasting' is that it risks being thought of as a specific type of electronic media, for example, over-the-air radio or television. However, in this book, it is used to refer to all radio and television services, and this is also explained in Chapter One. Of course, one of the current challenges for regulation in this area is how to define and/or delineate the matter for regulation: content delivery via the Internet, mobile phones and MP3-type players are undermining traditional classifications and assumptions about media. That raises another issue. Although the book does, particularly in the final chapter, consider some of the implications of this 'new media' for pluralism and diversity regulation, its primary focus is broadcasting. As such, it might be thought that this book is too concerned with old media and old debates, but the focus has been very deliberate. As the current reform debates show (examined in Chapter Seven), the rhetoric of new media is an attractive handle for governments and rule-makers keen to distance themselves from difficult decisions about media regulation. However, if there is to be an appropriate policy and regulatory response to the changing media environment, then it is important to understand how the current regulatory tools have developed and operated, and the policy basis for those rules. If pluralism and diversity is really the concern, then it is necessary to avoid simplistic 'old' and 'new' media divisions, in order to undertake a genuine inquiry into how the media regulatory framework should be adapted to meet the changes in media delivery and use. Indeed, it is one of the contentions of this book, that the developments in media delivery do not render redundant the need for regulation, particularly when a normative case for media regulation can be put forward, as I try to do in Chapter Two.

As the reader will observe, there is no consistent approach to the treatment of the topics. In some chapters, where it is more appropriate to the subject matter, the material is treated on a jurisdiction by jurisdiction basis, but in other chapters, the material is organised by aspects of the topic, with perhaps a brief overview of each jurisdiction. There is also no attempt to trace every relevant regulatory detail, rather regulatory measures are intended to illustrate the type of regulation which might contribute to pluralism and diversity promotion. Nevertheless, because this book has a narrower focus, than say a comparative work on broadcasting regulation generally, it has been able to be more detailed than might otherwise have been possible, and, hence, to illustrate more fully the type of regulation under discussion. For a different reason, the discussion, in Chapter Three, of the history of ownership and control regulation in the three jurisdictions is particularly detailed, tracing as it does the history of that regulation from its origins. A common argument in the current ownership and control reform debates is that such regulation is not suitable for the current media environment. However, if one examines closely the history of such regulation, it is clear that the design of the regulation was often the product of poorly thought-out policy and the need to accommodate particular interest groups. As such the historical account in Chapter Three takes the opportunity to examine, across the three jurisdictions, each stage in the development of ownership and control regulation to demonstrate this assertion.

Whether or not I have succeeded in the aims for this book, a number of people have at least tried to help me on the way. I am particularly grateful to those who read and commented on chapters: Eric Barendt, Gianluca Gardini, Tom Gibbons, Zhongdong Niu, and Derek Wilding. Particular thanks goes to Gianluca Gardini, who read all the chapters, and whose enthusiasm for discussing the issues explored in the book, whilst on a research stay in Australia, from the University of Bologna, sustained my interest in the final stages of writing. Of course, all the weaknesses and errors remain my responsibility. I am grateful also to Zhongdong Niu for providing me with some valuable references for Chapter Five, and to Emma Armson for clarifying a point on UK takeover law. Jonathan Gadir and Cathy Hunter provided valuable research assistance at various stages of the book. Simon Curtis deserves particular acknowledgement: although not providing research assistance on this book, his excellent work on other projects ensured that valuable time was created to allow me to concentrate on finishing this book. There are institutional debts to be acknowledged also. Birkbeck College, London, provided me with an office and other assistance during a research visit to the UK. The Senate House

Library, University of London, through the assistance of Catherine Phillpotts, was especially helpful in providing me with particular materials. My Faculty assisted with research funds. There have been a number of other colleagues, past and present, who have provided help in many and varied ways, and to them I am grateful, especially David Brennan, Andrew Choo, Simone Degeling, Fiona Macmillan, and Dallal Stevens. Hart Publishing—Richard Hart and Mel Hamill—have ensured that the production process has been efficient and pleasant.

The book has tried to state the law for the three jurisdictions as at February 2006, but it has been possible to include a couple of further developments in the brief note below.

Lesley Hitchens
Sydney, 2006

Note on Further Developments

Australia

As anticipated in Chapter One (pp 4-5), the government has announced its intention to introduce legislation to reform ownership and control into Parliament in 2006. In March 2006, a discussion paper on options for media reform was issued,[1] and in July, the Minister, Senator Coonan, issued a statement announcing the government's legislative intentions.[2] Contrary to expectations, although consistent with statements made by Senator Coonan in 2005,[3] the Government's legislative plan involves not only changes to media ownership, but also to other aspects of broadcasting regulation, including digital television; although it has to be said that these proposals are still relatively modest, and illustrate once again the accommodations which seem to be considered necessary in Australian broadcasting policy.[4] With regard to media ownership reform, the proposed changes are consistent with previous indications of intention.[5] Foreign ownership rules will be removed, although the media industry will remain as a 'sensitive sector' under the

[1] *Meeting the Digital Challenge: Reforming Australia's Media in the Digital Age* (March 2006), http://www.dcita.gov.au/__data/assets/pdf_file/37572/Media_consultation_paper_Final_.pdf. Despite the discussion paper, the policy making process was generally consistent with past reform processes (see Chapter Three). Only a month was given for responses to the discussion paper and there was no follow-up paper in light of the submissions received, only the announcement of the government's plans.
[2] Senator H Coonan, 'New Media Framework for Australia', Media Release 068/06 (13 July 2006), http://www.minister.dcita.gov.au/media/media_releases/new_media_framework_for_australia.
[3] See Chapter Seven at pp 299-300.
[4] See, Chapter One at p 28. The government couldn't have avoided making some changes to the digital broadcasting and datacasting regime, as some of current regulatory arrangements were due to expire at the start of 2007, and it was clear that the planned date for switch-off of analogue (2008) would not be met: see further Chapter One, at pp 28-30.
[5] See Chapter Seven at p 299.

government's foreign investment policy. Cross-media rules will be relaxed to permit mergers provided that no fewer than five independent 'voices' remain in metropolitan markets and four in regional markets. Although the government intends to introduce the legislation this year, the proposals have been put forward with very little detail. This may have been intentional to give the government room to respond to any significant opposition. Despite its control of both Houses of the Federal Parliament, the government may face opposition from some Members of Parliament who represent regional interests.[6] It is also clear that the reforms might not come into force for some time, since the government intends that the changes will only become effective upon Proclamation on a date to be announced in 2007.

With regard to digital television, the government has announced changes that will relax some of the previous restrictions on digital, which have inhibited its development and contributed to lack of consumer interest.[7] The most significant changes are that commercial television broadcasters will be allowed to provide one standard definition multichannel, although only from 2009, with full multichannelling after the analogue signal has been switched-off. In addition, current requirements to simulcast in high definition standard will be removed, leaving broadcasters free to meet their high definition quota by providing other programming. The current genre restrictions on the national broadcasters' multichannels will be removed. The spectrum currently allocated to datacasting will be allocated to two new digital channels with the intention that these channels will offer new services such as mobile television. The government has also announced a new date for switching off the analogue signal—2010–2012—and the development of a digital action plan to encourage digital take-up. Unless the digital action plan suggests some very pro-active measures, even this date seems unrealistic, and it is curious that the commercial broadcasters' right to multichannel, in standard definition, will only commence in 2009, since it is likely that it will be multichannelling which will drive consumer uptake.

Finally, the government has announced some changes to the anti-siphoning regime, although, again, the details are sketchy.[8] The government has stated that it will include a 'use it or lose it' requirement, whereby events on the anti-siphoning list will be removed if they have not received adequate coverage on free-to-air services. Given the problematic nature of the current regime, as discussed in Chapter Five, this is a very limited reform, although a review of the regime, to take place in 2009, has been announced.

United States
In 2003, the Federal Communications Commission (FCC) announced extensive reform of media ownership and control rules, but the new rules were stayed as a

---

[6] See Chapter One at p 5 and Chapter Seven at p 294.
[7] See Chapter One at pp 28-30.
[8] This regime protects certain sporting events for free-to-air services, see Chapter Five at pp 226-29 for details of the current regime.

result of a successful court challenge.[9] In July 2006, the FCC announced a new rule making process.[10] Although the new process will review again all the rules which were part of the 2003 process, there are no clear proposals at this stage. The *Further Notice* essentially seeks comments on the issues raised by the *Prometheus* decision. The comment period will expire in September 2006, although it is likely to be some time before the rule making is completed.

---

[9] *Prometheus Radio Project v FCC* 373 F 3d 372 (2004); see also Chapter One, at p 4 and Chapter Seven, at p 280ff.

[10] *Further Notice of Proposed Rule Making,* FCC 06-93 (24 July 2006), http://hraunfoss.fcc.gov/edocs_public/attachmatch/FCC-06-93A1.pdf.

TABLE OF CONTENTS

PART III: REGULATORY FUTURES

TABLE OF CASES

European Court of Human Rights

European Court of Justice

REGULATORY AGENCY DECISIONS

Australia

United States

TABLE OF LEGISLATION

AUSTRALIA, UNITED KINGDOM, UNITED STATES

STATUTES

SECONDARY LEGISLATION

Australia

United Kingdom

United States

TABLE OF ABBREVIATIONS

General

Convention	European Convention for the Protection of Human Rights and Fundamental Freedoms
DTV	Standard Definition Digital Television
EC	European Community
ECHR	European Court of Human Rights
EEA	European Economic Area
EPG	Electronic programme guide
EU	European Union
EU Television Directive	Council Directive 89/552/EEC of 3 October 1989, as amended (Television without Frontiers Directive)
HDTV	High Definition Digital Television
UK	United Kingdom
US	United States

Australia

ABA	Australian Broadcasting Authority
ABC	Australian Broadcasting Corporation
ABC Act	Australian Broadcasting Corporation Act 1983
ABT	Australian Broadcasting Tribunal
ACCC	Australian Competition and Consumer Commission
ACMA	Australian Communications and Media Authority
Board	Australian Broadcasting Control Board
BSA (Aus)	Broadcasting Services Act 1992
PMG	Postmaster-General
SBS Act	Special Broadcasting Service Act 1991
SBS	Special Broadcasting Service
TPA	Trade Practices Act 1974

United Kingdom

BA 1990 (UK)	Broadcasting Act 1990
BA 1996 (UK)	Broadcasting Act 1996
BBC	British Broadcasting Corporation
Broadcasting Code	OFCOM Broadcasting Code
BSC	Broadcasting Standards Commission
CC	Competition Commission

Comms Act (UK)	Communications Act 2003
DCMS	Department for Culture, Media and Sport
DTI	Department of Trade and Industry
DTT	Digital Terrestrial Television
HRA	Human Rights Act 1998
IBA	Independent Broadcasting Authority
ITA	Independent Television Authority
ITC	Independent Television Commission
ITV	Independent Television Association
Ofcom	Office of Communications
OFT	Office of Fair Trading
Oftel	Office of Telecommunications
RA	Radio Authority

United States

Comms Act (US)	Communications Act of 1934
DBS	Direct Broadcast Satellite
FCC	Federal Communications Commission
TA 1996 (US)	Telecommunications Act of 1996

Part I

Introductory Matters

1

INTRODUCTION

Media Ownership and Control—A Subject for Reform

In April 2003, the then Australian Minister for Communications, Senator Alston, suggested that it was necessary to reform existing rules which limited cross-media ownership between radio, television, and newspapers:

> Like a number of countries, Australia is currently reviewing and reforming its media regulatory framework. Globalisation, new technologies and convergence make reform essential if we are not to become a media backwater. Australians are increasingly able to draw their news and information from new outlets and through new formats. The commercial media outlets are just some of the options available to Australians. . . . Our national broadcasters have a strong voice and a growing presence across a number of platforms. There are a growing number of community broadcast licences, especially in radio. Pay television and the Internet also provide Australians with choices for their news and information requirements. Australia can no longer rely on the current ownership regime to provide the kind of flexible, innovative and responsive legislative framework that our dynamic communications situation requires to ensure its continued strength and sustainability. The existing regime penalises the 'old' media and robs them of their ability to grow and develop their businesses to the benefit of themselves and the Australian consumer.[1]

As the Minister states, Australia is only one of a number of countries which have been engaged in reviewing their media regulatory framework, particularly in relation to rules prescribing the level of media ownership and control which is permitted. Elsewhere in his speech, he makes specific mention of the United Kingdom (UK) and the United States (US). The need for reform of media ownership rules is a familiar theme, as are the justifications. These are alluded to by the Minister: technological developments have provided the public with opportunities to access more media and information; scarcity is no longer a constraint; existing rules no longer reflect the current media environment; industry must be allowed to expand so as to exploit the opportunities offered by new technologies; and regulation

---

[1] Senator R Alston, 'Regulating a Converging Environment' (speech delivered at the ABN AMRO Communications Conference 2003, Sydney, 30 April 2003) http://www.dcita.gov.au/Printer_Friendly/ 0,,0_4-2_4008-4_114143-LIVE_1,00.html, accessed 24 June 2003.

should be removed where the marketplace can provide. Indeed, it is suggested that to continue to retain present limits would actually inhibit the potential offered by new media technologies to expand the number of media services available to the public. Accompanying these statements about the necessity for reform is invariably an acknowledgement of the need to continue to ensure that the public has access to a diversity of voices, information, ideas, and opinions. Whilst Senator Alston makes passing reference to the need to ensure that 'consumers continue to have access to a diverse range of media services,'[2] and his reference to the public as 'consumers' is telling, a UK Government Consultation Paper spells this out more strongly:

> 1.2 The current ownership rules are being overtaken by a changing media landscape. In devising new, forward-looking legislation, we have two main aims. We want to encourage competition and economic growth, by being as deregulatory as possible. However, we must also allow the media to continue to perform its vital role in democratic society, as a forum for public debate and opinion.

> 1.3 We want to ensure that citizens receive a diverse range of content from a plurality of sources. . .[3]

This statement highlights also the inherent tension that is to be found in this area of media regulation and reform. On the one hand, there is a recognition that, in the public's interest, diversity must be protected, whilst, on the other, there is a desire to serve certain economic and industrial goals. However, despite enthusiastic descriptions of a media environment of abundance, reform proposals have been more about relaxation, albeit substantial, rather than total removal of existing regimes. Nor has the enthusiasm for reform, displayed by the UK, the US, and Australia, translated equally into actual change. At the time of writing, only the UK has implemented reform of media ownership regulation. The reform, introduced by the Communications Act 2003, was part of a major reshaping of the communications regulatory environment in the UK, covering both telecommunications and broadcasting. For the US and Australia, the reform process has been more convoluted. In the US, new media ownership and control rules, effecting substantial change to the existing regime, were introduced in June 2003 by the Federal Communications Commission (FCC), the regulatory body responsible for communications in the US. However, the FCC's new rules were challenged by public interest groups; the challenge was upheld and the rules were stayed.[4] The FCC will have to undertake a new rulemaking process, but at the time of writing this had not commenced. In 2002, the Australian government introduced legislation proposing major reform of the existing media ownership regime. However,

---

[2] *Ibid.*

[3] Department for Culture, Media and Sport (DCMS) and Department of Trade and Industry (DTI), *Consultation on Media Ownership Rules* (November 2001), paras 1.2–1.3.

[4] *Prometheus Radio Project v Federal Communications Commission* 373 F 3d 372 (2004). The FCC did not appeal the decision. Various industry groups sought to appeal, but the Supreme Court declined to hear the appeals: *Media General Inc v FCC* 125 S Ct 2902 (2005).

despite attempts at compromise, the legislation failed to pass through the Senate, the Australian Parliament's Upper House. The Australian Federal Parliament consists of two divisions: the House of Representatives and the Senate. It has been common for the government of the day to lack a majority in the Senate, a House of review, and for minor parties or independent senators to hold the balance of power. This can make it difficult for the government to carry legislation through the Senate unless it is willing to compromise and make changes to the proposed legislation. Parliamentary elections, for the Federal Parliament, were held in October 2004 and the government was returned to power, but this time with majority control of both Houses. It is expected that legislation to reform media ownership will be introduced into Parliament in 2006.

Despite the stalled efforts of the US and Australia to institute reform, pressure for reform will continue, and it is likely that changes will eventually be effected. Yet reform of media ownership continues to generate anxiety and controversy. Indeed, in general, media ownership and control regulation has been controversial. Although it has been a long-established regulatory instrument in jurisdictions as varied as the UK, the US, and Australia, doubts remain as to its design and effectiveness, and even its purpose. However, there is also suspicion as to whether new outlets, platforms, and technologies, such as the internet and digital broadcasting, have rendered regulation superfluous. This is as true in the UK, which has succeeded in bringing in reform, as it is in the US and Australia, where reform attempts have been impeded. The media are viewed as a resource and an arena for public debate, which is regarded as essential for the proper functioning of a democratic society, whilst regulation of control has been seen as necessary to ensure that the public has access to a variety of voices and sources of information. Rules limiting the extent of ownership and control of media have been designed to prevent any one person being able to gain undue dominance and stifle debate. However the focus of media ownership and control regulation has been radio and television, although cross-media controls have meant that newspapers have also been brought into the framework. This regulatory focus on the broadcasting media (in contrast to the print media) has contributed to the controversial nature of this regulation. The reasons put forward to justify the specific regulatory treatment of broadcasting, such as spectrum scarcity and the potential influence of broadcasting, have been subject to much debate.[5] Always controversial, these familiar justifications are now seen as having even less validity, hence the impetus for reform. However, the debate over the different treatment of broadcasting and the press has tended to skew consideration about what should be the appropriate policy and regulatory approach if the media are to provide a space for public debate. This is a matter which is explored further in Chapter Two. Media ownership regulation has been a central element of media policy. But it is not the only regulatory measure designed to promote pluralism and diversity, although it is certainly the measure which receives most attention, and where the recent moves for reform

---

[5] See EM Barendt, *Broadcasting Law: A Comparative Study* (Oxford, Clarendon Press, 1995), 3–10.

have been concentrated. Other measures such as content regulation, sectoral diversity, and competition controls will also have an impact. The focus on media ownership tends to mean that the significance of these other measures and the part they play in pluralism protection are overlooked. One of the arguments of this book is that regulatory measures which promote, or have an impact on, diversity cannot be considered in isolation from each other. Thus, it is impossible to understand the significance of media ownership reform without examining also what other relevant regulatory measures are in place. Hence, Chapters Three, Four, and Five will examine these other regulatory measures in addition to media ownership and control rules.

A major aspect, therefore, of media policy and regulation is the promotion of pluralism and diversity in recognition of the role the media play in the democratic process, and any reform of the regulatory framework needs to take that into account. This may indicate why regulatory changes in this area can be so controversial and problematic. Of course, it might be doubted how much these claims about the importance of media accord with reality. As television, in particular, is increasingly devoted to lifestyle programmes, (surely misnamed) reality television, and 'infotainment', these claims might seem rather overblown. Yet, world events of the last few years are a reminder of how important the media remain as a source of information for the public. When there are important issues affecting the national interest, the public will seek out news and current affairs which reflect this importance.[6] Recent evidence from the UK shows that news is still regarded by the public as one of the most important elements of broadcasting, and television as the most reliable news source.[7] As debased as it may often seem, it is clear that the media, and particularly broadcasting, remain an important source of information for the public. In the past few years, the UK, the US, and Australia have all experienced controversies related to the way in which their governments have processed and presented information, whilst traditions of public servants providing independent, disinterested, even unpalatable, information and advice appear to have been eroded. This has been particularly apparent in the controversy surrounding the existence of weapons of mass destruction and military intervention in Iraq. Despite the advent of the internet, and the wealth of information to which it can provide access, it may be that the traditional media, with their resources for gathering and verifying information, have an even more vital role to play than previously envisaged, in enabling the public to receive and access independent information. In assessing the continued role and design of media regulation, this renewed need for strong and independent media needs to be borne in mind.

---

[6] Early in 2003 it was reported that Australian viewers were turning to public broadcasting news and current affairs programmes and away from commercial television's current affairs programmes, which had become dominated by 'infotainment'-type reporting: D Dale, 'Calling Ray: it's time for Nine to get serious', *Sydney Morning Herald* (Sydney), 26 January 2003, 3, and 'Munro's Affair Over', *Sydney Morning Herald* (Sydney), 25–26 January 2003, 6.

[7] Ofcom, *The Communications Market 2004—Television* (August 2004), para 6.9.

Approach and Themes

This book is a study of the policy and regulatory measures relating to pluralism and diversity which have been adopted in three jurisdictions: the UK, the US, and Australia. It explores the approaches towards pluralism policy and regulation which have been developed over time, as well as current regulation and reform agendas. As such, the book is both a comparative and an historical study. It does not, however, pretend to offer an encyclopaedic collection, or detailed account, of every relevant regulatory measure across the three jurisdictions. Specific regulatory measures are presented to illustrate the various types of measure which might be relevant to pluralism and diversity. Over the past decade or so there have been a number of studies of media regulation, with particular reference to broadcasting, which have helped to generate academic interest in the study of media regulation and policy.[8] These books have also examined regulation of pluralism and diversity, and some have offered comparative studies; reference will often be made to them in this study. So far in this chapter, reference has been made to the media generally, although, as the title of this book shows, the focus is broadcasting. This is not to suggest that the press is not important to the promotion of pluralism but, as already indicated, and as will be explored further in the following chapter, it is broadcasting which has been the focus for regulation. Unlike the press, which has largely been left to the general law, broadcasting has been subject to quite specific sectoral regulation. The asymmetrical approach to the press and to broadcasting has not been entirely coherent and, as suggested in the following chapter, has skewed policy formation in relation to broadcasting. However, an examination of what specific press pluralism regulation might look like is outside the scope of this book. Nevertheless, reference to the press will be made from time to time as a discussion of broadcasting policy and regulation inevitably draws in the press to some extent. Moreover, by referring only to 'broadcasting' in the title, it is not intended that the study will ignore what might for now be conveniently referred to as the 'new media'. The new media are an important element of the debate over how broadcasting should be regulated, and a consideration of what impact they have on pluralism policy and regulation cannot be ignored.

The three countries which form the subject matter of this study have been chosen because they offer useful points of comparison and contrast. All three are undergoing or attempting reform of media ownership regulation using similar

---

[8] Notable examples are EM Barendt, *Broadcasting Law: A Comparative Study* (Oxford, Clarendon Press, 1995); R Craufurd Smith, *Broadcasting Law and Fundamental Rights* (Oxford, Clarendon Press, 1997); M Feintuck, *Media Regulation, Public Interest and the Law* (Edinburgh, Edinburgh University Press, 1999); T Gibbons, *Regulating the Media*, 2nd edn (London, Sweet & Maxwell, 1998); D Goldberg, T Prosser and S Verhulst (eds), *Regulating the Changing Media: A Comparative Study* (Oxford, Clarendon Press, 1998); W Hoffmann-Riem, *Regulating Media: The Licensing and Supervision of Broadcasting in Six Countries* (New York, The Guilford Press, 1996), pp 297–300; and ME Price, *Television, the Public Sphere, and National Identity* (Oxford, Clarendon Press, 1995).

grounds for justification. The UK, the US, and Australia share a common law heritage, they operate within liberal democratic traditions, and they acknowledge the principle of freedom of expression, although the realisation of this principle is quite different in the three jurisdictions. The three countries have all imposed sector-specific regulation on broadcasting, although to differing degrees, and they have broadcasting environments which have both similarities and significant differences. Whilst each of the jurisdictions has a well-established private commercial broadcasting sector, they differ in the extent to which that sector has dominance. For the US and Australia, broadcasting began with the private sector, and, although Australia later developed a publicly funded broadcasting sector, it has never had the central place and significance of UK public broadcasting. In the UK, the concept of public service broadcasting has been a major influence on broadcasting policy in both the public and private broadcasting sectors. In the US, public broadcasting has only a marginal role. Over time each of the three countries has developed regulatory frameworks which rely heavily on independent regulatory bodies to supervise broadcasters, although the role of these regulatory bodies, and the degree to which they exert regulatory control, also differs in the three jurisdictions. In the final section of this chapter, a brief overview of the broadcasting environments of the three countries will be provided as background.

Two assumptions inform this study. The first, which has already been mentioned, is the claim that pluralism regulatory measures cannot be considered in isolation. Hence, although it tends to be media ownership and control regulation which attracts attention and which is the focus of reform, a proper assessment of such reform can be made only if one considers that this measure is part of a network of regulatory measures which are interdependent. The second assumption relates to the policy which informs pluralism. This will be explored in Chapter Two, but, briefly, it will be asserted that much of the policy informing pluralism regulation, although making reference to the importance of media's role in the democratic process, has been skewed by a futile focus on the different regulatory treatment of the press and broadcasting, with the result that it is this which is influencing reform debate rather than a proper focus on the place of media in a democracy. It will be argued that a different approach to the role of media, using the concept of the public sphere, needs to be adopted and used as a standard against which regulatory reform can be assessed.

Terminology

Two matters of terminology need to be clarified. So far, this chapter has referred without explanation or distinction to 'pluralism' and 'diversity'. In the context of broadcasting ownership policy and regulation, these do not by nature have distinctly different meanings. Terms like 'pluralism' and 'diversity' can have several meanings. First, they may refer to a situation in which the media environment is structured in a way which ensures that there are a number of different kinds of media outlets; for example, public broadcasting and private broadcasting services. Secondly, they may refer to a media environment which is structured so as to ensure that there is a diversity of owners of the media outlets. Thirdly, they may refer to the desirability of a diversity of opinions being broadcast, and, fourthly, to the broadcasting of a diverse range of programming including both information and entertainment programmes.[9] Each of these meanings is contemplated by the pluralism and diversity regulatory measures examined in this book, although there are variations between the three jurisdictions as to how explicitly or directly each is translated into regulation. It can be seen that the first two meanings relate more to how the broadcasting environment is structured, and another way to refer to this is to speak of 'external pluralism'. 'Internal pluralism' can be used to describe the third and fourth meanings, which relate more to what is broadcast: that is, the content. Each of the jurisdictions makes different use of terms 'pluralism' and 'diversity'. In the US, where the focus of regulation is on ensuring a diversity of ownership, 'diversity' is the term commonly used. In Australia, not much attention is given to the choice of terminology, but the tendency is to use 'diversity' to cover all four meanings. Only in the UK has the practice developed of using 'pluralism' and 'diversity' in two quite distinct ways, whereby 'pluralism' is more closely aligned to the meanings encompassed by 'external pluralism', and 'diversity' to the meanings encompassed by 'internal pluralism':

> By diversity, we mean the range of different programmes and services available to viewers and listeners. Plurality, on the other hand, is about the choices viewers and listeners are able to make between different providers of such services. Society benefits from both a diversity of services between and within genres (such as news, entertainment, documentaries etc) and a plurality of suppliers of such services (since this increases exposure to a variety of editorial styles and a range of views and opinions).[10]

This book will distinguish between 'pluralism' and 'diversity', and use these two terms to differentiate the different ways in which pluralism/diversity can be understood. Hence, 'pluralism' will used to refer to the way in which the media environment is structured, and this will embrace both the first and second meanings described above. 'Diversity' will refer to the third and fourth meanings, and, therefore, will be more relevant to regulation which focuses on content.[11] In parts of the text it will not be necessary to make a distinction between pluralism and diversity, and so the term 'broadcasting pluralism' will be used to embrace both these concepts more generally.

---

[9] See also E Barendt, 'Structural and Content Regulation of the Media: United Kingdom Law and Some American Comparisons' in EM Barendt, *The Yearbook of Media and Entertainment Law 1997/8* (Oxford, Oxford University Press, 1997), 75 at 84–86 for a discussion of the meanings of these terms.

[10] DTI and DCMS, *A New Future for Communications*, Cm 5010 (2000), para 4.2.1.

[11] This may distinguish it slightly from the way in which it is used in the UK, where the explanation of the term quoted above seems to refer only to plurality of ownership and not to a plurality of services also.

Terminology to describe the media is becoming increasingly problematic as new technologies develop and content can be delivered in a variety of ways. Even the apparently straightforward distinction between print media and non-print (or electronic) media may no longer be as clear as it once seemed. The focus of the book is on broadcasting rather than the press, but the term 'broadcasting' also needs clarification as it has been so far used in a way which might imply that it is always understood to refer to all non-print media. One of the difficulties of terminology in this area is that media services have often been identified and distinguished on the basis of delivery technologies. Now with content able to be transmitted via a variety of delivery platforms, technology is a less satisfactory way of sorting radio and television services. Thus, although the word 'broadcasting' is by definition technologically neutral, a reference to 'broadcasting' has tended to mean radio and television services delivered over-the-air, using wireless technology, because in the past this was the only way radio and television were available. However, with the advent of other delivery technologies such as cable and satellite delivery, broadcasting was not necessarily the appropriate term if it was to imply a certain delivery platform. For regulatory purposes, the need to be clear about the type of service can be important because the rules may vary according to the delivery platform. One finds also differences in usage by the different jurisdictions. However, throughout this book, the term 'broadcasting' will be used to refer generally to radio and television services, regardless of whether those services are delivered over-the-air, by cable, or by satellite. Where it is necessary to make a distinction, because the different types of services are accorded different regulatory treatment, this will be made clear in the text. Further, where it is necessary to distinguish between subscription and non-subscription services, the terms 'subscription' and 'free-to-air' will be used. 'Free-to-air' services will generally also be services delivered 'over-the-air'. The adoption of a generic term, like 'broadcasting', arguably leaves open the question of whether the term takes account of radio and television services (or like services) delivered over the internet, and even other forms of 'new media' such as podcasting. Although the implications of internet delivery and other developments will be relevant to this study and will be considered, the book's reference to 'broadcasting' will not automatically include such services; they will be referred to separately. Aside from helping to keep the discussion clear, this separation makes sense because there are still differences in the way traditional broadcasting services and internet services are regulated.

Outline of Regulatory Approaches

In the previous section, it became apparent that different regulatory approaches might be used depending upon the outcomes being sought. In this section a brief survey will be given of the main types of regulatory approaches used in connection with broadcasting pluralism and diversity, which will be considered in more detail in the rest of this book. It is convenient to classify broadcasting pluralism and diversity regulation into two main categories: the first is structural regulation, and the second, content regulation.

Structural regulation addresses the architecture of the broadcasting environment by establishing rules which will determine the type of broadcasting services which can be established and who can control those services. The rules which are designed to ensure that ownership and control of broadcasting is not dominated by one or only a few individuals or enterprises are an example of structural regulation. These rules will include limits on the accumulation of interests within media of a certain type (mono-media interests), and limits on ownership interests which can be held across different types of media, usually radio, television, and newspapers (cross-media interests). However, there are other forms of structural regulation which contribute to the architecture of the broadcasting environment. For example, measures may be in place to ensure differently constituted broadcasting services by enabling public and private broadcasting sectors. The public sector may be funded differently from the private sector in order to minimise some of the programming limitations which can arise when broadcasting is financed through advertising revenue. These different structures, sometimes with different programme mandates, ensure that diversity is built into the system. The public broadcaster can act as a counterbalance to the private commercial broadcaster. For example, if a public broadcaster does not have to be concerned with maximising audience size in order to attract advertising revenue then it will be able to present programming which may be of interest only to a small audience. Equally, the private broadcasting sector can act as a balance to the public sector, which may have more limited funding or be constrained by government controls. Structural regulation, then, is concerned with the design of the overall environment and with the make-up of individual broadcasters.

Content regulation will be more concerned with what programmes are actually being broadcast. Content regulation can serve other objectives apart from diversity. For example, content regulation might include rules designed to protect children from unsuitable content, to control the portrayal of violent or sexual material, or to prevent audiences being misled by certain advertising claims. However, in the context of diversity goals, content regulation will be concerned with trying to ensure that audiences have available to them a range of programme types covering both information and entertainment. Other rules may focus more on the content of actual programmes, such as rules which require news and current affairs programmes to present a balanced range of opinions. Another important area of content regulation will be concerned with access; for example, there may be rules which ensure that political candidates or parties are able to make broadcasts during election periods. Rights of reply may be available to individuals who have been attacked by the broadcasting service.

As the delivery of broadcasting has become more complex, competition law has had an increasing impact on the broadcasting environment, often accompanied by the development of sector-specific competition rules. Such rules may be concerned with ensuring that those who control delivery systems such as cable are not able to block access to other programme providers, or there may be rules governing exclusive agreements for major sporting events. Although these competition rules may spring from a concern about anti-competitive practices, they are also relevant to the protection of broadcasting pluralism. Controls which are in place to prevent, say, abuse of a dominant position can open up access for the public to a wide range of services or programmes. It is no longer possible to consider broadcasting pluralism and its regulatory protection without also including a consideration of the impact of competition law.

A Brief Overview of Three Broadcasting Systems

In order to provide a background for the matters covered in the following chapters, this section will provide a brief overview of the broadcasting environment and regulatory framework for each of the three jurisdictions.

United Kingdom

Whilst sharing similarities with the US and Australian broadcasting systems, the UK system is also markedly different. The contrast can be seen most clearly in its long-standing commitment to public service broadcasting, a set of principles which has influenced the structure and content of both the public and private free-to-air sectors of broadcasting, and which, in turn, has led to close regulatory supervision of broadcasting. Even now, after major reform of UK broadcasting, the influence of public service broadcasting can still be observed. Despite its influence there was no precise definition of the concept, although the following explanation illustrates its main features:

> [T]wo features are distinctive. One is the idea of universality, in the geographical sense that the material which is produced should be available throughout the country, and in the consumer sense that it should cater for all tastes and interests. The other feature is the idea of cultural responsibility, that material should have the object of informing and educating the public, offering a high standard of quality, as well as entertaining them.[12]

The Communications Act 2003 (Comms Act (UK)) now includes a statutory statement of the purposes of public service television broadcasting which reflects the description just given.[13] The public service mandate no longer applies to the commercial radio sector.

Another difference in the UK environment is the dominant role played by the public broadcaster, the British Broadcasting Corporation (BBC). Initially radio

---

[12] T Gibbons, *Regulating the Media*, 2nd edn (London, Sweet & Maxwell, 1998), 56.
[13] Comms Act (UK), s 264. See further Chapter Four, at p 145.

and television services were offered only by the BBC. Commercial television did not begin until 1955, whilst local commercial radio only began in 1972, and national commercial radio in 1992. The structure of the BBC and its operations are governed by Royal Charter and an agreement made between the BBC and the relevant Secretary of State (currently the Secretary of State for Culture, Media and Sport), although for some aspects of its operations, it will also be accountable to external regulatory authorities.[14] The current Charter and Agreement expire in 2006, but the government has announced that the BBC will be given a new Royal Charter for a further term of 10 years, and that it will continue to be funded by the licence fee.[15]

The commercial sector is regulated by the Office of Communications (Ofcom), a statutory regulatory authority, which has been established as the regulator for all aspects, including infrastructure and content, of electronic communications in the UK. Its powers and duties were formally vested in it in December 2003. Until the recent reforms, the UK communications sector, particularly broadcasting, had been answerable to a plethora of regulatory bodies, but, as part of that reform, Ofcom was established to replace the former regulators for both the broadcasting and telecommunications sectors: the Independent Television Commission (ITC), the Radio Authority (RA),[16] the Broadcasting Standards Commission (BSC),[17] the Office of Telecommunications (Oftel),[18] and the Radiocommunications Agency.[19] In relation to radio and television services, Ofcom's regulatory responsibilities include licensing, competition and economic regulation, and content regulation. For the most part, Ofcom's powers and duties in relation to broadcasting will be determined by the Comms Act (UK), the Broadcasting Act 1990 (BA 1990 (UK)) and the Broadcasting Act 1996 (BA 1996 (UK)). It was unfortunate that, as part of the reforms, the government did not take the opportunity to introduce a comprehensive legislative source. Instead the Comms Act (UK) amends, inter alia, the 1990 and 1996 legislation, and so it is frequently necessary to consult all three Acts. The Comms Act (UK) is the key legislative source for the

---

[14] Department of National Heritage, *Royal Charter for the Continuance of the British Broadcasting Corporation*, Cm 3248 (1996); Department of National Heritage, *Agreement Dated the 25th Day of January 1996 Between Her Majesty's Secretary of State for National Heritage and the British Broadcasting Corporation*, Cm 3152 (1996); and DCMS, *Deed of Variation dated 4th December 2003*, Cm 6075 (2003).

[15] DCMS, *Review of the BBC's Royal Charter: A Strong BBC, Independent of Government*, PP 789 (March 2005).

[16] The ITC was the main regulatory body for commercial television services covering such matters as licensing, ownership and control, and content regulation. The RA had similar responsibilities in relation to radio.

[17] The BSC was responsible for investigating complaints about standards of taste and decency and privacy and fairness in relation to both commercial and public radio and television services. Its functions often overlapped with those of the ITC and the RA. The BSC was the result of a merger, in 1996, of two other regulatory bodies, the Broadcasting Standards Council and the Broadcasting Complaints Commission.

[18] Oftel was primarily responsible for telecommunications regulation, but, as new delivery platforms developed for radio and television services, Oftel also had an impact on broadcasting.

[19] The Radiocommunications Agency was responsible for spectrum management.

recent reforms and Ofcom's role, and it injects a different regulatory policy approach into the communications sector. In carrying out its functions, its principal duty will be

> (a) . . . to further the interests of citizens in relation to communications matters; and
> (b) to further the interests of consumers in relevant markets, where appropriate by promoting competition.[20]

Ofcom's duties, in furtherance of this principal duty, include ensuring the availability of a wide range of television and radio services of high quality, appealing to a wide range of tastes and interests, and maintaining a plurality of providers.[21] However, there is now a much clearer preference for lighter regulation. For example, the legislation requires Ofcom, in carrying out its duties, to have regard to 'regulatory activities . . . [being] proportionate, consistent and targeted only at cases in which action is needed'[22] and to 'the desirability of promoting and facilitating the development and use of effective forms of self-regulation.'[23] The Chief Executive of Ofcom, Stephen Carter, has referred to Ofcom's 'bias against intervention'.[24] Although the legislation refers to 'self-regulation', in practice the model will be more one of co-regulation, whereby industry regulation will be backed by statutory enforcement by Ofcom. The Ofcom Board, which has overall responsibility for the implementation of the Comms Act (UK), is comprised of mainly part-time members, but with some full-time members from the Ofcom Executive. Ofcom exercises its regulatory functions through a series of groups which tend mainly to be organised around functions rather than the type of electronic communication service. Of particular relevance to broadcasting is the Content Board, a committee of the Ofcom Board, which has responsibility for content regulation, although the Content Board is not responsible for applying sanctions for breach of content rules.[25] This is left to another committee of the Ofcom Board, the Content Sanctions Committee. Further committees of the Board are also relevant to broadcasting content: the Fairness Committee deals with complaints about fairness and privacy; and the Election Committee addresses disputes relating to party political broadcasts such as allocation of time. Under the new regulatory regime, broadcasting content is regulated according to tiers.[26] Tier One applies to all broadcasters, radio and television, regardless of the mode of

---

[20] Comms Act (UK), s 3(1).

[21] *Ibid*, s 3(2).

[22] *Ibid*, s 3(3)(a).

[23] *Ibid*, s 3(4)(c).

[24] S Carter, 'The Communications Act: Myths and Realities' (speech delivered to Media and Legal Practitioners, 9 October 2003) www.ofcom.org.uk/media_office/speeches/carter_mlp.htm, accessed 15 October 2003.

[25] Ofcom is required to establish the Content Board: Comms Act (UK), s 12(1).

[26] Whilst the commercial services will have their obligations set out in legislation, the BBC's obligations will be found in the Charter and Agreement, as amended. Compliance with these tiers by the commercial services will generally be monitored by Ofcom with some industry regulation, whilst the BBC's compliance will for some matters be determined by the BBC's Board of Governors, and for others by Ofcom.

delivery, and encompasses basic broadcasting standards and obligations such as impartiality, fairness and privacy, content likely to cause harm or offence, advertising and sponsorship, ensuring access to services for people with disabilities, and, where applicable, compliance with EU obligations. The second tier applies to those broadcasters which are designated as public service broadcasters. The public service broadcasting services are the traditional free-to-air television services: Channel Three, Channel Four, and Channel Five; as well as the BBC in respect of both its radio and television services.[27] The second tier addresses quantitative requirements such as quotas for independent productions and regional programming, provision of news and current affairs, and schools programming. The second tier requirements apply in different degrees to the broadcasters. The third tier refers to the qualitative obligations of the public service broadcasters: in short, obligations requiring the broadcasters to provide a range of diverse and high-quality programming.

The UK offers a mix of radio and television services transmitted using the radio frequency spectrum (usually referred to in the UK as 'terrestrial' services, but in this book as 'over-the-air' or 'free-to-air', as appropriate), and cable and satellite broadcasting services. The television and radio services provided by the BBC and the free-to-air commercial television services all retain public service broadcasting obligations although to varying degrees, whilst the commercial radio sector retains obligations relating to programme format and, where appropriate, local content. Free-to-air television continues to be transmitted in analogue mode, but simulcasting, via spectrum allocated to the traditional broadcasters, ensures that the same services are now also broadcast by digital. National public and commercial radio services are also simulcast, and simulcasting of some local services occurs. Broadcasters who were allocated spectrum for digital transmission are able to use any spare spectrum for additional broadcasting or services. After a slow start, digital television penetration has grown quickly; by June 2005, 63 per cent of UK households were receiving digital television.[28] The government has announced that the analogue signal will be switched off over a phased period commencing in 2008 and finishing in 2012.[29] The exploitation of digital technology has expanded the number of television channels available: for example, the BBC offers six digital-only channels in addition to its two traditional analogue services, BBC One

[27] Also included in the category of public service television broadcasting is the public teletext service and Channel S4C, the Welsh language television channel: Comms Act (UK), s 264(11).

[28] Ofcom, 'Digital Television UK Household Penetration reaches 63%' (News Release, 15 September 2005), http://www.ofcom.org.uk/media/news/2005/09/nr_20050915, accessed 1 October 2005. This constituted an increase of around 18% from the previous 12 months: DCMS, 'Tessa Jowell Confirms Digital Switchover Timetable and Support for the Most Vulnerable' (Press Notice 116/05, 15 September 2005),http://www.culture.gov.uk/global/press_notices/archive_2005/dcms116_05.htm, accessed 19 October 2005.

[29] DCMS, 'Digital Switchover Statement by the Secretary of State' (21 July 2005), http://www.digitaltelevision.gov.uk/press/2005/statement_ds.html, accessed 21 August 2005. Currently DTT is able to reach only 75% of the population, but switching off the analogue signal should ensure that the population reach of digital matches what is currently available under analogue: Ofcom, *The Communications Market 2005* (July 2005), 184.

and BBC Two, which are also simulcast. In the commercial sector, two analogue channels are offered, also on a free-to-air basis: Channel Three (also known as ITV), organised on a regional basis (although all the English and Welsh licences are now under common control), and Channel Five. Although not of the scale of the BBC, the UK is also served by another free-to-air public broadcaster, Channel Four.[30] Channel Four differs from the BBC because it is allowed to raise revenue from advertising. However, it is owned and controlled by a statutory corporation and is non-profit-making. Channel Four was established in 1982 and has a specific remit which includes obligations to be innovative and experimental, and to cater for a culturally diverse society.[31] Channels Three and Four each offer additional digital channels. Digital television transmitted over-the-air is referred to as 'DTT' (digital terrestrial television) in the UK. In addition to the simulcast and additional channels provided by the traditional broadcasters, there is also available a subscription over-the-air service, Top Up TV, which offers eleven channels, not all of them transmitted simultaneously.[32] DTT is limited by its spectrum in the number of channels which can be offered; currently 32 channels are available,[33] but full capacity has almost been reached.[34] The limitations of DTT are evident when one compares this with digital satellite: currently, BSkyB offers around 350 television channels.[35] After slow beginnings, cable and satellite services are now well established in the UK. Although the traditional over-the-air broadcasters, particularly the BBC and Channel Three, still dominate audience share,[36] they have been under pressure regarding both revenue and audience share.[37] Digital satellite services offered by BSkyB were introduced in 1998 offering an increased number of channels and interactive services, and in 2001 BSkyB switched off its analogue service. Cable services are also available in digital, and offer around 240 channels. Digital uptake in the UK has been assisted by pro-active industry measures. Freeview, which commenced in October 2002, has been a major contributor to growth in digital penetration,[38] and, indeed, appears to be contributing to an expansion of the terrestrial audience reach at the expense of the cable and satellite services.[39] Equipped with a relatively inexpensive digital set-top box, viewers can access all the digital free-to-air television channels, about 20 radio digital channels, and some interactive services. Another, more recent, measure, also designed to contribute to the uptake of digital is Freesat, which is a service promoted by

---

[30] In Wales, there is a similar service known as Channel S4C which broadcasts a substantial amount of programming in the Welsh language.

[31] Comms Act (UK), s 265(3).

[32] Top Up began broadcasting in March 2004. It is designed to build on the success of Freeview. Subscription services on DTT have had limited success. The first subscription DTT service, ITV Digital (formerly known as On Digital), collapsed in May 2002.

[33] Ofcom, *The Communications Market 2005* (July 2005), 10.

[34] Ofcom, *The Communications Market 2004—Television* (August 2004), 17.

[35] Ofcom, *The Communications Market 2005, Quarterly Update* (August 2005), 72.

[36] Ofcom, above n 34, 25, figure 10.

[37] *Ibid*, 11 and 22.

[38] *Ibid*, 16.

[39] Ofcom, above n 35, 69–70 and 72.

BSkyB. Freesat enables viewers to access free-to-view digital services via satellite delivery, but without the necessity of taking out a subscription. Obviously BSkyB would hope to convert these viewers to subscription services in time.[40]

Although generally receiving less notice than television, radio is undergoing significant change in the UK, particularly with a growth in the ways in which radio services are received, such as via the internet.[41] Over the past few years, there has been a significant increase in radio listening via digital platforms such as DAB (Digital Audio Broadcasting), digital television, and the internet.[42] This includes stations available in analogue and being simulcast, as well as stations being transmitted only in digital. There has also been growth in the number of radio stations, both AM and FM, available.[43] Like television, terrestrial radio services are provided by the BBC and by a commercial sector, with a mix of local, regional, and national services. There are presently no plans for switching off the analogue signal, although it is likely that simulcast obligations will eventually be removed.[44] The Comms Act (UK) has also introduced a new form of radio service, community radio.[45] The first community radio licences were awarded in 2005. Community radio services, which must be non-profit-making, are designed to provide community access, catering for either a community area or community interests, and to be broadcast over a limited geographical range. Radio services are also available under a restricted service licence which can either be short term (maximum of 28 days), usually for a special event, or long term, but linked to a particular site such as a university.

The European Union is also an important influence on UK broadcasting policy and regulation. The most direct influence is felt with regard to regulation of content, because Member States must comply (by adopting national laws) with the EU Television Directive, which lays down rules affecting certain areas of broadcasting content such as advertising, European content, independent programming, and protection of children.[46] A proposed revision of the Directive was published in 2005.[47] One of the main aspects of the proposal is to expand the Directive with the

---

[40] Ofcom, above n 34, 17.

[41] Delivery via mobile phones, PDAs and MP3 players is also becoming more common. Although television is less developed in this respect, there are also limited broadband television services.

[42] DAB refers to broadcasting in digital mode delivered over-the-air: Ofcom, *The Communications Market 2005* (July 2005), 35. However, most radio listening still takes place via broadcast rather than the internet: *ibid.*

[43] Ofcom, *The Communications Market 2004—Radio* (August 2004), 17.

[44] Ofcom, *Radio—Preparing for the Future, Phase 2: Implementing the Framework* (19 October 2005), 5.

[45] Comms Act (UK), s 262, and Community Radio Order 2004, SI 2004, No 1944.

[46] Council Directive 89/552/EEC of 3 October 1989 on the coordination of certain provisions laid down by law, regulation or administrative action in Member States concerning the pursuit of television broadcasting activities [1989] OJ L 298/23, as amended by Directive 97/36/EC of the European Parliament and of the Council of 30 June 1997 [1997] OJ L 202/60.

[47] Proposal for a Directive of the European Parliament and of the Council Amending Council Directive 89/552/EEC on the coordination of certain provisions laid down by law, regulation or administrative action in Member States concerning the pursuit of television broadcasting activities, COM (2005) 646/final.

intention that television content, and television-like content, will be regulated consistently, regardless of the means of delivery. Thus, 'linear' services are scheduled content, whether delivered via traditional broadcasting, or, for example, the internet or mobile phones—in another sense, content which is 'pushed' to the viewer. 'Non-linear' services will comprise content, such as on-demand news, which can be 'pulled' by the viewer. Linear services will be subject to the existing content rules, whilst non-linear services will be subject only to a minimum set of protective rules covering, for example, children, surreptitious advertising, and prevention of religious and racial hatred.[48] The proposal also alters the nomenclature of the Directive by introducing the term 'media service provider' in place of 'broadcaster', and 'audiovisual media service' in place of 'broadcast', although the term 'broadcaster' is still used where appropriate to describe the provider of 'linear audiovisual media services'.[49]

Another area of potential EU influence relates to ownership and control regulation. Aside from general EU competition law, which will be relevant to the UK, there have been for some time, indeed since 1992, discussions around the introduction of an EU media pluralism measure which would focus on regulation of ownership and control. However, Member State disagreement has meant that there have been no real advances towards such a measure. There is also a conflict of goals for the EU, given the recognised need to build up national or European champions able to compete with US industry. This, and the current regulatory climate, makes it unlikely that an EU media pluralism measure focusing on ownership and control would be introduced.[50]

United States

Regulation of broadcasting in the US is a matter for federal law, although the degree of responsibility varies depending upon its type. Radio services, using the radio frequency spectrum, began in 1920. Whilst the number of services quickly multiplied, the lack of spectrum planning and regulation meant that there was often interference between the stations' signals. The airwaves chaos led to the enactment of the Radio Act of 1927 which established the Federal Radio Commission, whose role it was to plan the spectrum and to assign frequencies to broadcasters. The Radio Act established the principle that the spectrum was to be treated as a public resource, access to which could be obtained by private users,

[48] See, also, European Commission, *The Commission Proposal for a Modernisation of the Television Without Frontiers Directive: Frequently Asked Questions*, Memo/05/475 (13 December 2005). The proposal also incorporates a substantial relaxation of some of the traditional rules on advertising; for details see Chapter Four, 'Regulatory Measures: Advertising', at p 190.
[49] Proposal for a Directive of the European Parliament and of the Council, above n 47, Art 1.
[50] For a recent European Commission statement, see 'Media Pluralism—What Should be the European Union's role?', Issues Paper for the Liverpool Audiovisual Conference (July 2005), available at http://europa.eu.int/comm/avpolicy/revision-tvwf2005/ispa_mediapluralism_en.pdf.

such as radio broadcasters, through a licensing process.[51] The Radio Act was replaced by the Communications Act of 1934 (Comms Act (US)), which remains the core legislative source for regulation of communications, although major amendments were introduced by the Telecommunications Act of 1996 (TA 1996 (US)).[52] The Comms Act (US) also renamed the Federal Radio Commission the Federal Communications Commission (FCC) and expanded its jurisdiction. The FCC is an independent regulatory agency which has control over all forms of electronic communications, including broadcasting and telecommunications services.[53] It has extensive policy- and rule-making powers, in addition to its general administrative and enforcement powers. The Act sets out the specific duties and powers of the FCC, which it is required to carry out as 'public convenience, interest, or necessity requires'.[54] This phrase, frequently referred to as the 'public interest standard', has encouraged the FCC at various points in its history to move beyond acting simply as a spectrum monitor, and to adopt a much more proactive role in the regulation of broadcasters.[55] The FCC is specifically denied any power of censorship.[56] Although the FCC's powers are broad, it is constrained also by the First Amendment guarantee of free speech, and the Comms Act (US) expressly prohibits interference with those free speech rights.[57] Consequently, many of the FCC's rules and regulatory decisions have been challenged on First Amendment principles.

The FCC's powers and responsibilities vary depending upon the broadcasting delivery platform. Its regulatory attention is most focused on radio and television services delivered via the radio frequency spectrum: in other words, over-the-air broadcasting.[58] These services are provided free-to-air and depend mainly on advertising for their revenue. Those wishing to operate broadcasting stations must be licensed by the FCC. Broadcasting services are licensed as either commercial stations or non-commercial educational stations. Although the FCC is required to consider the public interest in licence grants and renewals,[59] legislative and policy changes in recent years have meant that most licence awards and renewals for commercial services, are virtually automatic with an auction process (in place of a discretionary, merits-based process) being used where there are competing

[51] JD Zelezny, *Communications Law: Liberties, Restraints, and the Modern Media*, 4th edn (Belmont, CA, Thomson Wadsworth, 2004), 362.

[52] The Communications Act of 1934, as amended, is incorporated into the United States Code (USC) under title 47. Citations will generally be to the USC.

[53] There are five members, who serve for a term of five years. They are appointed by the US President, although their appointment must be confirmed by the Senate, and no more than three members may be from the same political party: KC Creech, *Electronic Media Law and Regulation*, 4th edn (Burlington, MA, Focal Press, 2003), 8.

[54] 47 USC § 303.

[55] Zelezny, above n 51, 362, and Creech, above n 53, 69–72.

[56] 47 USC § 326.

[57] *Ibid.*

[58] Although a viewer may receive a broadcast television station by cable, this will not change the regulatory character of the broadcast station: FCC (Mass Media Bureau), *The Public and Broadcasting* (June 1999), 2.

[59] 47 USC § 307(a).

applications.[60] Although over-the-air broadcasting's audience share is declining, losing out to the multichannel services provided via cable and satellite, free-to-air television still commands about 48 per cent of prime-time viewing of all US television households.[61]

When radio broadcasting began in the US, it began as a commercial service. There was never any question that radio broadcasting would not be a private commercial enterprise, and commercial broadcasting has remained the dominant form of broadcasting.[62] A form of public broadcasting does exist, although it differs from the traditional form, seen in the UK and in Australia. Public broadcasting services in the US, licensed as non-commercial educational stations, are operated as not-for-profit and are prohibited from broadcasting advertisements. Only limited government funding is available, and public broadcasters must rely on sponsorship and members' subscriptions for funding. Although marginal compared with the commercial broadcasting sector, there are around 3,000 public broadcasting radio and television services spread across the US.[63] Another non-commercial service available is low-power FM radio (LPFM) which, with a very limited broadcast range, is designed to serve local community needs. The development of LPFM, which was established in 2000, has been hindered by moves from the commercial broadcasting sector to protect the latter's position. As a result of lobbying, legislation was passed which limited the number of LPFM services.[64] Both commercial and public broadcasting services are subject to a degree of content regulation, notwithstanding the constraints of First Amendment free speech protection. As will be explored in later chapters, spectrum scarcity has been one of the main justifications for regulation, although the enthusiasm for such regulation has waxed and waned depending upon prevailing political philosophy.

Cable television, which developed in the 1940s, operates extensively throughout the US. Its original purpose was to distribute, via cable, over-the-air television signals to communities which did not have adequate television reception. By the 1960s, however, cable's ability to offer a much greater range of programming made it attractive even in areas where the broadcast signal was not a problem.[65] It is local

---

[60] W Overbeck, *Major Principles of Media Law*, 15th edn (Belmont, CA, Thomson Wadsworth, 2004), 439–52. Licences can also be acquired through transfers, which must also satisfy the public interest standard: 47 USC § 310(d).

[61] FCC, *Eleventh Annual Report, In the Matter of Annual Assessment of the Status of Competition in the Market for the Delivery of Video Programming*, FCC 05-13 (14 January 2005), para 77.

[62] W Hoffmann-Riem, above n 8, 12.

[63] About three quarters of these are radio stations. By contrast, as at June 2005, there were about 11,000 commercial over-the-air radio stations and around 1,300 television stations: FCC, *Broadcast Station Totals as of June 30, 2005* (29 August 2005), http://hraunfoss.fcc.gov/edocs_public/attachmatch/DOC-260747A1.doc, accessed 20 October 2005.

[64] Curiously, the public broadcasting sector also supported the legislation: Media Access Project, *Low Power Radio Overview: Communities Ask for a Small Slice of the Airwaves*, http://www.mediaaccess.org/programs/lpfm/Background9-02.pdf, accessed 20 October 2005. There are moves to have Congress remove the current limitations. Low-power television services have operated since the 1980s, but unlike LPFM, they can operate as commercial services.

[65] FCC, *Cable Television Fact Sheet* (June 2000), http://www.fcc.gov/csb/facts/csgen.html, accessed 10 September 2001, and Overbeck, above n 60, 480–81.

municipalities, and not the FCC, which are responsible for licensing cable systems, although the Commission does exercise some regulatory authority over cable. Because cable is not subject to spectrum constraints, it was not, initially, considered necessary for the FCC to exert authority over cable, but this changed as cable began to compete with local over-the-air television. The impact of cable on broadcasting's viability was considered likely to be detrimental to the public interest, so rules were imposed in 1965 which sought to protect local broadcasters by requiring cable operators to carry local television signals and prohibiting them from importing distant television signals.[66] Gradually, the FCC's regulatory control over cable broadened to include further regulation to protect local television viability, provide access channels, and control rates, as well as some content regulation. Cable broadcasting has experienced a particularly volatile regulatory environment, having experienced phases of regulation, deregulation and re-regulation, although the TA 1996 (US), which relaxed substantially much of the then-existing regulation, seems to have also brought with it a more stable environment.[67]

The other main delivery platform is satellite. The main service is referred to as Direct Broadcast Satellite (DBS); it delivers video and audio programming and has a much greater channel capacity than cable.[68] After a precarious beginning in the 1980s, DBS has now become much more successful.[69] Legislation has also facilitated DBS's development: the TA 1996 (US) allowed the FCC to overrule local regulations which limited the permissible size of receiving dishes, whilst the Satellite Television Home Viewer Improvement Act of 1999 allowed DBS to transmit local television stations.[70] As well, DBS operators have been proactive in encouraging new subscribers offering free or heavily discounted receiving equipment and niche programming.[71] By June 2004, there were approximately 23 million US households subscribing to DBS; this represented a growth of 13 per cent from the previous 12 months.[72] DBS now represents 25 per cent of multichannel service subscriptions, and DBS's growth can be contrasted with a decline in the number of cable subscriptions in 2003 and 2004.[73] DBS is also subject to some FCC competition and content regulation.

Although the US already enjoys a multichannel environment with a mix of deliveries,[74] the introduction of digital will have an even greater impact on the

---

[66] Creech, above n 53, 82, and Overbeck, above n 60, 481–82.

[67] Creech, above n 53, 92–108, Zelezny, above n 51, 412–16, and Overbeck, above n 60, 481–89. A number of these rules have relevance to broadcasting pluralism and will be discussed in later chapters.

[68] Another satellite service, known as HSD (Home Satellite Dish), is also available. This was the original satellite-to-home service, and it operates in the C-band frequency, which is mainly intended for satellite transmission of programming to cable operators. HSD can receive programming from several satellites, but requires a much larger dish, compared with DBS, to receive the satellite service. Subscriptions to HSD are declining: FCC, *Eleventh Annual Report*, above n 61, para 64 and fn 338.

[69] Overbeck, above n 60, 497.

[70] *Ibid*, 498.

[71] FCC, *Eleventh Annual Report*, above n 61, para 54.

[72] *Ibid*.

[73] *Ibid*, paras 22 and 54.

[74] In addition to the delivery platforms described above, the US, like the UK, is also developing other delivery platforms such as broadband.

number of media services available to the public. Rules for the conversion of the analogue over-the-air television signal to digital were made by the FCC in 1997.[75] There has been no stipulation of the standard to be used. The policy is to allow both standard definition (SDTV) and high-definition digital (HDTV) services to be available, leaving it to the market to decide.[76] Existing over-the-air television stations were allocated a channel for broadcasting in digital, and the larger stations were required to begin digital broadcasting by 1999 (which would be simulcast with the analogue signal).[77] However, many television stations failed to meet the deadlines set for commencement of digital broadcasting: the costs of conversion being a significant hurdle.[78] The Comms Act (US) had set a target date of end-2006 for switching off the analogue signal, although broadcasters will not be required to relinquish the analogue signal if 85 per cent of the viewers in that market do not have access to the digital service.[79] To date, digital uptake has been slow, and the date for switch-off has been extended to February 2009.[80] The FCC estimates that between 14 and 15 per cent of television households receive over-the-air television only, whilst there are many more households which have over-the-air sets in addition to their multichannel services.[81] Although the FCC has initiated consumer awareness programmes and encouraged industry also to do so, it is apparent that general awareness of digital is still low.[82] One report estimated that 40 per cent of the public had never heard of the transition to digital television.[83] There has been concern also about the number of new analogue-only television sets still being purchased each year: around 25 million in 2003.[84] Better progress has been made with cable and satellite. DBS already broadcasts in digital and offers digital television and radio services as well as some other services such as internet. Indeed, the competitive threat of the much greater channel capacity of DBS spurred cable into converting to digital so that it could also offer more channels and services.[85] Cable operators are gradually converting to digital technology, and many are adding digital-only tiers to their subscription packages.[86] Although

---

[75] Creech, above n 53, 367.

[76] HDTV provides greater picture and sound quality but uses more spectrum, thereby reducing the number of channels which can be provided when compared with SDTV. An Enhanced Standard is also available, which offers a quality somewhat lower than HDTV.

[77] Overbeck, above n 60, 493.

[78] *Ibid.*

[79] 47 USC § 309(j)(14).

[80] Deficit Reduction Act of 2005, § 3002(a), amending 47 USC § 309(j)(14)(A).

[81] FCC, *Media Bureau Staff Report Concerning Over-the-air Broadcast Television Viewers* (MB Docket No 04-210, 28 February 2005), paras 7 and 9.

[82] *Ibid*, para 22.

[83] *Ibid*, para 21, fn 69.

[84] *Ibid*, para 21.

[85] FCC, *Report and Order and Notice of Proposed Rulemaking, In the Matter of 2002 Biennial Regulatory Review—Review of the Commission's Broadcast Ownership Rules and Other Rules Adopted Pursuant to Section 202 of the Telecommunications Act of 1996*, FCC 03-127 (2 June 2003), paras 114–15. Transition to cable digital television has also been assisted by the FCC's plug-and-play rules which mandate that television sets allow a cable subscriber to receive digital cable without the need for an additional set-top box: FCC, *Media Bureau Staff Report*, above n 81, para 24.

[86] FCC, *Report and Order and Notice of Proposed Rulemaking (2003)*, above n 85, para 115.

cable and DBS are now offering digital radio services, over-the-air digital radio broadcasting has been slower to develop. Digital over-the-air radio services are now available via a standard, known as 'in-band on-channel', which does not require the allocation of additional spectrum to radio broadcasters to broadcast simultaneously in digital and analogue. This standard was approved by the FCC in 2002.[87]

Australia

The regulation of radio and television services in Australia is primarily a matter for federal law. The main legislative source is the Broadcasting Services Act 1992 (Cth) (BSA (Aus)) which, in relation to radio and television services, provides for spectrum planning and allocation, licensing, ownership and control regulation, and content regulation. When it was introduced, the BSA (Aus) represented a major overhaul of broadcasting regulation in Australia, and it was specifically designed to reduce the degree of statutory regulation in favour of industry regulation. Responsibility for supervision of the broadcasting services and their licensees, in accordance with the legislation, rests with an independent statutory authority. Until July 2005, the regulatory authority was the Australian Broadcasting Authority (ABA), which had been established in 1992 as part of the BSA (Aus) reforms. In 2005, a new regulatory authority was formed, the Australian Communications and Media Authority (ACMA).[88] ACMA follows the example set by Ofcom in the UK, because it is the product of a merger of existing regulatory authorities: the ABA, and the Australian Communications Authority, which had been responsible for telecommunications and (non-broadcasting) spectrum planning. Although the merged authority is meant to be a response to the changing and converging communications environment, the result has been more of an administrative achievement, because the legislation made no attempt to address substantively the type of powers and responsibilities such a body should have.[89] The BSA (Aus) makes explicit the objectives of Australian broadcasting regulation. Section 3 sets out these objectives, which include reference to promotion of a 'a diverse range of radio and television services offering entertainment, education and information,' and 'diversity in control of the more influential broadcasting services.'[90] Section 4 sets out the legislation's regulatory policy, and it gives a clear insight into the key elements of Australian broadcasting regulatory policy: the degree of regulation should be proportionate to the degree of influence which a broadcasting service is able to exert in 'shaping community views in Australia',[91]

---

[87] FCC, *FCC Selects Digital Radio Technology* (10 October 2002), http://hraunfoss.fcc.gov/edocs_public/attachmatch/DOC-227261A1.doc, accessed 23 May 2005.
[88] Australian Communications and Media Authority Act 2005 (Cth).
[89] Explanatory Memorandum, Australian Communications and Media Authority Bill 2004 (Cth), 1.
[90] BSA (Aus), s 3(1)(a) and (c).
[91] *Ibid*, s 4(1).

whilst regulation addressing the public interest in broadcasting must be balanced with the need to avoid undue financial and administrative burdens on industry.[92]

Pursuant to the BSA (Aus), broadcasting services are simply services which deliver television and radio programmes 'to persons having equipment appropriate for receiving that service, whether the delivery uses the radio frequency spectrum, cable, optical fibre, satellite or any other means or a combination of those means . . .'.[93] The BSA (Aus) classifies broadcasting services into categories according to the characteristics of the service. Determining the category into which the service falls is crucial because this will determine whether an individual or class licence is needed, and the degree of regulatory control which will apply to the service. One category of broadcasting service, national broadcasting services, is not actually licensed by the ABA, although it is specified in the legislation. The national broadcasting services are the over-the-air services provided by the publicly owned and funded broadcasters: the Australian Broadcasting Corporation (ABC) and the Special Broadcasting Service (SBS).[94] They are the Australian equivalent of the UK public broadcaster, the BBC, although SBS is allowed to broadcast some limited advertising. The BSA (Aus) regulatory regime does not apply to national broadcasting services unless expressly mentioned. Separate legislation sets out the nature and function of these broadcasters: in the case of the ABC, the Australian Broadcasting Corporation Act 1983; and, for SBS, the Special Broadcasting Service Act 1991. The ABC is intended as a traditional public service broadcaster, while SBS provides a more specialised service of multicultural and multilingual programming. Both provide radio and television services. The ABC provides a national television network, four national radio networks, and a range of local and regional radio services, whilst the SBS provides a national television network and a number of radio services.

A radio or television service will be a commercial broadcasting service if it is funded by advertising revenue, operated for profit, and provides general appeal programmes which are broadcast free-to-air, able to be received by commonly available equipment.[95] The commercial television and radio services dominate broadcasting in Australia. Of the services regulated by the BSA (Aus), the commercial services are seen as the most influential, and, consistent with the Act's regulatory policy, are subject to the greatest degree of regulation. Television commercial services are regarded as more influential than radio, and so are subject to a higher degree of regulation. The mainland capital cities, and some regional areas, have three commercial television stations, and most other areas have two commercial stations.[96] Most of the

[92] BSA (Aus), s 4(2)(a).

[93] *Ibid*, s 6(1). The original intention of a technology-neutral approach has not been sustained throughout the legislation. A 'program' is defined as 'matter the primary purpose of which is to entertain, to educate or to inform an audience; or . . . advertising or sponsorship matter': s 6(1).

[94] BSA (Aus), s 13.

[95] *Ibid*, s 14.

[96] Productivity Commission, *Broadcasting*, Report No 11 (Canberra, AusInfo, 2000), 76, and Communications Law Centre, 'Media Ownership Update' (2005) 168 *Communications Update*. Some

commercial television stations are owned by a metropolitan or regional network, and each of the regional networks is affiliated with one of the metropolitan networks, namely the Seven, Nine, and Ten Networks.[97] There is a prohibition on any further commercial broadcasting television licences being awarded until the end of 2006, although it is unlikely that the government will permit a fourth free-to-air commercial service to be licensed.[98] About 274 commercial radio services operate across the AM and FM bands, but, like television, most stations are part of a network.[99] Community broadcasting services are non-profit-making services, able to be received free-to-air on commonly available equipment.[100] Community broadcasting (originally known as 'public broadcasting') began in the 1970s, and, as the name indicates, is intended to meet the 'needs of a local community, or of a particular sector of the community'.[101] Services qualifying as community broadcasting might be local services, or services directed to a particular ethnic or religious community, or catering for specialised interests such as a particular genre of music. They are also expected to have in place mechanisms which will encourage community participation in their operation.[102] Community services have to rely mainly on membership subscriptions and sponsorship for their funding as they are prohibited from advertising, and they receive only very limited government funding. The community broadcasting sector is similar to the US public broadcasting sector and the new UK community radio services. There are approximately 350 community radio broadcasting services operating throughout Australia.[103] Community television trials began in 1994, and in 2004, four licences were awarded for the first permanent community television services.[104] Community television services are only available in metropolitan areas and because of spectrum limitations have only limited

more remote areas have only one service available (known as 'solus markets'). Through a practice of aggregation, which allowed some solus markets to be aggregated, most regional areas will have access to commercial services equivalent to what is available in metropolitan markets: Productivity Commission, above, 77. The Productivity Commission conducted an extensive investigation during 1999–2000 into the Australian broadcasting industry and its regulation. The Productivity Commission is a government agency which provides advice on microeconomic reform. It investigates industry regulation with a view to determining whether there are sufficient benefits to industry and the public interest to justify the regulation of a relevant industry.

[97] Productivity Commission, above n 96, 77, and Communications Law Centre, above n 96.

[98] BSA (Aus), s 28. Senator H Coonan, 'The New Multimedia World' (speech delivered to the National Press Club, Canberra, 31 August 2005), http://www.minister.dcita.gov.au/media/speeches/the_new_multimedia_world_-_address_to_the_national_press_club_-_canberra_-_31_august_2005, accessed 1 September 2005, 6.

[99] ABA, *Annual Report 2004–05* (2004), 17. This figure includes licences (13) operated outside the broadcasting services band spectrum; such services could be delivered via cable or satellite, for example.

[100] BSA (Aus), s 15.

[101] Explanatory Memorandum, Broadcasting Services Bill 1992, 23.

[102] BSA (Aus), sch 2, cl 9(2)(c).

[103] ACMA, *Community Radio Broadcasting Licences* (LIC031, 1 August 2005), http://www.acma.gov.au/acmainterwr/_assets/main/lib100052/lic031_community_radio_broadcasting_ licences.pdf, accessed 21 October 2005.

[104] These licences are known as 'CTV licences': BSA (Aus), s 6(1). It is intended that the remaining metropolitan markets will also be granted permanent licences in due course. There are also around 80 well-established community television services serving remote indigenous communities.

coverage and relatively poor transmission quality. The viability of community television is still uncertain.

Subscription broadcasting services are services which are only available to the
public upon subscription, designed to provide programmes of general appeal.[105] A
licence to offer subscription services is not tied to any particular mode of delivery.[106] Subscription television broadcasting did not begin in Australia until 1995,
because of long-standing government policy to protect the free-to-air services.[107]
Subscription television has been slow to develop and has struggled for profitability,
and there have been a number of failures. In addition to a pro-satellite policy, the
introduction of cable delivery was also problematic. The two major telecommunications carriers, Telstra and Optus, were encouraged, through government competition policy, to build cable networks. The result was that they both laid expensive
hybrid fibre-coaxial networks in metropolitan areas, resulting in 85 per cent duplication.[108] In a small market like Australia, it was unlikely that there would ever be
sufficient demand to deliver viability to two networks, and in 2002, Foxtel, the subscription service operated on the Telstra network, and Optus reached a content-
sharing agreement.[109] Subscription television services in Australia still represent a
relatively small share of the broadcasting market, although more recently the market has improved, and Foxtel is expected to reach profitability in 2006.[110] Around
25 per cent of Australian households now take subscription services, compared with
89 per cent in the US, and 45 per cent in the UK.[111] Apart from the impediments
produced by government policy at their start, subscription services are still affected
by restrictions designed to protect the free-to-air commercial services. For example,
subscription services are restricted in the amount of advertising revenue which they
can generate,[112] and extensive preservation of sporting events for the free-to-air
services limits the scope for subscription services to broadcast live sporting
events.[113] The BSA (Aus) also designates a category of service known as narrowcasting. These services can be provided either on a subscription or non-subscription

---

[105] BSA (Aus), s 16.

[106] When subscription television broadcasting was first permitted, it was tied to satellite delivery.
This was because the government was seeking to sell off the publicly owned satellite company,
AUSSAT, and envisaged that a satellite carrying subscription services would be more valuable. The
pro-satellite policy was not helped by the requirement that satellite services be delivered in digital, even
though the technology was not then available: Productivity Commission, above n 96, 292–93.
Television subscription services require an individual licence, but subscription radio services operate
under a class licence.

[107] Productivity Commission, above n 96, 292.

[108] T Barr, *Newmedia.com.au: The Changing Face of Australia's Media and Communications*
(Sydney, Allen & Unwin, 2000), 58–59.

[109] For further information, see ch 5.

[110] M Day, 'Foxtel About to Hit Paydirt', *The Australian* (Sydney), 18 October 2005,
http://www.theaustralian.news.com.au/common/story_page/0,5744,16900270%255E7582,00.html,
accessed 21 October 2005. The content-sharing agreement and Foxtel's move to digital are likely to
have contributed to the growth in subscription numbers: *ibid.*

[111] *Ibid.*

[112] It is a condition of a subscription television broadcasting licence that subscription income will
be the predominant source of revenue: BSA (Aus), sch 2, cl 10(2)(b).

[113] This is considered in ch 5.

(open) basis.[114] Narrowcasting services are intended to have limited reach because they are targeted, for example, to a special interest group or a particular location, or operated for a limited period. Narrowcasting services, which operate under class licences,[115] will have a limited impact on the broadcasting environment, and this is reflected in the minimal regulation to which these services are subject.[116] These services operate under class licences.

As flagged, the BSA (Aus) was intended to mark a change in the regulation of broadcasting services in Australia:

> [It] . . . represented a conscious attempt to implement good regulatory practice and was a major step towards a more market based, less interventionist approach to broadcasting regulation.[117]

The result is a combination of direct regulatory control in certain areas, and a co-regulatory approach in others, giving industry responsibility for rule-setting and compliance monitoring, and ACMA responsibility for enforcement of these industry codes. Thus, ACMA has direct control, through statutory provisions, licence conditions, or standards, of ownership and control rules, and some aspects of content regulation such as Australian content and children's programming. Where ACMA has direct control, it will also have direct enforcement powers. Other areas of content regulation are governed by codes of practice which are developed by industry groups representing the various broadcasting service categories. The matters to be covered in a code are set out in the legislation, and the codes are registered by ACMA.[118] However, unlike licence conditions and standards, the codes are not directly enforced by ACMA. A complaint about a breach of code must be made to the licensee, and only if the response is unsatisfactory, or not given within a specified time, can the matter be referred to ACMA.[119] Even then, ACMA has limited enforcement powers, as it can only

---

[114] BSA (Aus), ss 17 and 18, respectively.

[115] Although services may be able to operate under a class licence under the BSA (Aus), they may need a transmitter licence from ACMA under the Radiocommunications Act 1992. Other broadcasting services may also have to obtain a separate transmitter licence, depending upon their delivery format. Services using that part of the radio frequency spectrum known as the 'broadcasting services band' will not have to apply for separate transmitter licences. The broadcasting services band is primarily reserved for commercial, community, and national broadcasting. With regard to commercial and community broadcasting services, the licensing process will differ according to whether the service is to be offered via the broadcasting services band or not. This reflects the fact that if the service is to use the band, spectrum will be allocated to it. Thus, licences for commercial broadcasting services using the band will be allocated under an auction-type system, whilst licences for those not using the system are essentially issued on demand: BSA (Aus), ss 36(1) and 40(1). For community services, the difference will be between a merits-based award and one on demand: BSA (Aus), ss 84 and 82.

[116] There have been some concerns that services have inappropriately claimed narrowcasting status in order to take advantage of the lower regulatory burden: Productivity Commission, above n 96, 296–97. There are around 200 open narrowcasting services licensed: ABA, *Annual Report 2004–05* (2005), 17. Services operate for a variety of interests and needs, such as ethnic, sporting, tourist and educational: Productivity Commission, above n 96, 81.

[117] Productivity Commission, above n 96, 450.

[118] BSA (Aus), s 123.

[119] *Ibid,* s 148.

impose a licence condition requiring the licensee to comply with the relevant code of practice or, if it is satisfied that the code of practice, or a provision of it, is not providing effective community safeguards, it can determine a standard on the matter.[120] In recent years, there have been concerns about practices in the commercial broadcasting industry, particularly in relation to radio news and current affairs reporting, and the adequacy of the co-regulation scheme. ACMA's predecessor, ABA, was forced to undertake a major investigation of a number of commercial radio licensees in relation to allegations that radio presenters were accepting cash in return for favourable on-air commentary.[121] The Productivity Commission considered that the co-regulation model appeared to be closer to a model of self-regulation,[122] and was critical of ABA for its passive approach to monitoring and enforcement.[123] As will be suggested in Chapter Four, the adequacy of the regulatory framework can have an impact on protection of broadcasting pluralism.

Australian broadcasting policy and regulation has been heavily influenced by a determination to protect the over-the-air commercial broadcasters, so that developments with the potential to expand available services have often been restricted. This can be observed regarding subscription services, and the same pattern has been repeated with the introduction of digital technology. The regulatory framework is so framed that many of the potential benefits of digital technology, such as the opportunity to broadcast additional programming and other services, have so far not been realised.[124] Neither government nor industry has shown itself willing to encourage the spread of digital,[125] although in September 2005, the government announced a review to develop ways to encourage take-up of digital.[126] The mandating of high definition as the required standard, and a virtual prohibition on multichannelling, means that there is limited incentive for audiences to buy the still-expensive digital equipment. The commercial television broadcasting services have been allocated spectrum to enable them to simulcast their services in analogue and digital. Digital television began in the metropolitan areas in 2001 with a staged introduction in the regional areas. Currently, the take-up of digital is very low: digital television has been taken up by only 12 per cent of the population,

---

[120] BSA (Aus), ss 44(2)(a) (eg in relation to commercial broadcasting services), and 125(1). A standard will apply to all licensees for that broadcasting service. The government has been consulting on whether to provide ACMA with greater enforcement powers: Department of Communications, Information Technology and the Arts, *Proposed Reforms to the Broadcasting Regulatory Powers of the Australian Communications and Media Authority, Issues Paper* (November 2005).

[121] Discussed in ch 4.

[122] Productivity Commission, above n 96, 453.

[123] *Ibid*, 480.

[124] For further information on the regulatory constraints imposed on digital broadcasting, see L Hitchens, 'Digital Television Broadcasting—An Australian Approach' (2001) 12(4) *Entertainment Law Review* 112.

[125] Some of the free-to-air television broadcasters in Australia are able to exert considerable influence in shaping government communications policy, and their lack of interest in digital has no doubt contributed to the restrictive digital policy. For an account of their influence in relation to the introduction of digital, see Barr, above n 108, 203–8.

[126] Senator H Coonan, 'Review to drive digital take-up', Media Release 112/05 (27 September 2005).

although 96 per cent have access to digital.[127] Under current provisions, the analogue signal is set to be switched off at the end of 2008 (although there is provision
for this to be extended).[128] On current penetration rates it seems unlikely that this
date will be kept, and this has been acknowledged by the Minister; the matter is
under review.[129] It has been estimated that on the present rate of uptake, less than
50 per cent of households will have digital television by 2008.[130]

Digital also provides the opportunity for interactive services to be offered using
television receivers. The legislation made provision for these services to be
licensed, known in Australia as datacasting, but the conditions on what could be
provided were so restrictive that no one was initially willing to apply for the
licences when they were offered.[131] Currently only a few datacasting services operate under trial arrangements. The datacasting framework will have to be reconsidered, because the restrictions on what can be datacast are due to expire at the
beginning of 2007. Plans for digital radio were announced in October 2005; before
then digital radio was restricted to trials only. The proposals appear to favour
incumbent broadcasters, who will be given spectrum to enable digital broadcasting, although they will not have to simulcast their analogue services.[132] There have
been suggestions also that the choice of the digital standard, Eureka 147, will
favour existing broadcasters because it is not spectrum-efficient.[133] There will be a
moratorium for six years from the commencement of digital radio broadcasting
on the allocation of new digital commercial radio licences.[134] It will be at least a
couple of years before digital radio begins. Subscription services commenced
digital broadcasting in 2005, and this may help to stimulate demand, because
unlike the commercial and national services they will have much greater channel
capacity for additional programming, and flexibility in what they offer.

Government policy and a small market means that broadcasting in Australia is
still dominated by free-to-air radio and television services, which utilise the radio
frequency spectrum and analogue spectrum, whilst subscription services continue
to have limited penetration of the market. However, over the next decade there
could be considerable change in the broadcasting environment. Apart from the

---

[127] Senator H Coonan, above n 98, 8.
[128] BSA (Aus), sch 4, cl 6(c). The date will be later for regional areas which commenced digital
broadcasting in 2004.
[129] Senator H Coonan, above n 98, 9.
[130] Standing Committee on Communications, Information Technology and the Arts, *Inquiry into
the Uptake of Digital Television: Background Discussion Paper* (17 March 2005), http://www.aph.gov.au/
house/committee/cita/digitaltv/infopaper.pdf, accessed 28 May 2005.
[131] The datacasting services were restricted in order to ensure that no back-door commercial television services emerged.
[132] Senator H Coonan, 'Framework for the Introduction of Digital Radio', Media Release 119/05 (14
October 2005), www.minister.dcita.gov.au, accessed 15 October 2005. Spectrum will be allocated to
national, commercial, and wide-coverage community broadcasters.
[133] G Philipson, 'Battle on as the Wireless goes Digital', *Sydney Morning Herald* (Sydney),
6 September 2005, 29.
[134] Although the moratorium only applies to services offered in the broadcasting services band of
the spectrum.

likely reform of ownership and control rules, a number of government reviews are required by the digital regulatory framework. In accordance with the statutory timetable, these were taking place in 2005. It is difficult to envisage that the incumbent free-to-air broadcasters will be able to continue to restrain change and the expansion of digital.

2

POLICY RATIONALES AND
IMPLICATIONS FOR REGULATION

Introduction

As touched upon briefly in Chapter One, a policy promoting a media environment which represents or provides opportunities for a diversity of voices, information, ideas, and opinions is seen as desirable, even essential. This can be confidently asserted for countries embracing liberal democratic values, and certainly for the countries being considered in this book. Regulation which is designed to protect broadcasting pluralism obviously connects with these diversity values. However, the translation of policy into regulation has lacked coherence, and the justifications for regulation have been inadequate and vulnerable to criticism. This chapter will examine the policy framework underlying broadcasting pluralism regulation, since this has had, and continues to have, a significant influence on regulatory attitudes. It will suggest that the weaknesses in the current relationship between policy and regulation are likely to distort broadcasting pluralism reform agendas. It will also suggest that a more positive and coherent case can still be made for broadcasting regulation through the concept of the public sphere, and that the use of the public sphere model will better explain the place of regulation in the promotion of broadcasting pluralism. A normative case for broadcasting regulation will also enable a better understanding of what role the 'new media' will play in the public sphere, and how they should be treated within the regulatory space.

Valuing Media Diversity

Notwithstanding their entertainment role, particularly obvious in the case of television and radio, the media have an important function providing information, and facilitating and promoting the public debate which is seen as essential to the proper functioning of a democracy. There is an intimate relationship between democratic debate and the media. Governments, politicians, and public figures are rarely able to gain access to citizens in sufficiently large numbers except through the media. The media have become the town square. For citizens, the media are a major source for information and commentary on public issues. To be an effective contributor to this democratic process, the media, as a channel for ideas and information and generator of debate, must be able to offer a variety of voices and views, and operate independently, without undue dominance by public or private power. As Gibbons has stated this requirement for diversity is

> a practical recognition of the way that complex democracies work, with ideas and opinion being channelled into the constitutional process through the media, from discussions taking place in a whole range of overlapping constituencies and representative groups.[1]

To the extent that the functioning of democracy requires the exchange and debate of information and ideas, the media is a participant in the democratic process, as well as forming a space which facilitates that interchange.[2]

In Western democracies, free speech is valued and protected, sometimes expressly, sometimes implicitly.[3] In recognising the importance of free speech, and its claim to protection, consideration needs to be given to its relationship with the media. Whilst free speech protection might be readily accorded to individual citizens, it might be appropriate also to accord that protection to the media, although the nature of that right may require more exploration. It is helpful first to look at the justifications traditionally presented for free speech protection.[4] One justification is labelled 'the argument from truth'. This justification asserts that enabling free discussion will help to arrive at a discovery of the truth. Free speech, it is argued, is necessary if true facts and reliable opinions are to be ascertained, and false claims discerned. This justification derives particularly from the work of John Stuart Mill. Apart from the value inherent in the discovery of truth, there is also an implicit assumption that enabling truth to be discerned will be beneficial to society.[5] This is an argument for freedom of speech which might be thought to be most closely associated with the interests of those receiving the speech, rather than those producing it, although, as Barendt suggests, even speakers will have an interest in being free to assert their particular beliefs.[6] However, it is questionable whether it

---

[1] T Gibbons, *Regulating the Media*, 2nd edn (London, Sweet & Maxwell, 1998), 31.

[2] The role of the media in the democratic process has been explored in detail in other media studies. See, eg, Gibbons, above n 1, particularly 21–35; W Hoffmann-Riem, *Regulating Media: The Licensing and Supervision of Broadcasting in Six Countries* (New York, The Guilford Press, 1996); 297–300; M Feintuck, *Media Regulation, Public Interest and the Law* (Edinburgh, Edinburgh University Press, 1999), ch 1; and R Craufurd Smith, *Broadcasting Law and Fundamental Rights* (Oxford, Clarendon Press, 1997).

[3] E Barendt, *Freedom of Speech*, 2nd edn (Oxford, Oxford University Press, 2005), 1.

[4] The justifications will be considered here only briefly. For a full discussion see Barendt, above n 3. The brief outline presented here is taken from Barendt at 7–21. The justifications for free speech protection are also fully summarised in Gibbons, above n 1, 21–25 and Feintuck above n 2, 11–13.

[5] See, eg, JS Mill, *On Liberty and Other Essays* (Oxford, Oxford University Press, 1991), 59 and generally.

[6] E Barendt, 'Interests in Freedom of Speech: Theory and Practice' in KF Sin (ed), *Legal Explorations: Essays in Honour of Professor Michael Chesterman* (Sydney, Lawbook Company, 2003), 175 at 175 and 178.

is possible to reach and to recognise an objective conclusion as to what is truth, and even whether truth is the most important public value. From a practical viewpoint also, this seems a hazardous way to ensure the discernment of truth, since it would be necessary to ensure that no one voice or view is drowned out, accidentally or otherwise, by another. Nevertheless, the argument from truth has been very influential in the US, particularly in relation to media, specifically broadcasting, regulation.[7] The argument from truth, in its guise as the 'marketplace of ideas', is illustrated by Schauer:

> truth will most likely surface when all opinions may freely be expressed, when there is an open and unregulated market for the trade in ideas. By relying on the operation of the market to evaluate any opinion, we subject opinions to a test more reliable than the appraisal of any one individual or government.[8]

The second justification focuses more on the individual, rather than on societal and utilitarian aims. Here the argument is that speech must be unrestricted to enable individuals to develop; if they are to develop as persons with their own sets of beliefs and opinions, then they must be free to engage in discussion and to hear ideas. This is an argument for free speech which appears to be more concerned with the interests of the speaker, although it may also be in the interests of the individual, and his or her development and self-fulfilment, to be able to have access to speech as a recipient, since the ideas and opinions of others may contribute to the individual's development.[9] Whatever the validity of this claim to justify free speech protection,[10] it appears to have little relevance to the media, except in so far as it enables the dissemination of material which may contribute to the individual's self-development. Finally, there is the argument from democracy. Whilst this would appear to have particular relevance for the media, it is also, of the justifications (assuming that they can be so neatly isolated from one another, or that one justification will be applicable in all speech situations),[11] the one which is most attractive for modern democracies as a basis for upholding free speech protection for individual citizens.[12] This justification asserts that freedom of speech is necessary for the proper functioning and accountability of democratic government. Freedom of speech enables citizens to receive information, to debate and assess government actions and policies, and so to participate in the democratic process. In this sense, it is a basis for free speech which will be concerned with the interests of those who speak and those who receive speech.[13] In the second, and latest,

---

[7] See *Red Lion v FCC* 395 US 367 (1969), 390.

[8] F Schauer, *Free Speech: A Philosophical Enquiry* (Cambridge, Cambridge University Press, 1982), 16. Barendt argues that the marketplace of ideas argument is a distortion of the argument of truth put forward by Mill: Barendt, above n 3, 11–13.

[9] Barendt, above n 6, 177–78.

[10] See Barendt, above n 3, 13–18 for a critique of this justification.

[11] Barendt, above n 6, 178. Although the argument from democracy will be seen as likely to be most relevant to the issues under discussion in this book, it should not be assumed that the other justifications have no relevance.

[12] Barendt, above n 3, 18.

[13] Barendt, above n 6, 178.

edition of his free speech study, Barendt includes a fourth argument for free speech protection: suspicion of government.[14] Unlike the other justifications canvassed, this theory is essentially a negative argument; free speech is justified because government cannot be trusted. For example, governments cannot be trusted not to suppress speech which may be threatening to or critical of their power. But its negative nature means that this justification is unable to provide much guidance as to what speech can be regulated and what cannot: that is, when government can be trusted and when it should not. The negative argument is not without its value, however; it is often used in conjunction with, and to bolster, the positive justifications. As Barendt states:

> The negative case for free speech is parasitic on positive arguments; it reinforces the latter, providing reasons why government should not be trusted to make distinctions in this area, but it does not itself show why speech is special.[15]

However, this justification raises an obvious, but, in the context of a study on media, important question: why should government be singled out for distrust? In modern societies, where economic interests can exert considerable power, there might be a comparable suspicion of corporations. But if this is so, then something more than distrust is needed to work out how to draw the lines between the occasions when speech should be protected, and those occasions where it is appropriate to regulate.[16]

The media are able to play a role in the democratic process as participants in, and by providing a forum for, public debate; and, since free speech protection can be justified by reference to the importance of free speech to the democratic process, it makes sense to extend that free speech protection to the media. This application to the media is not, however, straightforward, and describing that application, and the differential treatment given to the press and to broadcasting, provides an early indication of the troublesome relationship between the policy and regulatory framework of broadcasting pluralism, something which is crucial to the subject matter of this book. This is a point which will be explored further in the next section, but first something needs to be said briefly about the application of free speech principles to the media. There are a couple of issues to be addressed here: first, who can assert this protection; and secondly, how free speech principles differ between the press and broadcasting.

The application of free speech protection to individuals should not ordinarily be problematic: free speech protection should apply to them in their capacity as individual citizens. It is not an unlimited or absolute freedom. One individual's right to speech may have to be constrained, so that another individual might also enjoy that same freedom. Similarly, there may be circumstances where in the interests of the community it will be appropriate to constrain the freedom, such as

---

[14] Barendt, above n 3, 21–23.
[15] *Ibid*, 22
[16] *Ibid*, 22.

for national security purposes.[17] For media, the issue is more complex. Who has the right to claim free speech? It hardly seems appropriate to guarantee protection to all individuals associated with a media organisation, for how then does one determine the priority of claims between the newspaper proprietor, the editor, and the journalist, or the broadcasting station owner, and the producer and the scriptwriter?[18] The relationship between free speech protection and the media can be better understood by characterising freedom of speech, as it applies to media, in a way which is different from freedom of speech when applied to individuals. Barendt suggests that, when speaking of the media, it is not appropriate to view freedom of speech as being simply about individual rights of expression, which arise as a protection against arbitrary government intervention.[19] Instead, it is necessary to focus on the institutional nature of the media, rather than characterising the media as a collection of individuals each claiming rights. In considering the nature of freedom of speech in the media context, it is helpful to refer to it as 'media freedom' to distinguish it from traditional understandings: as Barendt suggests, media freedom can be viewed as a freedom which is a derivative of the free speech principle.[20]

There are two, not entirely unrelated, aspects of this media freedom which need to be emphasised. The first is that media freedom should be understood not as having value in itself, but as an instrumental freedom. In other words, media freedom is valued and protected because it can serve and promote other values which are regarded as important within the community, such as the promotion of public debate.[21] Equally, it may be necessary to restrict media freedom to ensure that it serves, and not undermines, these values.[22] Hence, as shall be seen in the following chapters, regulatory measures may be imposed which are designed to promote pluralism and diversity, even though they may restrict the freedom of media organisations and the individuals associated with them.[23] The second aspect of media freedom which needs to be addressed is to clarify what is actually sought to be protected.[24] Here, the focus is on two free speech principles: the

[17] For a fuller discussion of these issues, see Barendt, above n 3, 23–30.
[18] EM Barendt, *Broadcasting Law: A Comparative Study* (Oxford, Clarendon Press, 1995), 32–33.
[19] E Barendt, 'Press and Broadcasting Freedom: Does Anyone Have Any Rights to Free Speech?' (1991) 44 *Current Legal Problems* 63 at 65–66.
[20] *Ibid*, 67.
[21] J Lichtenberg, 'Foundations and Limits of Freedom of the Press' in J Lichtenberg (ed), *Democracy and the Mass Media* (Cambridge, Cambridge University Press, 1990), 102 at 104–5, and Barendt, above n 19, 66.
[22] Barendt, above n 19, 67.
[23] In seeking to explain media freedom, it is not being asserted that the instrumental nature of this freedom has no application to individual citizens. In some circumstances it will be appropriate to view the free speech rights of individuals as being instrumental in nature also; this may be particularly so when free speech rights rely upon the argument from democracy. Equally, by focusing on media freedom as an institutional freedom, it is not being claimed that those individuals responsible for, or involved in, the media organisation's operations will have no individual claim to free speech protection. However, there may be practical and regulatory limits on those individual rights: Barendt, above n 18, 40–42.
[24] This too may have relevance to individual citizens, but the principles to be described here are particularly useful in understanding the nature of media freedom, and the implications of that freedom.

'non-interference principle' and the 'multiplicity of voices principle'.[25] The former, and perhaps more readily recognisable, principle can be understood as
meaning that speech should be able to proceed without interference.[26] In the
media context, this will be reflected in measures which provide protection from
arbitrary government interference or censorship. The 'multiplicity of voices principle' suggests that media freedom is maintained when 'expression and diversity of
expression flourish'.[27] Although not necessarily in conflict, there may be situations
in which these two principles will conflict, so that one principle will have to be subordinated to the other; one's right to non-interference might be constrained, so as
to enable others to have the opportunity to speak in order to ensure a multiplicity
of voices.[28] The relevance of this second principle to the media is clear when the
previous point, about media freedom being an instrumental freedom, is recalled.
The media offer an especially suitable vehicle to encourage diverse expression to
flourish and to be accessible, so it may be necessary to regulate media freedom in
order to ensure that the multiplicity principle which values 'discussion, debate,
diversity of ideas and sources of information' is promoted.[29] The multiplicity of
voices principle is operative in both pluralism and diversity regulatory measures.
Promotion of a multiplicity of voices might be threatened if there was only one
source of media, or if all media outlets were controlled by the state or one corporate entity. To address this risk, it is usual to restrict the number of media outlets any one corporate entity can control. Equally, regulation might be imposed
which facilitates a range of views being aired. Finally, ensuring that there are a
number of media outlets, separately controlled, provides journalists, and others
involved in the media, with greater opportunities for employment. Limited
opportunities for employment might mean journalists and other media workers
would feel constrained in their choice of topics or ideas to present, if they knew or
believed that their employer would disapprove. The risk of the so-called 'chilling
effect' can be minimised if there are a number of independently controlled media
outlets between which journalists and other media workers can move.

Two further issues need to be addressed. So far this discussion of freedom of
speech and media freedom has been conducted in a jurisdictional vacuum, yet
these free speech principles can be realised in quite different ways. Something
needs to be said about these differences, because they have influenced the policy
and regulatory approaches towards broadcasting pluralism. Secondly, this discussion has so far not distinguished between press and broadcasting, leaving the
impression that free speech principles might impact in the same way on these different media. This impression needs to be corrected, and, in so doing, will lead on
to the next section of this chapter, which addresses some of the reasoning behind
the differing policy and regulatory approaches to the press and broadcasting.

---

[25] For a full discussion of the nature of these principles, see Lichtenberg, above n 21, 102–35.
[26] *Ibid*, 107.
[27] *Ibid*.
[28] *Ibid*.
[29] *Ibid*, 122.

Although the focus of this book is broadcasting, these differences are important for the examination of broadcasting pluralism policy and regulation.

The free speech approaches adopted in the three jurisdictions will be outlined here. It is convenient to begin with the US, because it has the longest tradition of providing express recognition of free speech rights. The US Constitution's First Amendment provides that 'Congress shall make no law . . . abridging the freedom of speech, or of the press'. Despite the simplicity of the statement, the Amendment, as Barendt has noted, has given rise to much interpretative complexity.[30] The absolutist terms of the protection have not in fact been realised, and the US Supreme Court has always recognised the impracticality of allowing entirely unregulated speech.[31] Other interests, also of importance to society, may need to be protected or promoted. More importantly, there has been recognition that 'regulation, and on occasion even the prohibition, of speech may be justified to protect the free speech rights of others'.[32] The result has been that the Supreme Court has developed a set of balancing tests to determine whether a law which restricts free speech will be constitutional. The wording of the First Amendment appears to be more in line with the non-interference principle and, despite the qualifications in the application of this principle, as noted above, it (coupled perhaps with a marked wariness of government intervention) has been an important influence on US free speech jurisprudence.[33] This may help to explain also the interpretation given to the First Amendment guarantee of press freedom. Press freedom has not generally been interpreted as offering the press any special protection; the press will have the same protection offered under the free speech guarantee, rights which will be enjoyed by 'owners, editors, and journalists'.[34] Although Lichtenberg has argued that in the context of modern, large-scale press organisations, press freedom should be treated as an instrumental freedom,[35] this is not an interpretation with sits easily with US free speech jurisprudence.

For obvious historical reasons, the First Amendment makes no reference to broadcasting, but it is here that the differences in treatment of the press and broadcasting begin to emerge. Although First Amendment protection is relevant to broadcasting, the protection it offers has always been much more limited compared with what it offers to the press. Regulation applied to broadcasting has been treated as constitutional, which, if applied to the press, would almost certainly have been regarded as infringing the First Amendment. The right of reply principle provides a good illustration of this. A state law which required newspapers which had published criticism of a political candidate to publish a right of reply was held by the Supreme Court to be an infringement of the First Amendment.[36]

---

[30] Barendt, above n 3, 48.
[31] *Ibid*, 49.
[32] *Ibid.*
[33] See also *ibid*, 53–54.
[34] *Ibid*, 419–20 and 422–23, but, see also 432–33.
[35] See generally Lichtenberg, above n 21.
[36] *The Miami Herald Publishing Company* v *Tornillo* 418 US 241 (1974).

Even though the court acknowledged the arguments about restricted entry to the newspaper market and the risk of monopoly control,[37] it was unwilling to supplant editorial control; any intrusion into the editorial process was inconsistent with the constitutional guarantee of a free press.[38] The decision affirms the autonomy of the newspaper editor—the speaker's rights—whilst rejecting any notion that the First Amendment might confer positive rights which would recognise the interests of the readers of the newspaper to receive another perspective.[39] However, when it comes to broadcasting, the Supreme Court has been willing to reach a different First Amendment perspective. A rule requiring broadcasters to offer a right of reply was held not to infringe First Amendment rights: because broadcasting used a scarce resource (the radio frequency spectrum), the interests of the viewers and listeners took preference over the interests of the broadcaster.[40] A free and uninhibited marketplace of ideas required regulation if it was not to be dominated by monopoly interests: access to scarce resources had to be shared.[41] Although the *Red Lion* decision can be seen as conferring positive speech rights,[42] this cannot be taken too far, for, as Barendt notes, the decision was seen by many commentators as an exception to the orthodox First Amendment jurisprudence.[43] It was only the circumstances of frequency scarcity which justified what is ultimately seen as an interference with the rights of the owners and controllers of the broadcasting station.[44] This also explained the differences in the approach to regulation of cable compared with over-the-air broadcasting. The broadcasting right-of-reply obligation was part of a more general set of responsibilities, referred to as the 'Fairness Doctrine', but over time the Federal Communications Commission (FCC) has removed the obligations which made up this Doctrine, justifying its decisions by reference to the demise of spectrum scarcity.[45] Despite the *Red Lion* precedent, the FCC has always adopted a cautious approach to regulation, particularly in relation to content regulation. Where regulation has been considered necessary, the preference has been for structural regulation, such as rules limiting ownership and control of broadcasting stations, and must-carry rules.[46] Structural regulation, rather than content regulation, has been regarded as a more acceptable means, in a free speech context, of creating the conditions for the promotion of pluralism and diversity of voice. It is debatable

---

[37] *Ibid*, 254, per Burger CJ.

[38] *Ibid*, 258, per Burger CJ.

[39] M Chesterman, *Freedom of Speech in Australian Law: A Delicate Plant* (Aldershot, Ashgate Dartmouth, 2000), 40–42.

[40] *Red Lion*, above n 7, 390.

[41] See *ibid*.

[42] Chesterman, above n 39, 40–42.

[43] E Barendt, 'Structural and Content Regulation of the Media: United Kingdom Law and Some American Comparisons' in E Barendt (ed), *The Yearbook of Media and Entertainment Law 1997/98* (Oxford, Clarendon Press, 1997), 75 at 77.

[44] Barendt, above n 3, 445.

[45] The Fairness Doctrine and its current status is discussed in ch 4 (at p 147).

[46] For a discussion of 'must-carry rules', see ch 5 (at p 235).

whether that distinction can really be justified.[47] Thus, US guarantees of speech and press freedom have generally been understood and applied in a manner which is more consistent with the classical view of free speech—protection from state interference. Even though there has been a greater willingness, in the field of broadcasting, to recognise that free speech protection might require measures which positively ensure a diversity of voices, there has been no general recognition that free speech in the context of the media, media freedom, should be treated as an instrumental freedom. The free speech jurisprudence does not provide a strong basis for a regulatory framework designed to promote broadcasting pluralism.

The incorporation into UK law of the European Convention for the Protection of Human Rights and Fundamental Freedoms (the Convention) introduced an express free speech guarantee but, as Barendt suggests, the move may not be as dramatic as it might at first appear.[48] The Human Rights Act 1998 (HRA) incorporates the freedom of expression guarantee found in Article 10 of the Convention. Unlike the US free speech guarantee, Article 10 is not written in such absolutist terms and, specifically, does not preclude the licensing of broadcasting, whilst Article 10(2) also recognises a number of other situations which would justify a restriction on freedom of expression:

1 Everyone has the right to freedom of expression. This right shall include freedom to hold opinions and to receive and impart information and ideas without interference by public authority and regardless of frontiers. This article shall not prevent States from requiring the licensing of broadcasting, television or cinema enterprises.

2 The exercise of these freedoms, since it carries with it duties and responsibilities, may be subject to such formalities, conditions, restrictions or penalties as are prescribed by law and are necessary in a democratic society, in the interests of national security, territorial integrity or public safety, for the prevention of disorder or crime, for the protection of health or morals, for the protection of the reputation or rights of others, for preventing the disclosure of information received in confidence, or for maintaining the authority and impartiality of the judiciary.

Similarly, the enjoyment of freedom of expression rights will have to be balanced with other Convention rights.[49] Although an express guarantee of free speech will be valuable in bringing the existence of the right into public and judicial consciousness,[50] the UK courts had, prior to the HRA, already moved away from the traditional common law approach, whereby free speech was recognised only to the extent that it was not precluded by the law—a residual freedom only. Courts were willing to acknowledge 'a common law presumption in favour of free speech',[51] and they had already become accustomed to referring to, and taking into account,

---

[47] For a critique of the US approach to structural and content-based regulation, see Barendt, above n 43. The preference for structural rather than content-based regulation will be referred to also in later chapters.

[48] Barendt, above n 3, 39.

[49] *Ibid*, 44. This is so, notwithstanding HRA, s 12(4), which appears to give particular precedence to freedom of expression: see, further, *ibid*, 43–44.

[50] See *ibid*, 40–42 for a discussion of other ways in which an express right might have an impact.

[51] *Ibid*, 40–41.

the Convention right to freedom of expression.[52] Article 10 does not expressly mention freedom of the media, and, as in the US, there has been no recognition that the media should enjoy special free speech rights.[53] However, the important role the media can play in disseminating information and ideas, and the relevance of that to freedom of expression, has been acknowledged by the European Court of Human Rights (ECHR):

> The Court reiterates that freedom of expression constitutes one of the essential foundations of a democratic society and that the safeguards to be afforded to the press are of particular importance. Whilst the press must not overstep the bounds set, inter alia, in the interest of 'the protection of the reputation or rights of others', it is nevertheless incumbent on it to impart information and ideas of public interest. Not only does the press have the task of imparting such information and ideas: the public also has a right to receive them . . . Although formulated primarily with regard to the print media, these principles doubtless apply also to the audiovisual media.[54]

In contrast to the US, the Convention and its jurisprudence reflects the greater European tolerance for regulation of broadcasting, and the recognition that media freedom operates as an instrumental freedom:

> The European Court of Justice considers that, in the light of Article 10.2 of the Convention, there is a compelling public interest in the maintenance of a pluralistic radio and television system, which justifies restrictions on fundamental freedoms. Article 10 of the Convention accordingly not only enshrines an individual right to media freedom, but also entails a duty to guarantee pluralism of opinion and cultural diversity of the media in the interests of a functioning democracy and of freedom of information for all.[55]

Nevertheless, any restrictions on the right of free expression have to be justified— the starting point is the protection of the freedom. This point, and its interface with the notion of an instrumental freedom, is illustrated in the ECHR decision, *Informationsverein Lentia v Austria*.[56] In this case, an Austrian law which permitted only a public monopoly to broadcast was held to infringe Article 10(1). The restriction was a disproportionate response to the demands of pluralism, because, for example, there was spectrum available which could enable other entities to broadcast. Thus:

> In cases such as the present one, where there has been an interference with the exercise of the rights and freedoms guaranteed in Article 10(1), the supervision must be strict because of the importance—frequently stressed by the Court—of the rights in question. The necessity for any restriction must be convincingly established. . . .

---

[52] Barendt, above n 3, 39.

[53] *Ibid*, 424, and PA Bruck *et al, Media Diversity in Europe, Report Prepared by the Advisory Panel-Media Division* (Strasbourg, Council of Europe, 2002), para 6.

[54] *Jersild v Denmark* (1995) 19 EHRR 1, para 31.

[55] Bruck, above n 53, para 10.

[56] *Informationsverein Lentia v Austria* (1993) 17 EHRR 93.

The Court has frequently stressed the fundamental role of freedom of expression in a democratic society, in particular where, through the press, it serves to impart information and ideas of general interest, which the public is moreover entitled to receive. Such an undertaking cannot be successfully accomplished unless it is grounded in the principle of pluralism, of which the State is the ultimate guarantor. This observation is especially valid in relation to audio-visual media, whose programmes are often broadcast very widely.

Of all the means of ensuring that these values are respected, a public monopoly is the one which imposes the greatest restrictions on the freedom of expression . . . . The far-reaching character of such restrictions means that they can only be justified where they correspond to a pressing need. [57]

The Convention's understanding is not at odds with UK approaches, and the recognition that regulation of media might be necessary in order to ensure that the media serve other public goals has been an underlying influence on UK broadcasting policy and regulation. As such, it is not clear that the incorporation of the Convention into English law will have a significant impact on existing approaches to broadcasting pluralism regulation or policy, although, as noted above, the presence of an express freedom of expression right provides a more transparent framework for challenging regulation as an infringement of freedom of expression rights.[58] On this point, however, there may be some concern regarding whether the incorporation of the Convention into UK law will accord the freedom of expression right the primacy which might have been expected. In *R v BBC (ex parte ProLife Alliance)* a challenge was made to a decision by broadcasters refusing to broadcast a party election broadcast during a general election on the ground that it breached content rules on taste and decency.[59] The party bringing the challenge was the ProLife Alliance, which campaigned on an anti-abortion platform, and the advertisements showed images of aborted foetuses. The House of Lords upheld, by a majority, the lawfulness of the BBC's decision not to allow the broadcasts, but, as Barendt discusses, the real concern about the decision is its failure to give due weight to the Convention right of free expression.[60] The House of Lords did not seem to recognise the necessity of deciding whether the decision to refuse to allow the broadcast could be justified under Article 10(2): was it a necessary and proportionate restriction? By contrast, this had been approach of the Court of Appeal: it was for the BBC to justify a prior restraint on the exercise of freedom of speech.[61] Whilst Strasbourg jurisprudence has continued to emphasise the heavy burden required in justifying restrictions on freedom of expression, UK jurisprudence, at least as evidenced by the House of Lords in this instance, appears to be more

---

[57] *Ibid*, paras 35, 38–39.

[58] D Feldman, *Civil Liberties and Human Rights in England and Wales*, 2nd edn (Oxford, Oxford University Press, 2002), 752–53, and Barendt, above n 3, 41–42.

[59] [2003] UKHL 23.

[60] E Barendt, 'Free Speech and Abortion' [2003] *Public Law* 580.

[61] *Ibid*, 581. See *ProLife Alliance v BBC* [2002] EWCA Civ 297. In the House of Lords, Lord Scott, dissenting, also considered that the crucial question was whether the refusal could be justified under Art 10(2): above n 59, para 92.

willing to tolerate such infringements.[62] Accepting that restrictions on freedom of expression may be necessary is uncontroversial, but the failure to recognise the necessity of rigorously testing the validity of those restrictions is regrettable.

Although Australia has a written constitution, it contains no express free speech guarantee. Yet this has not meant that there has been no recognition of free speech. The common law has recognised a general freedom of speech, but, as was the case in the UK, this freedom has been treated as a residual freedom: a freedom which exists to the extent that existing law allows.[63] It is a negative freedom in the sense that it confers no enforceable right. However, the absence of express constitutional rights does exclude the possibility of implied freedoms. The Australian High Court has held that a freedom of political communication can be implied from the Constitution, because it establishes a system of representative government. It should also be noted that freedom of speech might be protected and/or promoted through specific legislation (or even specific instances of case-law).[64] Within the media context, aspects of broadcasting regulation can be seen to illustrate this point.[65] Rules directed at ownership and control of broadcasting (and the press, in relation to cross-media interests) and some aspects of content regulation can be seen as measures designed to promote speech and the communication of ideas. Certainly, the importance of broadcasting to the operation of democracy and public debate forms part of the rhetoric justifying broadcasting regulation.[66] In the absence, however, of an underlying free speech guarantee, these discrete free speech protections are, as Chesterman acknowledges, vulnerable to parliamentary or judicial reconsideration.[67] This can be seen in the broadcasting context, where the demise of spectrum scarcity is regarded as justification for relaxing ownership and control rules.[68]

The implied freedom of political communication was first acknowledged by the High Court in 1992 through two decisions, *Australian Capital Television Pty Ltd v The Commonwealth of Australia (No 2)*[69] and *Nationwide News Pty Ltd v Wills*.[70]

---

[62] Barendt, above n 60, 585 and generally.

[63] G Brennan, 'Foreword' in Chesterman, above n 39, vii, and E Barendt, 'Free Speech in Australia: A Comparative Perspective' (1994) 16 *Sydney Law Review* 149 at 149–50. As Williams notes, this residual category will apply even though the fundamental freedom might be described as a right: G Williams, *Human Rights under the Australian Constitution* (Melbourne, Oxford University Press, 1999), 16, fn 69.

[64] Chesterman, above n 39, 7–13.

[65] Although Chesterman's discussion relates more to the negative sense (freedom from government interference), whereas the example of broadcasting can be seen to represent the positive sense (speech is promoted): Barendt, above n 63, 159–61.

[66] Commonwealth, *Parliamentary Debates*, Senate, 4 June 1992, 3599 (Robert Collins, Minister for Transport and Communications), and Explanatory Memorandum, Broadcasting Services Bill 1992 (Cth), 10.

[67] Chesterman, above n 39, 4.

[68] It is ironic that the same argument (demise of spectrum scarcity) is being used to justify reform in the US, where there is an express guarantee of free speech, but this can be explained by the First Amendment jurisprudence: see, for example, Barendt, above n 63, 159–60 and generally.

[69] (1992) 108 ALR 577.

[70] (1992) 108 ALR 681.

The High Court held that the system of representative government established by the Constitution required 'for its efficacy that the Australian people be free to discuss matters relating to Australian government'.[71] However, it was not an absolute freedom: '[t]he guarantee does not postulate that the freedom must always and necessarily prevail over competing interests of the public'.[72] Somewhat ironically, the legislation struck down in the *Capital Television* case sought to regulate the broadcasting of political advertising during federal election periods, in order to ensure that access to broadcasting would not be the preserve of the political candidates or parties with the best funding resources. Later High Court decisions, building on the 1992 decisions, appeared to widen the scope of the implied freedom.[73] In *Theophanous v Herald & Weekly Times* it was held that the implied freedom could be used as a defence in defamation proceedings, whilst the majority appeared also to broaden the idea of what was contemplated by 'political communication':[74]

> Indeed, in our view, the concept is not exhausted by political publications and addresses which are calculated to influence choices. Barendt states that: '"political speech" refers to all speech relevant to the development of public opinion on the whole range of issues which an intelligent citizen should think about.' It was this idea which Mason C.J. endeavoured to capture when, in Australian Capital Television, he referred to 'public affairs' as a subject protected by the freedom.[75]

The *Theophanous* decision also appeared to suggest that the implied freedom might accord individual rights.[76] Certainly, the majority judges felt no need to clamp down on the possibility that the implied freedom could create positive rights.[77] However, in 1997, the High Court, in a unanimous decision, significantly reined in the more expansive claims for the implied freedom, again in the context of defamation proceedings.[78] Abandoning the broader statements of previous decisions, the High Court held that the constitutional basis for the freedom was to be found in the text and structure of the Constitution, rejecting earlier statements that the basis was to be located in concepts of representative democracy or

---

[71] Williams, above n 63, 165.

[72] *Capital Television*, above n 69, 597, per Mason CJ.

[73] *Theophanous v Herald & Weekly Times Ltd* (1994) 182 CLR 104, and *Stephens v West Australian Newspapers Ltd* (1994) 182 CLR 211, both concerned with defamation proceedings, and *Cunliffe v Commonwealth* (1994) 182 CLR 272, concerned with the registration procedures for migration agents. See D Meagher, 'What is "Political Communication"? The Rationale and Scope of the Implied Freedom of Political Communication' (2004) 28 *Melbourne University Law Review* 438 at 450.

[74] Meagher, above n 73, 450.

[75] *Theophanous*, above n 73, 124, per Mason CJ, Toohey and Gaudron JJ. The High Court is quoting from the first edition of Barendt's *Freedom of Speech*, 152.

[76] See Meagher, above n 73, 450, and Williams, above n 63, 62.

[77] *Theophanous*, above n 73, 125–26, per Mason CJ, Toohey and Gaudron JJ. See also *Cunliffe*, above n 73, 299, per Mason CJ.

[78] *Lange v Australian Broadcasting Corporation* (1997) 189 CLR 520. Although the High Court in *Lange* rejected the *Theophanous* constitutional defence, it did expand the common law defence of qualified privilege to ensure the protection of the freedom of political communication.

government.[79] There appeared also to be a narrowing of what constituted 'political communication' to that which was necessary to enable 'the people to exercise a free and informed choice as electors'.[80] The High Court reaffirmed the position that the implied freedom was not an absolute freedom, and established a new test for determining the validity of a law, which appeared to mark a move away from the influence of US jurisprudence to a 'more deferential approach'.[81] Under the new test, a law which burdens the freedom of communication will be invalid, unless that law is 'reasonably appropriate and adapted to serve a legitimate end'.[82] Wary perhaps of earlier decisions which appeared to open up the scope for individual rights, the High Court also clarified the nature of the freedom: the constitutional provisions, from which the implied freedom was derived, did 'not confer personal rights on individuals. Rather they preclude the curtailment of the protected freedom by the exercise of legislative or executive power.'[83]

The decisions referred to here which preceded *Lange* appeared to be strongly influenced by US First Amendment jurisprudence, displaying that traditional distrust of government regulation.[84] Chesterman has noted that *Capital Television* showed a preference for the rights of the individual speaker, although he points also to instances where the judgments made reference to the need to ensure that all viewpoints are represented.[85] In *Lange*, there appears to be a much stronger preference for a freedom of communication which protects public debate, evident by the court's references to the necessity of public being able to 'receive and disseminate information'.[86] However, in the context of broadcasting pluralism regulation this may be of limited assistance. It has been noted that the freedom does not give positive rights; thus, one can not claim under the implied freedom that the government should be compelled to regulate broadcasting, or even the media more generally, to promote the freedom of political communication. Indeed, there might be concern that the implied freedom could render regulation vulnerable, when it is recalled that *Capital Television* arose out of attempts to regulate political advertising. In that case, the government had argued that the rules restricting political advertising were necessary 'to safeguard the integrity of the political system' and to promote political debate.[87] The court has moved on from its earlier preference for speaker's rights, a preference which appears to have influenced the *Capital Television* decision, and so there may not be the same antipathy towards such measures. Nevertheless, broadcasting regulations, like other laws, must be read in terms of their consistency with the implied freedom. However,

---

[79] A Stone, 'Freedom of Political Communication, the Constitution and the Common Law' (1998) 26 *Federal Law Review* 219, 251–52.

[80] *Lange*, above n 78, 560.

[81] Stone, above n 79, 230 and 254.

[82] *Lange*, above n 78, 567–68.

[83] *Ibid*, 560.

[84] Stone, above n 79, 230, and Barendt, above n 63, 149.

[85] Chesterman, above n 39, 31–32.

[86] *Lange*, above n 78, 561.

[87] *Capital Television*, above n 69, 587.

notwithstanding the limitations of the implied freedom, Williams argues that such freedoms can have an extra-legal impact: they can 'shape attitudes' and act as 'cultural symbols'.[88] Barendt makes a similar point in relation to free speech:

> [t]he absence of individual free speech rights does not mean that decisions in this area are uninfluenced by arguments about the particular interests of speakers and listeners. The judgment of Mason CJ in *Australian Capital Television* clearly attached importance to the interests of speakers. The *Lange* ruling, in contrast, emphasised the listener interests in access 'to relevant information about the functioning of government in Australia and about the policies of political parties and candidates for election' . . . This emphasis is inevitable in the context of a Constitution without an explicit formulation of a right to free speech; it goes hand in hand with the rejection by the court in *Lange* of implicit individual free speech rights. In their absence the (limited) role enjoyed by freedom of expression can only be justified by reference to the argument from democracy, more generally associated with the interests of listeners.[89]

This brief review of free speech law and jurisprudence reveals also that there is generally a difference in approach depending upon whether it is the press or broadcasting which is under consideration: for example, Article 10 of the Convention expressly permits broadcasting licensing but makes no reference to the press. Although it might be appropriate to talk generally of media freedom as an institutional and instrumental freedom, the concept does not have the same practical effect on the press compared with broadcasting. In general, the press has been more able to resist regulation which might be viewed as serving an instrumental purpose. The differing regulatory treatment of the press and broadcasting has been an ongoing matter for debate, and various explanations have been offered as to why broadcasting has, virtually from its inception, been subjected to sector-specific regulation, whilst the press has in general been left to general law constraints. The justifications, reviewed in the next section, have had limited success in rationalising the differences in treatment, but, nevertheless, they continue to influence and, as will be suggested later in this chapter, to distort current debates on pluralism and diversity regulation.

Rationalising Broadcasting Regulation

Although others can be identified,[90] four of the justifications or rationales explaining the need for specific broadcasting regulation are presented here.[91] Whilst the rationales are usually presented in the context of broadcasting regulation generally, they are also relevant to the specific issue of broadcasting pluralism policy and

---

[88] Williams, above n 63, 68.
[89] Barendt, above n 6, 181.
[90] See Hoffmann-Riem, above n 2, 267–80.
[91] This brief review has been adapted from Barendt, above n 18, 3–10.

regulation. The first rationale to be discussed here arises because broadcasting is dependent upon the use of a public resource: the airwaves. As such, its right to use those airwaves will be subject to such terms and conditions as government, or a relevant regulatory authority, considers appropriate. There are, however, some difficulties with this justification. As Barendt has argued, it confuses the opportunity to regulate with whether it is right to do so.[92] Nor is it so clear that the airwaves are necessarily a public resource. This is a regulatory choice, and other options, such as sale of the frequencies, would be possible. One might argue that regulation of frequencies is necessary in order to avoid interference.[93] Hence, in order to ensure that the broadcasting signal of one broadcasting station does not interfere with the signal of another, regulation will be required to control the allocation of frequencies. Whilst this may be a valid reason for regulation, it does not explain all of the different aspects of broadcasting regulation, such as content regulation.

Spectrum scarcity has offered a particularly strong claim for regulation. It is argued that, because of limited spectrum, access to broadcasting is limited, and therefore those who have been allocated, through licensing, the privilege of broadcasting must share this with others. Hence, the opportunity for speech must be shared. This could, for example, lead to rules which require a broadcaster to present a balanced set of programmes or views. Although an influential rationale, there are weaknesses. For example, does this scarcity arise naturally or is it created? Governments have tended to allocate a certain number of frequencies for broadcasting, whilst reserving other frequencies for other purposes, and at times even leaving frequencies unallocated. This weakens the argument that scarcity justifies regulation. Secondly, the rationale focuses on one particular type of scarcity—physical scarcity. Another type of scarcity might be economic. If the concept of scarcity is broadened to include economic scarcity, then it is even less clear that the case can be made for regulation of broadcasting alone. It may now be as difficult in terms of cost to establish a newspaper as it is to start up a broadcasting station or channel.[94] More importantly, the spectrum scarcity argument has become less relevant with the development of alternative delivery platforms, such as cable and satellite, and new technological applications like digital which have opened up the possibility of numerous radio stations and television channels. It may be that there are new forms of scarcity, but physical scarcity appears less tenable.

Another influential rationale has been related to the perceived power of broadcasting. Regulation has been justified because broadcasting has been seen as likely to exert more influence on its viewers and listeners compared with the press and its readers. This argument is even more relevant to television, because of its visual impact, and helps to explain the differences in regulation between television and radio. Broadcasting has also been seen as more influential because of its intrusive nature, coming, it is argued, into the home uninvited—although it is hard to see what difference there is between a person's ability to decide to buy a newspaper or

---

[92] *Ibid*, 4.
[93] Hoffmann-Riem, above n 2, 268–70.
[94] Barendt, above n 18, 6.

to switch on the television or radio. This rationale helps to explain restrictions over certain types of content such as sexually explicit programming, or what can be broadcast during the hours when children might be watching. It can also be relevant to diversity measures, such as rules requiring news and current affairs programmes to provide a balanced range of views. However, a justification for regulation based on the influential and intrusive nature of broadcasting assumes a rather passive and gullible audience. This might, possibly, have been appropriate in the early days of broadcasting, but it is more difficult to accept in the modern multimedia environment when viewers and listeners can access images and sound from a variety of sources. On the other hand, there may still be some relevance to this argument, although the visual and sound impact may be felt in different ways. For example, new communication technologies have brought an immediacy to reporting which was not always possible, and this very immediacy, which can allow the audience to witness international events as they happen, such as the fall of the Berlin Wall or the conflict in Iraq, might mean that broadcasting provides a different quality of impact or influence, one which the press probably continues to lack.[95] The debate over television's influence could also take on a new dimension given current fashions for extremely large television screens and home cinemas.

Finally, an explanation for the differential treatment has been given by Bollinger.[96] Bollinger suggests that although there is no real difference between the press and broadcasting, they have been perceived differently, and this different perception has led to the regulation of broadcasting as the new and more different technology.[97] In this respect Bollinger is probably right, and the differences in regulatory treatment can be more easily explained by history than by coherent theory.[98] There has always been a predisposition for governments to control new technologies. But, 'newness' does not provide a very reliable basis for regulation, particularly for broadcasting, which can hardly still be characterised as new. Bollinger's argument goes on to suggest that this differential treatment can be further justified on the grounds that regulation of one media can make up for the lack of regulation of another media: regulation of broadcasting can compensate for the failings of the press. For anyone wishing to make a case for regulation of broadcasting, this is not an attractive argument. There is no guarantee that regulation can be designed in a way which will redress the deficiencies of one media, and it hardly seems good governance to expect one industry to bear the regulatory costs, whilst leaving the targeted industry free of the regulatory burden. Bollinger's attempt at rationalising the different treatment of the press and broadcasting is

---

[95] At least in relation to the paper versions of the print media; the internet versions may have a different impact more akin to television.

[96] See LC Bollinger, 'Freedom of the Press and Public Access: Towards a Theory of Partial Regulation of the Mass Media' (1976) 75 *Michigan Law Review* 1, and 'The Rationale of Public Regulation of the Media' in J Lichtenberg (ed), *Democracy and the Mass Media* (Cambridge, Cambridge University Press, 1990), 355, cited in Barendt, above n 18, 8, fn 24.

[97] Although there is a substantive difference between the press and broadcasting, which may require them to be viewed differently, and that difference relates to the economics of broadcasting (see ch 6).

[98] Barendt, above n 18, 9. On this point, see also Barendt, above n 3, 446–48.

not satisfactory, and it is not one advanced in policy discussions. However, in highlighting the lack of coherence in the regulatory treatment of media, it serves as a warning that in analysing the basis for broadcasting pluralism regulation, it is important to avoid assuming that the lack of regulation of the press justifies the removal of regulation of broadcasting. Indeed, although outside the scope of this book, the issue may really be not why broadcasting is regulated, but why the press is not.[99]

These rationales then have limits to their validity. The scarcity and influence rationales have had the most mileage, and they may still play some role, but they present no convincing basis for justifying the different regulation of broadcasting and the press. For anyone familiar with this debate, this will have seemed a rather tedious reiteration of the arguments and, perhaps, an unnecessary one given the move from scarcity to abundance. However, unsatisfactory as they may be, it is contended that the rationales (and the scarcity rationale especially) continue to have an important influence on media regulation debates and drives for reform. For those advocating reform, it is convenient to point to these rationales, and their declining relevance, as making the case for change, thereby obscuring any positive or normative case for regulation. The problem with these rationales is that they are negative and reactive in nature; they arise out of a need to explain why broadcasting is treated differently from the press, in other words to give coherence where there may be none.

As suggested earlier in this chapter, a strong positive value associated with the media is the role that it can play in contributing to a diversity of voices and opinions. However, whether appropriately or otherwise, the achievement of this goal has been played out differently for the press and broadcasting and, instead of evaluating whether or what regulation would serve this goal, the focus has been on trying to rationalise the seemingly irrational, and to explain why broadcasting is regulated whilst the press is not. The shift in focus has resulted also in a tendency to see the press as the ideal state. In other words, once the justifications for treating broadcasting differently have diminished, then broadcasting, like the press, can be returned to the ideal state whereby the general law will be sufficient. Bound up with this is the idea that 'the market should be regarded as the natural order from which departures should be justified'.[100] This is perhaps to put the matter rather crudely because, as will be discussed in Chapter Six, there are still particular characteristics of broadcasting which make it vulnerable to market failure. Certainly none of the jurisdictions considered here, in seeking to relax media ownership and control rules, has been willing to eradicate completely this form of structural regulation. But crude or otherwise, what is being suggested here is that the real focus for regulatory decision-making has been lost sight of, because of an unhelpful tendency to see the issue as one of regulation versus non-regulation—where regulation is an aberration which can be overcome fully, or at least partially.

---

[99] See, eg, Lichtenberg's discussion and her argument that, in the American context, it would be constitutionally feasible to propose specific regulation of the press: Lichtenberg, above n 21.
[100] Gibbons, above n 1, 9.

It is suggested that one has to accept the historical legacy and the asymmetrical approach to regulation, and concentrate instead on constructing a more positive case for the regulation of broadcasting (albeit one that may be applicable also to the press). In other words, it is necessary to move away from a focus on broadcasting regulation and its relationship to the press model, and to clarify instead a normative perspective for the media centred on pluralism and diversity, which may have relevance for all forms of media. A more coherent policy approach will also require a more inclusive concept of regulation, one which does not draw artificial distinctions between regulation and the market. It is suggested that one way of articulating a more coherent policy approach is through the concept of the 'public sphere'. This will be addressed in the next section.

Reclaiming the Public Sphere

As suggested, a way forward may be through the model of the 'public sphere', and it will be argued that this model can provide a coherent and normative framework and standard against which media policy and regulatory design can be measured. The public sphere can embrace all forms of mass media, and so, in this section, the discussion should be understood to refer to both print and broadcasting media, save where it is necessary to make a distinction between the press and broadcasting. It is also necessary to keep separate descriptions of the public sphere and considerations about regulation. Although it may be anticipated that a properly functioning public sphere would require some regulatory intervention, this is a separate issue. For the purposes of the discussion in this section, the term 'regulation' will be used loosely, in a non-specific manner; in the following section, the concept of regulation will be considered further.

It is the theorist, Habermas, and his work, *The Structural Transformation of the Public Sphere*,[101] who has been most responsible for the development of the public sphere concept in contemporary thinking. The interest amongst scholars generated by Habermas' work has included reflection on the relevance of the public sphere to the role played by the media.[102] However, given the manner in which the concept is used by Habermas, its application to the media is not entirely straightforward. Through a study which is intended to be both historical and normative, Habermas sets out to examine the nature of the 'space' where individuals could come together to consider rationally the issues of the day, and through which political opinion and will would be formed and exerted:

[101] J Habermas, *The Structural Transformation of the Public Sphere* (Cambridge, Polity Press, 1989).
[102] See, eg, P Dahlgren, *Television and the Public Sphere: Citizenship, Democracy and the Media* (London, Sage Publications, 1995); N Garnham, 'The Media and the Public Sphere' in C Calhoun (ed), *Habermas and the Public Sphere* (Cambridge, MA, and London, The MIT Press, 1992), 359; C Barnett, *Culture and Democracy: Media, Space and Representation* (Edinburgh, Edinburgh University Press, 2003); and S Venturelli, *Liberalizing the European Media: Politics, Regulation, and the Public Sphere* (Oxford, Clarendon Press, 1998).

In ideal terms, Habermas conceptualizes the public sphere as that realm of social life where the exchange of information and views on questions of common concern can take place so that public opinion can be formed. The public sphere 'takes place' when citizens, exercising the rights of assembly and association, gather as public bodies to discuss issues of the day, specifically those of political concern. . . . Habermas' concept of the public sphere insists on the analytic centrality of reasoned, critical discourse. The public sphere exists, in other words, in the active reasoning of the public. It is via such discourse that public opinion is generated, which in turn is to shape the policies of the state and the development of society as a whole.[103]

Habermas argued, using his study of Britain, Germany, and France in the eighteenth and nineteenth centuries, that a public sphere (or at least a new form) developed in eighteenth-century Europe as a result of the spread of capitalism, which facilitated the development of a new bourgeois class. The bourgeois class, because of its own resources and economic power, was able to exist separately from both State and Church.[104] Importantly, for Habermas, this new public sphere is part of the private realm and separate from the sphere of public authority and the market: '. . . it was a public sphere constituted by private people'.[105] The public sphere was able to mediate between the private realm and the public or state realm.[106]

The political role of the public sphere was able to develop via a well-established literary public sphere, with its institutions and 'forums for discussion'.[107] Thus,

[t]his public sphere functioned primarily through face-to-face interaction in coffee-houses and salons, and through an independent press, which both staged reasoned debate and represented public opinion to government.[108]

Both critical reasoning and equality of access to the public sphere for all citizens and views, provided that the participants sought the general interest, were central to the legitimation of this democratic public sphere.[109] Indeed, to close off access to this diversity would result in coercion.[110] As Calhoun points out, 'a public sphere adequate to a democratic polity depends upon both quality of discourse and quantity of participation'.[111] One can see in this the attraction of the public sphere concept to attempts to develop an understanding of the role of the media. The potential for media to be a focal point for a diverse set of views and ideas would seem ideally suited to the functioning of the public sphere, and certainly Habermas attributes the growth of the press and its development of a critical role

---

[103] Dahlgren, above n 101, 7–8.

[104] N Garnham, *Capitalism and Communication: Global Culture and the Economics of Information* (London, Sage Publications, 1990) at 106–7. See Habermas, above n 101, 1–26.

[105] Habermas, above n 101, 30.

[106] Venturelli, above n 102, 98–99.

[107] Habermas, above n 101, 51.

[108] J Curran, *Media and Power* (London, Routledge, 2002), 33.

[109] N Garnham, *Emancipation, the Media, and Modernity* (Oxford, Oxford University Press, 2000), 169–70, and see Habermas, above n 101, 54–55 and 87–88.

[110] Habermas, above n 101, 87.

[111] C Calhoun, 'Introduction: Habermas and the Public Sphere' in C Calhoun (ed), *Habermas and the Public Sphere* (Cambridge, MA, and London, The MIT Press, 1992), 1, at 2.

as important in the development of the eighteenth-century public sphere, particularly as the ideal of face-to-face 'coffee-house' or 'salon' discourse became impractical.[112] However, for Habermas the role of the media in the public sphere also contributed to the public sphere's decline or 'transformation', and this needs to be considered if the public sphere model is to be useful in providing a normative role for the media. However, before looking at Habermas' account of the decline of the public sphere, some of the criticisms of his theory should also be mentioned.

First, it has been suggested that Habermas' account of the public sphere in the eighteenth century, although purporting to be an historical study, represents an idealised portrait of the public sphere and of rational debate. At the same time, as he recounts the decline of the public sphere, he fails to acknowledge the intellectual history of the nineteenth and twentieth centuries—the contention being that he is overly influenced by the Frankfurt School's cultural industry critique.[113] Thus, Calhoun notes, Habermas ignored the trivial, the lurid, and the less than rational aspects of public life in the eighteenth century, such as the 'penny dreadfuls', the scandal sheets, and street gatherings,[114] whilst Curran points to instances where the press 'deviated from Habermas's model of rational-critical exchange':

> Some London newspapers received secret subsidies in return for political favours; some scandal sheets demanded fees in return for the contradiction or suppression of scurrilous stories; and some local papers were small, marginal businesses fearful of powerful local interests.[115]

Another concern is that Habermas' public/private split, and his focus on rational debate, has resulted in the exclusion or marginalisation of others, along with a failure to recognise the presence of other public spheres.[116] In particular, it has been noted that Habermas' construct of the public sphere excluded women and the working class, so that in fact the liberal public sphere was really a privileged arena to which only some (white, male, bourgeois) had access. What was accepted as constituting matters of public interest, to be brought into public discourse, were really only the interests of this privileged group. Much of the work flowing out of Habermas' initial study has been to demonstrate the existence of other public spheres, so that a more multi-layered and complex picture of civil society has emerged.[117] Habermas himself has acknowledged some of these

---

[112] Habermas, above n 101, 20–26 and 51.

[113] Curran, above n 108, 44, Garnham, above n 102, 359–60, Calhoun, above n 111, 33, and W Outhwaite, *Habermas: A Critical Introduction* (Cambridge, Polity Press, 1994), 11.

[114] Calhoun, above n 111, 33.

[115] Curran, above n 108, 45.

[116] N Fraser, 'Rethinking the Public Sphere: A Contribution to the Critique of Actually Existing Democracy' in C Calhoun (ed), *Habermas and the Public Sphere* (Cambridge, MA, and London, The MIT Press, 1992), 109, at 113–16, Curran, above n 108, 45, and Garnham, above n 102, 359–60.

[117] Curran, above n 108, 233. See, eg, MP Ryan, 'Gender and Public Access: Women's Politics in Nineteenth-Century America' in C Calhoun (ed), *Habermas and the Public Sphere* (Cambridge, MA, and London, The MIT Press, 1992), 259, which provides evidence of women's 'public spheres' in nineteenth-century North America, and G Eley, 'Nations, Publics, and Political Cultures: Placing Habermas in the Nineteenth Century' in C Calhoun (ed), *Habermas and the Public Sphere* (Cambridge, MA, and London, The MIT Press, 1992), 289.

weaknesses,[118] and, in fact, as Curran notes, his later work also offers a more complex perspective on the public sphere:

> Instead of viewing it as an aggregation of individuals gathered together as a single public, he now views it as 'a network for communicating information and points of view' which connects the private world of everyday experience to the political system. This network is multiple rather [than] unitary. It 'branches out into a multitude of overlapping international, national, regional, local, and subcultural arenas'.[119]

Although Habermas has acknowledged a greater complexity, both in terms of themes and interests, and in the means of coming together—what he refers to as 'manifold differentiations'[120]—these many 'publics'[121] and levels still coalesce into 'the' or 'the universal' public sphere:

> Despite these manifold differentiations, however, all the partial publics constituted by ordinary language remain porous to one another. The one text of 'the' public sphere, a text continually extrapolated and extending radially in all directions, is divided by internal boundaries into arbitrarily small texts for which everything else is context; yet one can always build hermeneutical bridges from one text to the next.'[122]

The concept of the public sphere, in its more intricate and rearticulated form, continues to have normative value in facilitating democratic functions. Thus, the public sphere: can act 'as a sounding board for problems that must be processed by the political system because they cannot be solved elsewhere'; will be 'a warning system with sensors that, though unspecialized, are sensitive throughout society'; and, must 'detect and identify problems but also convincingly and *influentially* thematize them, furnish them with possible solutions, and dramatize them in such a way that they are taken up and dealt with by parliamentary complexes'.[123] The ability of the public sphere to solve problems is limited;[124] its role is opinion-forming and not decision-making,[125] but '[d]emocratically constituted opinion- and will-formation depends on the supply of informal public opinions that, ideally, develop in structures of an unsubverted political public sphere'.[126] It

---

[118] J Habermas, 'Further Reflections on the Public Sphere' in C Calhoun, (ed), *Habermas and the Public Sphere* (Cambridge, MA, and London, The MIT Press, 1992), 421, 430, and generally. It is relevant to recall that *Structural Transformation* was written in 1961, but was translated into English only in 1989.

[119] Curran, above n 108, 234, quoting from J Habermas, *Between Facts and Norms* (Cambridge, Polity Press, 1996), 360 and 379.

[120] J Habermas, *Between Facts and Norms* (Cambridge, Polity Press, 1996), 374.

[121] *Ibid.*

[122] *Ibid.*

[123] *Ibid*, 359.

[124] *Ibid.*

[125] This is the idea of the public sphere as a 'weak' public. The public sphere, as an opinion-forming public is a weak public, whereas the parliamentary bodies, with their scope for opinion-forming and decision-making, are strong publics: Fraser, above n 116, 134. This notion of weak and strong publics was adopted by Habermas, above n 120, 307. This separation of the weak public from the strong, and more formally organised, public provides scope for a much more inclusive network of 'sub-publics': *ibid*, 307–8.

[126] Habermas, *ibid*, 308.

is easy to see that there may be a role for the media in this complex public sphere with its manifold differentiations: '[t]he currents of public communication are channeled by the mass media and flow through different publics . . .'.[127] But the place of the media in the public sphere may also be problematic. Habermas is certainly aware of this, and the role of the media is relevant to his account of the decline of the public sphere.

Habermas' early work on the public sphere also included an account of its decline (or, perhaps more appropriately, its distortion), which came about because of 'the structural transformation of the relationship between the public sphere and the private realm in general'.[128] In what Habermas termed a '"refeudalization" of society',[129] he argued that from the end of the nineteenth century changes in the economic order, marked by increasing concentration and growth of large-scale enterprise, required also a counterbalancing growth in state power, with the result that the state, as it sought to redress the impact of large-scale capitalism, increasingly encroached upon the private realm.[130] With these changes, the public sphere is displaced or invaded by associations of 'collectively organized private interests' and by political parties which, 'fused with the organs of public authority,' establish 'themselves, as it were, *above* the public whose instruments they once were'.[131] For Habermas, the public sphere was invaded by these collective interests:

> Competition between organized private interests invaded the public sphere. If the particular interests that as privatized interests were neutralized in the common denominator of class interest once permitted public discussion to attain a certain rationality and even effectiveness, it remains that today the display of competing interests has taken the place of such discussion. The consensus developed in rational-critical public debate has yielded to compromise fought out or simply imposed nonpublicly.[132]

Related to these aspects of the transformation is the transformation of the media itself. The public sphere of critical-rational debate was replaced by 'the pseudo-public or sham-private world of culture consumption'.[133] For Habermas, the media are crucial to this change. Alongside the invasion of the public sphere and the undermining of its place within the private realm,[134] the influence of large-scale capitalism on the media contributes to a change from participation in rational debate to one of passive consumption.[135] Habermas does not deny that a debate takes place through the media, but for him it is a sham debate—one that is manufactured and staged:

[127] *Ibid*, 307.
[128] Habermas, above n 101, 142–43.
[129] *Ibid*, 142.
[130] *Ibid*, ch 5.
[131] *Ibid*, 176.
[132] *Ibid*, 179.
[133] *Ibid*, 160.
[134] For Habermas, the public sphere had '. . . evolved from the very heart of the private sphere itself': *ibid*, 160.
[135] Calhoun, above n 111, 22–23.

Today the conversation itself is administered. Professional dialogues from the podium, panel discussions, and round table shows—the rational debate of private people becomes one of the production numbers of the stars in radio and television, a salable [sic] package ready for the box office. . .[136]

As the media have become commercialised and the public sphere invaded by (collectively organised) private interests and opinion management, so the public (now consumer-citizens) reaches consensus not by means of rational discourse, but through 'a kind of integration of mass entertainment with advertising,'[137] and the public sphere is transformed or refeudalised.[138] Habermas' account of the decline of the public sphere, and the role of the media in that decline, has been seen as too negative.[139] This negativity, in relation to the media, has been attributed to the influence of the Adorno and the Frankfurt School's critique of the cultural industries.[140] Habermas himself has acknowledged this influence.[141] He has also accepted that his analysis of the move from a 'culture-debating to a culture-consuming public' was too simplistic.[142] The limits to Habermas' critique need to be emphasised if, as will be asserted in this chapter, the media are to be recognised as having a role to play in the operation and energising of the public sphere. At the same time, it would be a mistake to ignore entirely his critique of the media. Ironically, that critique can indicate the way in which the media may be able to contribute positively to the modern public sphere.

In his later work, Habermas clearly acknowledges that there is a place for the media within the public sphere. Not only are the media able to act as a channel of communication between the various publics, they also help to expand the public sphere. The media actually contribute another level of differentiation to the public sphere: '. . . the *abstract* public sphere of isolated readers, listeners, and viewers scattered across large geographic areas, or even around the globe, and brought together only through the mass media'.[143] Habermas also seems to accept that the public sphere can be made more inclusive through mass communications.[144] However, he is still wary of the media as a participant in the public sphere, although his wariness stems from a much more sophisticated analysis than his earlier critique. Habermas' negative view of the media was perhaps also influenced by an idealised harking back to a form of rational discourse which takes place through a face-to-face mode. The press was seen as an acceptable part of this discourse, but only because they acted 'merely as conduits for the transmission of information between locales'.[145] Thus, what concerns Habermas is not the involvement of the

---

[136] Habermas, above n 101, 164.
[137] *Ibid*, 195.
[138] *Ibid*, 192–95.
[139] Outhwaite, above n 113, 11, and Calhoun, above n 111, 33.
[140] Outhwaite, above n 113, 11, and Garnham, above n 102, 360.
[141] Habermas, above n 118, 438.
[142] *Ibid*.
[143] Habermas, above n 120, 374.
[144] *Ibid*.
[145] Barnett, above n 102, 57.

media in this discourse, but the fact that, in his view, they no longer simply transmit and amplify the debate of private people, but also shape the very debate.[146]
This concern about the way the media behave has some important elements to it.
On the one hand, it would be clearly unrealistic to expect that the public sphere
today can be confined to a discourse which occurs only in some localised arena,
and so the media is able to provide a space, within the public sphere, which is able
to reach out to, and connect, large numbers. This has an importance not just in
some crude numerical sense. The risk of intimate gatherings is always that they
may only include those who naturally share common backgrounds, perspectives,
and interests. Thus, one of the great contributions that the media can make to the
quality and depth of discourse is its capacity to act as a channel, and even inter-
preter, for these diverse perspectives—shaping the debate may help to ensure then
that the public sphere remains open and inclusive. As noted above, Habermas, in
his rethinking of the public sphere and greater tolerance of the media, has recognised this potential.

However, one of Habermas' concerns is that as the public sphere broadens into
a more abstract form, there is the risk that participants are separated out into roles
of either actors or spectators.[147] An important set of actors will be the media professionals. Whilst this might indicate a reference back to the problem of passivity,
associated with the decline of the public sphere, Habermas' concerns about actors,
and the role of the media in shaping debate, also raise some important issues for
the normative role of the media. Habermas clearly remains concerned that the
media might dominate the public sphere.[148] He would see the role of the media as
independent of 'political and social pressure', their task being to take up issues and
concerns raised by the public which will be presented to the political process.[149] In
this way, Habermas sees that '[t]he power of the media should thus be neutralized
. . .'.[150] Although he acknowledges that the media may have a role in the presentation, to the larger public, of issues, which move in from the 'outermost periphery'
to the centre, there seems also to be a sense in which he expects the media to be
reactive only. Issues can be augmented and presented controversially in the media,
but the role of the media seems only to be to take up issues generated by the public.[151] One might question whether the media needs to be confined to this conduit-
like role. Given their scope for reaching across and throughout the public sphere,
it may be that the media should also have a voice in identifying issues to which the
public will either respond or not. Be that as it may, one can understand the
concerns behind Habermas' wish to neutralise media power. As actors within
the public sphere, the media, or more particularly, the media professionals have
the power to:

---

[146] Habermas, above n 101, 188.
[147] Habermas, above n 120, 374.
[148] *Ibid*, 379.
[149] *Ibid*, 378.
[150] *Ibid*, 378–39.
[151] See *ibid*, 378, 381–2.

make decisions about the selection and presentation of 'programs,' and to a certain extent control the entry of topics, contributions, and authors into the mass-media-dominated public sphere. As the mass media become more complex and more expensive, the effective channels of communication become more centralized. To the degree this occurs, the mass media face an increasing pressure of selection, on both the supply side and the demand side. These selection processes become the source of a new sort of power.[152]

Habermas' worry about media power and its ability to shape debate relates particularly to his concern that that power will be captured by political and large-scale economic organisations which will have privileged access to or control of the media.[153] Habermas is right to express this as a concern. If the media are to facilitate debate, then it is essential that they are not suborned by particular interests. However, this does not have to be an inevitable tendency of the media (or, at least, one which cannot be contained): what it points to is the need to design carefully the media environment, and media's place within the public sphere. This is not to suggest that Habermas does not recognise this also, but he seems sceptical; there seems in his analysis always a sense that the media are inherently a negative influence, and that it is only an energised civil society which can and must restrain their power.[154]

Habermas has moved way from his earlier view of the media as promoting a climate of passive consumption but, as noted above, there is still, in his account of the place of the media in the public sphere, a trace of this passivity when he divides up the public sphere into actors and spectators.[155] Indeed, this division seems to stem from the media's role in widening the public sphere.[156] This may, still, be an overly simplistic assessment in which 'spectator-activity' is equated with non-engagement. In the case of broadcasting, for example, listening or viewing does not have to mean a passivity in which active critical assessment is suspended. The fact that the nature of broadcasting does not allow a dialogic engagement with those participating in the broadcast (except, of course, by way of 'talk-back' or 'call-in' programmes) does not mean that there is no engagement—it is simply that the debate or contemplation which arises as a consequence of the broadcast may take place in a different context. Of course, the internet is also changing the level of engagement, as emails, web postings, and online forums allow for interaction either during or immediately after the broadcast programme. Although Habermas acknowledges that, ultimately, the spectators, in their 'galleries', will determine who are the successful actors, he is clearly concerned also that the spectators may not be capable of autonomous assessment—in part because the debate has been distorted by the media-actors.[157] Habermas seems to suggest that 'the

---

[152] Habermas, above n 120, 376.

[153] Habermas, above n 101, 188–89, and above n 120, 376–77 and 380.

[154] Habermas, above n 120, 379.

[155] See also *ibid*, 377.

[156] *Ibid*, 374.

[157] *Ibid*, 374–75.

information-processing strategies' employed by the media, which serve to depoliticise public communication, whilst they may not be overtly manipulative, will at least also have the effect of de-activating the public or lowering the level of public discourse.[158] There is another, connected, concern here, and that is the place of entertainment values. On the one hand, there is the traditional concern that the commercialisation of the media leads to a growth in entertainment programmes at the expense of information or more serious programming. For Habermas, an entertainment-rich media also contributed to the changed nature of the public sphere, whereby the object becomes more 'stimulating relaxation than [. . .] a public use of reason'.[159] This, of course, has been a common complaint about the media, particularly television, and it reflects a myopic view of the role which entertainment programmes can play. For just as non-fictional programming, such as current affairs and documentaries, can help people to understand their lives and the society in which they live, so too can fictional programming. Recalling the justifications for free speech protection, one can see that entertainment programmes might be relevant to the self-fulfilment or growth justification, but equally such programmes can contribute to public debate and, through the use of imagination, a broadening understanding of issues and different perspectives. Such a view is unlikely now to be controversial, but even those accepting this argument might contend that contemporary media have given way to programming which could not be said to be enriching in any sense. On the other hand, some would argue that the inclusion of the seemingly trivial, the personal, or the trashy is actually providing a more inclusive and representative perspective of society.[160] It would be a mistake to think this is a new debate. The subject matter may have changed, but one needs to be careful about harking back to a so-called 'golden age'. Nevertheless, here again it is worth heeding Habermas' concerns. A concern which comes out more clearly in his later work is the influence of entertainment values in the media's presentation of public issues, a process which patronises the public and lowers the level of discourse.[161] In a quest to make reality 'more palatable for consumption',[162] Habermas argues that the media follow market strategies in the presentation of news and related programming:

> Reporting facts as human-interest stories, mixing information with entertainment, arranging material episodically, and breaking down complex relationships into smaller fragments—all of this comes together to form a syndrome that works to depoliticize public communication.[163]

---

[158] *Ibid*, 377 and 380. Habermas acknowledges that there are no clear conclusions about the effect of the media on audiences: *ibid*, 377.

[159] Habermas, above n 101, 170.

[160] A McKee, *The Public Sphere: An Introduction* (Cambridge, Cambridge University Press, 2005), chs 2–3, and generally, and see, also, Curran's account of this debate: above n 108, 237–39.

[161] Habermas, above n 120, 378–79 and 380.

[162] Habermas, above n 101, 170.

[163] Habermas, above n 120, 377.

Habermas' comments will certainly resonate with contemporary experiences of the media and their modi operandi. There may be room for concern, for example, about the way in which society seems only to be able to be viewed through the perspective of the individual and the personal experience. Hence, it seems that an understanding of the past can now only be gained by a group of modern individuals recreating some past living experience, or that values of toleration, for example, can only be examined via a programme built around the fiction of a group of people living together.[164] Equally, a commercialised media seeking to maximise audiences may be too ready to merge entertainment and information; the resulting 'shock-jock' programming may be popular, but offer little real understanding or communication and not much more than a sharing of prejudices. Here, again, the design of the media environment becomes important, with issues such as the relationship between commercial interests and news and information programming having to be considered. This is a matter which is taken up in Chapter Four.

Habermas' work on the public sphere has been much debated, and, as discussed above, Habermas himself has refined the concept in a way which addresses more appropriately contemporary society. As an historical description, it clearly had weaknesses, but the concept of the public sphere, in its revised and more developed form, remains of normative value. As Fraser describes it:

> It designates a theater in modern societies in which political participation is enacted through the medium of talk. It is the space in which citizens deliberate about their common affairs, and hence an institutionalized arena of discursive interaction.[165]

The public sphere, then, provides an important space for the generation, consideration, and formation of public opinion, which in turn facilitates the democratic process. Despite Habermas' concerns, it would be difficult to envisage today the public sphere operating without the media participating: indeed, the media have become 'the chief institutions of the public sphere'.[166] The media are able to provide a focus for citizens within that space, to provide access to different voices, and to facilitate debate. However, the mere presence of the media within the public sphere will not be enough to secure this role. It is essential that the media are not subverted by political or economic power, but are able to function as independent servant-actors within the public sphere. This requires careful attention to the way in which the media are structured and operate. In turn, the recognition of the public sphere model, and media's role within it, can provide the normative basis for determining the shape of, and practices within, the media environment. A media environment which values and promotes pluralism and diversity will help to guarantee that the media fulfil their proper role within the public sphere. The public

---

[164] McKee has argued that programmes like *Big Brother* raise important questions about how people live together and communicate across cultural differences: McKee, above n 160, 67. However, it is difficult to envisage what real understanding can be gained from these pseudo-reality programmes, with their highly artificial situations and encounters.

[165] Fraser, above n 116, 110.

[166] Dahlgren, above n 102, 8.

sphere model can help discussions about broadcasting (if not media) regulatory policy to move beyond the somewhat futile quest to justify the regulation of broadcasting and the non-regulation of the press. Of course, for each of the jurisdictions examined in this study, this disparity will remain, but, as suggested earlier in this chapter, it is a disparity which provides little help when one is trying to determine the appropriate regulation of broadcasting. Habermas has expressed concern that media power, with its ability to control access, is not sufficiently restrained by professional standards. Although he refers to regulation as another form of restraint, he appears pessimistic.[167] Indeed, he seems to think that the only issue regarding legal form, is whether it will incline the media to be more subject to political or economic power, rather than how regulation might enhance the independence of the media from either source of power.[168] Yet, this does seem too negative a view. This is not to deny that there are significant concerns about the way media operate, and about their vulnerability to political or economic influence, but this should not mean that a normative role can not be asserted for the media, and that it is not appropriate to explore the measures which might help that role to be realised.

For broadcasting, some writers have suggested that the public service broadcasting model, or the public broadcasting model, embodies or fulfils the public sphere concept.[169] However, if the broadcasting media are to fulfil their task within the public sphere, it is necessary to look more broadly, and to embrace all forms of broadcasting, even those not imbued with public service obligations or structures. Thus, both commercial and public broadcasting should be expected to serve the public sphere. From a practical perspective, it is unrealistic to expect, within the UK commercial broadcasting context, a reversion to the traditions of public service broadcasting such as they applied during the days of the broadcasting duopoly, and it is a tradition which has not had a central place in US and Australian broadcasting. Secondly, for any regulatory model to be convincing it has to take into account media developments such as subscription, new digital services, and the newer forms of media—something which will be considered in Chapter Seven. But, all media have the potential, even when they might be predominantly about entertainment, to tell us something about ourselves and the society in which we operate. All media, then, will, to a greater or lesser extent, contribute to the public sphere. It will be the role of policy and regulation to articulate the manner in which these different forms of media communications will contribute to the public sphere. One of Habermas' concerns was the risk that the public sphere might be vulnerable to political or economic pressure, and, as noted earlier, he saw the media as particularly vulnerable, bringing with it the risk that they might thereby 'infect' public discourse. To argue that both public and

---

[167] Habermas, above n 120, 376.

[168] *Ibid.*

[169] See, eg, F Webster, *Theories of the Information Society* (London, Routledge, 1995), 106ff, and N Garnham, 'The Media and the Public Sphere' in P Golding, G Murdock, and P Schlesinger (eds), *Communicating Politics* (Leicester, Leicester University Press, 1986), 37 at 45.

commercial broadcasting ought to serve the public sphere might be thought to exacerbate that risk. However, it is this very risk which makes it important to expect that both these sectors will play a part in the public sphere, so that they can act as counterweights to one another. Public broadcasting can be structured in a way which is independent of the state, but questions of funding, appointments, and so forth can mean that the state is able to exert indirect influence over the broadcaster, or at least have a chilling effect. Commercial broadcasting can operate as another voice to counteract these possibilities. In the same way, public broadcasting can counteract some of the constraints which a broadcasting sector relying on private commercial funding may experience. In short, it is unrealistic to expect that there can be complete independence from the influences of the state and the economy, but it is equally unrealistic to expect that the public sphere can function adequately without the media. Hence, the task must be to structure an environment which recognises the media's potential to enhance public discourse, but minimises its capacity for distortion of that same discourse.

The Regulatory Space

So far, the term 'regulation' has been loosely used. It has been argued that regulation of the media can be justified by reference to the role that it can and should play within the public sphere. Of course, as already discussed, whilst there has been a willingness to apply industry-specific regulation to broadcasting, that same willingness has not extended to the press. It has been argued that this disparity has tended to skew consideration of broadcasting regulation—particularly evident in recent attempts to reform ownership and control regulation. It has also been suggested that, although outside the scope of this book, the lack of a more targeted regulatory framework for the press might be open to question. However, there is another way of looking at this matter, which may also help the debate to move beyond the 'broadcasting-regulated, press-not-regulated' barrier. References to 'regulation' may too readily give the impression that broadcasting, even the media more generally, must inexorably be subjected to some form of heavy-handed, command and control legal regulation.[170] It might be more helpful to consider the issue in terms of a 'regulatory space', which moves beyond stark dichotomies such as regulated/unregulated, regulator/regulated, and public/private.[171]

The regulatory space concept recognises that regulatory power and authority will not be held within a single formal body, but may be dispersed between any

---

[170] J Black, 'Critical Reflections on Regulation' (2002) 27 *Australian Journal of Legal Philosophy* 1, at 2.
[171] For a much more sophisticated analysis and use of the regulatory space metaphor than will be found here, see: C Scott, 'Analysing Regulatory Space: Fragmented Resources and Institutional Design' [2001] *Public Law A Reader on Regulation Regulation* (Oxford, Oxford University Press, 1998) at 148. See also C Parker *et al* (eds), *Regulating Law* (Oxford, Oxford University Press, 2004).

number of entities, both private and public, within the relevant space.[172] There is an acknowledgement also that resources which can influence and determine regulatory power will be varied, and may include 'information, wealth and organisational capacities', and be 'fragmented among state bodies, and between state and non-state bodies'.[173] There will almost certainly be a variety of 'regulatory modalities' within the regulatory space.[174] The regulatory space concept can be seen as a way of understanding 'the relationship between the events being regulated and the mechanisms used to regulate those events'.[175] This understanding of the complexity of regulatory activity can be used as a means of improving institutional design.[176] For the purposes of this study, the concept of regulatory space is useful, because it provides a broader conception of the resources and tools which might be relevant 'to support the public policy objectives of the regulatory regime'.[177] The regulatory space concept avoids setting up a false construct whereby the market, and the discipline of the market forces, is viewed as beyond regulation or non-regulation. As Gibbons has suggested, this allows a different way of viewing regulation. Rather than viewing it as a departure from the norm, which is the market, one can instead view the market as simply another instrument within the regulatory space, which may be selected to serve the public policy objectives of the particular regulatory environment.[178] Using the regulatory space concept might also help to smooth out the lack of symmetry between broadcasting and the press, although questions might remain as to whether the institutional design is the most appropriate one. Similarly, it can also clarify the different responses to the broadcasting regulatory framework which are evident in the UK, the US, and Australia. Within each of these jurisdictions the regulatory choices made will be influenced by a range of values and priorities: an obvious influence on regulatory choices and outcomes, in the context of this study, will be the recognition given to free speech values in the relevant jurisdiction.

Conclusion

As this chapter has discussed, the media can have a crucial role facilitating public discussion and debate, and informing the public about that debate. The recognition of this critical role has influenced the regulation of broadcasting, but the case for regulation, although often acknowledging this role, has been dependent, for its

---

[172] Scott, above n 171, 331.
[173] *Ibid*, 330.
[174] N Lacey, 'Criminalization as Regulation: The Role of Criminal Law' in Parker, above n 171, 144, at 148.
[175] A Corbett and S Bottomley, 'Regulating Corporate Governance' in Parker, above n 171, 60, at 62.
[176] Scott, above n 171, 330–1.
[177] *Ibid*, 330.
[178] Gibbons, above n 1, 9–10.

justification, on arguments being put forward to explain why it is that broadcasting and not the press should be subject to regulation. This provides a weak basis for determining appropriate regulation, particularly when the traditional arguments used to justify broadcasting regulation are becoming increasingly open to challenge. Instead, it has been argued in this chapter that the model of the public sphere can provide a useful normative framework for articulating the role of the media, and determining the best way of giving effect to that role. Within this framework, for example, broadcasting pluralism policy can be shaped and the appropriate regulatory tools determined. Equally, it might be appropriate to look at whether regulatory attitudes towards the press are sufficient to guarantee that the press can fulfil its proper role within the public sphere. But this question is outside the scope of this study—the point is, however, that the public sphere model provides a normative role for the media which makes irrelevant the traditional debate which tries to justify broadcasting regulation. Equally, embracing a broad understanding of regulation means that debates over the choice of regulatory instrument can rise above crude dichotomies and simplistic definitions of what counts as regulation.

However, despite the attempt in this chapter to make a positive case from which broadcasting pluralism policy and regulation might be understood, it is accepted that the public sphere model is not one which has expressly influenced the regulatory measures being examined in this book, nor is it being articulated in the discussions about reform of media ownership rules. Abundance of media and demise of spectrum scarcity are much more convenient rallying calls for the jurisdictions examined here, which are eager to relax traditional forms of regulation. Even if the public sphere model were to be embraced, it is likely that the solutions found would differ considerably between the UK, the US, and Australia, given the different treatment of free speech principles and regulatory traditions. Nevertheless, the public sphere model can provide a useful standard by which current approaches to broadcasting pluralism and diversity regulation can be tested, and future policy, in the light of a changing media environment, assessed.

Part II

Regulatory Approaches

3

STRUCTURAL REGULATION

Introduction

Structural regulation is probably the most complex type of broadcasting plural-ism, because it attempts to engineer the environment within which broadcasting operates. As discussed in Chapter One, structural regulation, although generally focused on media ownership and control rules,[1] will also include regulation designed to produce differently constituted broadcasting sectors, such as, for example, public and private broadcasting sectors. In broad terms, it is believed that structural regulation which results in a plurality of ownership or differently constituted broadcasting outlets will help to promote diversity of voice and idea, because of the availability of media outlets which are owned and controlled by dif-ferent persons, or which have different programme mandates or sources of financ-ing. There are problems with this assumption, and these will be considered in this chapter but, nevertheless, it is an assumption which has influenced broadcasting regulation in all three jurisdictions. Structural regulation, particularly in relation to ownership and control rules, also tends to be controversial, and it is the form of media regulation for which reform is most consistently sought. The fact that it is controversial seems paradoxical, because it might also be viewed as a more accept-able form of regulation, since it does not directly interfere with, or determine, the content of what is broadcast. Whilst it is reasonable to assume that most forms of regulation are undesired by business, ownership and control rules are probably also the form of media regulation which business finds most unacceptable. In set-ting limits on ownership, these rules seem to interfere directly with property rights, and the freedom of business to determine its investments and direction. Thus, business may be less likely to view structural regulation as just a cost of busi-ness. Nevertheless, unlike other regulatory instruments designed to promote broadcasting pluralism which are reviewed in this book, structural regulation, and particularly ownership regulation, is the approach which finds the most common ground across the UK, the US, and Australia. Likewise, in recent times, the

---

[1] The reference to 'media' ownership and control rules rather than to 'broadcasting' is to reflect the fact that ownership and control rules can include newspapers also, through cross-media rules. For brevity, 'ownership' rather than 'ownership and control' will frequently be used, but it should be understood to encompass the concepts of ownership and control.

jurisdictions have shared a determination to reform this component of structural regulation.

The main focus of this chapter on structural regulation will be ownership and control regulation. Other forms of structural regulation will also be considered, but more briefly.

Sectoral Pluralism

This section examines the way in which the broadcasting environment can be designed to provide diversity by establishing services which differ in the way they are structured and financed. The most obvious example is by having a private broadcasting service funded by advertising revenue and a public broadcasting service financed by public funds, with either no advertising revenue or limited advertising revenue. Sectoral pluralism might also be provided by authorising broadcasting services which are operated on a non-profit, non-commercial basis, and which may receive some public funding, or none. These services will be funded through a mix of sponsorship, member subscriptions, and audience support. Australia provides an example of this type of diversity in the form of community broadcasting services, as does the US, with its public broadcasting sector which, despite its name, receives only limited public funding. The 2003 reforms led to the establishment of a community radio sector in the UK also. Further diversity might be obtained by having some services funded by subscription revenue instead of advertising revenue.

All three jurisdictions have structured their broadcasting environments to include differently structured and funded sectors, but it has been the UK, in particular, and Australia, which have shown the greatest commitment to sectoral pluralism. Although other factors, such as a specific programme mandate, will have a part to play, the lack of dependence upon advertising as a funding source is generally seen as one of the most important factors contributing to sectoral pluralism. One of the problems with a broadcasting service delivered free-to-air and financed by advertising is that the service will of necessity be more responsive to the advertisers' needs than the needs and interests of the audience. Thus, it is likely that programming which delivers the largest audience will be broadcast, even though there may be programmes which the audience might prefer more. This may also tend to produce a relatively homogeneous range of programming which pays little regard to minority interests.[2] A broadcasting environment which provides services with different funding sources is considered more likely to provide programming which will cater for a much wider range of tastes and interests. Making services available by subscription does not completely address the limita-

---

[2] Productivity Commission, *Broadcasting*, Report No 11 (Canberra, AusInfo, 2000), 94. The effect of funding on broadcasting is examined in Chapter Six.

tions of advertising-funded services; such services may raise access issues, since many people may not be able to afford the cost of subscription services.[3] However, if the mechanism of sectoral pluralism is to be an effective counterbalance to an advertising-funded broadcasting system, then the structural elements need to be carefully designed. In the following paragraphs, the public broadcasting sector in the UK and in Australia will be examined, followed by an examination of the community broadcasting sector in Australia and the public broadcasting sector in the US.

Public Broadcasting in the UK and Australia

The Australian public broadcasting service is modelled on the UK service, but there are important differences. Certainly, the most developed approach towards sectoral pluralism is found in the UK, with its pervasive public broadcasting service, the British Broadcasting Corporation (BBC), which operates alongside the private commercially-funded broadcasting sector. In addition to the BBC, the UK provides another public broadcaster, Channel Four. Channel Four differs from the BBC because it is financed through advertising, but it is run as a non-profit statutory corporation so that, although subject to the limitations of an advertising-funded system, it has greater freedom than private broadcasters, because it does not have to generate returns to shareholders. It also has a specific programme mandate which, within a general obligation to provide 'a broad range of high quality and diverse programming', requires it to demonstrate 'innovation, experiment and creativity in the form and content of programmes', to appeal 'to the tastes and interests of a culturally diverse society', to exhibit 'a distinctive character', and to provide educational programming.[4] But it is the BBC, with its range of television channels and radio stations, which provides the most characteristic example of a public broadcasting system.

However, it would be a mistake to assume that the current broadcasting environment arose out of a clearly articulated and planned pluralism policy. When the BBC began broadcasting in 1922, it was run as a monopoly by a private company, owned by the radio manufacturers as a way of helping the sale of radio equipment.[5] It became a public corporation in 1927 following the recommendations of the Crawford Committee in 1925, which was concerned that the power of broadcasting was such that it should not be left to private interests.[6] It was not until the mid-1950s that private commercial television broadcasting began in the UK, and commercial radio did not begin until the 1970s. Craufurd Smith suggests that the

---

[3] *Ibid*, 94–95.

[4] Comms Act (UK), s 265(3).

[5] RH Coase, *British Broadcasting: A Study in Monopoly* (London, Longmans, 1950), 15–16. The BBC was then called the British Broadcasting Company.

[6] T Gibbons, *Regulating the Media*, 2nd edn (London, Sweet & Maxwell, 1998), 57. These concerns about the power of broadcasting had also been expressed by an earlier inquiry into broadcasting by the Sykes Committee: *ibid*, 56–57.

adoption of a public broadcasting monopoly, and its maintenance, had more to do with political concerns about the potential influence and persuasiveness of the medium, rather than with any more lofty or practical concerns for broadcasting.[7] Likewise, the introduction of commercial television probably had less to do with pluralism promotion than with a Conservative government's view that broadcasting was a matter for private industry.[8] However, there was strong opposition to the introduction of commercial television, on the ground that it would diminish the tone of broadcasting.[9] Notwithstanding the genesis of British broadcasting services, the justification for public and private broadcasting sectors is now firmly embedded in pluralism policy.[10]

The BBC's structure is quite unusual. Rather than being established under statute, it is formed under Royal Charter. This Charter sets out the overall structure and objectives of the BBC.[11] The Charter is supplemented by an agreement made between the BBC and the relevant Secretary of State, which provides more detail on the terms of operation of the organisation.[12] Funding is provided by the income generated through collection of a licence fee which is payable by anyone who possesses a television set.[13] Although the BBC has other sources of funding, such as programme sales, the licence fee is still its major source of revenue.[14] Whilst a lack of dependence upon advertising revenue should have an effect on programme provision, this factor alone has not been treated as sufficient. Central to the BBC's operations is its public service obligation. The concept of public service broadcasting will be considered in more detail in Chapter Four, but it has been a concept which has influenced both public and private broadcasting policy in the UK.[15] Under the Charter, the BBC is required to provide 'programmes of information, education and entertainment for general reception'.[16] The BBC's terms of operation are set out in more detail in the Agreement, which elaborates

---

[7] R Craufurd Smith, *Broadcasting Law and Fundamental Rights* (Oxford, Clarendon Press, 1997), 30–31.

[8] J Curran and J Seaton, *Power Without Responsibility: The Press, Broadcasting, and New Media in Britain*, 6th edn (London, Routledge, 2003), 160–61.

[9] Craufurd Smith, above n 7, 38.

[10] Department of Trade and Industry (DTI) and Department for Culture, Media and Sport (DCMS), *A New Future for Communications*, Cm 5010 (2000) ('White Paper'), 35–36.

[11] Department of National Heritage, *Royal Charter for the continuance of the British Broadcasting Corporation*, Cm 3248 (1996) ('Charter').

[12] Department of National Heritage, *Agreement Dated the 25th Day of January 1996 Between Her Majesty's Secretary of State for National Heritage and the British Broadcasting Corporation*, Cm 3152 (1996), amended by DCMS, *Deed of Variation dated 4th December 2003*, Cm 6075 (2003) ('Agreement').

[13] Wireless Telegraphy Act 1949, s 1(1). Possession of a radio no longer gives rise to a licence fee obligation, but licence fee revenue funds both television and radio services.

[14] Independent Panel on BBC Charter Review, *Emerging Themes* (December 2004), para 4.1 (available from www.bbccharterreview.org.uk). The licence fee accounts for around 95% of the BBC revenue: J Smith, 'Financial Challenges for the BBC' (2003) 43 *Corporate Sector Review*, http://www.accaglobal.com/publications/corpsecrev/43/822086, accessed 27 July 2005.

[15] The public service broadcasting obligation was imposed on both the public and private sectors to ameliorate opposition to the introduction of commercial television: Craufurd Smith, above n 7, 38.

[16] The Charter, above n 11, Art 3(a).

on the Charter's shorthand public service statement, specifying the programme areas or audiences which should be catered for.[17] Traditionally, the BBC has been a self-governing organisation, with the governors bearing responsibility for ensuring that the BBC meets its Charter obligations. However, over the past decade or so, the BBC has been made increasingly subject to external regulation for certain of its activities, alongside other broadcasters. With the 2003 reforms, that trend has continued, so that the Office of Communications (Ofcom) is now responsible for regulating many of the BBC's obligations; the government's intention is that regulation should be consistent between the BBC and other public service broadcasters.[18]

The structure of Australian public broadcasting services (or national broadcasting services, as they are known) follows more expected lines. Section 3(1)(a) of the Broadcasting Services Act 1992 (BSA (Aus)) requires the promotion of 'the availability to audiences throughout Australia of a diverse range of radio and television services offering entertainment, education and information'. Although Australia has followed a similar pattern to the UK, with the development of public broadcasting, it has also built up a more complex pattern of sectoral diversity, with the presence of both national (public) and community broadcasting services. Initially, as in the UK, broadcasting was provided by the radio manufacturers but, within a short time, an Australian version of the BBC, the Australian Broadcasting Corporation (as it is now known) (ABC) was established. Radio broadcasting commenced in 1932, and television broadcasting began in Sydney in 1956, extending nationally in 1960. However, unlike the UK, Australia began commercial broadcasting at much the same time.[19] The ABC is established under the Australian Broadcasting Corporation Act 1983 (ABC Act), and receives about 80 per cent of its funding through government grant.[20] The ABC Act incorporates a charter of obligations for the ABC, which requires it to meet traditional public service broadcasting programming standards.[21] The broadcaster is governed by the ABC Board, which is responsible for ensuring the ABC's independence and performance of the broadcaster's statutory functions.[22] Although the ABC deals with complaints about its programmes, the Australian Media and Communications Authority (ACMA) also has power to investigate if the ABC has failed to do so within a certain time, or the response has been inadequate.[23] Australia's other public broadcaster, the Special Broadcasting Service (SBS), was established in 1978

---

[17] The Agreement, above n 12, cls 3.1–3.2.

[18] DTI and DCMS, *The Draft Communications Bill—The Policy*, Cm 5508-III (2002) ('Policy Statement'), para 8.2.1.1. See also DTI and DCMS, *Draft Communications Bill, Proposed Amendments to the BBC Agreement* (2002), para 4.

[19] See M Armstrong, *Broadcasting Law and Policy in Australia* (Sydney, Butterworths, 1982), paras 302–5, and Productivity Commission, above n 2, 270.

[20] Productivity Commission, above n 2, 96. The ABC was funded by licence fee, but this was abandoned in 1948.

[21] ABC Act, s 6.

[22] *Ibid*, s 8(1).

[23] BSA (Aus), s 150.

to provide radio services, and began television broadcasting in 1980.[24] Like the ABC, it is a national broadcaster financed through government grants, although it is also allowed to receive funding through a limited amount of advertising.[25] SBS is incorporated under the Special Broadcasting Service Act 1991 (SBS Act), and is governed by the Special Broadcasting Service Board. SBS has a specific and distinctive remit, set out in the statutory charter, 'to provide multilingual and multicultural radio and television services that inform, educate and entertain all Australians, and, in doing so, reflect Australia's multicultural society'.[26] As with the ABC, complaints about the SBS can be taken to ACMA.[27]

Possibly nothing illustrates more clearly the sensitivity of the relationship between governments and the media than the existence of public broadcasting. Publicly funded and established, yet not a state broadcaster, it will be essential that a public broadcaster can maintain its independence if it is to contribute to the public exchange of information and ideas. Hence, the way in which the public broadcaster is structured, funded, and allowed to operate will be crucial if it is not to be the subject of interference, even indirect interference. The BBC and the Australian national broadcasting services provide a contrast in their method of establishment: the BBC by way of Royal Charter, the Australian services by statute, but this does not mean that the pressures faced by the broadcasters will differ. The use of a royal charter for the BBC was deliberate, because it was thought that a statutory instrument could make parliamentary interference more likely,[28] although, in practice, this does not prevent questions about the BBC being raised in Parliament, since questions can be asked of the Minister responsible for the broadcaster,[29] nor the BBC being required to appear before parliamentary committees. However, Ministers usually observe the convention of adhering to the independence of the BBC, and refuse to answer questions about day-to-day editorial and programming policy.[30] There are, however, disadvantages associated with the use of a charter. It is a creature of Crown prerogative, and so the government of the day will have broad control over the Charter's operation and renewal.[31] Both the Charter and the Agreement permit the government to revoke the BBC's mandate.[32] The Charter is also only granted for a fixed period of time. There has been no consistent practice for this; it has varied between 10 and 15 years, and the current Charter is for 10 years, shorter than the 15-year term of its predecessor. This shorter term reflected the uncertainty at the time it was granted about the con-

---

[24] Productivity Commission, above n 2, 270.

[25] SBS receives about 75% of its funding from government grants: *ibid*, 96.

[26] SBS Act, s 6(1).

[27] BSA (Aus), s 150.

[28] EM Barendt, *Broadcasting Law: A Comparative Study* (Oxford, Clarendon Press, 1995), 67, citing T Burns, *The BBC: Public Institution and Private World* (London, 1977), 15–16.

[29] Gibbons, above n 6, 247.

[30] *Ibid*.

[31] *Ibid*, 245, and E Barendt, 'Legal Aspects of BBC Charter Renewal' (1994) 65(1) *The Political Quarterly* 20 at 21.

[32] The Charter, above n 11, Art 20(2), and the Agreement, above n 12, cl 15.

tinuing role and funding of the BBC, especially in the light of emerging media platforms. Charter renewal provides the government with an opportunity to make major changes to the BBC. This prospect can lead to uncertainty for the broadcaster, its plans, and future activities, and it may also have a chilling effect on its preparedness to broadcast material which may be controversial, or unlikely to be appreciated by the government of the day.[33] A public broadcaster, formed under statute, may risk greater parliamentary interference, but it may also have a greater sense of permanency. It is a fine balance, although the difference may be largely one of perception. A charter, having been renewed, may create a sense in which it is 'hands-off' the public broadcaster until the next renewal process, whereas the statutory framework, incorporating the opportunity for amendment, may create the impression that it is legitimate to interfere with the broadcaster on a more regular basis. And other means, such as government inquiries, regardless of the legal form of the public broadcaster, may serve to intimidate the public broadcaster.

The Charter renewal process (for 2007 and beyond) was seen as particularly sensitive, coming in the wake of the Hutton Report, which arose out of an inquiry into the death of a government scientist, David Kelly, who had leaked information to a BBC journalist.[34] The journalist had broadcast reports concerning the basis for the government's claims about the existence of weapons of mass destruction in Iraq. The Hutton Report, which was highly critical of the BBC, led to the resignations of the Chairman and Director-General of the BBC, and to changes in journalist and editorial procedures and complaint-handling processes. Whilst the establishment of the Hutton Inquiry, in the aftermath of Dr Kelly's death, might have seemed legitimate, attacks on the ABC in Australia can be blunter.[35] In May 2003, the then Minister for Communications, Senator Richard Alston, made 68 formal complaints to the ABC alleging that a current affairs radio programme, *AM*, had been biased and anti-American in its reporting of the Iraqi war. The Minister claimed to be representing the public, having received a number of complaints, but it transpired that there were only eight written complaints (and an unknown, and unlogged, number of telephone calls).[36] Eventually, Senator Alston took the complaints to the Australian Broadcasting Authority (ABA), ACMA's predecessor, after the complaints had already been dealt with by the ABC Complaints Review Executive and the Independent Complaints Review Board (established by the ABC). Of the original 68 complaints, the ABA was asked to review 43. It upheld only six of the complaints (three of which related to one

---

[33] Curran suggests, citing Briggs (A Briggs, *The BBC: The First Fifty Years* (Oxford, Oxford University Press, 1985)), that Charter renewal periods have often been the time when the BBC has been most sensitive to government opinion: J Curran, *Media and Power* (London, Routledge, 2002), 214.

[34] Lord Hutton, *Report of the Inquiry into the Circumstances Surrounding the Death of Dr David Kelly* CMG, HC 247 (January 2004).

[35] It is the ABC, rather than SBS, which usually incurs government ire—this reflects the fact that SBS is a much smaller broadcaster, as well as the different mandates of the two broadcasters.

[36] None of the written complaints mentioned *AM*: ABC Television, 'The Minister's Complaint', *Media Watch* (3 November 2003), http://www.abc.net.au/mediawatch/transcripts/s981335.htm, accessed 16 July 2005.

segment of one programme) but, like the two earlier bodies, it found that, overall, the programmes were of a high standard and balanced.[37] As with the BBC, this series of complaints prompted the ABC to review its internal complaints procedure. In effect, regardless of the outcome of these types of issues, public criticism of the broadcaster, or complaints against it, will have a tendency to provoke the public broadcaster into making changes to its processes in order to demonstrate its integrity and accountability. One ABC commentator refers to the ABC's 'ritual appeasement', and the 'pre-emptive buckle', a reference, used within the ABC, to mean 'the practice of making changes in response to the perception of coming political pressure from the government'.[38] Perversely, however, the Hutton Report may have constrained the UK government in the Charter renewal process and plans for the BBC's future, because it emerged that, despite the Hutton Report's conclusions (which had also exonerated the government of any wrongdoing), the general public were much more willing to trust the BBC than the government.[39] The government has now made clear that the BBC will be granted a new Charter for a term of 10 years. Although it considered the option of moving to a statutory basis for the BBC, it decided to retain the Charter for much the same reasons as have been canvassed here.[40]

Neither of the approaches adopted by the UK and Australia provides a satisfactory approach to the appointment of members to the broadcasters' governing bodies. The BBC governors (including the BBC chairman), and the ABC Board members and chairman (with the exception of the managing director and a staff-elected director), and the SBS Board members and chairman (with the exception of the managing director) are appointed by the government.[41] Appointments to these significant positions have frequently been seen as politically motivated, and those appointed have often had close connections to the government of the day. Two former BBC chairmen, Marmaduke Hussey and Stuart Young, were related to Cabinet Ministers at the time.[42] The same perception also applies in Australia, and there have been appointments to the ABC Board of known critics. Indeed, a recent appointment, Janet Albrechsten, has a record of being openly hostile to the ABC. The UK Labour government changed the appointment process in 2001 by introducing a formal application and interview process for candidates for a governor position (or for chairman), and by establishing an interview panel, which makes a recommendation to the government. However, as Curran suggests, this

[37] ABA, *ABA Investigation Report: AM broadcast by ABC Radio National: 21 March–11 April 2003* (Investigation Report No 1362, March 2005).

[38] Q Dempster, 'The Slow Destruction of the ABC' in R Manne (ed), *Do Not Disturb: Is the Media Failing Australia?* (Melbourne, Black Inc, 2005), 101 at 107–8.

[39] N Watt, 'New poll reveals public mistrust', (2004) *The Guardian* (London), 30 January, http://guardian.co.uk/hutton/story/0,13822,1134981,00.html, accessed 16 July 2005.

[40] DCMS, *Review of the BBC's Royal Charter: A Strong BBC, Independent of Government*, PP 789 (March 2005), paras 3.3–3.4.

[41] In the case of the BBC, it is strictly the Queen in Council: The Charter, above n 11, Art 8(1), and in the case of the ABC and SBS, it is the Governor-General: ABC Act, s 12(2) and SBS Act, s 17(1).

[42] Curran, above n 33, 213. Hussey was chairman of the BBC between 1986 and 1996, whilst Young was chairman from 1983 until 1986. See also Barendt, above n 31, 24–25.

was a limited reform because the panel itself was comprised of people who were close to the governing party, and it ultimately recommended a 'New Labour insider, Gavyn Davies' as chairman.[43] However, both Davies and his successor, Michael Grade, were well qualified to hold the position. The government has recommended that the system of BBC governors should be replaced with a new governing entity, the BBC Trust, which will have ultimate responsibility for the licence fee and assessing the BBC's performance. An executive board will be responsible for the delivery of the BBC's services.[44] This new structure aims to provide greater separation of governance and management, and is a response to what has been perceived as a confused role for the governors, whereby they must both regulate the BBC and be its advocate.

Another major area of vulnerability for a public broadcaster will be funding. Here, again, the UK and Australian structures offer different approaches—the primary funding mechanisms being the licence fee in the UK, and government grant in Australia. A licence fee is generally seen as a more acceptable form of funding for a public broadcaster, because it will provide a more long-term and stable source of funds. It will lessen the broadcaster's dependence upon government, which can ensure a greater degree of independence, compared with a system of government grants which may have to be renewed annually or every few years. On the other hand, the Charter renewal process means that the case for the licence fee as a funding mechanism may have to be repeatedly made. This is made more problematic because the licence fee is not a particularly popular form of funding with the public (and therefore with politicians). Its popularity is not served either by being essentially a regressive form of taxation, since it takes, with some limited exceptions, no account of ability to pay.[45] Another difficulty is that the licence does not allow much room for growth. In the past, new markets, first television, and later colour television, enabled the licence fee income to increase naturally, but as the market becomes more stable the broadcaster is more dependent upon government willingness to increase the fee, the value of which may also be eroded by inflation.[46] In 1998, the government established a review of BBC funding, but the terms of the review were limited to ways to supplement licence fee income.[47] However, the panel did explore other forms of funding. It considered that direct funding, via government grant or taxation, 'tended to create broadcasters that are inextricably linked to political moods and have the potential to lose management or editorial independence'.[48]

---

[43] Curran, above n 33, 213. See also Barendt for arguments for and against the appointments process: above n 31, 25–27. The appointment of Michael Grade was overseen by a cross-party group of Privy Councillors: D Sandelson and G Smith, 'The Future Shape of the BBC' (2004) 15(5) *Entertainment Law Review* 137 at 138.

[44] DCMS, above n 40, paras 5.24–5.33. The first chair of the BBC Trust (a working title) will be the current BBC chairman, Michael Grade.

[45] Independent Review Panel, *Report: The Future Funding of the BBC* (July 1999), 142–43.

[46] Curran, above n 33, 214.

[47] Independent Review Panel, above n 45.

[48] *Ibid*, 67.

The mixed funding solution offered by SBS does not really alleviate this risk, and indeed may exacerbate it, because it is likely that the broadcaster will still remain primarily dependent upon government grants, but with the constant pressure that it could be doing more to raise advertising revenue. Governments may also feel more reluctant to increase the public funds available to a broadcaster which also has the option of raising further revenue from advertising. However, the likelihood is that a small broadcaster like SBS would never be able to attract the amount of advertising revenue which would be needed to compensate for the public funding. Given its size and reach, the BBC would probably be quite an attractive option for advertisers, but the review panel rejected advertising as a form of funding for the BBC. In addition to the usual concerns about the impact of advertising upon programming, the panel was also concerned that it would diminish the availability of advertising revenue for other broadcasters, because advertising was likely to be a less certain form of funding as the number of competing services grew.[49] Although the licence fee has advantages over direct funding, the BBC, during the past couple of decades, has had to undergo major management restructuring because of increasing financial pressure.[50] In the future media environment, where programming may be delivered via a variety of means, the licence fee may be under renewed pressure if the television set becomes increasingly irrelevant. Similarly, with an increasing number of services available, the BBC's audience share may decline. The UK government has proposed that the BBC should continue to be funded for its renewed Charter term by the licence fee, although a review of funding mechanisms is intended during the post-2007 Charter period.[51] Interestingly, the government, in making its recommendations, reported that, although public support for the licence fee was equivocal, there was clear public opposition to government funding, because of the potential for government interference. In this respect, the licence fee was seen by the public more positively.[52] There was also strong public opposition to advertising on the BBC and, although there was more support for subscription services, this was seen as raising access concerns.[53]

It is clearly appropriate that a public broadcaster in receipt of public funds be accountable for the use of those funds, just as a private broadcaster will be accountable to its shareholders. However, a balance needs to be found between mechanisms which provide appropriate accountability and those which may erode the broadcaster's independence. Accountability mechanisms may be informal (such as providing opportunities for viewer or listener feedback) or formal. The number of accountability mechanisms has certainly increased over the last

[49] *Ibid*, 64.
[50] For an account of this period, see Gibbons, above n 6, 181–85. The ABC is also under constant financial pressure. The BBC receives, per capita, three times the funding of the ABC: G Withers, *Australian Financial Review* (22 March 2000), cited in Friends of the ABC, *ABC Funding for the 2003–2006 Triennium* (2003), http://www.friendsoftheabc.org/fund2003.pdf, accessed 27 July 2005, 6.
[51] DCMS, above n 40, 5.
[52] *Ibid*, para 4.6.
[53] *Ibid*, paras 4.7 and 4.12–4.13.

decade or so, particularly in the UK, with an increased emphasis on value for money—efficiency and value for money are key principles guiding the BBC Charter review.[54] Whilst accountability mechanisms have the potential to place the broadcaster under greater pressure, they may also provide some protection for the broadcaster. They are likely to involve more formal and public processes, thereby offering a greater transparency in dealings between the public broadcaster and government. As already noted, both the UK and the Australian public broadcasters are accountable in varying degrees to the statutory regulators, Ofcom and ACMA, respectively. The processes of Charter renewal, or, in the case of Australia, the determination of a new funding grant, will provide occasions for reviewing the broadcasters' performance. Both jurisdictions require the broadcasters to report on compliance with their Charter or statutory obligations. In each case this is done in the form of an annual report. This has a slightly curious aspect to it because it is the organisation itself which assesses how successfully it has met its obligations. However, in both jurisdictions, these reports are tabled in Parliament and can be debated there. Apart from these more regular forms of accountability, public broadcasters may find themselves having to appear before parliamentary committees to provide information, answer questions, and so forth. These appearances may be perfectly appropriate, but, once again, they can provide opportunities for making the public broadcaster aware of its vulnerability. With the 2003 reforms, the BBC has been made subject to a new form of accountability. Following amendments to the Agreement, the BBC's audit committee must consider whether plans for the use of licence money offer 'value for money'. This process also requires reviews to be carried out by the National Audit Office, and reports from the National Audit Office must be tabled in Parliament by the BBC.[55]

Regardless of the differences in the design, it is apparent that, both in the UK and Australia, there is a long history of political interference and displeasure with public broadcasting services. Accusations of bias, waste, and failing to fulfil their mandates have been heard regularly throughout the histories of these broadcasters. Governments frequently make the mistake of thinking that public broadcasters should be supportive of government policies and action, and are prone to confuse independence with bias—although when Baroness Thatcher was Prime Minister she was, on one occasion, displeased with the BBC for being too even-handed.[56] On the one hand it is apparent that, whatever the structural design of the public broadcaster, problems are likely to arise given the sensitive nature of an independent, but publicly funded, broadcaster, but it also shows clearly that the design is crucial if the public broadcaster is to have the best opportunity to carry

[54] *Ibid*, paras 6.5–6.7. However, the emphasis on accountability may also reflect the increased attention paid to governance within the community generally, which has affected both public and private sectors: Independent Panel on BBC Charter Review, above n 14, paras 5.5–5.7.

[55] The Agreeement, above n 12, Art 10B. The National Audit Office scrutinises public spending on behalf of the Parliament.

[56] M Cockerell, *Live from Number 10: The Inside Story of Prime Ministers and Television* (London, Faber & Faber, 1988), 270–71. The occasion was the BBC's reporting of the Falklands War.

out its mandate independently, particularly during times of major national controversy. It is the ABC, with its exposure to political board appointments, and dependence on government funding grants, which seems to be the most vulnerable.

Public Broadcasting in the US and Community Broadcasting in Australia

The 2003 reforms in the UK introduced a new radio broadcasting sector: community radio. Community radio was first licensed in 2005 (after a trial period), and is designed to serve specific communities—local or interest-based— and must be non-profit-making. These services will be broadcast over a small area, up to a maximum of five kilometres. They may include advertising and sponsorship, but at least 50 per cent of their funding must be from other sources.[57] However, it is the US and Australia which have the most developed community non-profit broadcasting sectors. These sectors can contribute to the pluralism of the broadcasting environment. However, their limited sources of funding may mean that their reach and impact are small and, although relieved of the constraints usually associated with an advertising-funded service, they may face other pressures because of the financing sources upon which they are dependent.

Community broadcasting in Australia (originally known as 'public broadcasting') began in the 1970s and, as its name indicates, it is intended to meet the 'needs of a local community, or of a particular sector of the community'.[58] Thus, services may be local services or services directed to a particular ethnic or religious community, or they may specialise in certain interests such as a particular genre of music. Community broadcasting services are not operated for profit, or as part of a profit-making enterprise, and they are made available free to the public.[59] They are also expected to have in place mechanisms which will encourage community participation in their operation.[60] The licensing process requires ACMA to consider the diversity of interests of the community, and the diversity of services offered by other broadcasters in that area.[61] Community broadcasting services can access some sources of government funding, but primarily they must look to audience and member subscriptions, donations, and sponsorships for their funding.[62] They also usually rely on some level of voluntary participation for their operations. As the Productivity Commission noted, although some community radio broadcasters have managed quite well with these sources of funding, others 'have suffered from a chronic lack of funds'.[63] Accessing sufficient funding is particularly a

---

[57] Community Radio Order 2004, SI 2004, No 1944.
[58] Explanatory Memorandum, Broadcasting Services Bill 1992, 23.
[59] BSA (Aus), s 15.
[60] *Ibid*, sch 2, cl 9(2)(c).
[61] *Ibid*, s 84(2).
[62] Productivity Commission, above n 2, 275.
[63] *Ibid*.

problem for community television, with its higher operating costs. Community broadcasters are prohibited from broadcasting advertisements,[64] but are allowed to broadcast sponsorship announcements provided these do not run for a total of more than seven minutes, in the case of CTV, or five minutes for community radio, in any hour of broadcasting.[65] Sponsorship announcements on CTV can be broadcast only 'during periods before programs commence, after programs end or during natural program breaks'.[66]

The US public broadcasting sector is similar to Australian community broadcasting, although the former has a much more established television service. The American public broadcasting sector offers radio and television broadcasting services on a non-profit, non-commercial basis. Licensed as 'non-commercial educational' broadcasting stations, public broadcasters are prohibited from broadcasting advertisements.[67] This proscription is consistent with the sector's objectives, namely that public broadcasters should be able to make programming decisions free of the usual pressures faced by commercially funded broadcasting services.[68] In the absence of advertising revenue, public broadcasting services are funded through a mix of sources. There is some government funding but, as with the Australian sector, viewer and listener membership and business support provide the most significant sources of funding.[69] Public broadcasting in the US is intended to offset the limitations of the commercially funded services, but it is marginal, accounting for only around two per cent of viewing audience, even at peak viewing times, and illustrates the dominance of the private commercial sector in US broadcasting.[70] However, this has not prevented it from being subjected to accusations of bias and attempts to cut its funding.[71]

Sponsorship funding can provide a practical means of increasing the revenue-raising capacity for these broadcasters, whilst avoiding the pressures produced by reliance on advertising revenue. Sponsorship, although in one sense a form of advertising, is thought to be more acceptable in a non-commercial context, because it lacks the intrusive nature of traditional 'spot' advertising. This idea was captured by an Australian working party established in the 1970s to consider recommendations for the development of community broadcasting:

[64] BSA (Aus), sch 2, cl 9(1)(b).

[65] *Ibid*, sch 2, cl 9(3). Community announcements and the like are excluded from these calculations.

[66] *Ibid*, sch 2, cl 9(4).

[67] 47 USC § 399b(2). See also 47 CFR § 73.621(e) (per television), and 47 CFR § 73.503(d) (per radio).

[68] Federal Communications Commission, *Second Report and Order, In the matter of Commission Policy Concerning the Noncommercial Nature of Educational Broadcast Stations*, 86 FCC 2d 141 (1981), para 3.

[69] Corporation for Public Broadcasting, 'Who pays for public broadcasting?', http://www.cpb.org/pubcast/#who_pays, accessed 25 August 2003.

[70] P Aufderheide, 'Public Television Now and Later' in H Lamb (ed), *The Encyclopaedia of Television* (5 November 2001), http://www.centerforsocialmedia.org/publictelevisionnowandlater.htm, accessed 27 July 2005.

[71] For information on attacks on public broadcasting in 2005, see Freepress, www.freepress.net/publicbroadcasting; Citizens for Independent Public Broadcasting, http://www.cipbonline.org/; and Common Cause, http://www.commoncause.org.

Sponsorship is considered to have a different objective to advertising. Certainly the prime one is to promote the interests of the sponsor, but if its nature is restricted, there should not be such pressure to consistently go for mass audiences. Public radio should lend itself to a class of sponsor who would certainly hope to gain some benefit for himself, but whose measurable return might be much less than an advertiser would normally contemplate. It could be a means of encouraging some interests to sponsor broadcasting as a public-spirited gesture.[72]

However, sponsorship can create pressures, so, if the non-commercial nature of the sector is to be maintained, what will, and what will not, be permissible in the sponsorship arrangements needs to be carefully considered. For example, sponsorship can permit a direct identification with particular programming, rather than just programming within a certain time slot, but the risk is that the sponsor might want to have a more direct influence over the programme's content. This is a matter which will be raised also in Chapter Four. There are some odd aspects to the Australian arrangements which illustrate the potential difficulties. Community broadcasting was introduced because of concerns that the commercial sector was not catering to needs across the whole community.[73] When first established, community broadcasting was not prohibited from broadcasting advertisements, although the sector volunteered not to do so, confining itself to sponsorship. This restraint did not seem to arise from a sense of what was appropriate to the nature of the sector but, rather, to ensure that the commercial sector was not deprived of revenue.[74] This voluntary forbearance was given statutory force in 1980. Until the BSA (Aus), the then legislation and policy was quite explicit as to what sponsorship permitted: mention of the identity of the sponsor was permitted, together with a description of the sponsor's business, but there could be no inducement to purchase the goods or services.[75] This explicitness has not been carried through to the current legislation. Indeed, the BSA (Aus) seems almost to have the opposite effect. There is no statutory definition of 'advertisement' or 'sponsorship', but the legislation does set out when a community broadcaster will be taken not to be broadcasting an advertisement—the effect of which is to permit a broadcaster making a sponsorship announcement to include promotion of the sponsor's goods or services.[76] As a result, community broadcasting sponsorship announcements could have the look and feel of an ordinary spot advertisement; the only difference will be the presence of a 'tag', disclosing the presence of sponsorship. If the purpose of community broadcasting is to promote sectoral pluralism, then a fairly relaxed regulatory attitude appears to have been taken to preserve the funding distinctions between the commercial and non-

---

[72] Working Party on Public Broadcasting, *Public Broadcasting: Report by the Working Party to the Minister for the Media* (Canberra, AGPS, 1975), 44.

[73] Productivity Commission, above n 2, 275.

[74] Armstrong, above n 19, para. 503.

[75] See Broadcasting and Television Act 1942, as amended, s 111BA(3), and Armstrong, above n 19, para 503.

[76] BSA (Aus), sch 2, cl 2(2).

commercial sectors. Presumably, it is thought sufficient to rest upon the assumption that community broadcasting, with its smaller audience and reach, will be less attractive to advertisers and, therefore, less likely to be subject to commercial pressures.

The US has a more clearly articulated policy concerning the non-commercial broadcasting sector. Here, sponsorship announcements have several clear functions. For example, if a programme has been underwritten, then a sponsorship announcement must be made in order to identify who has provided funding.[77] Hence, the sponsorship announcement is not for the benefit of the sponsor, but is made in the public interest, because the public is 'entitled to know by whom they are being persuaded'.[78] The approach is illustrated by a phrase which appears regularly in relevant Federal Communications Commission (FCC) policy: 'identification not promotion'.[79] It is less clear that this concern applies in Australia. However, even in the US, there has been a gradual relaxation as to what is permissible by way of identification; sponsorship announcements can now include 'logograms' which relate to the sponsor's business.[80] Whilst the use of logograms still has to be seen in the context of identification, the FCC has recognised that allowing sponsorship announcements to include logograms could help the sector's revenue-raising capacity.[81] It is obvious that in both jurisdictions fine judgements may be needed to ensure the community or public broadcaster keeps separate revenue-raising activity and the determination of programme policy. Certainly, in Australia there have been instances of programmes being little more than 'advertorials',[82] whilst the FCC has had to remind broadcasters of their obligations in relation to sponsorship announcements.[83]

Structural Control Over Who Can Broadcast

Each of the jurisdictions has controls in place over who can broadcast. These may be specific controls such as restrictions on foreign ownership, or they may arise less explicitly through licensing processes and the exercise of discretion. These controls may not be directed specifically towards promotion of broadcasting

---

[77] 47 USC § 317 and 47 CFR § 73.1212(e). These requirements apply to commercial and non-commercial services.

[78] FCC, *Public Notice, In re Applicability of Sponsorship Identification Rules*, 40 FCC 141 (1963).

[79] See, eg, FCC, *Public Notice, In the Matter of Commission Policy Concerning the Noncommercial Nature of Educational Broadcasting Stations*, FCC 86-161 (1986), and FCC, *Memorandum Opinion and Order, In the matter of Commission Policy Concerning the Noncommercial Nature of Educational Stations*, 97 FCC 2d 255 (1984).

[80] Logograms are defined to include aural or visual words, signs, or symbols: Communications, 47 USC § 399a(a).

[81] FCC, *Second Report and Order* (1981), above n 68, para. 37.

[82] ABA, *Annual Report 2000–2001* (2001), 132–33.

[83] FCC, *Public Notice* (1963), above n 78.

pluralism but, indirectly, they may have some impact. Such controls will be considered only briefly, but they are worth a brief review because they illustrate the belief that there is a connection between ownership and voice—something which is so important to the regulation of media ownership.

Structuring the Market through Licensing and Discretionary Powers

It is through the exercise of licensing powers that these controls are most apparent. Even where there has been a change in licensing procedures, from discretion-based to price-based systems or auctions, controls over who can hold a licence are still in place. For example, in the US, the FCC will have to be satisfied that a broadcasting licence applicant meets certain basic qualifications, which include character.[84] The character qualification is not so broad-ranging as it might appear: the FCC has stated that a character determination will be focused on determining whether there is a risk of the licence candidate not dealing honestly with the FCC, or operating the licence in accordance with regulatory requirements.[85] The character qualification is a manifestation of the requirement that the FCC must consider whether a licence grant would be in the public interest.[86] Australia has a similar requirement in its licensing procedures, which addresses the suitability of an applicant: suitability will be determined by considering whether or not an applicant is likely to commit an offence under the broadcasting legislation or breach a licence condition, although there is a presumption that an applicant is suitable.[87] A suitability inquiry will examine the business record, and record of trust and candour, of the applicant and those who would be associated with the licence.[88] The UK also has a character-type qualification, found in the requirement that only fit and proper persons may hold licences.[89] The legislation does not define the term, and it is left to Ofcom's discretion to determine what is 'fit and proper'. The former regulator of radio, the Radio Authority (RA), decided on one occasion that the majority shareholder of companies which held a number of local radio licences was not fit and proper because he had convictions for rape and sexual assault,[90] whilst the former regulator of television, the Independent Television

---

[84] 47 USC § 308(b). As expected, these requirements will apply also to licence transfers: 47 USC § 310(d).

[85] FCC, *Report Order and Policy Statement, In the Matter of Policy regarding Character Qualifications in Broadcast Licensing* 102 FCC 2d 1179 (1986), para. 21. The FCC later broadened the type of evidence it would take into account for this inquiry; eg, it decided that it was relevant to consider not just broadcast-related anti-trust violations, but all media anti-trust violations: FCC, *Policy Statement and Order, In the Matter of Policy regarding Character Qualifications in Broadcast Licensing*, 5 FCC Rcd 3252 (1990).

[86] 47 USC § 309(a).

[87] BSA (Aus), s 41 for commercial broadcasting licences. Similar suitability requirements apply to other licence categories.

[88] *Ibid*, s 41(3).

[89] BA 1990 (UK), ss 3(3) and 86(4).

[90] RA, 'Radio Authority Agrees Transfer of Control of Licences Held by Owen Oyston' (News Release 28/98, 9 April 1998).

Commission (ITC), had indicated that evidence of collusion between applicants for a licence could be an indication of a lack of fitness and propriety.[91]

A character qualification does not bear an obvious connection with pluralism, but it can be seen as a reflection of the attitude that the right to broadcast is imbued with the characteristics of a public trust. In that sense, those who are licensed are akin to trustees, and they must be fit to bear that responsibility. One might push this further by suggesting that it is important that those who have privileged access to the public sphere should be persons who will treat that space with respect. As such, what is included in a character determination will be important. Australia, for example, has a relatively limited character test, compared with the open-ended UK requirement. The matters to be taken into account in determining suitability for Australian licensees are probably appropriate, given that they relate to business record and matters of honesty, but such facts may not give much indication of the suitability to operate the special sort of business which is the media.

If character qualifications can be seen as one way of eliminating unsuitable persons from holding licences, another way is by specifying categories of persons or organisations who are disqualified from holding licences. Apart from foreign control, which is considered separately below, setting up categories of disqualified persons has been a concern more evident in the UK than in the other jurisdictions. Until the 2003 reforms, the UK disqualified political organisations, local government authorities, advertising agencies, and religious bodies from holding licences, although there was provision for the latter to hold some television licences (satellite and cable services) and some radio licences (but not national services). Concerns about undue influence and threats to the traditional impartiality of the broadcasting system seem to be at play here.[92] The 2003 reforms have brought some relaxation. Political organisations are still prohibited from holding licences, because the government was not convinced that a political organisation could operate a broadcasting service with the requisite degree of impartiality.[93] However, local government authorities can now hold licences, provided that the services are run in connection with the functions of the local authority, and to provide information to the local community.[94] Religious organisations are now allowed to hold licences, except for services where spectrum may be limited, such as a Channel Three or Five licence, a multiplex licence, or a national sound broadcasting licence.[95] Ofcom can make a determination allowing a religious organisation to hold a licence which would otherwise not be permitted.[96] The UK had intended to relax the prohibition on advertising agencies holding licences, but backed down, because of concerns that there might be, or might appear to be, a

---

[91] ITC, *Annual Report and Accounts 1995* (1996), 22–23. The possibility of collusion had arisen when two applicants for the Channel Five licence had submitted identical cash bids.

[92] Gibbons, above n 6, 213–15.

[93] Policy Statement, above n 18, para 9.3.2.

[94] Comms Act (UK), s 349.

[95] *Ibid*, s 348.

[96] *Ibid*, sch 14, para 15.

conflict of interest if advertising agencies were to hold broadcasting licences.[97] The US and Australia are much less concerned with specific disqualifications, although when allocating community broadcasting services ACMA is required to consider the undesirability of the Commonwealth, a State or Territory, or a political party being in a position to exercise control of a community broadcasting licence.[98] The restriction on certain persons or organisations holding licences illustrates once again the concern that ownership will affect content. It is debatable whether this is so, because there will be a variety of factors influencing content, such as the need to attract advertising revenue and rules about what can be broadcast.

The US probably offers the most unique example of this link between ownership identity and content. Rather than the negative link made in the UK, the US has tried to promote diversity by giving preference to minority applicants. In 1978, the FCC adopted a policy whereby minority ownership and management participation would operate as a positive factor in licence awards.[99] The FCC believed that minority viewpoints were not being adequately represented (despite other FCC equal opportunity policies), and that this was detrimental both for minority and non-minority audiences.[100] A constitutional challenge to the policy was narrowly defeated when the Supreme Court decided that it did not violate constitutional guarantees of equal treatment.[101] The court relied on the customary spectrum scarcity reasoning. Policies encouraging diversity through minority participation would be beneficial not only to members of minority groups, but to 'all members of the viewing and listening audience.'[102] However, the dissenting opinion of O'Connor J exposes the weaknesses in this link between ownership and voice. Justice O'Connor pointed to the policy's tendency to stereotype, because it implicitly rested upon an assumption that people of a certain racial group would think and behave in a particular way, and that their racial identification would be the key motivation for the operation of the licence.[103] O'Connor J's critique highlights also the difference in this US approach from the UK approach of disqualification. It is reasonable to assume that an organisation established for, say, political or religious purposes might have a particular voice—a particular view—to convey, but it is not so reasonable to assume that an individual who happens to belong to a certain racial or gender group will reflect the voice of that group, which, in any event, requires an assumption that there is a particular group voice. Justice O'Connor was also concerned that a policy which aimed to ensure that certain viewpoints were transmitted might constitute an infringement of the First Amendment.[104]

---

[97] Lord Evans, HL Deb, 2 July 2003, vol 650, col 942.

[98] BSA (Aus), s 84(2)(f).

[99] FCC, *Public Notice, Statement of Policy on Minority Ownership of Broadcasting Facilities*, 68 FCC 2d 979 (1978).

[100] *Ibid*, para 2.

[101] *Metro Broadcasting Inc v FCC* 497 US 547 (1990). An important factor in the decision was that Congress had approved the FCC policies: at 563, per Brennan J for the majority.

[102] *Ibid*, 568, per Brennan J.

[103] *Ibid*, 603–4 and 618–19.

[104] *Ibid*, 617.

Structural regulation rules tend to be acceptable in the US, because they appear as content-neutral, but the example of the minority policy illustrates how difficult it can be to separate out content-neutral and content-based regulation.[105] Although the court in *Metro* upheld the minority policy, other decisions exposed its fragility. In 1992, a similar policy, which gave preference to women, was declared, by the US Court of Appeals, unconstitutional, because there was no sufficient basis for expecting that preference to women would lead to programme diversity.[106] In 1995, in a matter concerning a minority preferential policy, but not relating to broadcasting, the Supreme Court ruled that such policies would be constitutionally valid only if they served a compelling government objective—in other words, they would be subject to strict scrutiny.[107] In overruling the standard set by *Metro*, the FCC was effectively forced into reviewing its minority policies.[108]

Foreign Ownership

Common to the three jurisdictions have been restrictions on foreign ownership of licences. The UK has now removed these restrictions, and Australia is also likely to do so, but the US shows no sign of relaxing its foreign ownership rules. Foreign ownership controls do not have a direct connection with pluralism protection, but once again they show this assumed link between ownership and voice. Earlier concerns about foreign ownership have diminished or changed over time, and, ironically, it is pluralism which is now being used as an argument in favour of removing or relaxing such controls.

Restrictions on foreign control of commercial television licences originated in Australia in 1956. Their purpose was to protect national sovereignty by preventing foreigners being able to influence domestic opinion. In recent times, the concern has been more about cultural domination, and the need to protect local cultural industry.[109] Current restrictions prevent foreign persons from being in a position to exercise control of a commercial television licence and prevent two or more foreign persons from having combined company interests of more than 20 per cent.[110] The only other broadcasting service affected by specific foreign ownership restrictions is subscription television broadcasting. Foreign persons must not hold company interests of more than 20 per cent, in the case of an individual, or more than 35 per

[105] For a more detailed discussion of this dilemma, see E Barendt, 'Structural and Content Regulation of the Media: United Kingdom Law and some American Comparisons' in EM Barendt (ed), *The Yearbook of Media and Entertainment Law 1997/98* (Oxford, Clarendon Press, 1997), 75.

[106] *Lamprecht v FCC* 958 F 2d 382 (1992). The majority distinguished *Metro* on the ground that there had been in that case evidence to support such a connection: at 390–94, per Thomas J.

[107] *Adarand Constructors Inc v Pena* 515 US 200 (1995).

[108] See W Overbeck, *Major Principles of Media Law*, 15th edn (Belmont, CA, Thomson Wadsworth, 2004), 443–44.

[109] Productivity Commission, above n 2, 332–33.

[110] BSA (Aus), s 57. A foreign person is defined in s 6 as a natural person who is not an Australian citizen, and, in the case of a corporation, where holdings by foreign persons (including companies controlled by foreign persons) exceed 50%. The foreign ownership restrictions also limit the number of directors who are not Australian citizens: s 58.

cent, when other foreign interests are added together.[111] The inclusion of company interests only, rather than any wider notions of control, seems strange.[112] This means that foreign persons could enter into contractual arrangements which would have the effect of putting them in a position to exercise control and influence. No specific foreign ownership restrictions apply to radio; the Foreign Acquisitions and Takeovers Act 1975 (Cth) gives the Treasurer power to block foreign investment in media generally, although Australian policy is generally positive towards foreign investment. In a small market, like Australia, foreign investment is seen as important in expanding markets and increasing competition. This is the type of attitude which is influencing the move to remove broadcasting foreign ownership restrictions; opening up opportunities for investment is seen as likely also to promote diversity. Specific restrictions on foreign control of radio were removed in 1992, and although foreign ownership of radio is now quite high, the Productivity Commission was unable to identify whether this had had any particular impact on the industry or radio content.[113] Notwithstanding the existence of foreign ownership restrictions on free-to-air television and subscription television, there is actually quite extensive foreign ownership, some of which has arisen in controversial circumstances.[114] Techniques have been devised which do not constitute formal control. One of the most controversial has been the interest of CanWest Global Communications Corp, a Canadian media company, in the free-to-air broadcaster, Network Ten.[115] Although it does not have formal control of the broadcaster, it clearly has a substantial economic interest. CanWest acquired the network when the latter was in receivership; it now holds a 56.6 per cent 'economic interest', which includes a 14.5 per cent shareholding (just below the 15 per cent required for formal control).[116] The economic interest arises through the use of debentures, which do not come within the definition of 'company interests', although CanWest's earnings on the debentures reflect the profit earnings of Network Ten, not a fixed rate of interest.[117] The CanWest experience points also to the difficulties generally of trying to devise rules regulating control. The Productivity Commission suggested that the current controls really had no place, given that they had not been able to achieve the statutory objective of giving Australians effective control over the more influential broadcasting services.[118]

---

[111] BSA (Aus), s 109.

[112] Company interests are defined to include shareholdings, votes, dividends, and winding-up interests: *ibid*, s 6.

[113] Productivity Commission, above n 2, 338–39. The Commission noted that regional broadcasting had suffered during the same period, but it considered that this was more likely to be the result of a growth in radio networks, which had coincided with the relaxation of foreign restrictions. For the issue of regional broadcasting, see further Chapter Four.

[114] Productivity Commission, above n 2, 335–38.

[115] The CanWest acquisition led to three ABA investigations and a Federal Court challenge: *CanWest Global Communications Corporation v ABA* (1998) 153 ALR 47.

[116] Communications Law Centre, 'Media Ownership Update' (2005) 168 *Communications Update* 4.

[117] J Given, 'Foreign Ownership of Media and Telecommunications: an Australian Story' (2002) 7(4) *Media and Arts Law Review* 253 at 259.

[118] Productivity Commission, above n 2, 338.

The US retains restrictions on foreign control of licences. Section 310 of the USC prevents non-US citizens from holding broadcasting licences.[119] The rationale for these restrictions has been the usual concern that foreign control might put national security at risk. Although there has been some relaxation—there is no longer a prohibition on foreign directors and officers—there seems to be no debate about removing the prohibition completely. This might seem strange for a country with such a huge and powerful media industry, but it possibly reflects also the size and strength of an economy which does not need to look abroad for investment capital.

The UK, because of its membership of the European Community, has had a different approach to non-national ownership. Until the 2003 reforms, restrictions applied only to non-European Economic Area (EEA) citizens, although even non-EEA citizens could hold licences for some types of services, such as cable and some types of satellite services. This was permitted in the hope that it might encourage North American investment into these newer services.[120] The 2003 reforms have removed all restrictions, so that EEA citizens and non-EEA citizens are now treated alike. It had not initially been the government's intention to make this change. In the White Paper, the government justified retaining the status quo on the grounds that foreign ownership restrictions were common in other jurisdictions, and because it believed that this was the best way to maintain 'high quality European content'.[121] In a later consultation paper, the government argued again that it would be inappropriate to lift restrictions on foreign ownership, whilst other countries, such as the US and Australia, retained them.[122] However, by the time the Bill was introduced into Parliament, the government had changed its position, arguing instead that the rules would be 'inconsistent and difficult to apply', and that it wanted to encourage inward investment in order to take advantage of new technologies and ideas. It now cited content regulation as a way of ensuring 'high quality, original programming'.[123] Some resistance to this change was expressed in Parliament: the main concern was that it was inappropriate to allow UK media to be open to foreign, notably US, control without reciprocal privileges.[124] This, of course, was the concern which the government had also expressed prior to the reversal of its position.

---

[119] Corporations must be organised under the laws of the US, and there are limits on non-US shareholdings: 47 USC § 310(b).

[120] Gibbons, above n 6, 214.

[121] White Paper, above n 10, para 4.9.5.

[122] DCMS and DTI, *Consultation on Media Ownership Rules* (November 2001) ('Consultation Document'), para 6.1.5.

[123] Policy Statement, above n 18, para 9.3.1.

[124] See, eg, the debate in the House of Lords: HL Deb, 2 July 2003, vol 650, cols 925–39.

Structural Regulation of Ownership and Control

In this section, the ownership and control rules, their evolution, and the policy generating the rules will be examined for each jurisdiction. Despite the substantial differences between the three jurisdictions in approach to broadcasting policy and regulation, an examination of the evolution of ownership and control policy and regulation is illuminating in revealing the troublesome nature of media ownership regulation as a tool of broadcasting pluralism. At various points in their regulatory history, each of the jurisdictions has experienced confusion in determining the policy attitude towards the involvement of players from one media sector in another sector. The three jurisdictions illustrate also that, despite different approaches, media ownership regulation is beset with design problems. Finally, the three jurisdictions reveal that a common experience has been the dislike of this form of structural regulation amongst the media industry, which has brought about reasonably consistent pressure for repeal or relaxation of the rules. This pressure, and the uneasy symbiotic relationship of governments and media, has meant that changes to the regulatory form have often been made to appease the media industry, or elements of it, rather than to address weaknesses in the design or to ensure that the rules embrace developments in the media industry.

The most recent reform moves of each jurisdiction will not be examined in this chapter, but will be covered in Chapter Seven. However, the current UK media ownership rules, which arose out of the recent UK communications reform, will be described below, although discussion of the policy generating those changes will be left to Chapter Seven.

United Kingdom

The UK's experience and development of ownership and control regulation differs from the US and Australia, possibly because until the 1990s it maintained a much more closely controlled commercial broadcasting sector. Another difference can be seen in the type of regulation; it was only in the 1990s that the UK moved away from a broad discretionary-based form of regulation to a pre-emptive rule-based system. Before then the pattern of ownership regulation was extremely stable. However, this does not mean that control issues were not present. From the introduction of commercial television in the 1950s, the question of what role newspaper interests could play in broadcasting was a matter for contention. An examination of cross-media interests, and the role they played in the history of early regulation of broadcasting ownership, is useful in illustrating both the UK approach and the ambivalence which marked ownership policy.

Early Regulatory Steps

The Television Act 1954 established the first commercial television service, but the legislation provided very little guidance as to how the service was to be structured, and none on matters of ownership and control. Indeed, the arrangements for the establishment of commercial television were curious. Legally, the broadcaster was to be the regulatory authority, then known as the Independent Television Authority (ITA), although it would not actually produce programmes, but would award programme contracts or franchises to programme companies. In the absence of legislative guidance, the ITA determined that it would award contracts on a regional basis, with one programme company to a region.[125] This regional arrangement for commercial television (now Channel Three) has continued, although most of the regional licences are now under common control. The first award of programme contracts led to criticism about press involvement. Apart from a specific concern that programme contracts had been awarded to companies associated with right-wing newspapers,[126] there was a more general concern that allowing newspapers to have interests in television would 'mean an undesirable extension of their sphere of influence'[127] and increase concentration of ownership.[128] In its defence, the ITA argued that the press had a constructive role to play in the development of commercial television.[129] This ambivalence about the role of the press would be a continuing theme in the early years of commercial broadcasting.

The Television Act 1963 made some provision for dealing with press interests. Every programme contract had to contain a provision whereby, in the event that a newspaper shareholding in a programme contractor led to, or was likely to lead to, a situation which was against the public interest, the ITA could, subject to the consent of the Postmaster-General (the then relevant Minister), suspend or determine the programme contract.[130] Consideration had been given to the introduction of rules which would impose specific ownership limits, but the proposals were relatively crude, because they equated control with share ownership of more than 50 per cent,[131] and the preference was for a more flexible test.[132] This preference probably also reflected the continuing ambivalence about the press's role: there was certainly agreement that the press should not be prevented from having a role

---

[125] Curran and Seaton, above n 8, 182. In fact, there were many ideas for how these franchises should be arranged, such as dividing the contracts according to types of programming or hours of broadcasting.

[126] ITA, *Annual Report and Accounts for the Period 4 August 1954–31 March 1955*, HCP 123 (1955–6), 6.

[127] *Ibid.*

[128] HC Deb, 23 November 1954, vol 533, col 1135.

[129] ITA, above n 126.

[130] Television Act 1963, s 8(1).

[131] Committee on Broadcasting, *Report of the Committee on Broadcasting 1960*, Cmnd 1753 (1962), para 632.

[132] Postmaster-General, *Further Memorandum on the Report of the Committee on Broadcasting 1960*, Cmnd 1893 (1962), para 23–24.

to play in broadcasting, but it was also acknowledged that any undue influence should be avoided.[133] A Royal Commission (the Shawcross Commission) which was concerned with economic aspects of the newspaper industry, following a number of closures, appeared more concerned. It observed that, where news-papers had a link with television companies, advantages were gained in the provi-sion of news services, the sharing of facilities, and the packaging of advertising rates. However, the Commission considered, given the programme companies' statutory monopoly, that the control of television companies by newspaper inter-ests was contrary to the public interest.[134]

Certainly, at the time of the 1963 legislation, there were some significant press holdings, in some cases shareholdings of between 20 and 40 per cent. Eighty per cent of the voting shares in Scottish Television were held by Roy Thomson, who controlled Thomson Newspapers. Thomson Newspapers also held all of the non-voting shares in Scottish Television.[135] The legislation did not impact on these holdings. In fact, the legislative provision, which continued until the Broadcasting Act 1990 (BA 1990 (UK)), was never directly used by the ITA, or its successor, the Independent Broadcasting Authority (IBA). Given the severe consequences if the provision were to be applied, the ITA, and its successor, were probably reluctant to exercise their power. Certainly the ITA was criticised for its lack of intervention when, in the early 1970s, Rupert Murdoch's press interests obtained a significant stake in one of the programme companies, London Weekend Television, and Murdoch became a director of the company.[136] Although the ITA warned the pro-gramme company that its contract was in jeopardy, it took the view that it would not be in the public interest to suspend the service, preferring, instead, to insist on changes to the company's management structure.[137] The ITA's failure to suspend or terminate the programme contract might be seen as indicative of the inappro-priateness of this form of regulation but, on the other hand, it also illustrates its flexibility, because the threat of suspension could lead television companies to respond to regulatory demands. Scottish Television may provide another example of this: at its contract renegotiation in 1963–64, the ITA was able to ensure that the Thomson holdings were distilled.[138]

The introduction of local commercial radio in the early 1970s highlighted even more clearly this ongoing ambivalence. One of the chief concerns was the impact local commercial radio would have on press viability and advertising revenue. This echoed earlier concerns. When the BBC had commenced radio broadcasting, arrangements were put in place to protect the press, which prevented the BBC

---

[133] Postmaster-General, *Further Memorandum on the Report of the Committee on Broadcasting 1960*, Cmnd 1893 (1962), paras 21–22.

[134] Royal Commission on the Press 1961–2, *Report*, Cmnd 1811 (1962), para 244.

[135] B Sendall, *Independent Television in Britain, Volume 2: Expansion and Change, 1958–68* (London, Macmillan, 1983), 125.

[136] Committee on the Future of Broadcasting, *Report on the Future of Broadcasting*, Cmnd 6753 (1977), para 13.32.

[137] ITA, *Annual Report and Accounts, 1970–1*, HCP 3 (1971–72), 4.

[138] Sendall, above n 135, 217.

broadcasting any news before seven in the evening, and it could broadcast only news which had been obtained from certain identified news agencies, all of which were owned by the newspaper sector.[139] When commercial radio was introduced, newspaper industry lobbying (representing the regional and suburban press) resulted in a form of positive discrimination. Preference, when awarding programme contracts, would be given to local newspaper interests, operating within the radio licence area, which were likely to be adversely affected by the radio service. In such circumstances, the newspaper proprietor would be given an opportunity to acquire shares in the broadcasting company, although the IBA would have to approve the level of shareholding, although, except in the case of a sole newspaper in the locality, it could amount to control.[140] The IBA could prohibit these cross-interest arrangements, if it was satisfied that they would be contrary to the public interest.[141] These proposals sparked much debate during the passage of the legislation, with concerns about the appropriateness of this type of industry assistance and the danger of increasing media influence, although there was no objection to the principle of press involvement.[142]

More conventional was the treatment of radio and television interests: television companies were prohibited from having an interest in local radio which broadcast within the same area, and vice versa.[143] The introduction of cable in 1984 followed a similar pattern: prohibiting television and local radio programme contractors and local newspapers from becoming licence holders if they were operating within the same area as the cable service.[144] The Cable Authority also had a discretionary power similar to that of the IBA in relation to award of cable licences.[145] However, even with the introduction of cable, the same ambivalence could be detected between the undesirability of a concentration of media interests and the benefit of media companies (particularly the press) contributing to the development of new media industries.[146]

Identifying Policy

Until the introduction of the BA 1990 (UK), with its major restructuring of the broadcasting regulatory environment, the regulation of ownership and control in the UK followed a reasonably stable pattern. The approach, particularly of

---

[139] J Tunstall, *The Media in Britain* (London, Constable, 1983), 48. These restrictions lasted until 1945, although there were attempts by the newspaper industry to have them extended: BBC Memorandum, *The Effect of Broadcasting on Newspaper Circulations*, Paper no 42, in Committee on Broadcasting, *Report of the Committee on Broadcasting 1960*, Cmnd 1753 (1962).

[140] Sound Broadcasting Act 1972, s 8.

[141] *Ibid*, s 9.

[142] See, eg, HC Deb, 11 November 1971, vol 825, col 1300, and Standing Committee F, 8 February 1972, cols 1123, 1129 and 1147. This preferential treatment ended in 1980: Broadcasting Act 1980, s 36.

[143] Sound Broadcasting Act 1972, s 6. There were also provisions dealing with the accumulation of interests in sound programme contracts: s 7.

[144] Cable and Broadcasting Act 1984, s 8(2).

[145] *Ibid*, s 8(3).

[146] Home Office and Department of Trade and Industry, *Report of the Inquiry into Cable Expansion and Broadcasting Policy*, Cmnd 8679 (1982), para 26.

cross-media interests, relied heavily on discretionary-based public interest tests; but these seemed generally to lie dormant in the regulators' hands, although there is evidence that these powers could be exploited as negotiating tools. The use of a discretionary test has its merits. It provides flexibility, enabling a variety of control circumstances, such as the appointment of directors, and commercial arrangements, which might otherwise be outside a set of formal rules, to be taken into account. However, in general, this flexibility seemed to be ignored, as the UK regulators tended to interpret control as manifested mainly by shareholding interests. These early regulatory approaches were no doubt shaped by the policy outlook, which seemed to be the product of an amalgam of competing or potentially incompatible issues. Commercial broadcasting had developed out of a desire to end the (BBC) monopoly on broadcasting, but it is apparent that not much detailed attention was given to how commercial broadcasting, and its control, would contribute to pluralism. From the commencement of broadcasting until the 1990s, UK broadcasting policy had been influenced by a series of committees established by the government to report on broadcasting—the Sykes Committee, the Pilkington Committee, and the Annan Committee, to name a few.[147] Whilst a concern that concentration of control of broadcasting could lead to abuse or undue influence was a familiar theme in these committee reports, these concerns did not seem to translate into very sophisticated thinking about how the regulatory design should be developed. Notwithstanding the reiteration of these concerns over the decades, there is a somewhat naïve quality about the way in which they were often addressed, something which can be contrasted with the US policy explication during much the same period. The Pilkington Committee provides such an example. Having been asked to consider the position of press interests in broadcasting (at that stage, television only), the committee explained the issue in the following terms:

> It refers to the threat which, some hold is currently presented to democracy by the participation by newspapers in the television companies. The threat is thought to reside in the fact that, because two of the media of mass communications are owned in some measure by the same people, there is an excessive concentration of power to influence and persuade public opinion; and that if these same people are too few or have broadly the same political affiliations, there will be an increasingly one-sided presentation of affairs of public concern. There might, too, be a failure to present some of these affairs sufficiently or at all.[148]

What is interesting is the way that the committee set about examining this concern: it asked whether there was any evidence of the press unjustifiably praising or publicising its related television service or ignoring or criticising the BBC or competitors in the commercial sector.[149] It concluded that there was no such evidence, and noted:

---

[147] The Broadcasting Committee, *Report*, Cmd 1951 (1923), Committee on Broadcasting 1960, *Report*, Cmnd 1753 (1962), and Committee on the Future of Broadcasting, *Report*, Cmnd 6753 (1977).

[148] Committee on Broadcasting 1960, *Report*, Cmnd 1753 (1962), para 627.

[149] *Ibid*, para 628.

On the contrary, the consensus of opinion was that it had had no material effect, good or bad. The press, we were told, on all sides, had entered independent television for commercial reasons and none other; if at the outset the experience of newspaper interests had helped independent television to develop programmes of news and comment, no help was needed now.[150]

Cross-promotion may be a matter for concern, but it is surely not the only issue which arises from cross-control of media. Equally, the way in which the committee defines the concern as being about one-sided presentation seems crude. Apart from the impact of content rules imposing impartiality and fairness obligations, the threat of concentration may be felt in less obvious ways, such as the narrowing of sources of information or programme ideas, or the limiting of employment opportunities. The Pilkington Committee, like other committees on broadcasting, did not neglect the risk of potential abuse or threat of undue influence, but the characterisation of the threat or potential threat led perhaps also to less clarity in the regulatory design. Attention to regulatory design was complacent, and the need to placate or protect other interests, such as the newspaper industry, when radio was introduced also tended to compromise policy development. But this relatively relaxed attitude towards matters of ownership and control would change with the 1990 reforms, which also marked the start of a more sophisticated discussion of pluralism and diversity concepts. The 1990 legislation introduced also a much more complex scheme of regulation, which ensured that ownership issues, and particularly cross-media ownership, would dominate the policy and regulatory agenda from then on. In contrast to the relatively stable period until the 1990s, the next decade and a half would be marked by substantial regulatory changes.

Ownership and Control Regulation and its Evolution

The UK approach to media ownership, which so differed from the US and Australia, was largely due to the UK's distinctive broadcasting environment. The preference for public service principles within the commercial sector meant that the sector was tightly controlled with limited scope for competition and change. Change came, however, with the BA 1990 (UK), and the changes meant that ownership regulation had to be rethought. The changes were borne out of the government's desire to apply its deregulation policy to the broadcasting sector, and its belief that market forces could play a greater role in developing competition and diversity.[151] At the same time, satellite broadcasting was developing as a feasible addition to the environment. Changes introduced by the BA 1990 (UK) included: the demise of the 'comfortable duopoly', and the expectation that the commercial sector would be full-scale public service broadcasters; the introduction of national commercial radio services; the separation of broadcaster and regulatory body; the

---

[150] *Ibid,* para 629.
[151] Home Office, *Broadcasting in the '90s: Competition, Choice and Quality: The Government's Plans for Broadcasting Legislation,* Cm 517 (1988), paras 2.5–2.6.

replacement of the IBA with two regulatory bodies, the ITC and the RA; and, the replacement of programme contracts with a licensing system using an auction-based process. The new approach to ownership regulation limited the scope for regulatory discretion and established a set of pre-emptive rules. As Gibbons has commented:

> the ownership provisions of the 1990 Act were very complex in an attempt to be all-inclusive and to trace corporate ownership to the controlling interest as far as possible. Predictability was obtained, but at the expense of excessive rigidity and the need to anticipate all difficulties in advance in order to avoid loopholes.[152]

In the lead-up to the BA 1990 (UK) there was little public consideration of the form which ownership regulation should take. A Home Affairs Committee Inquiry into the future of broadcasting had recommended retention of the status quo,[153] and even the government's White Paper provided little information, noting only the need for clear rules to limit concentration of ownership and excessive cross-ownership.[154] Announcement of the detail of the new regime was left to a ministerial statement.[155] Although no detailed explanation was given for the proposed change, it probably made sense, with the prospect of a more market-based, competitive broadcasting sector, to have in place rules which could provide greater certainty and transparency for industry players.[156]

Ownership and control regulation under the 1990 legislation constituted a set of detailed quantitative rules which addressed mono-media and cross-media accumulations.[157] The legislation prohibited the accumulation of licences beyond certain limits. Thus, for example, one person could not hold more than two regional Channel Three licences, whilst the two London Channel Three licences could not be held by the same person. It was permissible to own only one national radio licence. There were also limits on local radio ownership, although these were more generous than the television limits. Once these limits were reached, the holder was then restricted to a 20 per cent interest in another licence of the same type, and to five per cent in any further licence of the same type. Limits were also imposed on holding licences across different media services or sectors. Thus, for example, the holder of a regional Channel Three licence could not have an interest of more than 20 per cent in a Channel Five licence or a national radio licence. Cross-media interests between newspapers and broadcasting were also brought

---

[152] T Gibbons, 'Aspiring to Pluralism: The Constraints of Public Broadcasting Values on the Deregulation of British Media Ownership' (1998) 16 *Cardozo Arts and Entertainment Law Journal* 475 at 485.

[153] Home Affairs Committee, *Third Report: The Future of Broadcasting*, HCP 262 (1988), vol I, paras 41–42.

[154] Home Office, above n 151, para 6.48. Details were given for radio at para 8.4.

[155] HC Deb, 19 May 1989, vol 153, cols 318–19w.

[156] Home Office, above n 151, paras 6.5, 6.18 and 6.48. See also W Hoffmann-Riem, *Regulating Media: The Licensing and Supervision of Broadcasting in Six Countries* (New York, The Guilford Press, 1996), 98–99, and Gibbons, above n 152, 484–45.

[157] The ownership rules were set down in BA 1990 (UK), sch 2, and expanded through secondary legislation.

into the new scheme: proprietors of national newspapers could not have more than a 20 per cent interest in the holder of a Channel Three, Channel Five, or national radio licence, or five per cent in a further licence. Local newspaper proprietors were also limited, but only where there was overlap of the area served by the newspaper and the Channel Three service. Local newspapers were also limited in relation to local radio services and local delivery (cable) services. For the first time the cross-media restrictions between broadcasting and the press were reciprocal.[158]

Despite this more prescriptive approach, the rules, in some respects, still lacked precision. For example, the restrictions on Channel Three licences took no account of size, either of audience or revenue share. The holder of the Channel Three licences for the regions of Yorkshire and Tyne Tees was, under the rules, prohibited from acquiring any further licences, but the combined audience share for these two regions was less than half of either of two other Channel Three licensees, Carlton and Central, which were able to (and did) merge.[159] Another weakness was the approach to determining control, which focused on legal rather than practical control. This resulted in some merger arrangements falling outside the regime. For example, in a radio merger the parties agreed to a deadlocking arrangement which gave each party an equal share. The RA decided that it could not make a finding that either party was 'in control', and had no power to do anything other than confirm the merger.[160] It was these types of issues which gave rise to pressure for change, and which led to the Broadcasting Act 1996 (BA 1996 (UK)) reforms. However, even before the 1996 reforms, pressure had already produced change: in 1993, the prohibition on the common control of any two of the largest licensees (but not the London licences) was removed. Consolidation quickly followed.[161] The government had defended this relaxation on the basis that it enabled the Channel Three companies to be able to compete more effectively in the international marketplace.[162] This perceived need to promote national champions, in order to enable international participation, is a common claim in the debates about, and pressure for, media ownership reform.

However, it was the cross-media ownership provisions in the 1990 regime which proved most controversial, and created the most persistent clamour for reform. In particular, it was the treatment of News International plc, the media interests associated with Rupert Murdoch, which occasioned the concern. As one member of the House of Lords put it during the passage of the 1990 legislation, the term '"cross-media ownership" is rapidly becoming a kind of shorthand for the

---

[158] BA 1990 (UK), sch 2, Pt IV.

[159] ITC, *Memorandum on Media Ownership*, 25 February 1994, paras 15 and 17.

[160] *R v Radio Authority, ex parte Guardian Media Group plc; R v Radio Authority, ex parte Trans World Communications plc* [1995] 2 All ER 139.

[161] At the same time a moratorium on transfers of Channel Three licences ended. Prior to the 1990 reforms, the IBA had the power to prevent changes in control, but the 1990 policy viewed takeovers more favourably: Home Office, above n 151, para 6.18.

[162] Department of National Heritage (DNH), *Media Ownership, The Government's Proposals*, Cm 2872 (1995), paras 1.10 and 2.9.

anti-Rupert Murdoch club'.[163] The problem was that the satellite services, then known as non-domestic satellite services, were not part of the newspaper-broadcasting cross-media framework. This was particularly beneficial to News International, which had significant newspaper interests in the UK and operated a satellite television service, Sky Television.[164] The government tried to defend its approach on several grounds. One of these was the need to encourage the development of satellite broadcasting. However, this argument lacked consistency, given that the government had included another category (domestic satellite services) within the rules, and so it was curious that the same encouragement was not being given to the domestic satellite service, British Satellite Broadcasting. Indeed, shortly after the 1990 legislation came into force, British Satellite Broadcasting was forced into a merger with Sky Television, because the former could not viably compete with Sky. The merged service became British Sky Broadcasting, which would become, and remains, the dominant satellite broadcaster in the UK. Another argument used was that it would be wrong 'to move the goalposts when people have gone forward, quite legitimately, with massive investment programmes'.[165] However, this ignored the possibility of some form of structural separation of operations or a gradual divestment of interests. Indeed, if the intention was to open up diversity and competition, then providing opportunities for others to enter the market would have seemed a very satisfactory outcome. From the government's perspective there was also a risk that if non-domestic satellite services were regulated, then services like Sky could move offshore (but still broadcast to the UK), with the inevitable loss of jobs.[166] This was perhaps a more difficult argument to counter,[167] although it did not make for good legislation.

The omission of satellite services from the cross-media ownership regime,[168] and the sense by other media players that this created an uneven competing field, soon created pressure for further reform. There were other pressures also, such as a concern that other media groups within the European Union might gain control of the local companies, such as the Channel Three licensees, and there was also the more basic, but ever-present, industry desire to have the freedom to expand.[169] This was particularly acute at this time, because it was believed that, in the changing media environment, it was necessary for media companies to invest across different platforms, so as to be able to exploit, for example, resource-sharing opportunities.[170] The need to be able to compete internationally was also

---

[163] Lord Willis, HL Deb, 5 June 1990, vol 519, col 1285.

[164] The omission of non-domestic satellite services was also an advantage to another large newspaper group, Mirror Group Newspapers: Gibbons, above n 152, 489.

[165] D Mellor, then Home Office Minister, HC Standing Committee F, 30 January 1990, col 362.

[166] HC Standing Committee F, 25 January 1990, col 311, and 30 January 1990, col 384.

[167] Barendt, above n 28, 132.

[168] The inclusion of domestic satellite services within the cross-media regime had no practical effect, because after the merger of British Satellite Broadcasting and Sky there were no domestic satellite services, a situation which has continued.

[169] Gibbons, above n 152, 489–90.

[170] DNH, above n 162, paras 6.1 and 6.5.

asserted.[171] In 1994, in response to the lobbying, the government established a review of media ownership regulation. It was not only industry which was calling for change; the ITC had also suggested that there should be a review of cross-ownership.[172] The industry lobbying was well organised, as the media had formed themselves into the British Media Industry Group.[173] Their submissions to the review appeared to be influential in the government's recommendations for reform. It had been understood that the review was to recommend only minor changes to the 1990 regime, such as the relaxation of the permissible maximum interest but, ultimately, the proposals published were quite different, and much more in accord with a second submission made by the lobbying group.[174] The review had to straddle a number of competing concerns. On the one hand, there was a willingness to recognise that industry needed to be allowed to expand in order to take up international and new media opportunities, but there was also the need to ensure adequate protection of the public interest.[175] There appeared to be wholesale acceptance by the government of the industry and economic arguments for change, although the structure of the review provided little opportunity to test any of these claims. It was apparent that there was almost no independent analysis of the industry and economic claims, whilst departmental 'policy-makers apparently relied instead on their "intuitions" about what levels of media and cross-media concentration of ownership would seem acceptable'.[176] Research, carried out by Doyle, has shown that, within the ministry responsible for the review and the proposals, the industry arguments for liberalisation dominated, whilst there were few comparable advocates for the public interest concerns.[177] Doyle quotes one Department officer who described the process in the following terms:

> Broadly speaking, what we did was say [to the media] 'Well look, we are not in a position to wholly jettison the other side of the argument. We are satisfied, within Government, following months and months of examination, that there are still these positive goods on the plurality and diversity side.'
>
> I think, to be honest, what was done was simply to calculate how much needed to be done in order to buy off most of the media and, in particular, the newspaper sector of

---

[171] Gibbons, above n 152, 490.

[172] G Doyle, *Media Ownership: The Economics and Politics of Convergence and Concentration in the UK and European Media* (London, Sage Publications, 2002), 89.

[173] This lobby group was comprised of a number of the larger media groups, although it did not include News International or the Mirror Group. Indeed, a particular concern of this lobby group was the need to relax cross-media ownership rules in order to redress the unfair advantage obtained by these two groups. For further descriptions of the lobbying process, see Doyle, above n 172, 91–95.

[174] (1995) *The Guardian*, 10 March, 17. The review was not held in public: it was an internal review conducted within the ministry, and there were no public hearings, although there were meetings with industry groups. The review reported to the Secretary of State, but did not publish its findings. The only public outcome of the review was the publication by the government of what was termed a 'policy paper', which was something of a mix of White Paper and Green Paper. For a more detailed discussion of the process, see LP Hitchens, '"Get Ready, Fire, Take Aim": The Regulation of Cross Media Ownership—An Exercise in Policy-Making' [1995] *Public Law* 620.

[175] DNH, above n 162, para 1.10.

[176] Doyle, above n 172, 107.

[177] *Ibid*, 106.

the media, to the extent that they would say that they would back up our proposals and say that they were a good statesman-like thing. And that then, having sort of covered ourselves by going what we assessed as that far, or far enough in that direction, we could then (as indeed we *did* during the passage of the Bill) spend most of our time defending ourselves against attacks designed to engender yet further liberalization.[178]

Her analysis of the economic arguments has also shown that the case for allowing expansion of cross-media ownership could not really be sustained, because there was little evidence which indicated that expansion across sectors, particularly across the newspaper and television sectors, would lead to economies of scope or cross-synergies.[179] And although the evidence does point to benefits gained from expansion within a sector, such as television, the realisation of these benefits might be constrained by obligations, such as the provision of regional programming.[180] The result was that proposals for reform would amount to a substantial liberalisation which would level the playing field for those media companies which had missed out in the 1990 reforms. As Doyle has noted, there was virtually no attempt to take on board 'existing media power', whilst the industry under consideration was the very one which was able largely to control the debate and flow of information about the issues.[181] Even though the reforms were presented as driven by the benefits to be gained by exploiting media cross-synergies,[182] it was apparent that even within the industry there was considerable scepticism as to whether such synergies were really to be had.[183]

The 1996 reform proposals contained both an immediate and a longer-term strategy. As a longer-term measure, the government considered introducing a system whereby the traditional division of the media market into segments (of television, radio, etc) should be replaced with the concept of a total media market within which a media company would be permitted a certain share. The size of the media markets would be determined by measures such as audience size or revenue share, and media sectors would be weighted to reflect their influence in relation to other sectors, to produce a so-called 'exchange rate'.[184] Eventually, the government abandoned this proposal as too complex. The immediate strategy led to the introduction of a 'market share' concept based upon audience size for broadcasting, and newspaper sales for the press, which was intended to act as a measure of influence. The 1996 reforms also enabled some of the concerns about the 1990 regime to be addressed, such as the definition of 'control', which now took into account both practical and legal control concepts. In addition, the BA 1996 (UK) provided a regulatory structure for the introduction of digital broadcasting, and so this too had to be taken into account in the ownership regulatory framework. The

---

[178] Doyle, above n 106.
[179] *Ibid*, 114–15.
[180] *Ibid*.
[181] *Ibid*, 107.
[182] DNH, above n 162, paras 5.20–5.22.
[183] Doyle, above n 172, 115–16.
[184] DNH, above n 162, paras 6.4ff.

new ownership regime[185] was complex, because it combined elements of the old regime, upon which the new scheme was superimposed. For television, the new regime used a combination of market share and accumulation limits. Thus, for example, a person with more than 15 per cent market share[186] was prohibited from ownership of, for example, two or more regional Channel Three licences. The 15 per cent market share also applied to other services such as Channel Five, satellite television services, licensable programme services, and digital programme services.[187] The 15 per cent market share triggered a number of other restrictions, such as a prohibition on a person holding more than a 20 per cent equity interest in two or more licences for the services referred to above. As with the 1990 legislation, there were also cascading limits. There were blanket prohibitions in relation to certain services: for example, common control of a national Channel Three licence and a Channel Five licence was prohibited, as was common control of Channel Three licences in overlapping regions.[188] The choice of a 15 per cent market share as the trigger was never properly explained, and appeared to be the product of an intuitive sense of what was appropriate.[189] Another issue was whether it was appropriate to include, as it did, within the market share measurement, the audience share of the public broadcasters, which would result in a smaller market share for the commercial broadcasters. As Gibbons suggests, this might have been appropriate for Channel Three, where one could regard the commercial and public broadcasters as part of the one market, but it made less sense in relation to other sectors, such as subscription television.[190] It might also be questioned whether inclusion of the public broadcasting sector within an audience share measurement undermines the sectoral pluralism balance.

For radio, there was a different approach, although it too carried over some of the features of the 1990 regime. There was now less emphasis on setting maximum limits for the holding of licences, although only one national radio licence, one national radio multiplex licence, or one national digital sound programme service licence could be held.[191] A market share threshold of 15 per cent was established, but it related to a points system, which had been established under the 1990 regime. The points system was based on a potential audience size measurement for the relevant service, and different types of services were allocated a different number of points. Thus, a licensee was limited to interests of 15 per cent of the total number of points for all relevant licences in the areas serviced by that

---

[185] BA 1996 (UK), sch 2, Pt II.

[186] This was measured by reference to the total television audience time, and it included also the public broadcasters: the BBC, Channel 4, and the Welsh Channel (Channel S4C).

[187] Satellite television services were the programme services (channels) carried over satellite systems; licensable programme services were the services carried over cable networks; and digital programme services were the programme services provided in digital form only, and carried on terrestrial services.

[188] BA 1996 (UK), sch 2, Pt III, para 4. This prevented anyone from holding both London Channel Three licences.

[189] Gibbons, above n 6, 223. Doyle's research leads to the same conclusion.

[190] *Ibid*, 224.

[191] BA 1996 (UK), sch 2, Pt III, para 11.

licensee.[192] There were additional restrictions for local licences which shared audiences. Thus, a licensee was prohibited from holding two licences within a common area, unless one licence was for the AM band and one for the FM band, or the licensee was able to meet a public interest test. A licensee could hold three licences within the same area, provided that at least one licence was for the AM band and at least one for the FM band, and a public interest test was satisfied.[193] The public interest test provided the most direct reference to plurality and diversity of the regime, and it is worth noticing that it addressed not just plurality of ownership, but diversity also.[194] It required the RA to consider for the relevant area, as well as any likely diminution in plurality of ownership, the impact on the range of programmes available on commercial services, and the diversity of sources of information available and opinions expressed on local radio services.[195] The RA was required to apply the public interest test quite regularly. On most occasions it determined that the proposed acquisition was not against the public interest, although in some instances it imposed conditions; for example, in relation to sale of advertising, or sharing of news production facilities.[196] The RA was critical of the labour-intensive nature of the test and the commercial uncertainty which it created.[197]

Not surprisingly, it was the provisions for cross-media ownership in the 1996 reforms which were of most interest. The reforms introduced two new aspects to the cross-media regime: a market share test and a public interest test.[198] A person who operated a national newspaper or newspapers which had a combined market share of 20 per cent was prohibited from holding a Channel Three or a Channel Five licence, or a national or local radio licence.[199] Such a person was also prohibited from holding more than a 20 per cent equity interest in a Channel Three or Channel Five service, or a national or local radio service. At the local level, the controller of a local newspaper or newspapers with a 20 per cent share of that local market was prohibited from holding a regional Channel Three licence or a digital programme service licence relevant to that area. There were some further restrictions on cross-interests affecting local radio, such as a prohibition on a person operating local newspapers with a local market share of 50 per cent holding a local radio licence for that area, unless another service also operated in the area, and the person did not hold another licence for that area. Finally, certain cross-holdings were to be subject to a public interest test. Thus, a public interest test could be invoked where the proprietor of a national or local newspaper sought to control a

---

[192] BA 1996 (UK), sch 2, Pt III, para 8.

[193] *Ibid*, sch 2, Pt III, para 12(1)–(2).

[194] For a discussion of the test, and the approach to structural regulation generally, see Barendt, above n 105, 89–90.

[195] BA 1996 (UK), sch 2, Pt III, para 12(4).

[196] See, generally, RA, *Annual Reports*.

[197] RA, *Consultation on Media Ownership Rules: Radio Authority Response* (January 2002), http://www.culture.gov.uk/PDF/media_own_ra.PDF, accessed 9 December 2005, para 23.

[198] The cross-media regime is set out in BA 1996 (UK), sch 2, Pt IV.

[199] Market share for newspapers was based on circulation measures.

national Channel Three or Channel Five licence, a national radio licence, or a national digital sound programme service, or where a national or local newspaper (for that region or local area) sought to control a regional Channel Three or local radio service licence.[200] However, there was no requirement for the test to be 'passed' prior to the award or acquisition; it applied only in the sense that the ITC or the RA could make a determination that the award or acquisition would not be in the public interest. This public interest test differed from the public interest test described earlier; this test required the relevant authority to consider the desirability of promoting plurality of ownership in the broadcasting and newspaper industries, and diversity in the sources of information available and in the opinions expressed in newspapers and on broadcasting. However, these matters had to be balanced with an assessment of the economic benefits that might be expected, such as technical developments or employment, and the effects on the operation of the broadcasting and newspaper markets generally.[201] Like the RA, the ITC also formed the view that the certainty should be favoured over 'ad hoc plurality tests'.[202]

Prior to the 1996 reforms, only minority cross-holdings were allowed between broadcasting and newspapers, but the new regime allowed companies much greater freedom in acquiring broadcasting and press interests. The new regime did not bring into the cross-media scheme those interests previously, and sometimes controversially, omitted, such as cable and satellite services, but it appeased the media groups disaffected by the 1990 reforms. That this was the intention seemed likely when it became apparent that the 20 per cent market share threshold would conveniently prevent News International and Mirror Group from further acquisitions, but allow other media companies the opportunity to acquire broadcasting licences.[203] The 1996 reforms also made much more explicit the government's willingness to pursue economic and industrial goals in relation to the media industry. This can be seen in the cross-media public interest test. Thus, protection of broadcasting pluralism has to compete with these other policy goals. This is not to suggest that public interest concerns, such as broadcasting pluralism, should have absolute dominance, but as seen with the 1996 reform process, the economic and industrial arguments might be more easily able to find vocal 'friends in court'. A degree of scepticism about the operation of an economic benefits test might also be permitted, bearing in mind the ready acceptance of the unchallenged and untested economic and industrial arguments which were used to advocate reform of the media ownership regime. The 1990 reforms had sought to reduce the scope for regulatory discretion but, paradoxically, the 1996 reforms marked something of a reversal of this goal: the public interest test was a move away from a strict

---

[200] The public interest test would also be invoked where a licence holder was to become connected with a national or local newspaper.

[201] BA 1996 (UK), sch 2, Pt IV, para 13.

[202] ITC, *Consultation on Media Ownership Rules: ITC Response* (January 2002), http://www.culture.gov.uk/PDF/media_own_itc.PDF, accessed 9 December 2005, para 21.

[203] Hitchens, above n 174, 637.

pre-emptive approach, whilst the amended definition of 'control', which changed the focus from legal control to include additionally practical or functional control, also required a greater exercise of discretionary judgement on the part of the regulators.

Current Rules

Whilst the 1996 reforms marked a stage in the relaxation of media ownership restrictions, the Comms Act (UK) has been even bolder.[204] However, once again there is a curious mix of the new and radical with retention of the old. In this section, the new ownership and control framework will be described, since it is already in force, but the discussion of the policy and reform process leading up to these changes will be addressed, alongside reform attempts in the US and Australia, in Chapter Seven.

In relation to mono-media ownership, the previous rules which limited the common control of Channel Three licences have been removed. As the government anticipated (and favoured),[205] the effect of these changes has been to bring most of the Channel Three regional licences under common control. Shortly after the Comms Act (UK) came into force in 2003, Carlton and Granada merged to form ITV plc. This meant that all the English and Welsh Channel Three licences were now under common control. The removal of the Channel Three restrictions means that such mergers are now a matter for competition and merger law alone.[206] The 2003 reforms also removed any ownership constraints in relation to Channel Five. It was anticipated that, now there were no cross-media controls on Channel Five, Murdoch's News Group would bid for Channel Five, but this did not happen, and Channel Five is now wholly owned by one of its founding shareholders, the RTL Group, a pan-European media group, which itself is almost wholly owned by the Bertelsmann Group, the German-based media conglomerate.[207] There has also been significant relaxation in the ownership regime for commercial radio. The prohibition on holding more than one national radio licence has been removed, and local radio ownership relaxed. The aim of the local radio restrictions is that each local area should have at least two separate owners of local commercial radio services plus the BBC service. Thus, a person who holds two local licences cannot hold a further licence which overlaps with the two licences already held, unless it would also not breach the points limit.[208] The points limit would be breached if the licences held by the person exceeded 55 per cent of the

---

[204] The new ownership and control regime is set out in Comms Act (UK), sch 14.

[205] Consultation Document, above n 122, paras 6.2.1–6.2.6.

[206] As part of the Carlton–Granada merger, the companies had to agree to certain conditions which were designed to ensure that they did not abuse their dominant position in the television airtime sales market: Ofcom, *The Communications Market—Television 2004* (August 2004), 14.

[207] In fact, during the legislation's passage through Parliament, Murdoch apparently sent letters to members of the House of Lords stating his intention not to bid for Channel Five: Lord Peyton, HL Deb, 2 July 2003, vol 650, col 933.

[208] Media Ownership (Local Radio and Appointed News Provider) Order 2003, SI 2003, No 3299, art 5. Overlapping in these provisions will mean overlap (of audience) by at least 50%.

total number of points for the relevant area.[209] The removal and relaxation of restrictions on radio have resulted, as anticipated, in considerable consolidation activity.[210] Apart from cross-media ownership restrictions, the only other services regulated are digital multiplexes and local digital sound programme services. Not more than one national digital multiplex licence can be held and not more than one local licence in an area.[211] A person is prohibited from providing a further local digital sound programme service if it would mean providing more than four services in the area, and the number of points for the relevant services would exceed 55 per cent of the total number of points attributable to that market.[212]

Cross-media ownership restrictions have also been considerably relaxed.[213] Controllers of national newspapers, with a market share of more than 20 per cent, will be prohibited from controlling a Channel Three licence, and such persons will also be limited to a 20 per cent interest in a Channel Three licence. This rule has been carried over from the 1996 regime. Similarly, a local newspaper controller with more than a 20 per cent market share will be prevented from holding a regional Channel Three licence for that area. Channel Three licence holders are precluded from holding more than a 20 per cent interest in a national newspaper proprietor, but there are no longer any cross-media restrictions affecting Channel Five or national radio services. Local radio services are, however, still subject to cross-media restrictions. There is a prohibition on holding a local radio licence, a regional Channel Three licence, and controlling a local newspaper or newspapers with a 50 per cent market share within the same area. Further, in a market with three overlapping local licences, no person who also controls a local newspaper (or newspapers) with a 55 per cent market share, or a Channel Three licence for the relevant area, may hold a local radio licence, unless, under a points determination, the points allocated to that licence are not more than 45 per cent of the total number of points for that area.

Finally, some other provisions which address matters of control should be noted. First, the new legislation did not make significant changes to the definition of control, which had been amended in the 1996 reforms,[214] but it does impose an obligation on Ofcom to publish guidance on the matters it will take into account in determining whether someone has de facto control of a relevant company.[215] In its (revised) draft guidance, Ofcom explores a range of, not atypical, issues which

---

[209] Points are determined and allocated on the basis of overlap: Media Ownership (Local Radio and Appointed News Provider) Order 2003, SI 2003, No 3299, art 8. Thus, a licence which had an audience overlap of 75% or more would be allocated four points, but a licence with only 5% or less overlap would be awarded only one point.

[210] See Ofcom, *The Communications Market 2005* (July 2005), 35–37 and *The Communications Market 2005: August 2005, Quarterly Update* (2005), 11–13.

[211] Comms Act (UK), sch 14, paras 7 and 8.

[212] Media Ownership (Local Radio and Appointed News Provider) Order 2003, SI 2003, No 3299, art 11.

[213] Comms Act (UK), sch 14, Pt 1, for Channel Three services, and Media Ownership (Local Radio and Appointed News Provider) Order 2003, SI 2003, No 3299, arts 6 and 9, for local radio services.

[214] The statutory definition of control is found in BA 1990 (UK), as amended, sch 2, Pt 1, para 1(3).

[215] Comms Act (UK), s 357(2).

might expose de facto control. such as shareholding and voting interests, constitutional arrangements, management practices, shareholder agreements, and any relevant funding arrangements.[216] For the sake of certainty, Ofcom also establishes a deemed concept of de facto control. De facto control will be presumed where a shareholder holds at least a 30 per cent shareholding; is the largest shareholder; and could outvote the next two largest shareholders.[217] Compared to the test for deemed control under the Australian legislation, which is set at 15 per cent (see 'Current Rules' at p 130), this seems an unnecessarily cumbersome and lenient test, especially since in most large public companies with widely spread shareholdings, control could arise at a much earlier stage. However, the 30 per cent trigger is consistent with UK takeover regulation.

Ofcom has a responsibility in relation to changes of control of Channel Three and Channel Five licences, and local radio licences, to review the likely effect of the change on the service's programme output, having regard to matters particularly relevant to the type and range of programming.[218] If Ofcom determines that the change of control will be detrimental to any of these matters, it must vary the terms of the licence to ensure that the change will not be prejudicial. These provisions are interesting, not only because of their discretionary nature, but also because they indicate clearly the UK preference to protect broadcasting pluralism through a combination of regulatory approaches, in other words, both structural and content regulation. Indeed, as will be discussed in Chapter Seven, one of the justifications for relaxation of the ownership rules was the protection provided through content regulation. It can be seen too how these provisions might address concerns also about relaxation of foreign ownership, particularly since some of the matters which Ofcom has to address relate specifically to matters of local and regional programming. Finally, a general plurality public interest test has been included. Adding as it does another layer of discretionary regulation, it would seem that the 1990 attempts to move away from discretion-based regulation have been largely abandoned. The public interest test, examined in Chapter Five, will apply to a media merger if the Secretary of State serves a public interest intervention notice. In that event, Ofcom is required to advise the Secretary of State on the public interest considerations, whilst the competition aspects of the merger are dealt with by the Office of Fair Trading (OFT). For broadcasting and cross-media mergers, the public interest test will require a consideration of plurality of ownership, the availability of a wide range of programmes of high quality, and commitment to the attainment of programme standards such as impartiality and taste and decency.[219] However, there is a significant limitation on the application of the public interest test, because it is the Secretary's policy, except in exceptional

---

[216] Ofcom, *Consultation on Ofcom Guidance on the Definition of Control of Media Companies* (October 2005).

[217] *Ibid*, paras 3.9–3.10.

[218] Comms Act (UK), ss 351–56. Specific matters which have to be considered by Ofcom are listed in these sections.

[219] Enterprise Act 2002, s 58(2C).

circumstances, to intervene only in mergers of interests which would have come within the former media ownership regime.[220] This means that in general the public interest test will apply only to mergers concerning Channel Three or national radio, cross-media mergers between newspapers and Channel Five or national radio, or between Channel Three and Channel Five, or either of these channels and national radio, as well as mergers which would once have been prevented by the foreign ownership rules.[221]

United States

Despite its preference for market-driven solutions, the US has imposed specific restrictions on media ownership since the early 1940s. Since that time the pattern of ownership and control regulation has remained reasonably consistent, although substantive changes were introduced by the Telecommunications Act of 1996 (TA 1996 (US)), and the 2003 FCC reforms would have also brought significant change, had they been implemented. The 2003 reform attempts will be examined separately in Chapter Seven. In the US, ownership regulation has been the main regulatory instrument for promotion of broadcasting pluralism. Correctly or otherwise, structural regulation, particularly ownership regulation, has been viewed as more acceptable to First Amendment principles than content regulation.[222]

Early Regulatory Steps

Multiple ownership of radio stations was evident at the outset of broadcasting in the 1920s, although formal rules were not introduced until 1941.[223] Both the National Broadcasting Company, well known as NBC, and the Columbia Broadcasting System, CBS, became multiple owners virtually from the commencement of their operations.[224] However, prior to the introduction of rules, the FCC had developed, through its licensing powers, policies which addressed multiple ownership.[225] Although the Comms Act (US) made no specific provision for FCC supervision of broadcasting ownership, the FCC acted under its statutory mandate to regulate as 'public convenience, interest, or necessity requires'.[226] In 1938, the FCC refused to grant an application for a new broadcast station, because the

---

[220] DTI, *Enterprise Act 2002: Public Interest Intervention in Media Mergers* (Guidance Document, May 2004), para 8.2.

[221] *Ibid.* See further Chapter Five.

[222] Barendt, above n 105, 77–83.

[223] FCC, *Notice of Proposed Rule Making, In the Matter of Amendment of Sections 73.35, 73.240, and 73.636 of the Commission's Rules Relating to Multiple Ownership of AM, FM and Television Broadcast Stations,* 95 FCC 2d 360 (1983), para 2.

[224] HH Howard, 'Multiple Broadcast Ownership: Regulatory History' (1974) 27 *Federal Communications Bar Journal* 1 at 2.

[225] ME Price and J Weinberg, 'United States (2)' in V MacLeod (ed), *Media Ownership and Control in the Age of Convergence* (London, International Institute of Communications, 1996), 265 at 268.

[226] Howard, above n 224, 4.

applicant already operated a radio station in the same area.[227] The FCC considered that it would not be in the public interest to grant licences to persons who already controlled stations in the same community unless a compelling case could be made out.[228] The Commission noted also that in the facts of this application the second station would not provide 'a program service better in kind or quality, or more diversified or serving a wider range of interests than that now offered'.[229] The FCC also appeared to be influenced by the fact that the interests associated with, and in control of, both stations were identical, as was the managerial policy.[230] One can see here an early adherence to the assumption that ownership diversity can produce voice diversity.[231]

Formal rules, which prohibited duopolies and limited national ownership to six stations, were first adopted in 1941 with the introduction of commercial FM radio.[232] At the same time, television was being introduced on an experimental basis, and rules were also put in place which limited national ownership of television stations to three and prohibited duopolies.[233] When television was adopted as a permanent service in 1941, the limits were retained, although the national limit was raised to five in 1944, following a request from NBC.[234] These rules represented the FCC's judgement that ownership above the prescribed limit would constitute 'a concentration of control of . . . broadcasting facilities in a manner inconsistent with public interest, convenience, or necessity'.[235] Although the FCC had not introduced national ownership rules for AM radio, in 1946 it rejected an application by CBS for an eighth AM radio station.[236] This decision set a marker for future decisions, although the FCC acknowledged that, for AM, numerical limits were not the sole issue, and other matters, such as the power and frequencies of stations, were also relevant.[237] By then, the Commission had already prohibited AM duopolies.[238] A consolidated set of multiple ownership rules, adopted in 1953, retained the duopoly rules, and limited national common control of AM and FM radio stations to seven, and television to five stations, although the maximum for television was also increased to seven in 1954 provided that two were UHF facilities.[239] From early

---

[227] *Genesee Radio Corporation* 5 FCC 183 (1938).

[228] *Ibid*, 186.

[229] *Ibid.*

[230] *Ibid.*

[231] See also Price and Weinberg, above n 225, 267–68.

[232] By 'duopoly' the FCC meant the common ownership of more than one station of the same type of service within a community: FCC, *Notice of Proposed Rule Making* (1983), above n 223, paras 2–3.

[233] *Ibid*, para 3.

[234] *Ibid.* In fact, NBC had requested an increase of the limit to seven stations. At the time, there were only five stations operating across the nation, although this situation changed quickly once World War II was over: Howard, above n 224, 8–9.

[235] FCC, 9 Fed Reg 5442 (1944), quoted in Howard, above n 224, 9.

[236] FCC, *Notice of Proposed Rule Making* (1983), above n 223, para 4.

[237] *Ibid.*

[238] Order No 84-A-Multiple Ownership of Standard Broadcast Stations, 8 Fed Reg 16065 (1943), cited in *ibid*, para 5.

[239] The increase for UHF stations was designed to encourage exploitation of the UHF band: *ibid*, para 13.

on the US regulation adopted a broad notion of control: thus, the rules were triggered by ownership, operation, or control, directly or indirectly, of a licence, and control incorporated concepts of both legal and functional control.[240] There were objections to the setting of numerical limits by industry members, but the FCC took the view, although without giving reasons, that the problems created by multiple ownership were best dealt with by developing generally applicable rules.[241] There were industry objections also to the arbitrary nature of the rules because they made no allowance for market differences in respect of size of population and location. The FCC recognised this problem, but asserted that other approaches were impractical since they might require substantial divestment or undesirable grandfathering arrangements.[242]

An early area of concern for the FCC was networking. By the late 1930s, radio broadcasting was dominated by NBC and CBS through their networking arrangements.[243] As a result of complaints from a third networking company, Mutual Broadcasting System, the FCC initiated an investigation into the practices of the networks.[244] In its Report,[245] it noted with concern the practices of the networks which included: binding affiliates with long-term exclusive contracts; preventing them taking programmes from other networks; allowing affiliates only limited opportunities to reject network programmes; and, dominating prime-time periods, which made it difficult for the affiliates to attract advertising revenue and develop their own local programming.[246] The Report also noted that the network companies tended to align themselves with only the largest stations in an area, whilst refusing to supply their programming to smaller stations.[247] Whilst the FCC considered that these arrangements were not in the public interest, it also demonstrated a certain ambivalence about the practice of networking, because it recognised that networking constituted 'an important factor in the development of the broadcasting industry', since it enabled the financing and production of more expensive programming which might not otherwise have been available to smaller communities.[248] Despite the Commission's concern that the network companies were also station owners, it did not require divestment, since it had been earlier FCC decisions which had allowed the situation to develop.[249] However, it did require NBC, which operated two networks, to divest itself of one network; the sold network eventually became the American Broadcasting Company (ABC). It also introduced rules to address some of the practices noted above. The networks

---

[240] FCC, *Report and Order, Multiple Ownership of AM, FM and Television Broadcast Stations* (1953) 18 FCC 288. This broad approach has continued throughout the history of US regulation of media ownership, see 47 CFR § 73.5555, notes 1–3.
[241] FCC, *Report and Order* (1953), above n 240, para 4.
[242] *Ibid*, para 11.
[243] Overbeck, above n 108, 519.
[244] Howard, above n 224, 5.
[245] FCC, *Report on Chain Broadcasting,* Commission Order No 37 (Docket 5060, May 1941).
[246] *Ibid*, 48, 62–63.
[247] *Ibid*, 56.
[248] *Ibid*, 4.
[249] *Ibid*, 67.

challenged the rules but the Supreme Court held that the FCC was authorised, under its public interest mandate, to make rules designed to correct the type of abuses which had been identified in the Report, and that such rules would not infringe the First Amendment.[250]

Thus, by 1953, a pattern for broadcasting ownership regulation, covering local, national, and network ownership, was established. The regulatory pattern would be completed in the 1970s with the introduction of cross-media rules, and would continue, subject to some variations, essentially along the same lines until the TA 1996 (US).

Identifying Policy

In its recent reform of media ownership rules (see further Chapter Seven), the FCC observed that it had 'identified diversity, competition, and localism as longstanding goals that would continue to be core agency objectives in this area.'[251] When the FCC had established its presumption against duopolies, its policy motivation was the value to be had from 'diversification of service'.[252] The goals of competition and localism can also be detected in the early rule-making. When it adopted the national radio ownership rules it stated that the purpose was to 'obviate possible monopoly, and encourage local initiative.'[253] These policy goals, and particularly those of diversity and competition, come through in the 1953 rule-making which formally imposed national limits on common ownership of AM stations:

> This Commission has consistently adhered to the principle of 'diversification' in order to implement the Congressional policy against monopoly and in order to preserve competition.. . . It is our view that the operation of broadcast stations by a large group of diversified licensees will better serve the public interest than the operation of broadcast stations by a small and limited group of licensees. The vitality of our system of broadcasting depends in large part on the introduction into this field of licensees who prepared and qualified to serve the varied and divergent needs of the public for radio service. Simply stated, the fundamental purpose of this facet of the multiple ownership rules is to promote diversification of ownership in order to maximize diversification of program and service viewpoints as well as to prevent any undue concentration of economic power contrary to the public interest.[254]

Diversity is understood here as diversity through services and programmes, so that once again the assumption at play is that diversity of ownership will lead to diverse content and views. In these early efforts at ownership regulation, this is usually the understanding of the diversity concept, but in its presentation of the 2003 rule changes, the FCC referred to five different types of diversity: viewpoint; outlet;

---

[250] *National Broadcasting Co, Inc v United States* 319 US 190 (1943).
[251] FCC, *Report and Order and Notice of Proposed Rulemaking, In the Matter of 2002 Biennial Regulatory Review—Review of the Commission's Broadcast Ownership Rules and Other Rules Adopted Pursuant to Section 202 of the Telecommunications Act of 1996*, FCC 03-127 (2 June 2003), para 17.
[252] FCC, *Notice of Proposed Rule Making* (1983), above n 223, para 2.
[253] FCC, *Sixth Annual Report* (FY 1940) (1941), 68, quoted in *ibid*, para 3.
[254] FCC, *Report and Order* (1953), above n 240, para 10.

programme; source; and minority and female ownership.[255] The 2003 report also acknowledged the long-standing importance of localism:

> Localism is rooted in Congressional directives to this Commission and has been affirmed as a valid regulatory objective many times by the courts . . . Federal regulation of broadcasting has historically placed significant emphasis on ensuring that local television and radio stations are responsive to the needs and interests of their local communities.[256]

The FCC's early concern about networks also provides evidence that localism is recognised as an important policy objective.

There has certainly been a clearer articulation of policy in the US compared with the UK. Price and Weinberg suggest that media ownership policy rests on two assumptions: the first is that 'a speaker's identity will strongly influence the social narrative his speech conveys'[257]; and the second that 'the owner of the physical communications resources—printing press, broadcast station or whatever—used to disseminate speech should control that speech'.[258] Thus, the first assumption means that if the marketplace is structured so as to influence who are the speakers, then the content will also be affected. This, of course, is the presumption that ownership is linked with voice or narrative.[259] However, Price and Weinberg have questioned the coherence of FCC policy:

> [b]eginning in the 1940s, US policy makers built up a set of ragged, not always articulated, understandings flowing from these two assumptions. Different media owners would provide different media voices. More owners would mean more voices. A range of owners would lead to a range of views or social narratives, rendering the community of listeners more content with the responsiveness of the system. A multiplicity of owners would lead to competition; competition would lead to robust, open discussion.[260]

Coherent or otherwise, the policy objectives have remained consistent, although the policy has had to adapt to periodic relaxation of the rules, and to variations in the regulatory inclinations of the FCC.

Ownership and Control Regulation and its Evolution

Once established, the US retained the basic pattern of pre-emptive rules which set limits on media control although, under its public interest mandate, it retained discretion to act in relation to unacceptable control situations. Yet it would be a mistake to assume from this that there has been a happy acceptance of ownership regulation. In fact, the history of media ownership regulation in the US has been

---

[255] See FCC, *Report and Order and Notice of Proposed Rulemaking* (2003), above n 251, paras 18–52 for a discussion of these different types.

[256] *Ibid*, paras 73–74.

[257] Price and Weinberg, above n 225, 266.

[258] *Ibid*, 266–67.

[259] ME Price, 'An Access Taxonomy' in A Sajó and M Price (eds), *Rights of Access to the Media* (The Hague, Kluwer Law International, 1996), 1 at 4.

[260] Price and Weinberg, above n 225, 267–68.

characterised by continual pressure on the FCC to alter or relax the rules. Ownership regulation has also been subject to the variations in political and philosophical temperament, which differently constituted Commissions have brought to the role.

Relaxing Limits   The pressure to relax can be seen most clearly in the national multiple ownership rules. As described above, national ownership and duopoly rules were in place by the early 1950s. But the history of these rules from then on is one of reasonably regular revision, usually in the direction of relaxation. As Hoffmann-Riem put it: 'the history of the FCC's battle against concentration consists of step-by-step retraction of former restrictions'.[261] The rules remained stable until the 1980s, when a deregulatory-minded Commission was in place.[262] In 1984, the FCC relaxed the rules to set the limit at 12 for each type of service.[263] In fact, the FCC had wanted to remove all national ownership rules, but opposition, and pressure from Congressional committees,[264] caused it to back down. It confined itself to raising the numerical limits, but stated that this was to be a transitional move, and the limits would cease after six years.[265] The FCC's willingness to relax these rules was partly influenced by the increased number of media outlets, and the development of technologies, such as cable, which, in the Commission's view, created a very different media environment from that which had existed when the rules were imposed in the 1940s and 1950s.[266] As such, the Commission considered that the traditional justification of spectrum scarcity was no longer applicable, and concerns about broadcasting's power to influence were also weakened.[267] However, there were other factors influencing the Commission. It questioned the very purpose of a national ownership limit, arguing that such a rule might be counter-productive and that the real focus for viewpoint diversity and economic competition should be local markets.[268] Because of this, the Commission left the duopoly rule unchanged. It con-

---

[261]   Hoffmann-Riem, above n 156, 30.

[262]   H Geller, 'Ownership Regulatory Policies in the US Telecom Sector' (1995) 13 *Cardozo Arts & Entertainment Law Journal* 727 at 731.

[263]   FCC, *Report and Order, In the Matter of Amendment of Section 73.3555 [formerly Sections 73.35, 73.240, and 73.636] of the Commission's Rules Relating to Multiple Ownership of AM, FM and Television Broadcast Stations*, 100 FCC 2d 17 (1984). The television UHF/UVF rule was not carried through, although the FCC back-tracked slightly by deciding that a UHF channel would only be attributed with 50% of the audience share: FCC, *Memorandum Opinion and Order, In the Matter of Amendment of Section 73.3555 [formerly Sections 73.35, 73.240, and 73.636] of the Commission's Rules Relating to Multiple Ownership of AM, FM and Television Broadcast Stations*, 100 FCC 2d 74 (1985). This was to reflect the weaker signal.

[264]   Geller, above n 262. The FCC had noted that its review of the multiple ownership rules had been of its own motion: FCC, *Notice of Proposed Rule Making* (1983), above n 223, para 1.

[265]   FCC, *Report and Order* (1984), above n 263, para 5. Under pressure it dropped the automatic sunset clause: FCC, *Memorandum Opinion and Order* (1985), above n 263, para 49.

[266]   FCC, *Report and Order* (1984), above n 263, para 4.

[267]   *Ibid*, paras 7–8.

[268]   *Ibid*, paras 9–10.

sidered that there were benefits to be gained from group or multiple ownership, because the consequent economic strength would enable the development of voices independent from the networks, which could lead to greater diversity of views and programming.[269] However, national limits prevented the development of media groups strong enough to compete against the networks. This argument is an odd rationalisation, because it seems to be suggesting that, having created one form of dominance in the media market, it is necessary to create a new form to counteract the earlier form. Seen in this light, it resonates with the UK pressure for the 1996 reforms, which challenged what was seen as an unequal and unfair market. In a reconsideration of its new multiple ownership rules, the FCC also adopted an audience reach limit for television. Thus, the limit of 12 stations was combined with a permissible maximum audience reach of 25 per cent of the national television audience.[270] This appeared to undermine the FCC's earlier claim for the benefits of group ownership, particularly since it was clear that the addition of an audience reach limit was a response to concerns that the 12-station rule would introduce large-scale and rapid restructuring of the market, through consolidation.[271] The audience reach rule, however, dealt with the arbitrary nature of the 12-station limit.

Television limits remained unchanged until the TA 1996 (US) reforms were implemented in 1996, but national radio limits were increased in 1992, to 18 AM and 18 FM stations, with a planned increase in 1994 to 20,[272] although they were not removed completely as had been anticipated by the FCC in its 1984 decision. In its 1992 revision, the FCC again relied upon the justifications which were influential in the 1984 relaxation, but it was also conscious that radio was facing intense competition, from within the radio industry and from other media sectors, with the result that many radio stations, particularly small stations, were suffering financially.[273] In fact, the Commission initially decided to increase the national limit to 30 AM and 30 FM stations. This would strengthen the industry, but would not threaten competition or diversity; nor would it lead to a major restructuring of the industry, which might be the case if national limits were removed completely.[274] It was thought very unlikely that a single firm or group of firms would be able to exercise dominance over the industry.[275] Only a few months later, however, the FCC, as a result of petitions received and strong pressure from Congress,[276] revised its decision, to implement instead the 18-to-20 limit.

---

[269] *Ibid*, paras 58, 60–63, and 108.

[270] FCC, *Memorandum Opinion and Order* (1985), above n 263, para 39. Some adjustments were made for UHF services and minority ownership.

[271] *Ibid*, paras 35–40.

[272] FCC, *Memorandum Opinion and Order and Further Notice of Proposed Rule Making, In Re Revision of Radio Rules and Policies,* 7 FCC Rcd 6387 (1992).

[273] FCC, *Report and Order, In Re Revision of Radio Rules and Policies,* 7 FCC Rcd 2755 (1992), paras 4–9.

[274] *Ibid*, paras 12 and 23.

[275] *Ibid*, para 19.

[276] Hoffmann-Riem, above n 156, 29.

In part, this recurring process of limit relaxation was justified by assertions that local diversity was what really mattered: thus, the 1984 FCC decision left the local duopoly rule unchanged. However, by 1989, the local radio duopoly rule was also being modified. This rule prohibited common control of two or more commercial stations of the same broadcast type within the same market. The 1989 decision retained the duopoly concept, but it relaxed its impact by varying how a relevant area would be defined.[277] In 1992, however, the radio duopoly rule was effectively abandoned, although local ownership restrictions were maintained. Once again, the argument was that restrictions could be counter-productive to competition and diversity, because they prevented companies taking advantage of opportunities to achieve efficiencies and cost savings through consolidation. The Commission noted that stations were forced to find other cost-saving measures in order to remain competitive, and that these usually impacted upon programming budgets.[278] The new local ownership rule relied upon a combination of numerical limits, audience share, and market size. In markets of 15 or more stations, a licensee could own up to two AM and two FM stations, provided that the result did not lead to excessive concentration in the market. Excessive concentration was presumed where the combined audience share exceeded 25 per cent.[279] In smaller markets, control of up to three stations (but no more than two in the same service) was allowed, provided that the number of stations amounted to less than 50 per cent of the stations in the market.[280]

Thus from the time of the earliest regulatory measures, and notably during the 1980s, until the TA 1996 (US) reforms, there was a gradual relaxation of the ownership and control rules. This process was partly a reflection of changing attitudes about the role of the FCC and broadcasting regulation, but it was also the product of changed assumptions about pluralism. Starting with the 1984 decision, it was assumed that, provided there was protection of local diversity, national limits were largely irrelevant to the promotion of pluralism.[281] Their retention during this period was mainly the result of Congressional pressure. Secondly, there was a growing intolerance with the assumption that ownership controls were the way to achieve pluralism, or 'viewpoint diversity' as the FCC usually referred to it. Instead, enabling competition was seen as the appropriate instrument. Thus, if industry participants were allowed to expand, creating economic strength, competition would be encouraged, promoting, in its turn, greater diversity.[282] This is

---

[277] FCC, *First Report and Order, In the Matter of Amendment of Section 73.3555 of the Commission's Rules, the Broadcast Multiple Ownership Rules,* 4 FCC Rcd 1723 (1989). Markets were determined by reference to signal coverage areas. This method of determination of relevant markets would have been changed in the 2003 reforms, at least for most markets, to one based on geographic markets defined by a recognised ratings system.

[278] FCC, *Report and Order, In re Revision of Radio Rules and Policies,* 7 FCC Rcd 2755 (1992), para 37.

[279] FCC, *Memorandum Opinion and Order and Further Notice of Proposed Rule Making, In Re Revision of Radio Rules and Policies,* 7 FCC Rcd 6387 (1992), para 7.

[280] FCC, *Report and Order* (1992), above n 278, para 40.

[281] FCC, *Report and Order* (1984), above n 263, para 24.

[282] *Ibid,* para 58.

an argument which has pervaded the reform process in each of the jurisdictions, but it rests on an assumption which may be tenuous: namely, that the media company having realised economic efficiencies will reinvest these in programming rather than return them to shareholders.

Cross-Media Ownership   Restrictions on cross-media interests were not imposed until the 1970s, although by that time there was already a fair degree of cross-media ownership. By the late 1960s, there were approximately 1,600 combinations of station ownership across the country, including 1,200 AM–FM combinations, 124 AM–television combinations, 42 FM–television combinations, and 212 AM–FM– television combinations.[283] The first regulatory move dealt with broadcasting station combinations, although this initiative came as something of a surprise to the industry; the result, Howard suggests, of increased Congressional and Department of Justice scrutiny at that time.[284] In 1970, the FCC prohibited common control within the same market of two or more broadcasting stations, whether AM, FM, or television; known as the 'one-to-a-market rule', it was seen as an extension of the duopoly rule.[285] The ruling did not require licensees to divest any existing interests which might have breached the rule.[286] The new rules were based firmly on the policy grounds that diversifying control was essential for the promotion of diversity and competition.[287] In justifying its decision, the FCC rejected the argument that an economically strong 'multiple owner' could provide better programming, and thus enhance diversity: the evidence did not support this contention, and the FCC specifically noted that there was no evidence that the extra funds were channelled into programming.[288] However, it would be precisely this argument which would be used in the 1980s, and in 2003, to justify relaxation. There was strong opposition to the decision from the broadcasting industry,[289] and within a year, the FCC had modified its one-to-a-market rule by permitting AM–FM combinations,[290] because of viability concerns about independent FM

---

[283] *Broadcasting*, 25 March 1968, at 23, cited in Howard, above n 224, 57.

[284] Howard, above n 224, 56.

[285] Federal Communications Commission, *First Report and Order, In the Matter of Amendment of Sections 73.35, 73.240 and 73.636 of the Commission Rules relating to Multiple Ownership of Standard, FM and Television Broadcast Stations*, 22 FCC 2d 306 (1970), para 6. There were some minor exceptions to the rule to take into account very small services, and AM services which were day-time services only: para 51. Further, sales of AM–FM combinations were permitted where it could be shown that for technical or economic reasons they were interdependent and it was impractical for them to be sold or to operate as separate stations: para 48.

[286] *Ibid*, para 14.

[287] *Ibid*, paras 16–18 and 25.

[288] *Ibid*, para 23.

[289] LA Singleton and SC Rockwell, 'Silent Voices: Analyzing the FCC "Media Voices" Criteria Limiting Local Radio–Television Cross-Ownership' (2003) 8 *Communications Law and Policy* 385 at 388.

[290] FCC, *Memorandum Opinion and Order, In the Matter of Amendment of Sections 73.35, 73.240 and 73.636 of the Commission Rules relating to Multiple Ownership of Standard, FM and Television Broadcast Stations*, 28 FCC 2d 662 (1971), para 35.

stations.[291] Although local ownership rules were liberalised in 1992, the one-to-a-market rule remained.

The radio-television cross-ownership prohibition provides a good illustration of another aspect of FCC management of the ownership regime—the use of waiver policies. The FCC operates waiver policies in respect of radio–television ownership and the television duopoly rule.[292] These waivers amount to a case-by-case relaxation of the ownership regulations. The radio–television waiver was introduced in 1989, following a review of the rule; operating a waiver policy was seen as a more cautious way to proceed.[293] Under the policy, there was a presumption in favour of allowing radio–television combinations in the largest 25 television markets, provided that there would remain at least 30 separately owned and operated broadcast licensees (including non-commercial services).[294] The FCC was favourably disposed to combinations in these circumstances because it considered that there were economic efficiencies to be gained, which would not significantly put at risk diversity policy. It justified this view by reference to the large number of media outlets and to the unlikelihood of any one firm gaining undue economic power or influence.[295] Applications to waive the rule were likely to be granted where a broadcast station was failing, or no longer operating, on the ground that the public interest was better served by two commonly owned stations than one operating and one not operating.[296] The Commission was also prepared to consider other waiver requests on a case-by-case basis, although these would not benefit from the presumption. Such requests would have to demonstrate that the benefits of a combination could be balanced by diversity and competition goals.[297] The use of waivers could be beneficial because it can provide greater flexibility to respond to changing, or particular, situations without losing the safety-net of the rule itself. On the other hand, the use of waivers might raise concerns about the extent to which the rules are being undermined over time, particularly if the regulatory authority feels under pressure in the maintenance of its media ownership policy. In fact, the waiver policy may indicate why the ownership rules were able to remain relatively stable over a long period of time; indeed, the presumption could be seen as a de facto variation of the rule. Conversely, a waiver policy used regularly might increase the pressure for rule change, since it might provide evidence that the rule is otiose.

---

[291] *Ibid*, para 31.

[292] 47 CFR § 73.3555, note 7.

[293] FCC, *Second Report and Order, In the Matter of Amendment of Section 73.3555 of the Commission's Rules, the Broadcast Multiple Ownership Rules*, 4 FCC Rcd 1741 (1989), paras 3–4. The policy was modified slightly later in 1989: FCC, *Memorandum Opinion and Order, In the Matter of Amendment of Section 73.3555 of the Commission's Broadcast Multiple Ownership Rules*, 4 FCC Rcd 6489 (1989).

[294] Under the FCC's attribution rules, which were relevant to the application of the policy, network affiliates would not be counted.

[295] FCC, *Second Report and Order* (1989), above n 293, paras 77–78.

[296] *Ibid*, paras 86 and 89.

[297] *Ibid*, paras 90–91.

Cable was also brought into the broadcasting cross-ownership regulatory framework. In 1970, common ownership of a cable system and a television station serving the same market was effectively prohibited.[298] The prohibition was also given statutory force in 1984 by the Cable Communications Policy Act. Following a review in 1998, the FCC decided to retain it, despite a 1992 review concluding that the rule no longer served a purpose.[299] It now considered that the rule was necessary to prevent undue discrimination by cable operators against competitors.[300] It acknowledged that other rules, such as those dealing with carriage and channel position, did not manage to control all discrimination problems.[301] However, it was difficult to sustain this rule in light of the 1996 reforms, and a legal challenge resulted in the rule being vacated.[302]

The most contested area of cross-media regulation was, not surprisingly, newspaper–broadcasting combinations. The FCC first introduced rules prohibiting such combinations within the same market in 1975, although it had been formally contemplating the possibility from the time of the broadcast cross-ownership rules.[303] Once again, the policy lynchpin of ownership regulation was the belief that diversity of ownership could produce diversity of voice:

> The significance of ownership from the standpoint of 'the widest possible dissemination of information' lies in the fact that ownership carries with it the power to select, to edit, and to choose the methods, manner and emphasis of presentation, all of which are a critical aspect of the Commission's concern with the public interest.[304]

The FCC had long been concerned about press–broadcasting cross-ownership. As early as 1940, it had considered introducing rules, but it relied instead upon its public interest discretion in licence awards to deal with the matter on an ad hoc basis.[305] The attitude towards newspaper involvement in broadcasting has echoes

---

[298] FCC, *Second Report and Order, In the Matter of Amendment of Part 74, Subpart K, of the Commission's Rules and Regulations relative to Community Antenna Television Systems; and Inquiry into the Development of Communications Technology and Services to Formulate Regulatory Policy and Rulemaking and/or Legislative Proposals,* 23 FCC 2d 816 (1970) The 1970 rule-making also introduced a prohibition on the broadcast networks owning cable systems. This rule was repealed by the FCC in 1992: 7 FCC Rcd 6156.

[299] FCC, *Report and Order, In the Matter of Amendment of Part 76, Subpart J Section 76.501 of the Commission's Rules and Regulations to Eliminate the Prohibition on Common Ownership of Cable Television Systems and National Television Networks,* 7 FCC Rcd 6156 (1992), para 17.

[300] FCC, *Biennial Review Report, In the Matter of 1998 Biennial Regulatory Review—Review of the Commission's Broadcast Ownership Rules and Other Rules Adopted Pursuant to Section 202 of the Telecommunications Act of 1996,* 15 FCC Rcd 11058 (2000), para 102.

[301] *Ibid,* para 104. The TA 1996 (US) had directed the FCC to ensure that there were rules which would ensure carriage, channel positioning, and non-discriminatory treatment of non-affiliated stations, where there was common ownership of a network and a cable system: § 202(f)(2).

[302] *Fox Television Stations Inc v Federal Communications Commission* 280 F 3d 1027 (2002).

[303] FCC, *Second Report and Order, In the Matter of Amendment of Sections 73.34, 73.240 and 73.636 of the Commission Rules relating to Multiple Ownership of Standard, FM, and Television Broadcast Stations,* 50 FCC 2d 1046 (1975), para 4. The evidence about the extent and effect of newspaper–broadcasting combinations appeared to be equivocal, although there was evidence of combinations of the only local newspaper and the only local television station: para 40.

[304] *Ibid,* para 14.

[305] *FCC v National Citizens Committee for Broadcasting* 436 US 775, 781 (1978).

of the UK experience. In its early licensing decisions, the Commission had to balance public interest diversity concerns with the need to provide the best practicable service to the public. Thus, licences for broadcasting stations were often awarded to newspaper interests, because they were best able to meet licensing requirements, such as programme service.[306] The FCC acknowledged the industry's role in the development of broadcasting, although it did not consider that continued co-ownership was necessarily in the public interest.[307] Thus, the FCC, having tacitly encouraged, through licensing and renewals, newspaper ownership, was now acting because of concerns about the dominance of newspaper interests. It was not concerned to identify some optimal level of diversity, more with increasing opportunities for ownership diversity generally. This was the reasoning behind its decision to include radio in the cross-media rules, even though, as it acknowledged, there might be less of a case for regulation, given the greater number of radio outlets.[308] However, it stopped short of requiring divestiture of existing newspaper–broadcast combinations, except where they constituted monopoly combinations.[309]

The FCC noted in detail the various arguments raised against (and sometimes for) the imposition of a cross-ownership restriction, but it provided little in the way of review or assessment of these arguments. However, as it noted, many of these arguments related to anti-trust considerations.[310] In its conclusions, the FCC re-emphasised the policy objectives of both 'diversity of viewpoints' and 'economic competition', but it also made clear that there could be a priority of policy goals:

> Early in its history, the Commission acted to adopt rules to end common ownership of stations in the same service serving substantially the same area. Needless to say, such commonly owned stations could neither be true competitors nor could they offer true diversity. Since then the multiple ownership rules have been extended in a number of respects to better serve one or both of the above goals. As to competition in particular, the national public policy (expressed in anti-trust laws and elsewhere) in favor of competition and against actions which would curtail it, finds a reflection in the actions of the Commission. Sometimes, this policy will yield, however, to the even higher goals of diversity and the delivery of quality broadcasting service to the American people. This is a vitally important matter, for it is essential to a democracy that its electorate be informed and have access to divergent viewpoints on controversial issues.[311]

For the Commission, extending its rules to include newspaper interests in broadcasting gave greater consistency to its diversity policy, and better reflected the contemporary media environment, which was so different from the early days of broadcasting.[312]

---

[306] *FCC v National Citizens Committee for Broadcasting* 436 US 775, 782.
[307] FCC, *Second Report and Order* (1975), above n 303, para 100.
[308] *Ibid*, para 104.
[309] *Ibid*, paras 109 and 117. About 16 such combinations were required to divest: *National Citizens Committee for Broadcasting*, above n 305, 788.
[310] FCC, *Second Report and Order* (1975), above n 303, para 33.
[311] *Ibid*, para 99.
[312] *Ibid*, paras 100–1.

The new rules survived a Supreme Court challenge.[313] Not surprisingly, one of the arguments was that the Commission did not have authority under the communications legislation to make decisions which affected the newspaper industry, but this was rejected, as giving too narrow an interpretation to the duty to regulate broadcasting in the public interest.[314] It is significant to note also, given the pressure the FCC would later be under, that the court (and the Court of Appeals) found that the Commission had acted rationally, even though the rule-making record did not conclusively establish that the proposed rules would increase diversity. The court recognised the difficulty of making clear empirical links in this area, agreeing with the Court of Appeals that '[d]iversity and its effects are . . . elusive concepts'.[315] The new rules on cross-ownership did not satisfy either industry or public interest groups, the latter being concerned that too many combinations were allowed to continue.[316] Despite the FCC's later enthusiasm for relaxing ownership rules, the cross-media rules continued, although the 2003 reforms would have had a dramatic impact.

Telecommunications Act of 1996 and Current Rules

The TA 1996 (US) came with a deregulatory and liberalising agenda, and it had an impact, directly and indirectly, on FCC media ownership policy and rules. The Act was the most comprehensive reform of communications since the introduction of the Comms Act (US) in 1934, and it reflected a strong bias towards free market solutions over regulation.[317] Although the FCC, since the 1980s, had been steadily relaxing the rules, the Act reshaped media ownership regulation in a way which even the FCC had not felt able to do.[318] The direct effect of the Act was felt through the changes made by Congress to the then current rules. The Act directed the FCC to make certain changes. The changes were dramatic. National ownership limits for radio, both AM and FM, were removed.[319] For television, national ownership limits on the number of stations which could be owned were also removed; the audience reach cap was retained, but raised from 25 per cent to 35 per cent.[320]

---

[313] *National Citizens Committee for Broadcasting*, above n 305.

[314] *Ibid*, 794–95.

[315] *Ibid*, 796, quoting the Court of Appeals.

[316] Overbeck, above n 108, 523. Once again waivers were used to ameliorate the impact of the rules, although, in general, they were used only for newspaper–radio combinations: *ibid*.

[317] P Johnson, 'United States' in D Goldberg, T Prosser and S Verhulst (eds), *Regulating the Changing Media: A Comparative Study* (Oxford, Clarendon Press, 1998), 201 at 217 and 222.

[318] The FCC had instituted a proceeding in the 1990s which was contemplating a major relaxation of many of the rules, but this was overtaken by the TA 1996 (US): see FCC, *Notice of Inquiry, In the Matter of Review of the Policy Implications of the Changing Video Marketplace*, 6 FCC Rcd 4961 (1991); *Notice of Proposed Rulemaking, In the Matter of Review of the Commission's Regulations governing Television Broadcasting*, 7 FCC Rcd 4111 (1992); and *Further Notice of Proposed Rulemaking*, 10 FCC Rcd 3524 (1995).

[319] TA 1996 (US), § 202(a).

[320] *Ibid*, § 202(c)(1), now 47 CFR § 73.3555(e)(1). In 2004, Congress set the limit at 39%: Consolidated Appropriations Act 2004, § 629(1). This was a reaction to the FCC's proposal to increase the limit to 45% (see Chapter Seven, 'Reforming Broadcasting Pluralism: United States', at p 280), and was a compromise between this and a Congress proposal to take the rule back its 35% limit. The 39%

Local radio ownership rules were also relaxed. In the largest markets (a market with 45 or more commercial stations), it was now possible to own up to eight stations, provided that not more than five were in the same service. A sliding scale operated down to the smallest markets:

— in a market with between 30 and 44 commercial stations, up to seven stations, provided that not more than four were in the same service;
— in a market with between 15 and 29 commercial stations, up to six stations, provided that not more than four were in the same service; and
— in a market with 14 or fewer commercial stations, up to five stations, provided that not more than three were in the same service. Control of more than 50 per cent of the stations in the market was not permitted.[321]

The FCC was also directed to amend its waiver policy in relation to the one-to-a-market rule to allow the waiver to apply to the top 50 markets, a change from the previous limit of 25 markets.[322] The 1996 reforms set in train a massive restructuring of the media industry, accelerating 'a trend towards concentrated ownership of all media'.[323] As a result of the relaxation of radio rules, there was substantial consolidation in the industry, so that 'ten parent companies control two-thirds of listeners and radio revenues across the nation, with the largest company owning twelve hundred stations nationwide'.[324] Within two years of the reforms, some 4,000 out of 11,000 radio stations had changed hands.[325] Between 1996 and 2002, the number of radio stations increased by 5.4 per cent, but the number of owners decreased by 33.6 per cent.[326] The dramatic change can be understood when it is noted that prior to 1996, the largest radio company owned only 65 stations.[327] The largest company after 1996, with 1,200 stations, Clear Channel Communications Inc, had prior to 1996 owned only 36 radio stations.[328] Clear Channel has become something of a touchstone for the media ownership debate, because of its ownership reach and radio practices. It has been the impact of the 1996 reforms which has made the 2003 reform attempt so controversial.

The TA 1996 (US) also had an indirect impact on the media ownership regime. Congress did not itself amend the local television ownership rule, but it directed

cap prevented the Fox and CBS Networks, which were both already over the 35% cap, from expanding further.

[321] TA 1996 (US), § 202(b), now 47 CFR §73.3555(a)(1). No more than 25% of the total hours broadcast can comprise programming which is duplicated on another local station, if it is commonly owned or subject to a time brokerage agreement: 47 CFR §73.3556(a).

[322] TA 1996 (US), § 202(d).

[323] Johnson, above n 317, 205–6.

[324] BL Dorgan, 'The FCC and Media Ownership: the Loss of the Public Interest Standard' (2005) 19 *Notre Dame Journal of Law, Ethics & Public Policy* 443 at 448–49.

[325] GM Prindle, 'No Competition: How Radio Consolidation has Diminished Diversity and Sacrificed Localism' (2003) 14 *Fordham Intellectual Property, Media and Entertainment Law Journal* 279 at 305.

[326] *Ibid*, 306.

[327] Dorgan, above n 324, 449.

[328] Prindle, above n 325, 306.

the FCC to conduct a rule-making procedure to determine whether the rules should be retained or amended.[329] The Act also directed the FCC to review its ownership rules on a biennial basis, with a view to determining whether the public interest required their retention.[330] The biennial review requirement would lead to the 2003 reform process. Continuing in the spirit of the TA 1996 (US), the biennial reviews were biased towards liberalisation. Indeed, it had been held that the wording of section 202(h) created a presumption in favour of modification or repeal.[331] However, the US Court of Appeals, dealing with the 2003 reforms, rejected this: the deregulatory spirit of section 202(h) was to be found in the obligation imposed on the FCC to review and justify its rules regularly, but there was no presumption that it could only act to eliminate rules.[332]

In compliance with the directives of the Act, the FCC reviewed its local television duopoly rule and the radio/television cross-ownership rule, announcing their relaxation in 1999. The television duopoly rule, which had prohibited control of two or more television stations within the same market, was modified to allow control of two stations, provided that one of the stations was not one of the four highest rating stations, and there would be at least eight other independent television stations (commercial or non-commercial) remaining.[333] The grounds justifying relaxation were familiar: the increased number of local media outlets, the efficiencies to be gained from joint ownership, and consequential benefits for the public of such efficiencies.[334] A challenge to the new rule was upheld, and the rule remanded to the FCC for reconsideration, with regard to what would count as an independent voice. The court considered that the decision to include only television stations was not sufficiently explained.[335] The Commission had sought to justify it on the basis that it regarded television as the primary and most accessible source for news and information, and that it was not convinced about the extent to which other media were substitutes,[336] but the court did not consider this as a sufficient explanation, because the FCC had not explained why a different measure was used in its cross-ownership rule; nor was its 'wait-and-see' approach consistent with the TA 1996 (US) review requirement.[337] This rule would be rolled into the 2003 reform process. In its 1999 review, the radio–television cross-ownership rule (the one-to-a-market rule) was also relaxed. The FCC had contemplated eliminating it altogether, on the assumption that radio and television did not compete in the same

---

[329] TA 1996 (US), § 202(c)(2).

[330] *Ibid*, § 202(h). This has since been amended to require a quadriennal review: Consolidated Appropriations Act 2004, § 629(3).

[331] *Fox Television Stations*, above n 302, 1048.

[332] *Prometheus Radio Project v Federal Communications Commission* 373 F 3d 372, 394–5 (2004).

[333] FCC, *Report and Order, In the Matter of Review of the Commission's Regulations Governing Television Broadcasting*, 14 FCC Rcd 12903 (1999) at para 8 and 47 CFR § 73.3555(b). Waivers in certain situations would also be allowed.

[334] *Report and Order* (1999), above n 333, paras 7 and 65.

[335] *Sinclair Broadcast Group v Federal Communications Commission* 284 F 3d 148 (2002).

[336] *Report and Order* (1999), above n 333, paras 68–69.

[337] *Sinclair Broadcast Group*, above n 335, 164.

markets.[338] However, it decided to proceed more cautiously, but was prepared to relax the rule, using the now familiar justifications.[339] The cross-ownership rule now permitted cross-ownership of up to two television stations and one radio station, but these limits could be exceeded depending upon the number of independent voices in the market, so that at the most permissive level, ownership of two television stations and six radio stations (or one and seven) would be allowed, provided that there would be at least 20 independent voices in the market.[340] Here, 'independent voices' had a wider meaning because it could include television, radio, newspapers, and cable services. The Commission did not seek to justify why the two rules should have a different approach, although one might be able to see a difference given that the rules are dealing with different control situations. But the FCC's approach seemed weak, when in relation to cross-ownership it referred to the importance of newspapers and cable as a source of news and information, in competition with radio and television.[341] The cross-ownership rule would also be caught up in the 2003 reform process.

Australia

The Australian experience of media ownership regulation has, as with the other jurisdictions, been highly sensitive, but it has also been more transparently the product of interference from both political and media quarters. Australia's history of regulation in this area is also a curious combination of reasonably stable regulation and major upheaval. Another trait is the limited articulation of policy, although this could be said to be a feature of Australian media regulation generally. Although ownership and control regulation was introduced relatively early, Australia is frequently cited as having one of the most concentrated media industries worldwide.[342] This view has been questioned by the Productivity Commission, which suggested that such comparisons are difficult to make, although it acknowledged the high concentration in Australia's traditional media industries: newspapers, radio, and television.[343]

Early Regulatory Steps[344]

The early structure of Australian radio broadcasting saw two classes of stations. Class A stations were financed by receiver licence fees; Class B stations by adver-

---

[338] *Report and Order* (1999), above n 333, para 93.

[339] *Ibid*, paras 100–5.

[340] 47 CFR § 73.3555(c). The rules were subject to the other local ownership rules being met.

[341] *Report and Order* (1999), above n 333, para 113.

[342] Hoffmann-Riem, above n 156, 239, citing M Armstrong, *Communications Law and Policy in Australia* (Sydney, Butterworths, 1987–91, looseleaf service), no 6705, and Barr, cited in HJ Kleinsteuber, 'Medien und Medienpolitik in Australien' (1989) 4 *Media Perspektiven* 207 at 207, fn 2.

[343] Productivity Commission, above n 2, 303 and 308.

[344] The review of early ownership and control regulation and policy draws on two sources, in particular: M Armstrong, 'Competition and Group Control in Communications Law' (paper presented at

tising. By the late 1920s, the Class A stations had been acquired by the government and formed into the public broadcaster, the Australian Broadcasting Company, the predecessor of the present-day ABC. The Class B stations gradually developed into a regular commercial broadcasting service and by the 1930s were becoming more profitable.[345] At that stage, apart from a set of statutory regulations, there was no statutory framework for broadcasting; nor was there any established process for licensing. Licences were within the domain of the Postmaster-General, a government minister, and, as Armstrong has observed, their award became a means to further political and personal advantage.[346] Nevertheless, because of concerns about concentration, limits on radio ownership were imposed in 1935.[347] Even at that early stage, the press held substantial interests in radio broadcasting, although these cross-media interests would not be addressed in the rules.[348] However, this first attempt occasioned such hostility that within a few weeks the new rules were relaxed.[349] One of the main opponents was Sir Keith Murdoch, Rupert Murdoch's father, who held interests directly, and through his press interests, in a number of radio stations. When Murdoch complained to the then Prime Minister that his Cabinet was hostile (to Murdoch), the Prime Minister replied 'that far from being hostile, ministers realised what their Government and party owed to the papers Murdoch controlled'.[350] The revised rules proscribed any person being in a position to exercise control, directly or indirectly, of more than one metropolitan broadcasting station in any State or four across Australia, or four stations in any State or eight across Australia.[351] This attempt provides an early illustration of the sensitive issue media regulation would be for governments, and of their susceptibility to media industry pressure. It is noticeable too that the rules were introduced with almost no elaboration of the underlying policy, which presumably also made it difficult for the government to defend the regulation. The Royal Commission on Wireless, which reported in 1927, gave no consideration to the question of control of licences at all, although perhaps this was understandable given that, at the time, most of the broadcasting stations were operating at a loss and, having paid no dividends, it was difficult for them to attract investment.[352] Although the Gibson Committee reported, in 1942, on the dominance of newspaper control of commercial radio, there seemed to be

the Monash University, Faculty of Law and Australian Communications Law Association Seminar on Legal Regulation of Media Control, Melbourne, 6 May 1981), 1, and R Watterson, 'Independence and Control: an Analysis of the Law and Policy on Concentration of Ownership and Control of Commercial TV in Australia' in M Armstrong (ed), *New Media: Law and Policy* (Sydney, Faculty of Law, University of New South Wales, 1981), 106, and also on Armstrong, above n 19.

[345] Armstrong, above n 19, para 305.
[346] *Ibid.*
[347] Watterson, above n 344, 107.
[348] RB Walker, *Yesterday's News* (Sydney, Sydney University Press, 1980), 118 and 128, cited in Armstrong, above n 19, para 305.
[349] Armstrong, above n 19, para 305.
[350] P Chadwick, *Media Mates: Carving up Australia's Media* (Melbourne, Macmillan, 1989), xxiii.
[351] Wireless Telegraphy Regulations (Cth), reg 48A, as amended by SR 1935, No 120.
[352] Royal Commission on Wireless, *Report*, Parl Paper No 121 (1927), 2 and 4.

no will to tackle the question of cross-media ownership.[353] The Gibson Committee's Report led to the introduction of the first comprehensive broadcasting legislation, the Australian Broadcasting Act 1942, but the Act merely carried over the ownership rules established in 1935, although the language changed from 'ownership' to 'ownership' and 'being in a position to exercise control, either directly or indirectly'.[354] The Gibson Committee had suggested that there should be consideration of increased restrictions but this did not take place.[355]

The introduction of commercial television renewed concerns about concentration.[356] A Royal Commission was established to make recommendations for the introduction of television, but discussion of control of commercial television licences was confined to a few short paragraphs.[357] There was no discussion about the likelihood or desirability of press or radio broadcasting becoming involved in television. The Commission thought some limitations on concentration were necessary in the public interest, but there was no attempt to elaborate what this might mean, and it was content to recommend that limits similar to those which applied to radio should be carried over to television.[358] In a slightly different version of the industry promotion argument, compared with the other two jurisdictions, the Commission thought that a degree of common control of television stations could be useful in assisting the development of television in rural sectors.[359] However, the Commission was conscious that there might be developments which could not be anticipated, and it recommended that the licensing process could also be used to deal with control situations which, although within the prescribed limits, might be contrary to the public interest.[360] However, this flexibility was undermined by the lack of real decision-making power and independence of the regulatory body, the Australian Broadcasting Control Board ('the Board'). As shown below, the weaknesses of the Board's powers became apparent quite early on. The Royal Commission's Report led to the Broadcasting and Television Act 1956, which prohibited ownership or control of more than one commercial television station within in a capital city (or the Australian Capital Territory), or more than two across Australia.[361]

The use of licensing powers was seen as a means of dealing with an undesirable control situation. Grants of licences could not be made without an inquiry being conducted by the Board, although the Board could only make recommendations: the grant of a licence being a matter for the Minister. The first commercial television licences awarded were two in Sydney and two in Melbourne. These awards,

[353] Joint Committee on Wireless Broadcasting, *Report*, Parl Paper No 73 (1942), para 381.
[354] Australian Broadcasting Act 1942, s 53(1). For further background see Armstrong, above n 344, 9.
[355] Armstrong, above n 344, 9.
[356] Watterson, above n 344, 107.
[357] Royal Commission on Television, *Report of the Commissioners*, Parl Paper No 38 (1954), paras 362–66.
[358] *Ibid*, paras 365–66.
[359] *Ibid*, para 365.
[360] *Ibid*, para 366.
[361] Broadcasting and Television Act 1942–1956, s 91.

made in 1955, were made under interim legislation, the Television Act 1953, and the Board was conscious that it had to consider such issues, although much of this consideration was focused on the question of foreign control.[362] Otherwise, there was not much consideration of control, although the Board observed that most applicants already had extensive interests in the communications or entertainment sectors, and its brief discussion of the implications of this raised familiar issues.[363] It considered that there was some benefit to be gained if television could draw on the experience of other media sectors, but it observed also that the public interest required 'the widest possible diffusion of ownership of television stations'.[364] But this view had no specific impact on its conclusions.[365] It was the allocation of licences in Brisbane and Adelaide that proved most testing for the Board.[366] By this stage the Sydney and Melbourne television services had been successfully established, and a major concern for the Board in the Brisbane/Adelaide inquiry was the dominance, amongst the applicants, of interests connected with Sydney and Melbourne broadcasting and newspaper activities. The Board also noted the growing influence of newspaper interests in the Sydney and Melbourne licences.[367] Another influence was the existence of plans for network operations between the television licensees. Whilst acknowledging that networks could bring benefits for programme production, the Board was worried that network arrangements might undermine the independence of individual stations, and amount to indirect control by persons who were not the licensees.[368] The Board declined to recommend to the Minister that any of the applicants should be awarded the licence, concluding instead that new applications should be called for.[369] It recommended that only one licence should be granted in each of Brisbane and Adelaide, and that applications should be sought from interests independent of

---

[362] The Board, *Report and Recommendations to the Postmaster-General pursuant to the Television Act 1953 and the Television Regulations on Applications for Commercial Television Licences for the Sydney and Melbourne areas*, Parl Paper No 37 (1959), paras 33 and 34–41. The Board conducted its inquiry and completed its report in 1955.

[363] *Ibid*, para 42.

[364] *Ibid.*

[365] *Ibid*, although the Board did suggest that this principle should be kept in mind if its recommendations that there should be a reduction of foreign shareholdings were accepted, and there was to be a disposal of shares.

[366] Armstrong, above n 19, para 312.

[367] The Board, *Report and Recommendations to the Postmaster-General on Applications for Commercial Television Licences for the Brisbane and Adelaide areas*, Parl Paper No 38 (1958), paras 89 and 124. The Board investigated the changes in shareholdings in the Melbourne and Sydney licences: paras 85–87.

[368] *Ibid*, para 102. It was also revealed that a number of the newspaper companies had made arrangements to divide up the Adelaide and Brisbane licences to try to keep Rupert Murdoch out of the market: Chadwick, above n 350, xxix. The Board also referred to the meeting to discuss this proposal: *ibid*, paras 94–98.

[369] The Board, *Report* (1958), above n 367, para 136. In part, the reluctance of the Board to make a recommendation was because of the lack of certainty whether one or two licences were to be granted. The Board considered that only one licence should be available in the smaller markets of Brisbane and Adelaide, and that a fresh call for applications should be made on that basis. It was not convinced that competition necessarily provided a better service for viewers and cited the experience of the Sydney and Melbourne markets: para 112.

the current licensees.[370] The Board was concerned that the relationships between the applicants for the new licences and the Sydney and Melbourne licensees were such that the latter would be in a position to control the new licences, or that it was certainly their intention 'to exercise at least a very substantial influence in the establishment of the new stations'.[371] Another area of concern was the potential for increased influence of newspaper interests.[372]

As Armstrong noted, this decision was to occasion one of the greatest crises for the Board; the government rejected the recommendations, and required the Board to recommend licensees from the existing applicants, which it subsequently did.[373] In its supplementary Report, it again drew attention to the question of who would have control of these new licences, pointing out that a major newspaper company, The Herald and Weekly Times Ltd, which already controlled one of the Melbourne licences, would be a substantial shareholder in companies which would control a Brisbane and an Adelaide licence. This would mean that the company would be likely to be in a position to control indirectly three television licences across the country.[374] However, it did not feel that it could take the matter any further. Thus, from the outset, clear patterns of concentration were being tolerated, with existing broadcasting and press interests staking claim to new television licences throughout Australia. It is reasonable to assume that the lack of independence and separation of political interests from licensing powers probably exacerbated this situation. It was not until 1977 that licensing powers were handed over to the regulatory body, at which time the Board was replaced by a new regulatory body, the Australian Broadcasting Tribunal (ABT). This pattern of cross-interests tended to continue as new metropolitan licences were awarded. However, when regional licences began to be awarded through the 1960s, the government did concede the Board's recommendation that control of these licences should be independent of the metropolitan licensees.[375]

Identifying Policy

Whilst the UK and the US might not provide the best exemplars of considered and coherent policy, Australia lags well behind when it comes to articulation of the policy basis for ownership regulation. Indeed, apart from cursory acknowledgement of the public interest, there is virtually no attempt to identify what might be required to serve that public interest. References are made to the need to prevent undue concentration of control, but there is little attempt to explain why this is

---

[370] The Board, *Report* (1958), above n 367, para 140.

[371] *Ibid*, para 130.

[372] *Ibid*, para 131.

[373] Armstrong, above n 19, para 312.

[374] Australian Broadcasting Control Board, *Supplementary Report and Recommendations to the Postmaster-General on Applications for Commercial Television Licences for the Brisbane and Adelaide areas*, Parl Paper No 39 (1958), para 9.

[375] Watterson, above n 344, 121. For an extensive account of the ownership and control history, see Watterson. The government's position was contrary to the Royal Commission's view that common control of metropolitan and rural stations could assist the development of television in rural areas.

might be important. A government departmental unit, the Forward Development Unit, which carried out a study, in 1986, of ownership regulation, examined this policy deficit in some detail, and it is worth quoting from its concluding comments at length:

> Although ownership and control issues have been high on the political agenda of a variety of Governments, there is no single statement setting out the principles which should underlie the system and no comprehensive explanation of what is intended. No single party has created the scheme which now exists and the incremental approach adopted has ensured that it is marked by inconsistency rather than purpose.
>
> Ministers introducing legislation related to the subject have typically directed their statements only to particular aspects. When principles have been addressed, they have been couched in such broad, often ambiguous language that they are difficult to reconcile with the actual effect of the legislation.
>
> And although they appear to be of major political significance, there has never been a complete review of ownership and control rules, let alone of regulatory policy as a whole. Major amendments have been made (in 1960, 1965 and 1981) but on none of these occasions has the responsible Minister addressed guiding principles. Indeed it may well be misleading to refer to the existing legislation as a 'system'. It could more accurately be described as an accretion of measures: an enthusiast's collection, lovingly handed from one generation to the other, but lacking the scientific approach which distinguishes the professional from the amateur.[376]

In its report, the Forward Development Unit extracted from the regulatory history what it identified as 'key principles': avoidance of undue concentration; promotion of local and independent ownership; limitation of foreign control; preservation of licensing decisions; and encouragement of a diverse shareholding in licensee companies.[377] However, it is apparent from the Unit's discussion that these key principles were not necessarily consistently maintained or endorsed.[378] One of the few discussions of ownership and control policy came in the course of the Brisbane/Adelaide licensing decision (discussed in the previous section). The Board identified local ownership and the need to avoid concentration of ownership as the two key objectives, and referred to the 'great public importance' of a commercial television licence.[379] It included in its discussion reference to regulatory policy in the UK, the US, and Canada, but here too the discussion of the implications of its review were limited. Nevertheless, it certainly tried to shape its licensing decision in the light of its policy conclusions, although the government certainly did not endorse the Board's approach or conclusions.

None the less, there were issues present which called for a systematic policy basis: the press sector was heavily involved from an early stage in both radio and television; there were concerns about radio concentration, which also formed a backdrop to the plans for introducing television; and the first commercial

---

[376] Department of Communications, *Ownership and Control of Commercial Television: Future Policy Directions* (Canberra, AGPS, 1986), vol 1, paras 4.45–4.47.

[377] *Ibid*, para 4.4.

[378] *Ibid*, paras 4.5–4.44.

[379] The Board, *Report* (1958), above n 367, para 115.

Structural Regulation

television licensees showed themselves keen to establish their dominance as new television licences became available. There was a willingness to make some regulatory provision for ownership, but it was evident that there was a reluctance to explore the basis for that regulation. This failure to explore the policy basis, no doubt, also inhibited opportunities for a consideration of appropriate regulation. It was apparent also that, right from the beginning of Australian broadcasting history, governments experienced, or were likely to experience, pressure from industry interests whenever the issue of media regulation was in the spotlight. This, no doubt, contributed to the lack of government will for a full-blown examination or debate on pluralism policy and regulation but, likewise, the lack of clear policy development is likely to have made governments more vulnerable to pressure. The situation was probably not helped by the absence of an independent regulatory authority with real decision-making power—although, even when such regulatory authorities were in place, government seemed to be uneasy with the idea that they might actually exercise their regulatory independence and powers.

Ownership and Control Regulation and its Evolution

Remarkably, with one exception for a relaxation of limits for television, there were no changes to the limits or structure of the rules until 1987, but this did not mean that the regulatory scheme was devoid of commercial and statutory upheaval.[380] Two areas show the ongoing sensitivity of the ownership regime: the determination of control; and the supervision of transfers of interests in licences. The early legislative provisions dealing with radio ownership and control referred to ownership of a licence and to a 'person being in a position to exercise control, either directly or indirectly'.[381] However, there was no legislative guidance. The statute in adopting the phrase 'position to exercise control' had introduced a new concept, because the earlier statutory regulations had referred only to ownership, so it is curious that the legislation gave no guidance. The same concepts of ownership and 'position to exercise control' were continued through when the legislation was amended to introduce commercial television, but still without any legislative guidance. The Board, during its inquiry into the allocation of the Brisbane and Adelaide commercial television licences, examined the concept of control, and took the view that the intention was that a wide view of control, including de facto control, should be adopted.[382] Legislative amendments in 1960 clarified the position (although the provisions covered television only): control included both practical and legal control:

---

[380] In 1965, the limits for television were relaxed to no more than two licences within a capital city and no more than three across Australia: Broadcasting and Television Act 1942-1965, s 92(1).
[381] Australian Broadcasting Act 1942, s 53.
[382] The Board, *Report* (1958), above n 367, paras 124–27.

[T]he Government is desirous that there should be no frustration of that policy by sheltering behind a legal concept whilst in truth and in commercial reality the policy is being defeated.[383]

Control could arise through a wide variety of mechanisms, including arrangements and understandings, whether or not having legal and equitable force, and there was a recognition also that a person could be in a position to exercise control because they were able to exercise control over the operations of the licence, the management of the station, or the selection or provision of programmes to be broadcast.[384] However, to provide certainty, a concept of 'deemed control' was also introduced, whereby the ability to exercise control of 15 per cent of voting power would constitute control of a company.[385] This is an approach which has continued through to the current ownership rules. The new provisions would have placed some licensees in breach of the new ownership rules, but for the 'grandfathering' of existing arrangements. The provisions were of limited effect, and further amendments were introduced over a number of years to strengthen the regime. The result was a complex set of provisions, described by Armstrong as 'formidable and sometimes tortuous'[386], designed to capture direct and indirect control, shareholding and practical control, and avoidance mechanisms. Yet, despite the attempts from 1960 to clarify and tighten the concept of control, circumvention of the regime certainly occurred through a variety of legal techniques.[387]

Changes in control of licences were also significant, because they could be used as a means to circumvent licensing decisions which may have been made to promote policy objectives such as the need for local ownership and independent control.[388] The Broadcasting and Television Act 1942–1956 required the Minister to approve transfers of licences, and substantial changes in the beneficial ownership of shares in the licensee company.[389] Control over transfers was already part of the regulatory regime for radio, and the Royal Commission recommended that it should be extended to television, in order to prevent what was referred to in the Commission's report as ' undesirable trafficking in licences'.[390] Prior to 1960, the

---

[383] House of Representatives, 12 May 1960, vol 27 (1960 Session), 1705.

[384] Broadcasting and Television Act 1942–1960, s 92A(b).

[385] *Ibid*, s 92B.

[386] Armstrong, above n 19, para 1001.

[387] A Brown, *Commercial Media in Australia: Economics, Ownership, Technology, and Regulation* (St Lucia, Queensland University Press, 1986), 118. See also Watterson, above n 344, 124, and Armstrong, above n 19, para 313. From 1965, the legislation used the concept, at least in relation to television, of a 'prescribed interest', which was a general term to cover all the ways in which ownership or control might arise. Thus, a prescribed interest included, eg, a person who was the holder of a licence, a person who was in a position to exercise control of a licence, and a person who held shareholding interests in excess of 5%: Broadcasting and Television Act 1942–1965, s 91(2). Parallel provisions for radio regarding control and changes in control were introduced in 1969: Broadcasting and Television (No 2) Act 1969.

[388] Armstrong, above n 344, 3.

[389] Transfers of licences (radio and television) were dealt with by s 88; changes in beneficial ownership by s 90 (radio) and s 92C (television).

[390] Royal Commission on Television, above n 357, para 367.

Minister had a broad discretion to approve or refuse changes in control, but amendments in 1960 substantially qualified the Minister's powers, at least in relation to television: refusal could only be to ensure that there would be no breach of the ownership rules or breach of a licence condition.[391] This amendment applied only to approval of changes in shareholdings, not to transfers of licences. A good example of this type of circumvention can be seen in the fate of one of the Brisbane television licences. The licence had been allocated in the early 1960s to a local company, which was independent of companies holding licences in other cities. One of the unsuccessful applicants was part of a group of companies (the Ansett group) which controlled one of the Melbourne television licences. The Board had rejected its application because of this link, and because it appeared that much of the programming for these two stations would be combined.[392] Shortly after notification of the licence award, the company was listed on the stock exchange and, almost immediately, the Ansett Group acquired control through exchange trading, so that by the time the licence was formally granted it was in the hands of the Ansett Group. However, the Minister had no power to refuse the transfer because it was in compliance with the specific ownership regime.[393]

Following the outcry over this licence, the 1965 amendments reintroduced a broad discretion in relation to changes in control: approval could be refused if the change would not be in the public interest.[394] In effect, this meant that the prescribed ownership limits acted as maximum limits only; it would be within the power of the Minister to refuse a change in control which complied with these limits. This discretionary power thus gave flexibility to the regime and enabled the Minister to take into account other matters; this could be significant when it is remembered that at this stage there were no cross-media controls. However, the discretionary power, whilst in the hands of the Minister, was never used to refuse a transfer or change in control for either radio or television.[395] Of course, a separate issue was the appropriateness of placing this discretionary power in ministerial hands, with the inevitable risk of decisions being politically influenced. As one commentator, who has characterised Australia's media history as a series of 'pacts between politicians and proprietors', has noted: 'Australia's media owners could not have been so successful in concentrating their control and excluding competition without the connivance of politicians.'[396] Indeed, it was not until the late 1970s that these ministerial powers were removed. When the Australian Broadcasting Tribunal (ABT) was set up to replace the Board, the powers formerly exercised by the Minister were transferred to the ABT. A government inquiry had been established to inquire into Australian broadcasting and the role of the Board, and it recommended the establishment of a new tribunal, and the importance of

---

[391] Broadcasting and Television Act 1942–1960, s 92F.
[392] Watterson, above n 344, 128.
[393] *Ibid*, 129–30.
[394] Broadcasting and Television Act 1942–1965, s 92F(4).
[395] Brown, above n 387, 128.
[396] Chadwick, above n 350, xix.

the tribunal being independent of the Minister and 'aloof both from the broadcasting industry and the day-to-day processes of government'.[397] The ABT initially showed itself willing to exercise its discretionary powers, although its approach seemed to be somewhat quixotic. In 1979, the ABT refused, for the first time, a transfer of a licence of a radio station, 2HD. The acquisition would have meant that the group controlling Radio 2HD would have been in a position to control another commercial radio station in the area, as well as the only television station in that area. The acquisition did not breach the ownership limits, but the ABT considered that it was not in the public interest to have three of the four commercial broadcasting outlets in the area under common control. The ABT's concerns were not allayed by assurances from the applicants that the stations would be run independently.[398] The High Court affirmed that the ABT's discretion was not constrained by the presence in the legislation of specific ownership limits:

[The specific limits regime] . . . suggests that the purpose [of that regime] is to do no more than fix a maximum ceiling on the aggregation of prescribed interests in various licences that a person may have, leaving the Tribunal free to decide in the exercise of its discretion whether it is in the public interest that a licence should be transferred to a company which is so structured that there is a possibility that all, or a substantial proportion, of the television and broadcasting licences in the one city may be controlled or influenced by the same interests.[399]

However, shortly after the 2HD decision, but before the High Court had given judgment, the ABT appeared to falter when faced with another request for approval for a change in control. This transaction concerned the acquisition by News Limited of a controlling interest in a Sydney television licence, Station TEN-10. If the transaction proceeded, the only independently owned Sydney television station would have joined the News Limited group, which had extensive newspaper interests both in Sydney and across Australia.[400] Consenting to the transaction, the ABT seemed reluctant to take this matter into account: it considered that because it did not have a power to make general policy about media ownership concentration, it did not have the power to decide this in a specific case. It also seemed to be influenced by the fact that the other television stations, which were all controlled by newspaper or publishing groups, would be able to retain their cross-interests.[401] It was not entirely clear whether the ABT now had doubts generally about the scope of its discretionary power, or whether the doubt was the scope of its power when the other media interests in question were newspapers. The nature of its discretionary power fell for consideration again in 1980 when the Tribunal was called upon to approve another News Limited acquisition, this time a Melbourne television station, ATV-10. News Limited held, of course, the Sydney

[397] Postal and Telecommunications Department, *Australian Broadcasting: A Report on the Structure of the Australian Broadcasting System and Associated Matters*, Parl Paper No 358 (1976), para 224.
[398] *Re Australian Broadcasting Tribunal and Others; Ex parte 2HD Pty Ltd* (1980) 27 ALR 321, 324.
[399] *Ibid*, 328.
[400] Watterson, above n 344, 135.
[401] ABT, *Commercial Television Station TEN-10, Inquiry into Proposed Acquisition of Stock Units by News Limited* (July 1979, No 27/79 O(T)), paras 5.21–5.28.

station, TEN-10, as well as extensive newspaper interests. The ABT was also concerned about the influence common ownership of the Melbourne and Sydney stations would have on the smaller stations, Brisbane and Adelaide, which also formed part of the Ten network arrangements.[402] This time the Tribunal was willing to act more decisively. Although it noted with concern 'the extent of influence by the "Murdoch Press"',[403] its refusal to consent was based on the likely effect of common control of the Sydney and Melbourne stations on the Ten Network.[404] The Tribunal's decision was overturned on appeal. The Administrative Appeals Tribunal was of the view that common ownership of television stations was not only inevitable but beneficial, and it decided that the common ownership of the Sydney and Melbourne stations was in the public interest.[405] The Administrative Tribunal affirmed that consideration of all cross-media interests of an applicant was a relevant public interest matter.[406]

The ABT's willingness, although not without hesitancy, to exercise its discretionary power showed how it could deal with the potential limitations of a rigid set of ownership rules, which might not be able to cater for every inappropriate control situation which would arise. In the ATV-10 case, it was able to take into account the effect this control situation might have on programming decisions. At the same time, however, the presence of such discretion gives rise to uncertainty, something which might be minimised if only pre-emptive rules applied. The willingness of the Tribunal, bolstered by the High Court's decision in the 2HD case, to interpret its discretionary power broadly was to prove short-lived. It might be reasonable to attribute the Tribunal's formerly conservative approach to a lack of confidence in its authority and independence and, if this is correct, confirmation may be seen in the fact that in 1981, the government, displeased with the ABT's decision, acted to reduce significantly the scope of its powers. Consideration of whether to refuse changes in control and transfers in licences were no longer to be decided on a broad public interest ground; the ABT was now confined to an exhaustive list of matters such as fitness and propriety, and the financial, technical, and management capability of the applicant. Only in relation to non-metropolitan licences could undue concentration of influence be taken into account.[407] Armstrong suggests that one of the factors influencing the government was concern that the ABT's decision would prevent News Limited and the Publishing and Broadcasting Group (the Murdoch and Packer interests, respectively) from expanding;[408] the amendments were referred to as the 'Murdoch

---

[402] Brown, above n 387, 129.

[403] ABT, *ATV-10 Melbourne/Control Investments Pty Ltd Share Transaction Inquiry: Decision and Reasons for Decision* (September 1980), para 49.

[404] *Ibid.*

[405] *Re Control Investments Pty Ltd and ABT (No 3)* (1981) 4 ALD 1 at 60

[406] *Ibid,* 56.

[407] Broadcasting and Television Act 1942–1981, ss 89A and 90JA.

[408] Armstrong, above n 19, para 324. It also transpired that the then Prime Minister had passed drafts of the legislation to directors of News and Publishing and Broadcasting before anyone else in the broadcasting industry had seen them: *ibid.*

amendments'.[409] As Brown noted, the establishment of the Tribunal had been an attempt to move broadcasting regulation away from the political process, but the broad powers given to the ABT 'were severely restricted as soon as the tribunal demonstrated that it was prepared to exercise them'.[410] The 1981 amendments might be seen as a crude response by a government dissatisfied by independent regulatory decision-making, but they do no more than illuminate what has been a constant theme of Australian media policy and regulation: namely, the considerable influence exerted by certain media interests on successive governments, and the willingness of those governments to respond. It is a theme which continues to resonate right up to the present day.

It was not until 1987 that substantive reform of the ownership regime occurred. This reform had two main elements: first, a change in the way influence was measured, and, secondly, the introduction of cross-media regulation. The lead-up to these reforms displayed the characteristically blunt approach to Australian media policy-making with its mix of political and media baron influence, provoking one senator to ask of the then Prime Minister, Hawke, '[w]hy don't you tell us precisely how you want us to help your mates?', to which the Prime Minister responded, 'they're the only mates we've got'.[411] Information about the proposed announcements was available well before the actual legislation was introduced, leading to major upheaval in the broadcasting and newspaper industries, and resulting in some media owners being in breach of the existing ownership limits.[412] There were several factors contributing to the desire to change the rules. One was the government's inclination to lessen the dominance of television interests, but without 'any direct attacks on the interests of the major media proprietors'.[413] Another factor was the inappropriateness of numerical limits, which made no allowance for the differences in audience size. The Minister for Communications was interested in adopting a measure which limited control to a certain audience reach, whilst removing any station limits.[414] There was a considerable battle between the Minister and the Prime Minister as to what should be the appropriate percentage; the former wanted a figure of around 43 per cent; the latter wanted 35 per cent, which would ensure the continuing dominance of the (grandfathered) Packer and Murdoch interests, and prevent other groups from expanding.[415] In fact, it was the stalemate

[409] Chadwick, above n 350, xxxix.

[410] Brown, above n 387, 131.

[411] The mates being Packer and Murdoch: Chadwick, above n 350, 16. Referred to also in R Tiffen, 'The Revolution in Australian Media Ownership 1986–87' (Working Paper No 36, Sir Robert Menzies Centre for Australian Studies, Institute of Commonwealth Studies, University of London, 1988), 3.

[412] Tiffen, above n 411, 1, and generally, and Chadwick, above n 350, 191–92. Those in breach of the legislation were relying on the fact that changes to the legislation might be effected before the six-month period of grace to divest excess interests expired: Chadwick, above n 350, 191. See also Bureau of Transport and Communications Economics, *Australian Commercial Television 1986–1995*, report no 93 (AGPS, Canberra, 1996), 39.

[413] Tiffen, above n 411, 2.

[414] *Ibid*, 3.

[415] *Ibid*, and Chadwick, above n 350, 13–18. The 43% limit would prevent Packer and Murdoch expanding, but would allow others to expand.

between these two which led to the introduction of cross-media regulation, as a result of a compromise suggested by the then Treasurer, Paul Keating.[416]

The upshot of the negotiations was a proposal that a person could not hold a prescribed interest in television interests which, combined, had a reach of more than 75 per cent (changed later to 60 per cent in order to win necessary parliamentary support) of the Australian population, and there was to be a ban on cross-control of television, radio, and newspaper interests within the same area.[417] The effect of these changes, although controlling cross-interests, would be to increase concentration within the television industry. The changes would benefit Packer and Murdoch at the expense of other media proprietors, particularly Fairfax and the Herald and Weekly Times (HWT).[418] Shortly after the changes, News Limited launched a successful takeover of HWT.[419] The reforms appeared to be almost entirely politically driven; there had been no public process to consider reform of the media ownership rules and, yet, both Packer and Murdoch appeared to be well informed about the progress of the reforms.[420] Although a study of ownership and control rules had been undertaken by a government departmental unit, the report of this study seemed to epitomise the peculiarities of Australian broadcasting policy and law-making.[421] The report highlighted the policy deficit in relation to ownership and control regulation, and asserted the need for a clear statement of objectives to inform the regulation.[422] Yet, although the unit undertaking the study did not consider it appropriate for the unit to suggest such objectives, it nevertheless went on to suggest rule changes.[423] The 1987 reforms resulted, in relation to television, in a reduction in the number of owners and an increase in concentration; in radio, there was an increase in the number of owners, but an increase also in concentration with the largest owners accounting for a greater percentage of revenue. Both radio and television experienced a reduction in the number of cross-media interests held.[424]

Current Rules

Although the BSA (Aus) constituted a major redesign of the regulatory framework, the ownership rules were not significantly changed: the population reach

[416] Tiffen, above n 411, 3, and Chadwick, above n 350, 18–20.
[417] Broadcasting (Ownership and Control) Act 1987. Radio was not affected by the population reach measure; it was subject to the traditional approach of national and local limits on the number of licences controlled.
[418] Tiffen, above n 411, 4. In fact, Keating had used the argument that Fairfax and HWT were Labor's enemies as part of his argument to convince his political colleagues to accept the arrangements: Chadwick, above n 350, 22. Keating considered that newspaper had greater political influence than television: *ibid*, 19.
[419] T Barr, *Newmedia.com.au* (Sydney, Allen & Unwin, 2000), 15.
[420] Chadwick, above n 350, 19–20. Keating had visited Murdoch in New York.
[421] Department of Communications, *Report* (1986), above n 376.
[422] *Ibid*, paras 5.24–5.27.
[423] *Ibid*, para 5.25, and generally.
[424] Bureau of Transport and Communications Economics, Report No 71 (AGPS, Canberra, 1991), 75.

figure was relaxed from 60 per cent to 75 per cent, and the radio limits were relaxed, including the removal of national limits. A new approach to defining control was also introduced. This section sets out the current ownership and control rules, although there is pressure for change, in particular to relax or remove the cross-media rules—this is considered in Chapter Seven. For commercial television, a person must not be in a position to exercise control of:

— licences with a combined reach of more than 75 per cent of the Australian population;
— more than one licence in the same licence area.[425]

For commercial radio, a person must not be in a position to exercise control of more than two licences in the same licence area.[426] A person must not be in a position to exercise control of:

— a commercial television licence and a commercial radio licence having the same licence area; or
— a commercial television licence and a newspaper associated with the same licence area; or
— a commercial radio licence and a newspaper associated with the same licence area.[427]

It can be seen that the cross-media rules do not prevent cross-media interests altogether, they bite only on interests within the same market.

Schedule One to the Act sets out a guide to 'control' and to being 'in a position to exercise control'. Contrary to previous approaches, the BSA (Aus) does not set out to provide a comprehensive regime of what will constitute control: instead the Schedule is intended to be illustrative of ways in which control might arise. The intention is that the regulator will have the flexibility to take into account prevailing practices and structures.[428] This changed approach was intended to avoid loopholes, and to reduce incentives for developing avoidance mechanisms.[429] As expected, control can include practical and operational control as well as company interests. In the interests of providing some certainty, a company interest exceeding 15 per cent will be deemed to be control.[430] Determining whether someone is in a position to exercise control on the basis of practical or functional control can involve the consideration of a wide range of factors, as the following illustration shows. Alan Jones, who conducts a commercial radio talkback programme, is

---

[425] BSA (Aus), s 53. There are some exceptions to this in the case of particular regional markets. For both television and radio there are also restrictions on directorships of companies which may be in a position to control: ss 55 and 56, respectively.

[426] BSA (Aus), s 54.

[427] *Ibid*, s 60. Cross-media directorships are also regulated: s 61. Cross interests of commercial television broadcasting licences and datacasting licences are also prohibited: s 54A.

[428] Department of Transport and Communications, *A New Approach to Regulation: Broadcasting Reform* (29 January 1993) at 18.

[429] *Ibid*.

[430] BSA (Aus), sch 1, cl 6. Deemed control can be reached by tracing through company interests.

generally regarded as one of the most influential radio presenters in Australia. Whilst he was with Radio Station 2UE, it was revealed that he had regularly accepted undisclosed payments from commercial interests in return for providing favourable on-air comment and access. The disclosures about Jones, and other radio presenters across Australia, sparked a major investigation in 1999 by the ABA into what became known as the 'cash for comment' affair (discussed in Chapter Four). Sometime after the investigation, Jones moved to another station, Radio 2GB. The financial arrangements associated with this move resulted in him having a company interest in the company which controlled 2GB, Macquarie Radio Network Pty Ltd ('Macquarie'), but an investigation was also held into whether Jones' relationship with the radio station itself might have put him in a position to exercise control.[431] The ABA considered whether he was in a position to control a significant proportion of programmes or operations, or whether he was able to exercise direction or restraint over management. It was evident that because of Jones' rating power he would be able to exert some degree of influence at the station. In joining the radio station he was expected to have a role in motivating and leading the staff, and there was evidence that he made regular suggestions to the station manager about programming matters, such as the performance of other presenters and programme formats.[432] However, the ABA concluded that this did not amount to being in a position to exercise control. Despite his position of influence, the ABA accepted that the station manager retained his managerial discretion, and did not feel bound to follow Jones' suggestions.[433]

It will be seen that these pre-emptive ownership rules address only traditional free-to-air broadcasting services. No specific ownership restrictions apply to subscription broadcasting (apart from foreign ownership controls discussed earlier in this chapter). This has enabled a degree of cross-interests to develop so that the main subscription broadcasting service, Foxtel, is owned by News Corporation Limited and Publishing and Broadcasting Limited (each with 25 per cent) and Telstra (with 50 per cent), the former two companies have substantial interests in newspapers and free-to-air broadcasting respectively.[434]

Conclusion: Structural Regulation as a Tool to Promote Broadcasting Pluralism

This chapter has focused mainly on two types of structural regulation: the structuring of the market through the creation of different sectors (usually referred to

---

[431] ABA, *Report of the Investigation into Matters Relating to the Control of the 2GB and 2CH Licences* (May 2003). If Jones had been in a position to exercise control, then there would have been a breach of the BSA (Aus) because of a failure to notify the interest.

[432] *Ibid*, 22.

[433] *Ibid*, 36–39.

[434] For a detailed analysis of Australia's media industry ownership patterns, see CLC, above n 116.

in the text as 'sectoral pluralism'), and the use of rules constraining ownership and control within the media industry. In each of the three jurisdictions, pluralism has been sought through sectoral design, but sectoral pluralism will be effective only if the sectors, intended to be a counter-balance to the commercial sector, are sufficiently resourced. It is true that some diversity in the market can be created, but the impact may be relatively minimal, as can be seen with the example of US public broadcasting. In Australia, the non-commercial sectors, public and community, struggle, because their funding is limited. In fact, it has been argued that structural diversity measures in Australia, particularly the presence of community broadcasting, have actually reduced competition between broadcasters, because spectrum has been occupied broadcasting to very small audiences.[435] Although this concern presumably recedes as the limitations of spectrum also recede, it points to the dilemma that sectoral approaches will probably only be truly effective in promoting pluralism if there is a willingness to commit sufficient public funds. It is only in the UK, with its long-standing commitment to funding public broadcasting, that one can observe a broadcasting environment where structurally different sectors are able to match one another in reach and influence. However, as noted earlier in the chapter, public broadcasting and governments frequently enjoy an uneasy relationship. Given the scope that a public broadcaster, freed from reliance upon advertising revenue, may have for more rigorous programming, it is perhaps not surprising that governments have often reluctantly promoted strong non-commercial sectors. There may be an acknowledgement of the need to promote sectoral diversity, but it may be more expedient to pursue that diversity through establishment of relatively small-scale broadcasting sectors. Even the BBC regularly finds itself under pressure and, at least veiled, threat: this is why the regulatory arrangements for the non-commercial broadcasting sectors will also be crucial.

Although structuring the market through different sectors is accepted as a pluralism mechanism, this cannot be taken as an assurance that public broadcasting will continue to exist. With the demise of spectrum scarcity, and the growth of the subscription broadcasting market, the necessity for public broadcasting is being called into question. Even the UK, with its strong tradition of public broadcasting, effectively requires the case to be made again at each charter renewal process. If the market can provide, what is the place for public broadcasting? Of course, this assumes that the market can provide adequately, and, as discussed in Chapter Six, that is not guaranteed, even in a multi-channelled environment. Once again, it is important to be able to make a strong and positive case, rather than one which sees the role of public broadcasting as simply filling market gaps. If the public sphere is to function adequately, then it is important that as much diversity can be introduced into the market as possible—diversity in structure, in funding, and in programming. One facet of that diversity can be provided by a broadcasting sector which does not have to be driven from a commercial, shareholder-return perspective. The merits of

---

[435] Productivity Commission, above n 2, 267.

having a public broadcasting sector are as strong now as they were during the period when only a few broadcasters were operating in the market, and there were no mechanisms for audience-pays. Indeed, as will be seen in Chapter Six, the risk that the commercial sector will under-provide certain types of programming may actually be growing, as competition for advertising revenue increases. Far from becoming superfluous, the public broadcaster may actually become more necessary than ever. However, in a political and regulatory climate, which no longer sets a high priority on publicly provided services, and without a clear normative case for regulation of broadcasting, ensuring a strong public broadcasting sector may be a low priority. Whilst governments may be reluctant to strike the death knell of public broadcasting, they may be content to allow the sector to limp along without adequate funding. A public broadcaster which has limited funding but which is constantly accountable for its performance is unlikely to be able to fulfil its true place in the public sphere. Hence, sectoral regulation as a pluralism tool must pay close attention to the structure and funding of the sector and its participants.

Notwithstanding the sensitivities of sectoral pluralism, as sensitive, if not more so, has been the regulation of ownership and control of media. Yet, as a broadcasting pluralism measure, it is the one for which most commonality can be found amongst the three jurisdictions, and despite reform moves, and pressure for relaxation, each jurisdiction seems set to retain some element of ownership and control regulation. Indeed, media ownership regulation might be seen as the lynchpin of pluralism and diversity regulatory measures. But, as a regulatory tool, it is problematic for a number of reasons. The chief reason relates to the policy objective that ownership and control regulation is expected to serve. If diversity of information and opinion is a key objective, then regulation of ownership is viewed as a key factor in attaining that diversity. This comes through strongly in FCC policy discussions, as can be seen in the following:

> The diversity of viewpoints, by promoting an informed citizenry, is essential to a well-functioning democracy. The principal means by which the Commission has fostered diversity of viewpoints is through the imposition of ownership restrictions. In *Sinclair*, the Court of Appeals noted that ownership limits encourage diversity in the ownership of broadcast stations, which can in turn encourage a diversity of viewpoints in the material presented over the airwaves.[436]

However, this rationale rests on an important assumption, namely that there is a connection between ownership and voice—in other words, identity of ownership will be predictive of content.[437] Apart from general ownership and control regulatory policy, this assumption has had a strong influence on other ownership-related policies and regulation, such as foreign ownership and, in the US, minority ownership. Indeed, such policies often expose the problematic nature of making

---

[436] FCC, *Notice of Proposed Rule Making, In the Matter of 2002 Biennial Regulatory Review*, 17 FCC Rcd 18503 (2002), para 35.
[437] Price and Weinberg, above n 225, 266.

this connection between ownership and voice, and minority ownership policies, discussed earlier in this chapter, provide a good example of this.

Several factors render the link between ownership and voice tenuous. First, the commercial context within which broadcasters will operate and, particularly, the means of financing broadcasting are likely to act as a constraint and strong influence upon the selection of content. Secondly, even if there is a link between owner and content, it is by no means guaranteed that this will produce diversity of viewpoint. In view of the business and commercial context within which those in a position to control a broadcasting outlet will operate, it is more than likely that these persons will share certain political and social values. Thirdly, as Gibbons suggests, it may not always be clear where power resides in the operation of a media enterprise, which may be part of a large publicly owned corporate group[438] although, regardless of the size of the media enterprise, the media sector seems still to throw up examples of corporate groups which are strongly associated with individuals who seem keen to have their 'voice'—Rupert Murdoch, a figure of significance in each of the jurisdictions, is the obvious example. Finally, other regulatory measures might limit the scope of the owner-voice. This can be seen particularly in the UK where 'no-editorialising' rules apply. Nevertheless, there is an instinctive apprehension about monopoly control of media, regardless of how strong or weak the connection between ownership and voice is, and this probably explains why each of the jurisdictions, even where the preference is for market solutions, have been loathe to remove such rules completely. As Baker puts it: '[t]he key goal, the key value, served by ownership dispersal is that it directly embodies a fairer, more democratic allocation of communicative power'.[439] It is not possible to establish with certainty the impact separately controlled broadcasting outlets will have on content and views aired, compared with monopoly provision, but this has not been a reason to abandon such regulation, instead it calls for an intuitive and cautious response, to favour regulation over no-regulation.[440] Even if the owner–voice link is tenuous, it should not be discarded entirely. Whilst there may not be a conscious projection of a voice, the absence of a diversity of owners in the market may constrain voice. For example, if the resources and outlets are under monopoly control, then there may be much less scope for different voices and ideas to be heard, even within an outlet, simply because there may be less incentive to explore other perspectives. Monopoly control is likely also to have a chilling effect on journalistic and editorial voices, because they will have few alternative employment opportunities. A diversity of outlets, even those all firmly placed within the commercial context, simply because they will utilise a different blend of resources and media professionals, will have the potential to throw up at least different shades of a voice. More mundanely, the drive to achieve economies of scale or scope may lead to homogenised content. Therefore, it should not be necessary

---

[438] Gibbons, above n 6, 205–6.

[439] CE Baker, 'Media Structure, Ownership Policy, and the First Amendment' (2005) 78 *Southern California Law Review* 733 at 735.

[440] Gibbons, above n 6, 206.

to be too apologetic or cautious about a process which seeks to regulate the allocation of ownership of broadcasting. The integrity of the public sphere, given its role in the democratic process, means that there must be assurances that broadcasting will be open and independent. As Baker implies, control of broadcasting should embody the democratic principles of the community it serves. However, the tenuous link between ownership and voice does highlight the risk of relying simply on structural regulation as a means of promoting broadcasting pluralism. Other measures, such as those discussed in Chapter Four, may also be necessary to ensure diversity.

Structural regulation is also problematic because it is complex and difficult to design in a way which can ensure that it will serve its objectives. This can create difficulties for regulator and regulated alike. Although the US has been fairly consistent in its approach, the UK and, to a limited extent, Australia, have varied between a rule-based approach and the use of discretionary powers, or a mix of both. The risk of a rule-based approach is that it will not be able to cover every situation which can arise, or that the drafting will create opportunities for evasive approaches and exploitation of loopholes. Certainly, examples can be found in the experience of the jurisdictions discussed in this chapter. Definitions of what constitutes 'ownership' or 'control' can be especially difficult in this regard, and each of the jurisdictions has adopted control tests which incorporate concepts such as practical or operational control, as well as control which might arise through more orthodox means, such as the possession of company interests. However, these more inclusive approaches come at the expense of certainty and clarity, and their effectiveness will also depend upon the presence of a regulatory authority which is willing to be pro-active and rigorous. The use of discretionary-based approaches in regulating ownership and control has been especially relevant to the UK experience. Having moved away from discretionary tests to a more rigid rule-based approach, the UK's more recent experience has been a combination of rules and discretion—the latter in the form of 'public interest' tests. The advantage of regulating through discretion will be evident: it can provide flexibility to address new situations, and enable the inclusion of transactions which might otherwise be outside a set of closed rules. However, the risk of such an approach is that it can create uncertainty—a criticism made by both the ITC and the RA of the UK experience—and, once again, it will depend upon an effective and independent regulatory authority. Still, it should be remembered that the UK's experiment with a rule-based approach in the 1990s brought dissatisfaction also, and led to changes which saw a combination of rules and discretion. None the less, the effectiveness of the regulatory authority is a particularly important factor in the context of discretionary tests, because, unlike pre-emptive rules which apply universally and impersonally, the exercise of discretionary judgement can be more contentious, and, therefore, the process must be such that there can be confidence that any decisions are made independently and without any undue pressure or bias.

Another problematic aspect in designing effective structural regulation will be the media covered by the regulation. In each of the three jurisdictions, regulation of ownership and control developed at a time when broadcasting was delivered only free-to-air, via over-the-air transmission. Despite the development of other broadcasting platforms, the practice has generally been to continue to confine regulation of ownership to the traditional broadcasters. This has often caused controversy, particularly in the area of cross-media ownership, when non-free-to-air broadcasters have been able to expand, whilst traditional broadcasters were constrained. The UK, and the experience of BSkyB, provides a very clear example of this frustration. Yet governments have generally been reluctant to expand the scope of ownership regulation. This reluctance probably stems from the sensitivity they feel about ownership regulation, and pressure felt from the media industry, which tends to find ownership regulation a particularly irksome regulatory imposition. The instincts are to relax, not to tighten or increase the scope of such rules. But it also points to another dilemma: rules governing ownership and control are cumbersome, and, given their highly interventionist nature, they appear somewhat out of place in the current media environment. As a regulatory measure, rules about ownership and control appear to have a continuing role, but their selective coverage exacerbates the impression that the rules do not operate effectively, and are no longer relevant. None of the structural regulation reforms or proposed reforms takes on board this issue, although it is used to justify reform of existing rules.

Another design difficulty is how to define the limits. Different examples can be found in the accounts given in this chapter. Initially, the most common approach was to use a simple model based on maximum numbers of licences which could be held, but as each of the jurisdictions has learnt, this is a crude approach, which does not take account of the size of markets, or licence areas. This has led to other approaches, either to replace or supplement the numerical limit model, and one of the most common is to determine maximum limits based on audience or market share. However, regardless of the actual model chosen, the difficulty is still where to set the level. This too points to the sensitivity of this regulation. What the rules are trying to do is to prevent harm, or the possibility of harm, but it is not a harm which can be easily measured. Diversity is not easily measurable; it is not like a chemical, about which it can be determined, with reasonable certainty, what level of exposure will be harmful. It will not be possible to conclude with respect to a certain degree of concentration what the impact on the diversity of voice and ideas will be. Regulation of ownership and control will of necessity be prophylactic regulation. The choice then of the permissible limits will lack clear objectivity and certainty. For each of the jurisdictions, the choice has tended to be largely arbitrary, and very often the levels have been determined to accommodate or appease existing media interests. A difference can be discerned in the US approach, where the FCC rule-making reports are usually replete with economic data and anti-trust or competition analysis, presented as evidence of the degree of diversity to be found in the market. However, it is not always clear that this makes the outcome any less arbitrary, and the approach ignores the fact that one of the reasons media is subject to ownership and control rules, rather than competition law, is because competition analysis is more concerned with economic markets, than with public interest concerns about idea or voice diversity. Nevertheless, as will be seen in Chapter Seven, this type of analysis has a strong influence on US media ownership policy.

Structural regulation has been common to each of the jurisdictions considered in this chapter. Sectoral approaches have had less emphasis in the US, but it has been a pluralism approach which the US has had in common with the other two jurisdictions. There appears to be an ongoing commitment in all three jurisdictions to sectoral pluralism, although that commitment is often reluctantly given, and it is likely that in all three jurisdictions, the public broadcasters, particularly, will find that more is required in order to justify their continued place in the broadcasting sector. As the accounts of the history and experiences of the three jurisdictions has shown, structural regulation, in the form of media ownership and control regulation, has been in place almost from the beginnings of broadcasting, but it has been a particularly sensitive area of regulation, and that sensitivity has often had an important influence in shaping the regulatory design, and in bringing about relaxations in the rules. Although, the three jurisdictions have varied in their management of ownership and control regulation, the contentious nature of the regulation has been a common factor, and this has often contributed to deficiencies in the regulatory design, and exacerbated the complexity of the instrument. Structural regulation in its ongoing form is clearly not ideal, but its history, in each of the jurisdictions, means that it would be unrealistic to expect this to change significantly. Nevertheless, structural regulation continues to have a role to play, but it should not be looked upon as a sufficient regulatory measure. Structural regulation will have a place as part of a collection of regulatory measures; in this way, these other measures can accommodate some of the weaknesses of structural regulation, and tackle changing media practices through more flexible regulatory instruments.

4

CONTENT REGULATION

Introduction

In Chapter Three a major component of broadcasting pluralism regulation was examined. Structural regulation aims to promote broadcasting pluralism by ensuring a certain number and range of voices in the market. However, as this chapter will show, none of the jurisdictions has been willing to rely upon structural regulation as the sole guarantee of broadcasting pluralism. Another important component has been content regulation. Even the US, with its customary First Amendment aversion to content-based regulation, has some relevant content-based measures, not that such regulation is necessarily at odds with First Amendment principles. As Sunstein argues:

> government efforts to promote a well-functioning democratic order should not be invalidated even if they involve content regulation, so long as there is no discrimination against any point of view. If government seeks to ensure a certain level of educational programming, or if it allows free air time for candidates, or if it provides a right of access for those who attempt to speak on political issues, it is not violating the free speech guarantee merely by virtue of the fact that it is intruding on the discretion of those who own stations. A conclusion to the contrary . . . would tear the First Amendment from its theoretical underpinnings.
>
> On this view of the First Amendment, there is no tension between constitutionalism and democracy, or between individual rights and majority rule, properly understood; robust rights of free expression are a precondition for both democracy and majority rule, properly understood. In this way, private autonomy is in no tension with, but is on the contrary inextricably intertwined with, the notion of popular sovereignty.[1]

Content regulation which is designed to serve broadcasting pluralism objectives will comprise regulatory measures which focus not on the structure of the external broadcasting environment but on what is offered by individual broadcasting services, or categories of service, with regard to programming generally, or the presentation of content in particular situations. Here the regulatory focus (sometimes referred to as 'imperative regulation')[2] is on setting down rules for the conduct of

---

[1] CR Sunstein, 'Television and the Public Interest' (2000) 88 *California Law Review* 499 at 524.
[2] See W Hoffmann-Riem, *Regulating Media: The Licensing and Supervision of Broadcasting in Six Countries* (New York, The Guilford Press, 1996), 281 and 282–83.

the broadcasting services in order to ensure a diversity of information and opinions. Surprisingly, diversity regulation has not been as controversial or politically sensitive as structural regulation, although it certainly does have the potential to be both, because it can be seen to intrude more directly on a broadcaster's freedom. Broadcasters have generally been more willing to accept diversity regulation than they have structural regulation, but tolerance for such regulation may diminish as the traditional justifications for broadcasting regulation are undermined. It is significant that Australia and, more recently, the UK have moved towards greater use of co-regulation or self-regulation for content matters.

Brief mention was made in Chapter One of the meaning of the diversity concept, but it is appropriate to reiterate that here. Referring to the concept of pluralism generally, Barendt refers to three ways in which pluralism can be understood.[3] In the first sense, the focus is on a multiplicity of speakers or channels. Whilst this may have an impact on diversity, it is a meaning which is understood more in the context of pluralism, or external pluralism, and hence relevant to structural regulation. The second meaning ascribed by Barendt is more directly relevant to the measures examined in this chapter. Here Barendt refers to a diversity of views and opinions. Barendt also writes of a third sense of pluralism, namely where there is a variety of different programme types or genres. Barendt suggests that the first meaning relates more to 'the interests of different *speakers*', whilst the second and third meanings 'are at least as much concerned with the interests of viewers' (and listeners).[4] This third meaning to which Barendt refers may not be strictly necessary. As was discussed in Chapter Two, media freedom and the right to access a diversity of views and ideas is not limited to information content, but will also include entertainment. Entertainment programmes can reflect and convey ideas and values, and even information. Promotion of the objective of a diversity of ideas and opinions may implicitly lead to or require presentation of a range of programming types. Nevertheless, diversity regulation will usually include requirements for a range of programming. Thus, the second and third meanings given by Barendt are relevant to the matters covered in this chapter. In contrast to pluralism, diversity regulation will focus on the content of what is broadcast, rather than who controls the means by which that content is broadcast.

As reviewed in Chapter Three, there are some concerns about the ability of structural regulation to provide adequately for the range of voices, or views and opinions, which proper participation in the democratic community might require. Hence, diversity regulation has been used as a way to compensate for any deficiencies or limitations in structural regulation. The demise of traditional broadcasting regulation justifications, such as spectrum scarcity, threatens to undermine the case for diversity regulation but, as was argued in Chapter Two, a positive case can be made by focusing on the need to recognise the instrumental

---

[3] E Barendt, 'Structural and Content Regulation of the Media: United Kingdom Law and Some American Comparisons' in EM Barendt (ed), *The Yearbook of Media and Entertainment Law 1997/98* (Oxford, Clarendon Press, 1997), 75 at 84–85.

[4] *Ibid*, 85.

role played by the media in the public sphere, and the necessity for media to be able to fulfil properly that role. This, it is suggested, requires a full range of regulatory measures to be considered. Hence, if structural regulation is to fulfil its role in the promotion of broadcasting pluralism, effective diversity regulation must also be present. The use of content regulation to these ends has been most fully realised in the UK broadcasting sector, both historically and, despite recent reform, currently. In fact, the UK, the US, and Australia provide some interesting comparisons in this area, because each represents a different point on the regulatory spectrum: the UK at one extreme, having the most fully developed content regulatory system, both generally, and specifically in relation to diversity goals, and the US at the other end of the spectrum, exhibiting, in general, an aversion to content regulation. Australia reflects something of the experience of both these jurisdictions, but it lacks the comprehensiveness of the UK system (and, especially, in recent times, an effective enforcement process) and, whilst exhibiting something like the US aversion to regulation of content, does not appear to do so from any clearly articulated position. Of course, whatever the formal regulatory position, broadcasters and journalists in all three jurisdictions will generally be cognisant of standards of professional and ethical conduct for the media, although there may be varying degrees of respect and adherence. Another regulatory feature which can be observed is the difference in treatment between radio and television. For a variety of reasons, it is usually television which is seen as the most pervasive or influential medium, and so content regulation has also tended to focus more on television. Similarly, there will usually be differences in the nature and degree of content regulation imposed on different types of services, such as free-to-air broadcasting and subscription services.

Content regulation can serve a number of different goals, so not all content-related regulation will be relevant to diversity.[5] Some rules are directly related to the promotion of diversity, but there will also be content rules, although not directly related, which will impact upon broadcasting pluralism. Thus, in relation to a diversity goal, one would expect to see rules which aim to ensure that a range of programmes catering to different interests and needs are available, as well as rules which require a range of views and opinions to be presented. Rules which aim to give access to some particular voices in the community, such as political parties, might also be seen as part of diversity regulation. However, another set of content rules can also serve broadcasting pluralism: this set might be identified as rules which address the quality or integrity of the information and opinions that are broadcast. In other words, it will be important that a viewer or listener can trust the information or opinion being broadcast. Thus, rules which require accurate and fair reporting could be seen as part of this regulatory set. Some jurisdictions may also prohibit the broadcasting service adopting an editorial line. Another important element in commercial broadcasting will be the relationship between broadcasters and advertising interests, and rules may also be imposed to ensure

---

[5] See Chapter One, 'Outline of Regulatory Approaches', p 10.

that content is not inappropriately influenced by its commercial context. In the next section, a brief review of each jurisdiction's approach to content regulation, relevant to this study, will be provided, before considering separately a range of regulatory measures which might be used to serve diversity, or more generally, broadcasting pluralism.

Jurisdictional Experience

United Kingdom

The UK approach to content regulation, which applies, in differing degrees, to each of the broadcasting sectors, has been influenced both by the presence of the public broadcaster, the BBC, and the concept of public service broadcasting. Many of the elements of the public service broadcasting concept have a direct relevance to broadcasting pluralism, and some of the current rules date back to the early days of the British Broadcasting Corporation (BBC). The idea of broadcasting as a public service was developed by the first Director-General of the BBC, Lord (as he was to become) Reith, and taken up in the first Royal Charter. One aspect of Reith's ideas was national coverage: 'broadcasting could and should serve everybody in the community who wished to "listen"'.[6] National coverage relates closely to that aspect of media freedom which recognises the rights of viewers and listeners to be able to receive programming, and ideas and opinions. Reith believed that national coverage meant that the greatest number of homes should be reached, a radical idea at the time.[7] As can be seen from the Home Office statement below, there was no precise definition of public service broadcasting, and different elements might be stressed over others depending upon the context but, certainly, the concept embraced expectations of quality and diverse programming. Public service broadcasting was described by the Home Office, the government department then responsible for broadcasting, in 1988, in a submission to a House of Commons inquiry into broadcasting, in the following terms:

> 12. Although there may be differences of opinion about what precisely is public service broadcasting, the Home Office sees it as embracing the following features:
>
> (a) broadcasting is a national asset which should be used for the national good, rather than for the benefit of particular interest groups;
> (b) responsibility for broadcasting should therefore lie with one or more broadcasting authorities, appointed as the 'trustees for the national interest' in broadcasting;
> (c) viewers (or listeners) in all parts of the country who pay the same licence fee should be able to receive all public service channels; the concept of universality;

---

[6] A Briggs, *The History of Broadcasting in the United Kingdom, Volume 1: The Birth of Broadcasting* (Oxford, Oxford University Press, 1961), 236.
[7] *Ibid.*

(d) the broadcasting authorities should be free of Government intervention in their day to day affairs and in the content of their programmes.

13. In return for the allocation of scarce frequencies on the spectrum the broadcasters have been expected to accept public service obligations which have formed an integral part of the British tradition of public service broadcasting. In broad terms these obligations have required that:

(a) the service should inform and educate as well as entertain;
(b) high standards should be maintained in technical and other matters;
(c) programmes should cover a wide and balanced range of subject matter in order to meet all interests in the population;
(d) there should be a wide distribution for programmes of merit;
(e) a proper proportion of programmes should be of British (now European Community) origin and performance;
(f) a suitable proportion of material should be calculated to appeal specifically to the tastes and outlook of the persons served by the station, including broadcasting in languages other than English (ie for ethnic minority or Gaelic or Welsh communities);
(g) local sound broadcasts in the same area should not consist of identical or similar material.[8]

The BBC maintained its monopoly status until the early 1950s, when commercial television was introduced. Although there had been concerns about the BBC's monopoly, there were also concerns about the impact commercial television would have on broadcasting quality, particularly in the light of the perceived US experience.[9] These concerns, and the general opposition to commercially funded television, led to similar public service broadcasting obligations being applied to the commercial television sector as a safeguard.[10] In addition, advertising rules were imposed to ensure editorial independence, and a proper separation between programming and advertising.[11] The commitment to public service broadcasting across both sectors was able to be maintained by means of what was known as 'the comfortable duopoly',[12] which compensated for the normal weaknesses of an advertising-funded system. The comfortable duopoly meant that the commercial sector faced no competition for advertising revenue from competing commercial broadcasting services, whilst the BBC and the commercial sector were able to co-exist with their separate funding sources. Even when Channel Four, a public broadcaster funded from advertising, began broadcasting in the early 1980s, the private commercial sector was protected, because the latter was responsible for

---

[8] House of Commons, *Home Affairs Committee Third Report: The Future of Broadcasting* (1987–8, HCP 262), paras 12–13.

[9] B Sendall, *Independent Television in Britain, Volume 1: Origin and Foundation, 1946–62* (London, Macmillan Press, 1982), 4 and 15.

[10] *Ibid*, 32–33.

[11] *Ibid*, 33.

[12] See Committee on Financing the BBC, *Report of the Committee on Financing the BBC*, Cmnd 9824 (1986), ch 4.

selling Channel Four's advertising time.[13] In addition, the programme remit of Channel Four effectively ensured that it was not in direct programme competition with the commercial sector, because it was required to provide programmes for tastes and interests not usually met by the commercial sector.

Although the public service concept has a direct relevance to broadcasting pluralism, it is not clear that this was a consciously sought outcome. Sendall has suggested that the commercial regulatory framework was not just a response to the problem of finding a balance between the dangers of commercialism and the maintenance of the traditions of public service broadcasting, but that it stemmed also from a generally held belief that television was a particularly potent 'means of influencing minds'.[14] Although this concern about influence probably had more to do with a fear of broadcasting and a desire to retain control of this 'mass voice', understandable in the wake of World War II and the experience of fascist regimes, a drive to contain undue influence and control can all the same be seen as having a bearing on diversity.[15] The arrangement which enabled the commercial sector to undertake a public service mandate was changed drastically with the 1990 reforms, which saw the end of the comfortable duopoly, and the introduction of greater reliance on market forces and competition. Although the commercial sector could no longer be viewed as a public service broadcaster in the way it had traditionally been, particularly with regard to investment in programming, many content-related rules were retained.

Despite radical reforms to the broadcasting and communications environment, the 2003 reforms have retained a commitment to public service broadcasting. Notable is the much more explicit link made with broadcasting pluralism. The White Paper which led to the Communications Act 2003 (Comms Act (UK)) explained the reasoning for the continuation of the public service broadcasting principle. The explanation is useful in showing this connection:

> 5.3.9 The democratic importance of public service broadcasting is as great as the economic justification [for continued regulation of broadcasting]. First, public service broadcasting ensures that the interests of all viewers are taken into account. Broadcasting is now a key part of living in a modern society, and we should not tolerate a market which excludes viewers and listeners from the programmes they have grown used to, or which no longer makes programmes for everyone. With the growth of new technology, there is a real risk of a digital divide, which public service broadcasting can bridge, by offering new and interactive services of information and education, and ensuring the development of the Internet is not purely commercial.

> 5.3.10 Second, public service broadcasting is a counter-balance to fears about concentration of ownership and the absence of diversity of views. It means news and current affairs are available in peak time, as part of mixed schedules, where citizens are most likely to see them. It guarantees the availability of full and balanced information about

[13] This position changed in 1990.
[14] Sendall, above n 9, 34.
[15] See R Craufurd Smith, *Broadcasting Law and Fundamental Rights* (Oxford, Clarendon Press, 1997), chs 1 and 2.

the world at local, regional and global levels. Such scheduling, together with the invest-ment which public service broadcasters have put into news and current affairs, is the key foundation of an open, balanced public debate.

5.3.11 Finally, there are strong cultural justifications for public service broadcasting. The value of information, education—whether in specific schools programming and materials or in general programming—and entertainment is not limited to how much we are prepared to pay for them. Whether arts or sciences, fiction or documentaries, entertainment or news, the subjects of television and radio are central to how we live our lives and how we understand each other. They allow our community to talk to itself.[16]

The Comms Act (UK) includes explicit statutory reference to public service broadcasting[17] and identifies the public service broadcasters as the BBC and Channels Three, Four, Five, and S4C (a Welsh language public broadcaster).[18] Each public service broadcaster also has a specific public service remit in addition to the general public service broadcasting responsibilities.[19] With the exception of the BBC, public service principles apply only to television, although commercial radio retains some obligations in relation to programme remits. The legislation's reference to the purposes of public service broadcasting or, more precisely, public service television broadcasting, makes clear that the concern is with the provision of a wide range of programmes catering to a variety of interests, and with pro-grammes that meet standards of quality, professionalism and editorial integrity.[20] Greater detail is given in section 264(6), which sets out the manner in which those purposes would be taken to be fulfilled. This sub-section makes reference to dif-ferent types of programmes as well as regional interests, and refers also to the need for fair and informed debate. Hand in hand with these changes are new approaches to the monitoring of compliance and obligations imposed upon the Office of Communications (Ofcom) to review public service television broadcast-ing. Although only some broadcasters are identified as public service broadcasters, some content rules—relevant to diversity—remain applicable to all broadcasters.

United States

In contrast to the UK, the US has always been more willing to let the market organ-ise broadcasting. Early regulation was focused on reducing the chaos which had arisen because of a lack of planned allocation of space on the radio frequency spec-trum. Thus, the pattern, established early, was one whereby regulation would be introduced where there was market failure. The Communications Act of 1934

---

[16] Department of Trade and Industry (DTI) and Department for Culture, Media and Sport (DCMS), *A New Future for Communications*, Cm 5010 (2000) ('White Paper'), paras 5.3.9–5.3.11. It is interesting to see here also the reference to public service broadcasting (which might be understood also as content regulation) acting as a counter-balance to ownership and control concerns.

[17] Section 264(4).

[18] The public teletext service is also classified as a public service broadcaster: s 264(12)(d).

[19] Section 265. The BBC's remit will be its Charter.

[20] Section 264(4).

(Comms Act (US)) itself provided a clear reminder that First Amendment rights would have to be accommodated within the broadcasting regulatory environment:

> Nothing in this Act [chapter] shall be understood or construed to give the Commission the power of censorship over the radio communications or signals transmitted by any radio station, and no regulation or condition shall be promulgated or fixed by the Commission which shall interfere with the right of free speech by means of radio communication.[21]

However, content regulation has not been as minimalist as one might expect. The Comms Act (US) differs from the UK, and even the Australian, legislation, because the former provides little coverage of content matters, and, in general, sets out only the broad parameters of the communications environment, leaving it to the Federal Communications Commission (FCC) to provide the detail, through its rule-making powers. However, the FCC is commanded to act 'as public convenience, interest, or necessity requires'.[22] This mandate has enabled the FCC to take a more pro-active role in relation to programming, subject to First Amendment constraints.[23] This tolerance, however, must be seen in the context of the market failure analysis. The prime justification for content regulation was spectrum scarcity. Scarcity of spectrum limited opportunities for access, so the FCC was entitled to manage the spectrum, its access and use, in the public interest, to enable wider access, and to ensure that the interests of viewers and listeners were being catered for. Not surprisingly, this rationale has come under pressure as the problem of spectrum scarcity is seen as diminishing. Even so, as will be apparent in this chapter, the US has never adopted content-based rules on the scale of the UK, or even Australia.

In the early days of radio broadcasting, the FCC's predecessor, the Federal Radio Commission, was disposed to impose obligations, through its licensing and licensing renewal powers, which looked similar to UK public service principles, in their expectation that broadcasters would provide a range of programming designed to 'meet, in fair proportion, "the tastes, needs and desires of all substantial groups among the listening public"'.[24] The FCC regarded itself as having a positive duty to continue this policy and to attend to the programme service being offered.[25] Although the FCC accepted that most broadcast time would be devoted to commercial programming, it asserted that the public interest required the provision also of 'sustaining programming',[26] which could counteract the effects of programming driven by commercial ends, and cater for minority interests. However, Sunstein notes that most of these early programming expectations were

---

[21] 47 USC § 326.

[22] 47 USC § 303.

[23] Hoffmann-Riem, above n 2, 15–16.

[24] Federal Radio Commission, *Third Annual Report* (1929), 33–35 quoted in FCC, *Report: Public Service Responsibility of Broadcast Licensees* (7 March 1946), 10.

[25] FCC, *Report: Public Service Responsibility of Broadcast Licensees* (7 March 1946), 12.

[26] The FCC defined 'sustaining programming' as programmes which were not paid for by a sponsor or interrupted by a spot advertisement: *ibid*, 56.

exhortatory only, lacking 'systematic enforcement'.[27] The early FCC experience provides an insight into the US approach. On the one hand, the FCC understood its public interest responsibilities to include programme service; however, it was also of the view that improvement in the programme service should come not from regulation but from individual broadcasters and industry assuming that responsibility.[28] Yet, it was apparent that from early on there were problems with radio broadcasting. The FCC referred to concerns such as excessive numbers and frequency of advertisements, and inappropriate intrusions, such as during news broadcasts.[29]

The most notable example of US diversity-related content regulation has been the Fairness Doctrine. However, the Doctrine's history is in part the history of its demise. It was developed by the FCC during the 1930s and 1940s, and consolidated in 1949 in its Report, *In the Matter of Editorializing by Broadcast Licensees*.[30] The Report overturned earlier decisions which had prohibited licensees broadcasting their own editorial line, but imposed an obligation on broadcasters to devote time to the discussion of controversial public issues, and to present a balanced range of views.[31] In 1967, two further rules were introduced: the 'personal attack' rule required a broadcaster to provide a right of reply to a person who had been attacked during a broadcast programme on a public issue; the 'political editorial' rule required a broadcaster who had endorsed or opposed a candidate for public office to notify the other candidates and provide them with a right of reply.[32] These rules led to a constitutional challenge, but the Supreme Court, in its *Red Lion* decision, upheld the rules, and the Doctrine.[33] In the court's view, spectrum scarcity was the basis upon which such a doctrine could be justified. Spectrum scarcity meant that the free speech rights of the broadcaster could not override the free speech rights of others:

> Because of the scarcity of radio frequencies, the Government is permitted to put restraints on licensees in favour of others whose views should be expressed on this unique medium. But the people as a whole retain their interest in free speech by radio and their collective right to have the medium function consistently with the ends and purposes of the First Amendment. It is the right of the viewers and listeners, not the right of the broadcasters, which is paramount.[34]

The Fairness Doctrine was always controversial because of the First Amendment, and the fact that its justifying ground was the essentially negative one of spectrum scarcity also made it vulnerable. Certainly, there was reluctance on the part of the

[27] Sunstein, above n 1, 507.
[28] FCC, *Report* (1946), above n 25, 54–55.
[29] *Ibid*, 44–47.
[30] EM Barendt, *Broadcasting Law: A Comparative Study* (Oxford, Clarendon Press, 1995), 158.
[31] *Red Lion Broadcasting Co, Inc v Federal Communications Commission* 395 US 367, 369 and 377 (1969).
[32] *Ibid*, 373–74.
[33] *Ibid*, 385.
[34] *Ibid*, 390.

FCC to enforce it, either through licensing renewal processes[35] or general enforcement powers.[36] Despite many thousands of complaints alleging Fairness Doctrine breaches, few were passed on to broadcasters or investigated.[37] However, Hoffmann-Riem suggests that this does not mean the Doctrine was ineffectual. Broadcasters showed themselves willing to monitor their output and their compliance with the Doctrine, and citizens' groups were also active in monitoring broadcasters and raising issues of non-compliance.[38]

In 1985, a lengthy report prepared by the FCC questioned whether the Fairness Doctrine was still justified.[39] Perhaps not surprisingly, the FCC took the view that the Doctrine, at least in the sense of an imposed obligation, was no longer needed because there was now an abundance of media in the marketplace.[40] In fact, rather than promoting speech, the Doctrine was considered more likely to have a chilling effect, due either to the fear of falling foul of the rules or to the cost and burden of compliance.[41] The FCC saw the issue of compliance as a significant factor, although this seems questionable as a justification, given that it rarely pursued alleged breaches.[42] However, the FCC refrained from repealing the Doctrine because at the time the matter of repeal was being also considered by Congress.[43] Finally, in 1987 the FCC repealed the Doctrine.[44] The personal attack rule and the political editorial rule were not repealed at that time, but these rules came under further attack, and, in 2000, the FCC was ordered to repeal them.[45]

Thus, a central contribution to diversity promotion has disappeared—the casualty of a combination of a narrow view of free speech principles and a weak basis (spectrum scarcity) for rationalising broadcasting regulation. Although there are still some relevant rules, the US system no longer has in place any positive content regulation addressing either diversity in programming or the principles previously

---

[35] Barendt, above n 30, 30. However, an exception to this general practice did arise in the early 1970s when the FCC refused to renew the licence of a religious radio station which consistently broadcast only one religious viewpoint, ignoring other faiths. The FCC's decision was upheld by a federal court: *Brandywine-Main Line Radio v FCC* 473 F.2d 16 (1972), cited in W Overbeck, *Major Principles of Media Law*, 15th edn (Belmont, CA, Thomson Wadsworth, 2004), 461.

[36] Hoffmann-Riem, above n 2, 35.

[37] Overbeck, above n 35, 461.

[38] Hoffmann-Riem, above n 2, 35–36.

[39] FCC, *In the Matter of Inquiry into Section 73.1910 of the Commission's Rules and Regulations Concerning the General Fairness Doctrine Obligations of Broadcast Licensees,* 102 FCC 2d 142 (1985).

[40] *Ibid,* para 175.

[41] *Ibid,* paras 26–68.

[42] *Ibid,* para 37.

[43] *Ibid,* para 176. There were also doubts as to whether the FCC had the power to repeal the Doctrine. These concerns were later shown to be unfounded and cleared the way for its repeal: Overbeck, above n 35, 462.

[44] FCC, *In re Complaint of Syracuse Peace Council against Television Station WTVH Syracuse, New York, Memorandum Opinion and Order,* 2 FCC Rcd 5043 (1987). In a challenge to the FCC's decision, the Court of Appeals held that the FCC had power to repeal the Doctrine, but it did not deal with the broader constitutional questions: *Syracuse Peace Council v FCC* 867 F.2d 654 (1989).

[45] *Radio-Television News Directors Association v FCC* 229 F 3d 269 (2000). The court was critical of the Commission's procrastination in removing the rules, which it considered had acted to the detriment of free speech and broadcasters' editorial judgements: *ibid,* 271–72.

embraced by the Fairness Doctrine. Despite the view that the Fairness Doctrine was chilling speech, its repeal has not apparently resulted in any increase in the coverage of public issues.[46] The FCC's general mandate, which requires it to have regard to the public interest, remains, and that always leaves scope for the FCC to regulate where it considers it is necessary in the public interest. However, in general, the FCC displays little inclination for content regulation which might be relevant to the promotion of broadcasting pluralism, and has shown, instead, a greater preference, from the 1970s, for unravelling existing content regulation.[47] However, the disclosure, in 2005, that some broadcasters were airing, undisclosed, government-funded and prepared news packages, has forced the FCC to focus its attention on matters more relevant to the concerns of this chapter.[48] By contrast, the FCC has, in the past few years, exhibited a greater interest in content regulation and enforcement so far as it relates to matters connected with decency or morality. The infamous Janet Jackson 'wardrobe malfunction' was only one of several instances in 2004 where the FCC sanctioned broadcasters, both radio and television, for indecency.[49] There is evidence that the FCC's renewed vigour in this area may be having a chilling effect: in the same year, about 30 network affiliates decided not to broadcast Spielberg's film, *Saving Private Ryan*, which was being offered by the ABC network, because the film contained a number of expletives.[50] The FCC is also considering introducing rules to regulate the portrayal of violence.[51] It has been suggested that increased consolidation in the media industry has contributed to the increased incidence of indecency, because large media conglomerates will be less able to appreciate and reflect local community values.[52]

Australia

Australian broadcasting began with commercial radio, although a public broadcaster was established within the same decade. However, Australia's public broadcaster, although modelled on the BBC, has never been as well funded as the British public broadcaster, nor has it held such a central place within the broadcasting environment. It is worth making these, albeit repeated, points about the origins of the various broadcasting sectors, because the early broadcasting structures have had an impact on the development of content-related regulation. From its commencement, the Australian commercial broadcasting sector was marked out as being different from the public broadcasting sector. Unlike the UK, there

---

[46] Hoffmann-Riem, above n 2, 37.
[47] RE Wiley and LW Secrest, 'Recent Developments in Program Content Regulation' (2005) 57 *Federal Communications Law Journal* 235 at 235–36.
[48] This matter is examined under 'Advertising'.
[49] Wiley and Secrest, above n 47, 236–38.
[50] *Ibid*, 237.
[51] *Ibid*, 239.
[52] BL Dorgan, 'The FCC and Media Ownership: The Loss of the Public Interest Standard' (2005) 19 *Notre Dame Journal of Law, Ethics and Public Policy* 443 at 450.

was no expectation that commercial broadcasting would meet the same public interest standards:

> During this period [1901–1931], a pattern was set for Australian broadcasting which was to last for many years. Although the origins of the national and commercial sectors were very similar, at this stage the distinction between their roles was already clearly acknowledged. The national sector would be government owned; it would have the most powerful transmitters and the best frequencies; its programs would be nationally oriented and transmitted through national and country relays; it would cover small States and country areas where the population density was insufficient to support stations dependent upon the sale of advertising; and it would be financed from receiver licence fees. The commercial sector, on the other hand, would be privately owned; it would have less powerful transmitters; its programs would be locally oriented and so would its coverage and it would be financed from the sale of time to advertisers.[53]

Expectations about programming were imposed on commercial broadcasters, although there was little in the way of developed policy. In the early days, regulation of radio broadcasting was in the hands of a government department, the Postmaster-General's Department, and licensees were required to broadcast programmes to the satisfaction of the Postmaster-General (PMG). What satisfied or dissatisfied the PMG appeared to relate more to indecent or disloyal content than to anything related to the range of programming broadcast.[54] However, when the public broadcaster was established in 1932, it was required to broadcast 'adequate and comprehensive' programmes.[55] Although licensing powers remained with the PMG until the 1970s, other aspects of broadcasting regulation were transferred in 1949 to a statutory body, the Australian Broadcasting Control Board ('the Board'). It had a general mandate to secure the provision of adequate and comprehensive programmes, as well as responsibilities related to specific types of programmes.[56] However, these specific programming duties were removed from the Board in 1956, which coincided with the introduction of commercial television.[57] In general, the idea of content regulation, particularly with regard to matters such as the quality and range of programming service, seems to have been embraced reluctantly in Australia. The Board was criticised for its failure to use its powers to ensure better programming,[58] but Armstrong suggests that the exercise by the Board of programming powers and duties would not have been acceptable to the government.[59]

---

[53] Postal and Telecommunications Department (P & T Dept), *Australian Broadcasting: A Report on the Structure of the Australian Broadcasting System and Associated Matters*, Parl Paper No 358 (1976), para 24.

[54] M Armstrong, *Broadcasting Law and Policy in Australia* (Sydney, Butterworths, 1982), para 304.

[55] P & T Dept, above n 53, para 26.

[56] *Ibid*, para 30.

[57] Armstrong, above n 54, para 310.

[58] Senate Select Committee on the Encouragement of Australian Productions for Television, *Report*, Parl Paper No 304 (1962–63), cited in Armstrong, above n 54, para 314.

[59] Armstrong, above n 54, para 403.

Australian broadcasting's early history exhibits a pattern of scant policy development and a reluctance to implement the rules which were developed, certainly in so far as content regulation was concerned. In fact, the preference may have been for sectoral diversity rather than content regulation. Major changes to the regulatory framework were made in the late 1970s, following the report of the Green Committee[60] including: the establishment of a new regulatory body; the Australian Broadcasting Tribunal (ABT); the transfer of licensing powers to the ABT; and the establishment of the Special Broadcasting Service (SBS). The Green Report's discussion is useful because it provides some insight into the underlying principles of Australian broadcasting. Although Australia embraced elements of the public service broadcasting model, it certainly never implemented it to the detailed level of the UK system. Whilst the Green Report acknowledged the role and success of the commercial broadcasting sector in 'providing programs of wide popular appeal to the mass audiences of the Australian community',[61] it also considered that, consistent with the principle of broadcasting as a public trust, the commercial sector could do more:

> to introduce a measure of innovation and experimentation in programs catering to more sizeable, if not mass, audiences. This would also assist in achieving a diversity of programming over all three sectors of the broadcasting system.[62]

It is notable here that the Green Report seems to see the call for diversity of programming as part of the overall sectoral diversity of the broadcasting environment, rather than a call for any particular content obligations on the part of individual broadcasters. Following the legislative changes, there was in place a range of programme and advertising standards which commercial broadcasters, particularly television, were required to observe, although the obligations were relatively minimal, and were mainly concerned with Australian content, programme classification, and advertising rules, as well as matters such as the portrayal of sexual and violent material. Save for the responsibilities of the public broadcasters, there were few positive programme requirements of relevance to broadcasting pluralism.

Throughout the history of Australian broadcasting there has been pressure from the broadcasting industry for it to be allowed to regulate itself. This wish was finally realised with the commencement of the Broadcasting Services Act 1992 (BSA (Aus)), which introduced a model of co-regulation. Under this model, it was envisaged that industry would develop its own codes and monitor compliance, whilst the regulatory body, then the Australian Broadcasting Authority (ABA), now the Australian Communications and Media Authority (ACMA), would ensure enforcement. The codes of practice drawn up by the various sectors of the broadcasting industry are light on detail, and there have been concerns about the effectiveness of the codes. Although the statutory objectives set down in section 3

---

[60] P &T Dept, above n 53.
[61] *Ibid*, para 95.
[62] *Ibid*, para 104.

of the BSA (Aus) indicate that broadcasting regulation is concerned with diversity, both of services and of programming, and with matters such as fairness and balance, the regulatory model has not served these matters well. Although on the face of it, the Australian system appears more sympathetic to content regulation, there has been a lack of political will to provide coherent implementation and enforcement of objectives and rules.

Regulatory Measures

Programme Diversity

As already discussed, ensuring the availability of a range of programmes is not just about making certain that news and information-type programmes can be accessed; it is also concerned with making available a full range of programming, even if the primary purpose of some of these programmes will be entertainment. Entertainment can be just as important in addressing current or public issues, or providing different perspectives on community values and standards, and may have important flow-on effects for the audience's participation in the democratic process. Providing a full range of programming is also important because it means that different types of audiences, tastes, and interests can be catered for. One way (examined in Chapter Three) to encourage a range of programming is to structure the broadcasting environment so that there are different types of broadcasting sectors, which have different financing sources, and roles or responsibilities. But sectoral diversity's success in providing programming range may depend upon the adequacy of funding. Further, there is a risk that some programmes will be marginalised, or that public broadcasters will be left to fill the 'gaps'. Whilst sectoral diversity can help to ensure that across all sectors a range of programming is available, it will not ensure that particular types of programming can be accessed from all services. In other words, some types of programming may be provided by only one or two broadcasters; if news and current affairs programming (of a more serious or substantial nature) is only available from the public broadcaster, then this means that the sources for news and information will be limited. Another strategy, of course, is plurality of ownership: the assumption being that the presence of a number of competing owners will lead to diversity of content. The limitations of that approach have already been canvassed in Chapter Three (and some of the economic limitations are considered in Chapter Six)—in brief, there is no necessary link between ownership and output, particularly in an advertising-funded environment. Therefore, regulation which addresses the provision of certain types of programming may be necessary.

All of the jurisdictions have at various points in their regulatory history experimented with content regulation to promote diversity, but the ongoing preference in the US and Australia has been for structural measures, whereas it is the UK which offers the most coherent form of programming range regulation. The success of such regulation is likely to depend upon a number of factors, but one important matter will be the regulatory process which is established for enforcement of this type of content regulation. If the programming mandate is exhortatory only, then it is likely to have little impact; on the other hand, even where an enforcement mechanism is in place, the qualitative judgements involved may make a regulator reluctant to enforce the rules. Sometimes bound in with requirements for diversity of programming is an expectation of quality programming. Quality programming is not something which directly relates to the concerns of diversity and broadcasting pluralism, although it is reasonable to expect that programmes which are of high quality (assuming this can be measured) may be more likely to serve broadcasting pluralism than those which are not. The tendency to group together expectations about diversity and quality may have an impact on any formal assessment or enforcement mechanisms: the problematic nature of assessing quality may impede any rigorous assessment of range of programming.

Australia has some regulation addressing programming range. However, here too the preference for a sectoral approach is apparent. It is useful to look at the Australian approach first because this contrasts well with the US and the UK. The sectoral focus comes through clearly in the BSA (Aus) statutory objectives, which refer not to the provision of diverse programming, but to the promotion of 'the availability to audiences throughout Australia of a diverse range of radio and television *services* offering entertainment, education and information'.[63] The statutory objectives also refer to the provision by broadcasting services of 'high quality and innovative content',[64] although there is nothing in the legislation which specifically addresses this, or provides any mechanism for assessing whether this objective has been achieved. There are some programming format requirements in relation to some types of broadcasting services: it is part of the definition of commercial broadcasting services that they provide programmes of general appeal,[65] and each commercial broadcasting licence contains a condition which is in the following terms:

> the licensee will provide a service that, when considered together with other broadcasting services available in the licence area of the licence (including another service operated by the licensee), contributes to the provision of an adequate and comprehensive range of broadcasting services in that licence area.[66]

This is an odd provision. As an obligation imposed upon each licensee, one might expect that it would require the licensee to provide an adequate and comprehensive range of programmes, or at least to ensure that, taking into account the other services available within the area, the licensee provides programmes which contribute to an adequate and comprehensive range of programmes but, in fact,

---

[63] BSA (Aus), s 3(1)(a) (emphasis added).
[64] *Ibid*, s 3(1)(f).
[65] *Ibid*, s 14(a).
[66] BSA (Aus), sch 2, cl 7(2)(a) (for television), cl 8(2)(a) (for radio).

the obligation is expressed in terms that the licensee must provide a service which contributes to the range of broadcasting services. It is not entirely clear how a licensee can do this; all that a licensee can do is to provide the type of service for which the licence has been granted, for example, a commercial broadcasting service. A licensee will have no power to restructure the market in terms of what kinds of services are provided. That would be a matter for ACMA. The 'adequate and comprehensive' requirement has been inherited from earlier legislation, where the phrase was used specifically in relation to programmes, and its current meaning should be understood as requiring a licensee, consistent with its licence mandate, to provide programmes which, taken together with the other services in that area, will constitute an 'adequate and comprehensive range'. This would seem consistent with earlier legislative expectations.

The terms 'adequate' and 'comprehensive' also have well-established meanings. Whilst 'adequate' may seem to be aiming rather low, it is in fact understood to mean 'a high standard of quality—technical and artistic', and 'comprehensive' to mean 'an overall balance as to subject-matter, content and variety'.[67] Even if one interprets the current licence condition as suggested above, there is still a difficulty as to what this condition can achieve. The licence condition is drafted in such broad terms that it is difficult to envisage how it could be enforced. Consideration of one licensee's compliance can only take place by looking at all other services, and it would be difficult to attribute non-compliance to any one licensee. If there is a gap in the comprehensiveness of one service, how does one decide that the gap is the failing of one licensee and not another? There is also a problem with the term 'comprehensive', notwithstanding its known interpretation. Given the absence of detail as to what might contribute to a comprehensive service, the provision leaves itself open to arguments as to what constitutes a 'comprehensive' service. A more general regulatory difficulty also arises. The point was made earlier that effective regulation for diversity will be dependent upon the scope for enforcement. The BSA (Aus) provides no mechanisms for any ongoing or specific assessment of broadcasting service performance: there are no regular reviews of performance or compliance, and renewal of licences is virtually automatic. Although the legislation contains provisions to deal with breach of licence conditions, it is unlikely that a licence condition requiring provision of an adequate and comprehensive service could be easily enforced. Even apart from the difficulties of the licence condition itself, the current regulatory environment displays little evidence of a proactive regulatory authority.[68] One must conclude then that the licence condition imposed upon commercial broadcasting services is largely exhortatory, and is not intended to have any real substantive force. This is consistent with an approach which focuses upon sectoral diversity. There are some exceptions to this where

[67] Senate Select Committee on the Encouragement of Australian Productions for Television, *Report*, Parl Paper No 304 (1962–3), para 11 quoted in P & T Dept, above n 53, para 75.

[68] Given that the establishment of the new regulator, ACMA, has been mainly an administrative matter, there is little to suggest that ACMA will show itself any more proactive with regard to licensee compliance than its predecessor.

specific interest groups or needs, such as children, are catered for. These will be referred to later in this section.

Although more specific programme mandates are imposed upon the public broadcasters, the ABC and SBS, these too are within the context of a focus on sectoral diversity, so that the programme range to be provided by the ABC is intended to complement the commercial and community sectors. A specific link is drawn then between the use of structural diversity and content regulation. Although the ABC's charter requires it to provide a comprehensive service, it is expressly required to take into account the services provided by the commercial and community sectors.[69] In fact, the ABC's programming mandate is quite complex, because in addition to a comprehensive service, it is required to cater for certain attributes or aspirations. Hence, its programming must, inter alia, contribute to national identity, reflect cultural diversity, and take into account the multicultural character of the Australian community.[70] As would be expected of a public broadcaster, the ABC has to provide educational programmes but, otherwise, there is not much specific direction about programme type, apart from a requirement that it takes into account its obligation 'to provide a balance between broadcasting programs of wide appeal and specialized broadcasting programs'.[71] A similar approach can be seen with SBS. It is given a specific programme mandate which is 'to provide multilingual and multicultural radio and television services that inform, educate and entertain all Australians',[72] and, like the ABC, must also take into account a variety of aspirations which might be seen as consistent with a multicultural, multilingual service.[73] It is also required to 'contribute to the overall diversity of Australian television and radio services, particularly taking into account the contribution of the Australian Broadcasting Corporation and the community broadcasting sector'.[74]

Australian content regulation then, at least in relation to programme diversity, exists to flesh out sectoral pluralism. In other words, it does not assume that the market with its differing sectors will automatically produce programme diversity. On the other hand, it is doubtful how much these programming mandates are likely to add to the sectoral approach, given the wording and regulatory context. Even for the public broadcasters there must be some doubt as to how precisely their respective mandates can be assessed and monitored. The programme obligations of the public broadcasters form part of their statutory charters, and it is the responsibility of the respective boards to ensure that the broadcasters meet their obligations. Yet, it would be difficult for the boards, which are not part of the broadcasters' management, to try to prescribe too closely what the broadcasters should be doing to fulfil their programme remits. Of course, there are other ways

---

[69] ABC Act, s 6(2)(a)(i).
[70] *Ibid*, ss 6(1)(a)(i) and (2)(a)(iv).
[71] *Ibid*, s 6(2)(a)(iii).
[72] SBS Act, s 6(1).
[73] *Ibid*, s 6(2).
[74] *Ibid*, s 6(2)(g).

that influence can be brought to bear on public broadcasters, as was discussed in Chapter Three, although these are likely to intrude upon the broadcasters' independence. Nevertheless, there is no doubt a greater willingness to bring the public broadcaster to account for failures, perceived or otherwise, or at least to criticise, than is usually the case with the commercial broadcasters.

Like Australia, the US focus is characterised by reliance on the market, and market structure, to provide programme diversity, but it also differs from Australia, in the absence of any type of requirement regarding the range of programmes. Although the past practice of the FCC was to issue programme guidelines, these were abandoned during the 1980s. FCC rules require licensees to maintain a public inspection file disclosing information on specified matters, some of which relate to programme issues, such as (for television and radio) programmes treating community issues, and (for television) commercial limits and children's programming.[75] However, the impact of these files is likely to be mostly symbolic given the FCC's preference for virtually automatic licence renewals. As one of the FCC Commissioners has commented:

> The Commission has allowed fundamental protections of the public interest to wither and die—requirements like ascertaining the needs of the local audience, the Fairness Doctrine, teeing up controversial issues, providing demonstrated diversity in programming, ensuring decent quality programming for our children, to name a few of the safeguards we had once but have abandoned.
>
> At the same time, the Commission has pared back its license renewal process from one in which it examined whether the broadcaster was actually serving the public interest to one where companies need only send us a postcard every eight years and nothing more. Unless there is a major complaint pending against a station, the license is almost automatically renewed.[76]

It is clear that, even apart from First Amendment considerations, there seems to be little will for any closer regulatory supervision of the broadcasting environment.

The UK has been much more willing to impose programming requirements to promote diversity, on commercial as well as public broadcasters. Such obligations fall mainly upon the traditional free-to-air services. This is because spectrum scarcity is still viewed as a constraining factor, at least in relation to the services which can be accessed free-to-air. But other justifications for the maintenance of public service broadcasting and content regulation are also offered: the economic features of broadcasting (see further Chapter Six), and the role broadcasting plays in the democratic process.[77] Access has also been an important principle, and can be

---

[75] 47 CFR § 73.3526. Public broadcasting public inspection file requirements are dealt with at 47 CFR § 73.3527.

[76] FCC, *Report and Order and Notice of Proposed Rulemaking, In the Matter of 2002 Biennial Regulatory Review—Review of the Commission's Broadcast Ownership Rules and Other Rules Adopted Pursuant to Section 202 of the Telecommunications Act of 1996*, FCC 03-127 (2 June 2003), 'Statement of Commissioner Michael J Copps, Dissenting', 4.

[77] DTI and DCMS, above n 16, para 5.3.

seen to relate to the role of broadcasting in the democratic process. Although other services are available by other delivery mechanisms, most citizens will have access to free-to-air broadcasting, but many will not have access to subscription services. So, although subscription services theoretically create diversity by throwing into the mix more and different broadcasters, content diversity regulation is a recognition that it is important to ensure that the greatest possible diversity is created within the range of services to which most people are likely to have access. Thus, each free-to-air television service has to provide that diversity.[78] What this means in practice may be less easy to identify. On its face, it might look simply like duplication but it is more subtle than that. The Green Paper on the future of the BBC referred to the public service broadcasting system as one 'where a range of different broadcasters offer complementary and competing services'.[79] Thus, while the commercial broadcasters may be expected to provide a wide range of programmes, it will be understood that commercial funding may influence what is offered, whereas the BBC will be expected to be able to provide that full range of programming. This is something which the recent Green Paper has also emphasised:

> The BBC should continue to be a broadcaster of scale and scope, active in all the main genres and with the ability to adapt to new technologies and new consumer developments. However, it needs to recognise its obligations to concentrate on PSB, to avoid unnecessary overlap with other providers . . .[80]

One advantage of requiring a number of broadcasters to provide a range of programming is that it can provide greater choice for the viewer and listener. There is less risk of the public broadcaster being marginalised, or of a monolithic approach to certain types of programming.[81] The UK practice has been to specify specific types of programming rather than rely on a general statement promoting diversity. Thus, in addition to the broad remit of provision of a wide range of programmes, specific types of programmes are also mentioned. This was a practice which applied across the public and commercial sector, and which has largely been carried through with the 2003 reforms. The BBC, under its current Charter and Agreement, is specifically required to provide programming in areas such as: culture and comedy; news and current affairs; sport and leisure activities; and educational programmes (both formal, vocational and of general educational interest), as well as catering for particular audiences such as children and young people, and regional communities.[82] A similar approach was used for the commercial

---

[78] Even the public broadcaster Channel Four, which has a particular programme remit relating, inter alia, to experiment and cultural diversity, is still required to provide a broad range of diverse programming: Comms Act (UK), s 265(3).

[79] DCMS, *Review of the BBC's Royal Charter: A Strong BBC, Independent of Government*, PP 789 (March 2005), 15.

[80] T Jowell, Secretary of State for Culture, Media and Sport, Foreword, in *ibid*, 3.

[81] DCMS, *Review of the BBC's Royal Charter*, above n 79, 15.

[82] Department of National Heritage, *Agreement Dated the 25th Day of January 1996 Between Her Majesty's Secretary of State for National Heritage and the British Broadcasting Corporation*, Cm 3152 (1996), cl 3.2.

television sector, Channels Three and Five, and to a lesser extent, commercial local and national radio services under the Broadcasting Act 1990 (BA 1990 (UK)). However, the commercial broadcasters, and Channel Four, are now governed by the programming remit of the Comms Act (UK). This has retained the public service broadcasting concept, but for the television sector only, although commercial radio services, both local and national, continue to have programme obligations which, in the case of local radio, reflect the needs of the local community and, for certain national radio services, ensure specific programme formats, such as mainly speech or non-pop music, for each service. Changes to format must be approved by Ofcom.[83]

However, the new legislation has a different approach, because it identifies the public service (television) broadcasting concept and elaborates the purposes of the concept, much of which has a direct relevance to the promotion of diversity. The statement of purposes is aimed at what can be achieved across the spectrum of television services provided by the public service broadcasters, public and commercial; in other words, the BBC and Channels Three, Four, and Five.[84] Thus, section 264(4) includes amongst the purposes of public service television broadcasting:

   (a) the provision of relevant television services which secure that programmes dealing with a wide range of subject-matters are made available for viewing;
   (b) the provision of relevant television services in a manner which . . . is likely to meet the needs and satisfy the interests of as many different audiences as practicable;
   (c) the provision of relevant television services which (taken together and having regard to the same matters) are properly balanced, so far as their nature and subject-matters are concerned, for meeting the needs and satisfying the interests of the available audiences; . . .

This statement of public service television broadcasting purposes focuses on the provision of services, and can be said to be aimed towards structuring the relevant sector. Section 264(6) provides more detail on how these purposes might be fulfilled, and here one sees again the more detailed spelling out of programme areas or specific interest and needs. Thus, similar to the requirements for the BBC, section 264(6) refers to television services which disseminate information, and provide education and entertainment, reflect cultural activity and diversity, provide news and current affairs coverage, cover sport and leisure, and provide educational material and religious programming, programmes covering science, international issues, social issues, as well as children's and regional programming. These requirements are not imposed upon individual licensees, as was the case under the previous regime. Instead, the purposes, and the more detailed programming remit, apply across 'the relevant television services (taken together)'.[85]

---

[83] BA 1990 (UK), as amended, s 106.
[84] The Welsh Channel and the public teletext service are also classified as public service broadcasting services. These services will not be discussed.
[85] See, eg, Comms Act (UK), s 264(6)(a).

This suggests there is now a greater reliance upon sectoral diversity than was the case before, and the possibility that the public broadcasters, particularly the BBC, will be required more than ever to cater for more specialised, less popular programming. This is reflected in the BBC Green Paper. This could lead to a significant lowering in expectation with respect to the performance of the commercial services, because they can rely on the BBC to shoulder the public service burden, and thus argue that the requirements are met if one has regard to television services as a whole. The BBC, given that it is in receipt of public funding, may be more vulnerable to public (and government) criticism, if there is a general perception that television is not meeting public service purposes. However, this view needs to be considered also in the context of the review mechanisms for the public television service broadcasting mandate. This will be considered shortly. In the meantime, it is also important to remember that Channels Three, Four, and Five have their own specific public service remits. For Channels Three and Five, the remit is 'the provision of a range of high quality and diverse programming'.[86] No other detail is given as to what this might entail, although presumably section 264 provides some guidance. The remit for Channel Four repeats this requirement, with a slight variation on the wording: 'a broad range of high quality and diverse programming'.[87] This also suggests that in keeping with its status as public broadcaster, Channel Four has the traditional role of a public broadcaster, namely to provide a broad or wide range of programming, but that this is no longer necessarily the case for the private commercial sector. Channel Four's remit is consistent with its traditional role of providing innovative and distinctive programming.

A point that has been made already is that the effectiveness of diversity regulation will be dependent upon the processes for review and enforcement. Problematic as monitoring and enforcement may be, given the qualitative judgements required, diversity regulation which provides no compliance and enforcement mechanism will provide broadcasters with little incentive to respond. Thus, UK diversity regulation must also be considered in this light. For the BBC the position has not changed, at least in relation to the type of obligations addressed here. Thus, it is a matter for the BBC governors to review and report on how well the BBC has met its obligations under the public service standard, and it does this through its Annual Report. Prior to the 2003 reforms, a rather paternalistic assessment process operated for the commercial broadcasters whereby the television regulator, the ITC, would issue annual performance reviews of Channels Three, Four, and Five, which assessed how well the broadcasters had met their licence obligations and set out priorities for the licensees for the forthcoming year. These tended to be reviews without much force; given the qualitative judgements involved, it is unlikely that the ITC would have wanted to pursue non-compliance

---

[86] Comms Act (UK), s 265(2).
[87] *Ibid*, s 265(3).

on matters such as quality and range, unless the degree of non-compliance was severe. The regulator for radio, the Radio Authority (RA), tended to rely on complaints received as the means of monitoring licensees. The 2003 reforms have ushered in a quite different review process: one which appears to require a focus on the overall broadcasting environment, consistent with the observations made above. It needs to be remembered that this review process applies only to television, not to radio. For radio there is no proactive or regular programme review requirement, although changes in format have to be approved, and the usual obligation to comply with licence conditions could be relevant.

For television, the 2003 reforms operate at two levels. First, the Comms Act (UK), under section 264(1), requires Ofcom to carry out regular reviews of public service television broadcasting. The first review has been completed. Thereafter it is a matter for Ofcom to determine the period of each subsequent review, although it must be within a period of five years. These reviews require Ofcom to determine whether the public service broadcasters (including the BBC) have provided television services which, taken as a whole, fulfil the purposes of public service television broadcasting, and to make recommendations to secure and strengthen the quality of public service television. This then is a review of the overall environment, although the review necessarily involves Ofcom making assessments of individual broadcasters. The review process also shows the significant scope the regulator has for reshaping the broadcasting environment, and the relevance of the more holistic approach (that is, 'taken as a whole') to the functions of the public service concept. The first review published by Ofcom was done in three phases and was extremely detailed. The first phase concentrated mainly on assessing how adequately the broadcasters provided programmes which would meet the public service requirements,[88] whilst the second and third phase reports were more concerned with securing the future delivery of public service broadcasting.[89] To some extent, the Phase One Report assessment echoes the old ITC performance reviews, although the focus is no longer on individual licensees, but on different types of programming and public service values as delivered by the whole sector. Even so the Report's assessment is quite detailed, taking into account qualitative factors as well as more readily ascertainable measures such as programme expenditure, number of programme hours, and scheduling. Although Ofcom concluded that broadcasting across the free-to-air services was doing well in many areas, it identified some areas of concern, which might be indicative also of the increasing difficulty of maintaining a public service system in a commercial, multi-delivery context. The areas raised for concern included the following:

---

[88] Ofcom, *Ofcom Review of Public Service Television Broadcasting: Phase One—Is Television Special?* (2004) ('Phase One Report').

[89] Ofcom, *Ofcom Review of Public Service Television Broadcasting: Phase Two—Meeting the Digital Challenge* (2004) ('Phase Two Report'), and Ofcom, *Ofcom Review of Public Service Television Broadcasting: Phase Three—Competition for Quality* (2005) ('Phase Three Report').

— a decline in the delivery of dedicated educational programming;
— current affairs programmes being moved to 'the margins of the schedules', although news programmes were seen as attracting high investment and public support;
— arts and minority programming were also likely to be moved to the less popular schedule slots.[90]

The Phase One Report noted that these concerns were symptomatic of trends which would develop more fully with the increasing uptake of digital television and subscription services.[91] In fact, between the commencement of the review and the delivery of the Phase Three Report, digital uptake increased from 48 per cent to 56 per cent of households, and television subscription revenue overtook advertising revenue for the first time.[92] But it is not just competition for revenue which is challenging traditional broadcasting structures; changes in viewing patterns and loyalties, along with the growth of new recording mechanisms, such as personal video recorders, might also threaten traditional public service assumptions about, for example, provision of programming range:

> New technology has changed viewing patterns. Future technology threatens to do so in more dramatic fashion. In this context, the existing main terrestrial networks face an uncertain future. For the commercial channels, regulatory requirements may begin to weigh much heavier as the market becomes more competitive and advertising funding is squeezed. The licence fee may become harder to justify as fewer people watch the programmes it pays for, and over time licence fee funding may struggle to fund programmes sufficiently to satisfy viewers' expectations in a competitive market. Some of television's traditional strengths—its ability to provide a common reference point for society, or to bring people challenging content that they might not encounter elsewhere—become harder and harder to sustain as individuals begin to create their own schedules. The increasingly populist approach . . . is a direct consequence of the commercial pressures that broadcasters now face, and those pressures will intensify as time goes on.[93]

These concerns and trends identified in the Phase One Report have led to the development, in the Phase Two and Three Reports, of proposals to secure the future of public service broadcasting, in recognition also that even in a fully digital environment, there will be some types of programming which the market will provide inadequately or not at all.[94] Some of these proposals have a direct impact on the range of programming expectation. This can be seen first in Ofcom's move away from an identification of the type of programmes which would constitute

---

[90] Phase One Report, above n 88, paras 110, 112, 116, and 120.
[91] *Ibid*, para 124. BSkyB subscription revenue now exceeds the total amount raised by the BBC licence fee: para 127.
[92] Phase Three Report, above n 89, 2.
[93] Phase One Report, above n 88, para 136.
[94] Phase Three Report, above n 89, para 1.10. Ofcom's research also established that there was continuing public support for the collective provision of public service broadcasting: Phase Two Report, above n 89, paras 4.28–4.40.

public service broadcasting to a short set of broadly stated purposes and charac-teristics.[95] The other important change which Ofcom recommends is the break-down of a universal type of public service remit to the identification of different remits for different broadcasters. Thus, the BBC would be seen as main bearer of public service broadcasting, whilst other broadcasters would be able to focus on particular areas.[96] For example, Ofcom recommends that Channel Three should be required to focus on news and high value original programming.[97] Channel Five would be expected to be a primarily market-led broadcaster, with a public ser-vice commitment to UK original programming.[98] In effect, Ofcom's proposals would mark a move away from a broadcasting environment committed to public service broadcasting to one in which one broadcaster, the BBC, is the public ser-vice broadcaster, with specialised contributions coming from other broadcasters. Such a design brings with it risks, which have been mentioned before—in particu-lar, that public service programming is marginalised or becomes a ghetto area. Such risks would be exacerbated if the BBC was put under funding pressure. The impact of Ofcom's conclusions can already be seen. Ofcom has amended the Channel Three licences so that Channel Three's obligations to provide a certain number of hours of non-news regional programming have been reduced.[99] The other major element of Ofcom's proposals is the recommendation that a new Public Service Publisher (PSP) (or Publishers) should be established. The PSP would be publicly funded and required to develop free-to-view content which would be appropriate for new delivery technologies, particularly broadband. The content developed might be expected to have a particular focus on local and other community interests.[100]

A second level of review focuses on the individual licensees, and their compli-ance with their individual public service remits. This process provides further evi-dence of the changed regulatory philosophy, for it is no longer the regulator who reviews performance, but the licensees themselves. They must provide annually a statement of programme policy, which sets out the licensee's proposals for meet-ing its public service responsibilities, and an assessment of their own performance in meeting the current policy.[101] In a sense, these are the equivalent of the BBC governors' assessment of the BBC's programme obligations. However, there has not been a complete move to self-regulation, because Ofcom retains powers to act if it considers that the licensee is not meeting its public service remit.[102] Ofcom can

---

[95] Phase Three Report, above n 89, para 2.36.

[96] *Ibid,* para 2.67. Ofcom also concluded that Channel Four should remain a not-for-profit broad-caster and would be important to the public service landscape but with a particular remit for innova-tive programming. However, Channel Four with its dependence upon advertising revenue faces considerable funding pressures—Ofcom has recognised this and does not seem optimistic about the broadcaster's future: see *ibid,* ch Four.

[97] *Ibid,* para 2.69.

[98] *Ibid,* para 2.77.

[99] *Ibid,* para 7.1.

[100] Phase Three Report, ch Five; discussed further in Chapter Seven.

[101] Comms Act (UK), s 266.

[102] *Ibid,* s 270.

give directions to the broadcaster to revise their policies, or to take steps to rectify their failures, and, if a direction fails to ensure an adequate outcome, Ofcom can replace self-regulation with 'detailed regulation'.[103] However, Ofcom cannot act under section 270 if it is of the opinion that the failure of the provider is not serious, or can be excused by economic or market conditions—one can envisage that market and economic conditions might provide a useful escape route for broadcasters. The programme policy review process can also provide an opportunity for licensees to renegotiate their commitments. Under section 267, licensees have to consult with Ofcom if they propose to make a 'significant change' to their programme policy. This seems to provide an opportunity for licensees to negotiate relaxations to their public service commitment. In the statements of policy for 2005, Channel Three licensees proposed a reduction in children's programming from 11½ hours per week to eight hours, and a reduction for religious output from two hours to one. Ofcom accepted these changes on the basis that, in the case of children's programmes, there had been an increase across digital channels, and the level of religious output would be comparable to that offered by other broadcasters.[104] Here again one can see a willingness to look across the whole of the broadcasting environment. Despite the requirement of the Act for licensees to monitor their performance, the written reviews of performance tend to read like promotional documents, and contain little self-criticism. This lack of a self-critical perspective has been raised by Ofcom, which has suggested that broadcasters need to devise ways to ensure effective evaluation.[105]

Regardless of the measures a jurisdiction might adopt to promote diversity, it is recognised that there will be some areas of content which will be under-provided. This will usually be because the costs of producing such programming might be high compared with the size of the market; children's programming might be an example of this. Additionally, the costs of producing content locally might be well in excess of the costs to import programming produced elsewhere, usually from the US. Children's programming and local content are prime examples of the types of content which an ordinary advertising-funded market might under-provide, regardless of what the audience demand might be.[106] Although the problems here can be attributed to the market failure aspects of broadcasting, as discussed in Chapter Six, there is also a direct relevance for broadcasting pluralism. One way to address this issue is by imposing minimum content requirements, or quotas, which ensure that a certain 'amount' of such programming is produced and broadcast. These types of requirements involve something more than a generalised mandate to provide a range of programming, whether or not it includes

[103] *Ibid*, s 270(6).
[104] Ofcom, 'Ofcom Accepts Commercial Public Service Broadcasters' Proposals on Tier 3 Obligations' (News Release, 25 February 2005), http://www.ofcom.org.uk/media_office/latest_news/nr_20050225, accessed 16 March 2005.
[105] *Ibid.*
[106] Productivity Commission, *Broadcasting*, Report No 11 (Canberra, AusInfo, 2000), 383. Although a user-funded market should overcome these problems, the evidence appears to be that a subscription market cannot be relied upon to overcome fully this content deficit: see Chapter Six.

specific types of programmes; what they seek to do is to engineer the market to ensure that it provides the content considered desirable or important. Policies seeking to promote locally produced content are generally seen as relating to the promotion of a community's cultural values, but it is not usually as straightforward as this, since most such policies will also serve economic goals, because of their potential to support local industry. Unsurprisingly, the US does not impose local content regulations, but both the UK and Australia do. In the UK, local content policies derive from the EU Television Directive, and they are concerned with European content, not just UK content—although given language differences this might be a distinction in appearance only. Under the Directive, all television broadcasters are required to devote a majority of their transmission time to European works, although there are some programmes which cannot be counted towards this quota, such as news, sports, and games.[107] The Australian content standard uses a combination of hours and a points system to ensure that commercial television broadcasting services transmit a certain amount of Australian content.[108] The Australian regulation also includes quotas to cover specific types of content such as first release Australian drama programmes, documentaries, and children's programmes. Unlike the European regulation, almost any type of programme can be included in the general quota, including repeat programmes. Although the points system provides some incentive to produce the kind of high-value content that would be sought by a cultural policy, the evidence is that the commercial networks are providing less high-value drama productions.[109]

In both jurisdictions the mixed motives of cultural and economic concerns are explicit. The EU Television Directive, in its preamble, refers to the European content regulation as a means of promoting audio-visual production and industry, and to the need to 'promote markets of sufficient size for television productions'.[110] This last statement is a clear reference to the need to build up a European industry which is able to compete with the US audio-visual market. The BSA (Aus) includes as one of its statutory objectives the need to facilitate the development of

---

[107] Council Directive 89/552/EEC of 3 October 1989 on the coordination of certain provisions laid down by law, regulation or administrative action in Member States concerning the pursuit of television broadcasting activities [1989] OJ L 298/23, as amended by Directive 97/36/EC of the European Parliament and of the Council of 30 June 1997 [1997] OJ L 202/60, Arts 4–6.

[108] The Broadcasting Services (Australian Content) Standard 1999. In 2004 Australia entered into a Free Trade Agreement with the US: the agreement allows the existing local content regulation to continue, but no new requirements can be imposed: see also BSA (Aus), s 122(5). Subscription television services are also subject to an Australian drama content expenditure requirement: BSA (Aus), Pt 7, Div 2A; for a review of this obligation, see Department of Communications, Information Technology and the Arts, *Review of Australian and New Zealand Content on Subscription Television Broadcasting Services, Report* (February 2005), available at http://www.dcita.gov.au/__data/assets/pdf_file/24874/Pay_TV_Drama_Review_Report_Final.pdf.

[109] See ABC Radio National, 'Local TV Content', *The Media Report* (13 October 2005), http://www.abc.net.au/rn/talks/8.30/mediarpt/stories/s1481265.htm, accessed 22 October 2005, and S Maclean, 'Epic Shift in funding leaves TV drama in the Wings', (2005) *The Australian* (Sydney), 25 August, 15.

[110] EU Television Directive, above n 107.

an Australian broadcasting industry.[111] To some extent, the design of local content regulations almost forces an industry focus, because the only feasible way of providing such regulation is to focus on matters such as where the content is produced, and the place of residence or nationality of those who produce it—the 'creative control' test. In the absence of such an approach, one would be left with the unappealing prospect of trying to determine what qualitative factors made something 'Australian'—the so-called 'look and feel' test—or, perhaps even more problematically, 'European', apart from any concerns that such regulation might constitute an unwarranted interference with freedom of expression.[112] Thus, local content regulation results in a rather strange outcome: it contains elements of economic protectionism and, although it is intended to promote cultural values which resonate with a particular community, there is no guarantee that the content will in fact have any programmatic or thematic connection with that community or place.[113] Indeed, in Australia, because of a trade agreement with New Zealand, New Zealand content must be treated as Australian content. The Australian content requirements apply only to commercial television broadcasting licensees. It is implicit in the public broadcaster's (the ABC) statutory charter that it will provide such programming, given its charge to provide programmes which will 'contribute to a sense of national identity'.[114] Moreover, as discussed in Chapter Three, and also in this chapter, it is expected that one of the outcomes of having a broadcaster which is not dependent upon advertising revenue is that it will be able to address programme areas not likely to be provided by the commercial sector. However, this expectation breaks down if the public broadcaster is not sufficiently funded to enable it to meet the costs of providing such programming. In Australia, the commercial sector now provides about 50 per cent more Australian content than the ABC.[115]

In addition to the promotion of Australian content in children's programming, there is a separate standard which requires a certain amount of programming for children to be broadcast by commercial television licensees.[116] Despite the US aversion to programming prescriptions, children's programming is one area in

---

[111] BSA (Aus), s 3(1)(b).

[112] *Project Blue Sky Inc v Australian Broadcasting Authority* (1998) 153 ALR 490.

[113] For a comprehensive discussion of the European content requirement, and the complexities of regulating in this area, see B de Witte, 'The European Content Requirement in the EC Television Directive—Five Years After' in EM Barendt (ed), *The Yearbook of Media and Entertainment Law 1996* (Oxford, Clarendon Press, 1996), 101.

[114] ABC Act, s 6(1)(a)(i).

[115] Friends of the ABC (NSW) Inc, 'Key Facts and Figures' (2005) 15(4) *Update* 7. The ABC's budget has declined 25%, in real terms, in the past 20 years, and with about two thirds of the budget of just one commercial television station, the ABC must provide two television stations, four national and 60 local radio stations, two digital stations, and an online and international radio service: *ibid.*

[116] The Broadcasting Services Children's Television Standard 1992. In December 2005, ACMA announced its intention to review the Standard. It is expected that the review will take between 12 and 18 months to complete: ACMA, 'ACMA Decides to Review the Children's Television Standards' (Media Release 66/2005, 21 December 2005), http://www.acma.gov.au/ACMAINTER:STANDARD ::pc=PC_100392, accessed 23 December 2005.

which there has been a willingness to regulate. As a result of concerns about the type of programming being aimed at children, and specific recognition that market forces were not adequate, Congress passed the Children's Television Act of 1990, which was designed to increase the amount of educational and informational programming available for children.[117] Rules imposed by the FCC to implement the legislation, require commercial and public broadcasters to transmit at least three hours per week of regularly scheduled core educational programming, which is defined as programming designed to meet the educational and informational needs of children of 16 years and under, which is at least 30 minutes in length and is aired between 7 am and 10 pm.[118]

Whilst the provision of certain types of programming will be desirable if real diversity is valued, the tendency towards under-provision is usually a product of the particular economic characteristics of the broadcasting market. However, another deficit area might be viewed also as the consequence of media consolidation: that of local or regional content. In the US and Australia, there have been concerns, in the past few years, that local community audiences are being neglected. In each case, growing consolidation within the media industry appears to be a contributing factor. In Australia, in 2001, as a result of complaints from communities in regional areas, the then regulator, the ABA, commenced an investigation into the provision of local news and information programmes on commercial television services in regional and rural areas.[119] The community concerns arose because of the closure of local newsrooms in a number of regional and rural areas by regional media networks, and the lack of local news and information. As part of government policy in the late 1980s and early 1990s, many smaller regional and rural television areas had been aggregated into larger markets in order to provide these areas with three commercial television services, comparable with the cities. Licensees now operated over much larger markets, with the risk that the pre-aggregation, smaller, markets would no longer be catered for. As a result of its investigation, the ABA imposed a licence condition on a number of licensees, which, using a points system, required them to broadcast matters of local significance in the sub-markets (the areas which roughly corresponded with the pre-aggregation markets).[120]

---

[117] S Rep No 227, 101st Cong, 1st Sess 5–9 (1989), 7 and 9, cited in FCC, *Report and Order, In the Matter of Policies and Rules Concerning Children's Television Programming*, 11 FCC Rcd 10726 (1996).

[118] 47 CFR § 73.671(c). Digital multichannel broadcasters will have to meet similar requirements on their main programming stream: 47 CFR § 73.671(e)(1). It was intended that these obligations would become effective from January 2006, but the FCC delayed the date of commencement pending a reconsideration of the rules: *Order Extending Effective Date, In the Matter of Children's Television Obligations of Digital Television Broadcasters*, FCC 05-211 (16 December 2005).

[119] ABA, *Adequacy of Local News and Information Programs on Commercial Television Services in Regional Queensland, Northern NSW, Southern NSW and Regional Victoria (Aggregated Markets A, B, C and D)* (August 2002). In 2004, the ABA produced a second report with respect to the remaining rural and regional areas, although it did not recommend the adoption of any formal requirements in relation to these areas: ABA, *Adequacy of Local News and Information Programs on Commercial Television Broadcasting Services in Regional and Rural Australia (Solus Operator and Two Operator Markets)* (June 2004).

[120] Broadcasting Services (Additional Television Licence Condition) Notice (7 April 2003). The obligation came into force on 1 February 2004.

Although the ABA reported in October 2004 that all relevant licensees had met their local significance obligations, it is apparent that some of what is provided, whilst technically fulfilling the licence obligation, does little to provide new or original content.[121] A report by the former Communications Law Centre found that some of the local significance content was little more than collections of press releases and other media.[122] Often the content is run from centralised (not local) newsrooms, and presented without images.[123] It is ironic that the aggregated markets policy, which was intended to create economics of scale, has resulted in the introduction of regulation to provide the content which the market is not willing to provide. This experience would seem to undermine the claims of those who argue that the economies of scale and efficiencies realised by media consolidation will lead to provision of better content. Localism has been a key component of US policy, but in 2004, the FCC launched an inquiry into localism and broadcasting in order to consider whether new policies or rules were necessary.[124] It is noteworthy that the FCC focus on localism appears to have arisen as a result of concerns expressed during the 2003 media ownership reform process.[125]

Fairness

Content regulation which addresses matters of fairness will be particularly relevant to news, current affairs, factual, and documentary programmes, but it can also have an impact on other programming types; for example, drama. As mentioned in the introduction to this chapter, fairness regulation will be concerned with diversity through measures which aim to ensure a diversity of views and opinions. Measures which ensure that the public can rely upon the integrity of the views and information being broadcast will also contribute. This may mean that rules are in place to ensure that views and opinions are presented in a balanced manner and are not misrepresented or presented misleadingly, that relationships which might influence the opinion being given are adequately disclosed, and that information being given has been properly verified. Fairness regulation has a clear connection with one of the underlying justifications for free speech protection, namely the argument from democracy. Ensuring the integrity of what is broadcast will enhance the media's contribution to the public sphere. That fairness regulation is considered necessary is again recognition that pluralism measures to structure the market may not be sufficient to produce a sufficiently balanced range of views. It might also constitute an acknowledgement that it is expecting too much

---

[121] ABA, 'Regional Television Exceeds Local Content Quotas' (2004) 136 (October) *ABA Update* 3

[122] H Wilson, 'Local News on Regional TV' (2005) 167 *Communications Update* 2.

[123] *Ibid.*

[124] FCC, *Notice of Inquiry, In the Matter of Broadcast Localism*, 19 FCC Rcd 12425 (2004). The inquiry appears to be ongoing.

[125] *Ibid*, para 5.

to require viewers and listeners to explore a full range of programmes across the channels to obtain a variety of views.[126]

Once again, it is the UK which has been the most willing to regulate. Australia regulates for fairness, but it is part of the self-regulatory framework for commercial broadcasting, and weaknesses in the regulatory process have severely compromised the effectiveness of fairness measures. As discussed earlier in this chapter, the US historically addressed this area through what was known as the Fairness Doctrine, but this has now been abandoned. Apart from rules on political broadcasting, which will be examined in the section on 'Access', the US now relies primarily on the market to throw up an appropriate range of opinions. There is another aspect of the fairness principle which is sometimes associated with the requirement to present a balance of views, and that is whether the broadcaster is allowed to express a view on a matter under discussion, that is to 'editorialise'. In the UK all broadcasting services are prohibited from taking an editorial line. This has not been the tradition in the US, even when the Fairness Doctrine was extant, and in Australia, it is an obligation which applies only to the public broadcasters.[127] Prohibiting editorial opinion is not a necessary condition for the achievement of fairness, although allowing an editorial line might make it more difficult to achieve balance and, as the UK fairness rules show, it may not always be easy to separate out the two concepts.[128]

In the UK, fairness obligations form part of what are termed Tier One obligations, which means that they apply to all radio and television services, however delivered, and to all broadcasters, whether they are public service broadcasters or not. Most of the Tier One obligations are set out in the Ofcom Broadcasting Code ('the Broadcasting Code'), which is enforced by Ofcom.[129] The Broadcasting Code expressly links the obligations imposed by the Code to the right of the audience 'to receive creative material, information and ideas' pursuant to Article Ten of the European Convention for the Protection of Human Rights and Fundamental Freedoms ('the Convention').[130] In a change from past practice, the BBC now falls under Ofcom's jurisdiction for Tier One obligations, except for impartiality and no-editorialising obligations, which remain a matter for the BBC governors.[131]

---

[126] Hoffmann-Riem, above n 2, 299.

[127] A ban on editorialising by public broadcasters in the US was held by the Supreme Court to be in violation of the First Amendment: *FCC* v *League of Women Voters of California* 468 US 364 (1984).

[128] The term 'impartiality' is sometimes used to cover both the presentation of a range of views and opinions (balance) and no-editorialising. However, to avoid confusion, 'impartiality' will be used to refer only to balance. The 'no-editorialising' principle or rule will always be referred to separately. This separation becomes more difficult to maintain when discussing the UK fairness rules, but the text attempts to make clear the sense or senses in which the term 'impartiality' is being used.

[129] The Code came into force on 25 July 2005. Prior to this, Ofcom had been applying the various codes inherited from the previous regulators.

[130] Ofcom, *Broadcasting Code* (July 2005), 3.

[131] This is because these obligations are seen as being so closely tied in with the editorial independence of the BBC, and the responsibility of the governors to ensure that independence: White Paper, above n 16, para 5.6.4. Responsibility for broadcasting during elections and referendums also remains with the BBC. However, services operated by the BBC which are not funded by the licence fee will fall under Ofcom's jurisdiction. The BBC equivalent to the Broadcasting Code is its Editorial Guidelines. A

Some clarification of the UK approach, and the use of terminology should be given here. The section in the Broadcasting Code which deals with what are termed, in this chapter, 'fairness obligations', Section Five, goes under the title of 'Due Impartiality and Due Accuracy and Undue Prominence of Views and Opinions', whilst Section Seven of the Broadcasting Code, which is titled 'Fairness', deals with matters of fairness towards individuals and organisations who may be directly affected by a programme. Thus, Section Seven deals with whether a party has consented to be included in a programme, whether they have been fairly represented, and so forth. Matters dealt with this in this section can also be relevant to general fairness principles.[132] The Comms Act (UK) has not changed, to any significant degree, the impartiality and no-editorialising obligations which applied before the 2003 reforms, although the provisions are no longer as prescriptive as to the matters the regulatory authority has to cover in a relevant code. Those earlier provisions came about because of pressure from the House of Lords when the BA 1990 (UK) was being debated in Parliament.[133] Broadcasters have to ensure that news is presented with 'due impartiality', and that all programmes observe the 'special impartiality requirements' (which can be seen to incorporate a no-editorialising obligation) set out in section 320.[134] Ofcom is required to draft a code to help secure compliance with these obligations, or 'standards objectives' as they are referred to in the Act. The main 'special impartiality requirements' under section 320 are that:

— The providers of all radio and television services must not air their own views and opinions on those services on matters of political or industrial controversy or relating to current public policy.[135]
— All television services, national radio services, and national digital sound programme services must observe due impartiality on matters of political or industrial controversy, or relating to current public policy. This can be satisfied by a series of programmes taken as a whole.
— Local radio, local digital sound programme services, and radio-licensable content services must not give undue prominence to the views and opinions of particular persons or bodies on any of the matters referred to above. This can be satisfied by taking into account all of the programmes included in the service, considering them as a whole. This is a slightly relaxed version of the impartiality requirement applicable to television and national and digital radio services.[136]

revised version of the Guidelines came into force on 25 July 2005. The Guidelines were revised to be consistent with the Broadcasting Code, although the former are generally more detailed and rigorous than the Broadcasting Code.

[132] The BBC is also regulated by Section Seven.
[133] For an account of that pressure, see LP Hitchens, 'Impartiality and the Broadcasting Act: Riding the Wrong Horse' (1991) 12(2) *Journal of Media Law and Practice* 48.
[134] Comms Act (UK), s 319(2)(c). The special impartiality requirements encompass both senses of impartiality: balance and no-editorialising.
[135] There is an exception for restricted radio services, which are services provided for a particular event or establishment.
[136] 'Undue prominence' will mean a 'significant imbalance': Ofcom, *Broadcasting Code*, 29.

It is clear that the UK concept of 'impartiality' incorporates broader fairness considerations. This can be seen in explanation of the term 'due impartiality' which emphasises context over a rigid, stop-watch approach:

> 'Due' is an important qualification to the concept of impartiality. Impartiality itself means not favouring one side over another. 'Due' means adequate or appropriate to the subject and nature of the programme. So 'due impartiality' does not mean an equal division of time has to be given to every view, or that every argument and every facet of every argument has to be represented. The approach to due impartiality may vary according to the nature of the subject, the type of programme and channel, the likely expectation of the audience as to content, and the extent to which the content and approach is signalled to the audience.[137]

The Broadcasting Code also imposes obligations which emphasise other aspects of fairness protection, as can be seen in the following rules:

> 5.7 Views and facts must not be misrepresented. Views must also be presented with due weight over appropriate timeframes.
>
> 5.8 Any personal interest of a reporter or presenter, which would call into question the due impartiality of the programme, must be made clear to the audience. . . .
>
> 5.12 In dealing with matters of major political and industrial controversy and major matters relating to current public policy an appropriately wide range of significant views must be included and given the due weight in each programme or in clearly linked and timely programmes. Views and facts must not be misrepresented.[138]

As suggested, achieving fairness through a balanced range of views does not require a no-editorialising rule, although it probably assists in the process of creating balance, and it may be more likely to engender trust in the viewer or listener that what is being heard is a genuine attempt at balance. In retaining the no-editorialising obligation, the government's view was that impartiality (here meaning balance and no-editorialising) was a major factor in the promotion of broadcasting pluralism:

> One of the cornerstones of broadcasting in the UK has been the obligation on all broadcasters to present news with due accuracy and impartiality. There are also important impartiality obligations applying to other programming. The Government believes that these obligations have played a major part in ensuring wide public access to impartial and accurate information about our society and the opportunity to encounter a diverse array of voices and perspectives. They ensure that the broadcast media provide a counter-weight to other, often partial, sources of news. They therefore contribute significantly to properly informed democratic debate.[139]

---

[137] Ofcom, *Broadcasting Code*, 24. A separate section of the Broadcasting Code, Section 6, deals with the 'special impartiality requirements' in relation to elections and referendums.

[138] The rules cover national and international matters, although the requirements of balance may be less rigorous for a non-national matter, such as the US elections: Ofcom, *Guidance Notes, Section 5: Due Impartiality and Due Accuracy and Undue Prominence of Views and Opinions* (Issue three, 28 September 2005), 3.

[139] White Paper, above n 16, para 6.6.1.

The effectiveness or necessity of a no-editorialising obligation might be questioned. Certainly it can be seen as an appropriate requirement for public broadcasters,[140] but is it strictly necessary for other broadcasters, bearing in mind that the press are free to take an editorial line? The traditional scarcity argument cannot apply, because the requirement is across all broadcasting and not just those services delivered via scarce spectrum. Barendt questions whether the no-editorialising rule, and even the strict impartiality requirements, can continue to be justified, at least in so far as they impose obligations on each broadcaster, particularly when the print media are free of such obligations.[141] Indeed, Hoffmann-Riem's point that the public cannot be expected to try to access a range of opinions across a variety of channels does not really stand up when one compares broadcasting and the press; in the case of the latter, this is exactly what the public must do, and this is probably more burdensome, because it requires a reader to purchase a number of newspapers,[142] whereas, in the case of broadcasting, it may only require the viewer or listener to change between channels.

But, again, the point can be made that it is not useful to determine appropriate standards for broadcasting by reference to the press. What is appropriate for broadcasting should be determined by reference to the purpose broadcasting serves. Requirements of balance, and, perhaps, even no-editorialising, may be fitting if broadcasting is to contribute to, and provide a space for, public debate. Whether the press should be expected to play the same role in the same way is outside the scope of this study, but the case for broadcasting might be stronger, because the immediacy of broadcasting can create stronger impressions, with possibly less opportunity for the audience to reflect upon and process the material. Hoffmann-Riem's point may also remain valid, because it is more difficult to try to access a range of opinions across channels and programmes given that their timing may not always be convenient. Of course, a viewer could, at least in the case of television, time-record these programmes, but this might be time-consuming and burdensome, and he or she would have to be able to anticipate that a particular set of programmes was going to provide the necessary balance and full range of relevant views. Perhaps the greatest advantage of fairness requirements is that it requires the professionals, such as journalists, with their expertise and resources, to identify and present the various relevant perspectives on a given matter, enabling the viewer or listener to be informed efficiently and reliably about the

---

[140] The BBC is obliged to adopt an impartial and no-editorialising position on all matters of public policy, not just current policy.

[141] E Barendt, 'Judging the Media: Impartiality and Broadcasting' in J Seaton (ed), *Politics and the Media: Harlots and Prerogatives at the Turn of the Millennium* (Oxford, Blackwell Publishers, 1998), 108 at 110. Barendt notes, however, that the removal of the impartiality and no-editorialising rules would probably result in the commercial broadcasting media favouring a right-wing political perspective: *ibid*. This certainly seems to be the US experience.

[142] This may no longer be the case, given that internet access enables easy access to a vast range of daily newspapers. On the other hand, it is becoming more common for newspaper publishers to charge for access to the online versions of their newspapers, or to require some sort of registration procedure before permitting access.

matter, and to develop his or her own position. Another advantage of fairness regulation is that it might ensure that less popular attitudes or opinions are able to be voiced. In the absence of a rule requiring the presentation of a range of opinions, broadcasters, who may have to be mindful of the demands of advertisers, may be reluctant to air views which might not find favour with general audiences, or which might be attractive to only a minority audience. A no-editorialising policy could enhance the effectiveness of these fairness obligations, because it might contribute to the public's sense of trust and confidence in the material being presented by the broadcaster.

However, one difficulty with content rules, particularly on fairness matters, can be their enforcement. Obtaining balance may be a difficult task, requiring fine judgements to be made, and regulators may be reluctant to step in and second-guess such decisions. Nevertheless, the presence of such rules may not be futile, because they can act as a standard and a reminder for broadcasters of general expectations.[143] Further, the presence of such standards provides a measure of transparency, and can serve as a reflection of public expectations about the role and conduct of broadcasting.

Another notable difference between the UK and Australia is the extent of coverage of fairness issues, whether in the legislation, or in the rules or guidelines applicable to the different types of broadcasting services. Australia deals briefly with such issues. Different standards apply to different types of broadcasters. The most rigorous standard is applied to the public broadcaster, the ABC, whereby the ABC Board is required:

> to ensure that the gathering and presentation . . . of news and information is accurate and impartial according to the recognized standards of objective journalism . . .[144]

'Objective journalism' is not a defined term, but its import is reflected in the ABC's Editorial Policies, which include the ABC's Charter of Editorial Practice. It is clear from these documents that news and current affairs programmes must ensure both balance and a strict non-editorial line:

> It is one of the statutory duties of the ABC Board to ensure that the gathering and presentation by the ABC of news and information is 'accurate and impartial according to the recognised standards of objective journalism'. The Board requires ABC editorial staff to observe the highest standards and not allow their professional judgment to be influenced by pressures from political, commercial or other sectional interests or by their own personal views.[145]

The Charter of Editorial Practice, which relates specifically to news and current affairs, also emphasises no-editorialising, accuracy, and balance.[146] The fairness obligations of SBS are put in slightly different terms. The Board of the SBS is required:

---

[143] Barendt, above n 141, 112.
[144] ABC Act, s 8(1)(c).
[145] ABC, *Editorial Policies* (2002), s 6.3.1.
[146] *Ibid*, see s 5.1.

to ensure, by means of the SBS's programming policies, that the gathering and presentation by the SBS of news and information is accurate and is balanced over time and across the schedule of programs broadcast . . .[147]

The differences in wording between the two public broadcasters might imply that the SBS is not precluded from editorialising, but the SBS's own guidelines indicate that it takes a similar approach to the ABC:

> SBS believes in the right of its audience to make up its own mind after a fair, objective, balanced and professional presentation of the issues. SBS provides a forum for views on important issues to be communicated to audiences and seeks to present the widest range of opinion over time.[148]

The more relaxed statutory standard for the SBS is probably a reflection of the nature of the SBS service. The television service relies heavily on unedited foreign language news broadcasts, over which it will have little control. In broadcasting such programmes, SBS is required to inform viewers of the source of these programmes so that 'audiences can exercise their own judgement about how issues and information are presented'.[149]

For other categories of broadcasting services, the obligations are dealt with by industry codes of practice. The BSA (Aus) makes scant reference to fairness standards, simply listing the promotion of accuracy and fairness in news and current affairs programmes as a matter for industry codes of practice.[150] The codes of practice which are drawn up by industry representatives of the different categories of broadcasting service are brief in their coverage of fairness standards and, generally, provide little more than broad principles, even for those services which are regarded as the most influential. Typical of the approach is the code relating to commercial television:

> 4.3 In broadcasting news and current affairs programs, licensees:
>
> 4.3.1 must present factual material accurately and represent viewpoints fairly, having regard to the circumstances at the time of preparing and broadcasting the program; . . .
>
> 4.4 In broadcasting news programs (including news flashes) licensees:
>
> 4.4.1 must present news fairly and impartially;
> 4.4.2 must clearly distinguish the reporting of factual material from commentary and analysis.[151]

The contribution of community broadcasting to diversity is reflected in the codes of practice for community radio and community television which both refer to the

---

[147] SBS Act, s 10(1)(c).
[148] SBS, *Codes of Practice* (2002), s 2.4.1.
[149] *Ibid*, s 2.4.3.
[150] BSA (Aus), s 123(2)(d).
[151] Free TV Australia, *Commercial Television Industry Code of Practice* (July 2004). Impartiality here will be in the sense of 'no-editorialising'.

need to provide access to 'views under-represented by the mainstream media' and 'people and issues under-represented in other media'.[152] Although one of the statutory objectives refers to commercial and community broadcasters being encouraged to be responsive to the need for fair and accurate coverage of matters of public interest,[153] there is nothing in the regulatory scheme beyond the minimal statements in the codes of practices which elaborates on what this might mean in practice. It is clear, however, that the reference to fairness principles in the BSA (Aus) was intended to incorporate the idea of balance:

> [the objective] . . . recognises that for most people, broadcasting is a major source of information on issues and events in the world. It is intended that, in the reporting of events and the presentation of issues, providers of broadcasting services will report the facts and facilitate the presentation of the range of views on any particular issue.[154]

The Productivity Commission, in its inquiry into broadcasting, stated that the concept of fair and accurate reporting included 'editorial independence and integrity, and ethical news gathering and reporting practices', although it did not find much coverage of ethical matters in the codes.[155] The Commission thought that ethical news-gathering practices were increasingly important as the lines between news and current affairs, 'infotainment', and entertainment were becoming blurred, and it recommended that fairness was too important to be left to industry regulation, particularly because there was evidence of systematic compliance failures.[156] Hoffmann-Riem has suggested that:

> Australia is generally suspicious of officially mandated schemes designed to guarantee fairness . . .. The bonds between broadcasting regulation and the functioning of a democratic society have thus far not been made the subject of any special normative provisions under Australian broadcasting law.[157]

Hoffmann-Riem's suggestion of suspicion may be true, or it may simply be that the limited treatment of fairness, as with other broadcasting issues, is the product of a continuing failure in Australia to articulate policy about the place of broadcasting in the community, and the role for regulation—something Hoffmann-Riem also suggests with his reference to the lack of a normative position. The ongoing willingness of successive Australian governments to succumb to broadcasting interests, particularly those representing the commercial free-to-air sector (as described in Chapter Three), is probably also relevant. Hoffmann-Riem also remarks on the lack of regulation to deal with one-sided influence, particularly given the degree of media concentration.[158] Unlike the UK, Australia has not

---

[152] CBAA, *Community Broadcasting Codes of Practice* (2002), cl 2.6(a). The code for community television refers to coverage of under-represented people and issues as a guiding principle but does not make it a specific requirement in the rules: CBAA, *Community Television Code of Practice* (2004).

[153] BSA (Aus), s 3(1)(g).

[154] Explanatory Memorandum, Broadcasting Services Bill 1992, 10.

[155] Productivity Commission, above n 106, 457.

[156] *Ibid*, 460–61.

[157] Hoffmann-Riem, above n 2, 246.

[158] *Ibid*.

pursued a no-editorialising policy, except in relation to public broadcasters, and it may even be inappropriate to presume a strong commitment to matters of balance. Although the extract above, from the Explanatory Memorandum, assumes that broadcasting's contribution to debate and understanding of public issues will include the provision of balanced news and current affairs, there is little in the regulatory scheme which reinforces such expectations. Earlier regulation of commercial television and radio expected something akin to the US Fairness Doctrine for current affairs programmes: broadcasters were required to afford reasonable opportunities for the airing of significant viewpoints on controversial issues of public importance.[159] However, it is not clear that current fairness regulation expects this of individual broadcasters, although this requirement is retained in commercial radio's code of practice.[160] Commercial television's code refers to an intention that news and current affairs programmes be presented fairly, but there is nothing in the rules which specifically requires the presentation of a balance of views. The rules do state that viewpoints should be represented fairly, but this seems to relate more to the treatment of individual viewpoints. Given that the broadcasting regulatory scheme contemplates that the most influential services—commercial free-to-air television, followed by commercial free-to-air radio—should be subject to the greatest degree of regulation, it is remarkable that the code of practice should be so short of detail.

It will be important also that the public is able to rely on the integrity of the information and opinion which is being presented. The Australian commercial radio sector provides a stark illustration of how public debate can be distorted if there is a failure to address such matters. The so-called 'cash for comment' affair concerned the breach of three rules which are relevant to this chapter, two of which are directly relevant to fairness standards.[161] The matter concerned a number of prominent talk-back radio presenters from commercial radio stations throughout Australia.[162] Although their programmes were broadcast on local radio, syndication arrangements meant that some of them had a significant national audience reach. These radio presenters had in place, often very lucrative, commercial arrangements which obliged them to give on-air exposure to the commercial interests concerned. In some cases, the commercial interests were individual companies, but industry lobby groups were also involved. The basic pattern of

---

[159] Australian Broadcasting Tribunal, *Television Program Standard (TPS) 24* and *Radio Program Standard (RPS) 8*, cl 5(c).

[160] Commercial Radio Australia, *Codes of Practice and Guidelines* (September 2004), cl 2.2(c).

[161] The third rule related to breach of advertising rules and will be considered under 'Advertising'.

[162] The then broadcasting regulator, the Australian Broadcasting Authority (ABA), conducted an inquiry into the matter: *Commercial Radio Inquiry: Report of the Australian Broadcasting Authority Hearing into Radio 2UE Sydney Pty Ltd* (February 2000) ('2UE Report'), *Commercial Radio Inquiry: Report of the Australian Broadcasting Authority Investigations into 2AW Melbourne, 5DN Adelaide, and 6PR Perth* (August 2000), and *Commercial Radio Inquiry: Final Report of the Australian Broadcasting Authority* (August 2000) ('Final Report'). A more detailed examination of the 'cash for comment' matter can be found in L Hitchens, 'Commercial Broadcasting—Preserving the Public Interest' (2004) 32(1) *Federal Law Review* 79; see also R Baker, 'Political Payola: The "Cash for Comment" Scandal and Australia's Protection of Political Speech' (2002) 7(1) *Media and Arts Law Review* 27.

these arrangements was that the presenter would provide favourable publicity, informed commentary, and editorial comment relevant to the interests of the commercial entity, often based upon material supplied by the commercial interest, and related to current public policy issues. Usually these arrangements would also include a provision which prohibited the presenter making any statements which would disparage or adversely affect the commercial interest and its image. Very often the radio stations were not party to these agreements, and did not know of their existence. The existence of these arrangements was itself testimony to the influential role these presenters exerted. For example, one of the most prominent of the presenters, John Laws, had been a strong on-air critic of Australian banks, and so an industry lobby group for the banks, the Australian Bankers' Association, entered into an agreement with Laws in order to ensure that this negative publicity would be reversed.[163]

The ABA found that the commercial arrangements, the existence of which had not been disclosed to listeners, resulted in a breach of fairness obligations. One of the rules breached related to the presentation of viewpoints, which, under the then applicable Code of Practice, required that '[i]n the preparation and presentation of current affairs programs, a licensee must ensure that: . . . (d) viewpoints are not misrepresented, and material is not presented in a misleading manner by giving wrong or improper emphasis, by editing out of context, or by withholding relevant available facts'.[164] The ABA found that the failure to disclose the existence of the agreements to the listening public was misleading because it was a relevant fact. The ABA's concern was not with whether the agreements had influenced the presenters' opinions, but with the lack of opportunity for the listeners to assess this:

> Listeners are entitled to assume that presenters are 'disinterested', or lack a commercial interest.. . . Listeners are entitled to make up their minds as to whether an on-air comment by a presenter has been influenced by a commercial arrangement between that presenter and a third party.[165]

Although the ABA recognised that talk-back radio had an entertainment role, it was conscious also that, as a major component of commercial radio current affairs programming, it was enormously influential:

> Talkback radio is an important source of information for many Australians and some talkback presenters are highly influential figures in contemporary Australian society.[166]

---

[163] Ironically, Laws' bank criticisms probably arose out of another commercial agreement he had with a home loan company which competed with the major banks. Under that arrangement he regularly read out scripts provided by the company: 2UE Report, above n 162, 48 and 152.

[164] Commercial Radio Australia Limited (CRA), *Commercial Radio Codes of Practice and Guidelines* (October 1999), cl 2.2(d). The current code has amended the clause, slightly but significantly. It now refers to 'viewpoints expressed to the licensee for broadcast' and omits the reference to 'withholding relevant available facts'. These amendments seem likely to have been made to protect the licensee, but it is indicative of the regulatory climate in Australia that, after the 'cash for comment' affair, broadcasters still felt free to narrow the scope of the obligation.

[165] 2UE Report, above n 162, 25–26.

[166] *Ibid*, 24.

The circumstances of the 'cash for comment' affair illustrate the importance of fairness and ethical standards, and recall the Productivity Commission's concerns about the blurring of boundaries between information and entertainment. The affair revealed widespread complacency within the radio industry about such standards and code compliance.[167] Indeed, it was suggested that the lack of detail in the codes may have contributed to the indifference to ethical standards.[168] Indifference to ethical standards, as in the 'cash for comment' matter, affected the public's access to information and opinion. Without the relevant information, the public were unable to assess adequately the information and opinions being presented, and the weight to be given to them. Such standards will be relevant even where the nature of the current affairs programme might be regarded by some as relatively lightweight; indeed, they may assume even greater importance, because it is possible that regular listeners of talk-back radio may not access many other sources of information and opinion. Thus, if content regulation is to serve properly diversity values, it will be important that it ensures that what is being broadcast is not tainted or skewed by commercial arrangements or other undisclosed information.

Also breached was a licence condition which requires a broadcaster who broadcasts 'political matter' at the request of another person to 'immediately afterwards, cause the required particulars in relation to the matter to be announced'.[169] The required particulars are aimed at disclosing the identity and location of the person who has authorised the broadcast. A number of the broadcasts which were made in connection with the commercial arrangements were found by the ABA to have dealt with topics of significant political and/or media debate at the time of the broadcasts. The broadcasts were:

> concerned with matters of public policy and decision by governments that have had commercial consequences for affected companies. These broadcasts, whilst couched in terms of a broader public policy debate, advocated particular political positions advantageous to those affected companies or organisations.[170]

Since the broadcasts were 'political matter' being made at the request of others, the relevant particulars should also have been broadcast. Once again there was no disclosure of the commercial arrangements or of information which would have made the listener aware that the presenter was putting forward particular arguments and opinions, not disinterestedly, but having been requested, and paid, to do so. Whilst seeming formulaic, the 'political matter' obligation is also directly relevant to fairness principles. The ABA noted the importance of political broadcasting disclosure within the regulatory framework:

---

[167] Final Report, above n 162, 74–78.
[168] Communications Law Centre, *Submission on the Final Report of the Australian Broadcasting Authority Commercial Radio Inquiry* (September 2000), para 2.1.1.
[169] BSA (Aus), sch 2, cl 4(2).
[170] Final Report, above n 162, 56.

> Broadcasting services play an influential role in the course of Australian political debate, and Parliament recognised this in a number of places within the Act. . . .
>
> Whereas other matters were left to the Authority and industry to develop guidelines for regulation, Parliament regarded the disclosure of the sponsor of political advertisements as a matter of such singular importance that detailed guidance was included in the Act. In accordance with the regulatory policy set down for it by Parliament, the Authority regards it as a matter of the highest importance that, in the course of political debate, listeners and viewers clearly know who it is that is trying to persuade them.[171]

The 'cash for comment' affair led to new licence conditions being imposed on one of the licensees, and the introduction of three radio programme standards, applicable to all commercial radio broadcasters. These new obligations deal with on-air disclosure of commercial agreements, the maintenance of registers of commercial agreements, implementation of compliance programmes, and the separation of programmes and advertisements.[172]

However, the presence, or suspected presence, of commercial arrangements has continued to cause disquiet, and to highlight ongoing weaknesses in the regulatory arrangements for fairness standards. Two of the most prominent of the radio presenters who were the subject of the 'cash for comment' inquiry, John Laws and Alan Jones, have been the focus of further investigations in relation to commercial agreements. The matters in relation to Alan Jones throw up a particularly revealing illustration of the interplay between ownership rules and content regulation, and the ease with which the new regulations can be by-passed. At the time of the original 'cash for comment' investigations, Jones was a presenter for the radio station 2UE, but he later moved to another radio station, 2GB. It was decided that, in order to avoid further problems concerning commercial relationships, any such arrangements should be with the radio licensee.[173] Accordingly, a commercial agreement was entered into whereby the telecommunications operator, Telstra, would sponsor the programme presented by Jones. It was clear that after the date of the agreement, Jones made a number of positive comments about Telstra, whereas prior to that date, his comments had been critical of Telstra.[174] However, the agreement was made not with Jones, but with the parent company of the licensee, Macquarie Radio Network Pty Ltd (Macquarie), and this meant that there was no obligation to make disclosure under the Disclosure Standard, because it requires disclosure only of commercial agreements between presenters and commercial sponsors. But the arrangements were not quite as neat as this, because when Jones had joined 2GB he (or companies associated with him) had taken an interest in the company controlling the radio station, Macquarie. A

---

[171] Final Report, above n 162, 55.

[172] Broadcasting Services (Commercial Radio Current Affairs Disclosure) Standard 2000 (Disclosure Standard), Broadcasting Services (Commercial Radio Advertising) Standard 2000, and Broadcasting Services (Commercial Radio Compliance Program) Standard 2000.

[173] ABA, *Investigation Relating to Sponsorship of the Alan Jones' Program on Radio 2GB Pursuant to an Agreement Between Telstra Corporation and Macquarie Radio Network Pty Ltd, Report* (April 2004), 18–19.

[174] *Ibid*, 40.

separate investigation had been held in relation to whether Jones was in a position to exercise control of 2GB.[175] Jones' interest in Macquarie could have had an impact on obligations under the Disclosure Standard, because the Standard requires disclosure of commercial agreements between sponsors and associates of presenters. If Macquarie had been an associate of Jones, by reason of the interest Jones had in Macquarie, then the commercial agreement would have had to have been disclosed by Jones on air. Although the ownership and control investigation had considered what company interests were held, and whether Jones, through practical influence, was in a position to exercise control, the Disclosure Standard only bites on company or beneficial interests (and directorships), and then only interests of more than 50 per cent.[176] Thus, although Jones did have a company interest, it was not of a size which would make him an associate. Although Jones was found not to be in a position to exercise control through practical influence, the investigation highlights the weaknesses of the Disclosure Standard. In a regulatory context which tries to draw a wide net around situations which could give rise to control and influence, it seems strange that in the context of these fairness provisions, such relationships should be drawn so narrowly.

Access

Ensuring access rights to broadcasting outlets can be seen as a more targeted aspect of fairness principles. Although the concept of media freedom encapsulates the idea that the public has access to broadcasting, this right does not extend to the right of the public to have its own direct speech access. Apart from being obviously impractical, it might also be seen as a disproportionate incursion of the broadcasters' freedom. There are a variety of regulatory measures which might be described as 'access' measures. For example, rules, which were mentioned in the section on Programming Diversity, promoting locally made content and regional programming might be seen as promoting access, both in the sense that they ensure the public has access to specific types of programming which might otherwise be neglected, and also by providing opportunities (although no direct rights of access) for some programme producers to have their programmes broadcast. Similarly, a requirement that a certain proportion of broadcast programmes be acquired from independent producers will provide access opportunities.[177] There may also be rules about access to certain types of broadcasting delivery platforms to ensure that bottlenecks are not created. This type of access issue will be considered in Chapter Five. And, of course, structuring the broadcasting environment so that there are differently structured and financed broadcasting services available might also be a way of promoting access.

---

[175] ABA, *Report of the Investigation into Matters Relating to the Control of the 2GB and 2CH Licences* (May 2003). See Chapter Three, 'Australia: Current Rules', at p 130.

[176] Disclosure Standard, above n 172, s 6.

[177] Such an obligation is imposed upon all television licensees in the UK by reason of the EU Television Directive.

Although it is not feasible, and possibly not even useful, to provide all viewers and listeners with speech access rights to broadcasting, certain individuals or interest groups may be given particular access rights, on particular occasions, under certain conditions. In general, the group most privileged with regard to access rights will be political parties and political candidates. In connection with broadcasting pluralism this makes sense, because such access rights provide the most explicit link with the argument from democracy. Another form of access right, and one which may be more generally available, will be the right of reply. But again this is an access right which will arise in only certain circumstances. There is a difference in approach between, on the one hand, the US and Australia, and the UK, on the other, in relation to access for political broadcasts, and the differences may reflect the toleration in Australia and the US for paid political advertising. By contrast, the UK has reviewed and retained its prohibition on paid political advertising.

Some of the rules associated with the Fairness Doctrine were clearly relevant to access rights in the US but, with the demise of that Doctrine, access opportunities have diminished. However, there remains a statutory right of access for political candidates, which provides that where a broadcaster has given access to a legally qualified candidate for any public office, equal opportunities of access must be provided to all other candidates for that office.[178] The equal opportunities rule does not compel a broadcaster to provide broadcasting time to any candidate: the obligation arises only when a candidate has used airtime during a political campaign, and other candidates demand equal access. Equal opportunities will include equal time, with comparable time slots and charges.[179] For these provisions to operate, much will depend upon whether there has been use of a broadcasting station by a political candidate. Certain broadcast appearances are exempt. Thus, appearances on bona fide news programmes or news interviews, incidental appearances in news documentaries, and on-the-spot coverage of bona fide news events will not be classed as a 'use'.[180] The rationale behind this is evident: without such exemptions, the equal opportunities rule could have a chilling effect on ordinary broadcasting coverage of public matters, although the exemptions will also provide scope for avoidance, and may advantage a candidate who is already in office and, therefore, likely to be featured in news broadcasts. The FCC now gives a fairly liberal interpretation to what constitutes a 'bona fide news interview': thus, programmes which might be more readily classified as entertainment talk programmes, such as *The Howard Stern Show* and *Jerry Springer*, can fall within this category of exempted use, even though the programmes might include other

---

[178] 47 USC § 315(a). What constitutes a legally qualified candidate is defined under FCC rules: 47 CFR § 73.1940. Public broadcasters are also bound by the equal opportunities rule as well as cable services (47 CFR § 76.205) and DBS (47 CFR § 25.701). The application of the equal opportunities rule is very complex—only an overview is provided here in order to give an insight into access measures.

[179] There must be no discrimination by the licensee between candidates in relation to services, facilities and practices, and so forth: 47 CFR § 73.1941(e).

[180] 47 USC § 315(a)(1)–(4). A television journalist's appearances as a presenter or reporter on regular news broadcasts will constitute a 'use' if that person is also a candidate for office. In this situation, the exemption will not be relevant: *Branch v FCC* 824 F 2d 37 (1987).

segments which do not relate to news or current affairs. The FCC will look at factors such as whether the programme is regularly scheduled and the licensee has
editorial control, and whether the inclusion of the candidate is based on news-
worthiness.[181] Surprisingly, the on-the-spot coverage of news events exemption
includes political conventions, and so a broadcaster could choose to broadcast the
convention of one political party only, but be exempt from the equal opportunities rule. However, as the free-to-air networks cut back on coverage, it seems that
the risk nowadays is not so much of one-sided coverage of political conventions,
but of little or no coverage.

Determining whether there has been a 'use' may not be straightforward. Whilst
a campaign advertisement should present no difficulties, a use does not have to be
political. A broadcasting licensee needs to be alert to appearances by a candidate,
otherwise it may find itself being obliged to offer a large number of access opportunities to other candidates. For example, in 2002, a series of public service
announcements, which featured a candidate promoting his office's free 'Women
and Money' investment seminars, were aired. The broadcast station was subsequently obliged to offer a large number of spots to the other candidates. Even
worse for the broadcaster, these had to be offered free of charge, since there had
been no charge for the public service announcements.[182] An appearance by a candidate, who is also a professional entertainer, will constitute a 'use', even though
the appearance is a strictly entertainment one, and made in the person's capacity
as an entertainer.[183] As such, broadcasters have to be cautious in the case of actors-
turned-politicians.[184] This interpretation of 'use' might seem harsh, particularly
since the candidate may not have sought the exposure, but it makes sense as an
anti-circumvention measure. The FCC also has in place a supplementary policy,
known as the 'Zapple Doctrine', which applies the equal opportunities rule to supporters of a candidate.[185] This can also be seen as an attempt to prevent evasions
of the section 315 rule. During the 2004 presidential campaign, Democrat candidate John Kerry attempted to invoke the Zapple Doctrine. His campaign asserted
that a planned broadcast of a documentary, *Stolen Honour: Wounds that Never
Heal*, about Kerry's war record, entitled Kerry's supporters to equal time. It was

---

[181] FCC, *Declaratory Ruling, In re Request of Infinity Broadcasting Operations Inc* (DA 03-2865, 9 September 2003).

[182] JD Zelezny, *Communications Law: Liberties, Restraints, and the Modern Media*, 4th edn (Belmont CA, Thomson Wadsworth, 2004), 398–99.

[183] *Paulsen* v *FCC* 491 F 2d 887 (1974).

[184] The broadcasting of films that featured Ronald Reagan when he was an actor during the period when he was running for office constituted a 'use': *Adrian Weiss*, 58 FCC 2d 342 (1976). The FCC considered that it would be too difficult to try to distinguish between a political use and a non-political use: *ibid*, 343. In 1992, the FCC reversed its position that such appearances constituted a 'use', if the candi-
date did not have control over the broadcast: FCC, *Report and Order, Radio Broadcast and Television Broadcast Services, Cable Television Service; Codification of the Commission's Political Programming Policies*, 57 FR 189 (1992), para 35. However, it later reversed its position again: Zelezny, above n 182, 399.

[185] *In re Request by Nicholas Zapple*, 23 FCC 2d 707 (1970). The justification for the Zapple Doctrine was based on the Fairness Doctrine, but it appears to have survived the latter's demise.

argued that the programme was not a genuine documentary, but had been produced by supporters of President Bush's campaign as an attack on Kerry.[186]

In a sense it is misleading to refer to section 315 as providing access rights, because the equal opportunities rule does not provide an automatic right of access to candidates: 'no obligation is imposed . . . upon any licensee to allow the use of its station by any such candidate'.[187] Without more, the temptation might be for broadcasters to refuse all appearances by candidates, since the equal opportunities requirement will place a burden on broadcasters, intruding on programme schedules and broadcasters' opportunities to make the most profitable use of airtime. However, at least in relation to federal election candidates, commercial broadcasters will be expected to provide opportunities for access. Broadcasters who wilfully or repeatedly fail to allow candidates reasonable access or to purchase reasonable amounts of broadcast time can have their licences revoked.[188] There is no absolute or automatic access right, but there is an expectation that candidates should be allowed reasonable opportunities for access, and it would not be reasonable for licensees to establish a blanket policy of refusal.[189] Determining reasonable access will be a matter for licensees' 'good faith judgments', and it is expected that what will constitute reasonable access will have to be determined in the light of the particular circumstances of a candidate's request.[190] Licensees are however entitled to take into account

> their broader programming and business commitments, including the multiplicity of candidates in a particular race, the program disruption that will be caused by political advertising, and the amount of time already sold to a candidate in a particular race.[191]

Neither the equal opportunities rule nor the reasonable access rule obliges the licensee to provide access free of charge, although where the licensee has already given one candidate access without charge, the same will have to apply to another candidate. Thus access to airtime will always be tempered by the ability to pay. There is some attempt to control the cost of political broadcasting. Section 315(b) provides that within certain time periods leading up to the election, candidates can only be charged what is known as the 'lowest unit charge' for advertisements of the same kind and frequency.[192] Thus, for example, if discounts are given to commercial advertisers—as they may well be for high-volume advertising—the same rate would have to be offered to the candidate. However, outside these particular periods only comparable rates have to be offered.[193] Despite these rules, practices

---

[186] C Limbacher, 'Kerry Demands Sinclair Stop Film or Give Equal Time', *NewsMax* (15 October 2004), http://www.newsmax.com/archives/ic/2004/10/15/184520.shtml, accessed 8 December 2005. As a result of public pressure, the documentary was not aired.
[187] 47 USC § 315(a).
[188] 47 USC § 312(a)(7).
[189] *CBS Inc v FCC* 453 US 367, 387–8 (1981).
[190] FCC, *Report and Order* (1992), above n 184, paras 6 and 8.
[191] *Ibid*, para 9(h)(i).
[192] 47 USC § 315(b)(1)(A).
[193] 47 USC § 315(b)(1)(B).

of broadcasters (particularly in television) have meant that candidates are often paying rates which are higher than necessary. One reason for this is that broadcasters usually offer advertising rates in two categories: a higher rate category which ensures that the airtime slot is fixed, and a lower rate category which means that the airtime slot is 'pre-emptible', if someone offers to pay more for that slot. Most candidates will need to pay for time in the higher-rate category, because they cannot be as flexible about when their broadcasts go to air. Another difficulty for candidates is that the lowest unit charge is only measured over the limited time periods set by the legislation; for example, 60 days in the case of a general election, which means that during this period broadcasters will often increase their advertising rates.[194] It has been suggested that a better approach would be to measure the lowest unit charge over the 365 days prior to the election, but attempts to amend the legislation to address this, and the pre-emptible problem, have not been successful.[195] Although, during the Clinton presidency, there was some pressure for the introduction of free political broadcasting time, and there was some support within the FCC, the matter has never advanced further, and it is likely that any such move would be strongly opposed by the broadcasting industry.

The question of campaign funding and advertising is an ongoing issue in the US, and, in 2002, the Bipartisan Campaign Reform Act attempted to address many of the concerns around campaign fundraising, such as 'soft money' fundraising.[196] The Act has some impact on broadcasting, and can be seen as a means of trying to prevent 'indirect' political advertising. For example, the public file that broadcasters must keep of requests to purchase broadcast time has now been expanded to include not only requests by candidates, but also requests about communications:

relating to any political matter of national importance, including—

(i)   a legally qualified candidate;
(ii)   any election to Federal office; or
(iii) a national legislative issue of public importance.[197]

Further, corporations and labour unions are prohibited from funding broadcast 'electioneering communications' during a specified period prior to the relevant election.[198] An 'electioneering communication' is one which refers to a clearly identifiable candidate for Federal office, is made within a certain specified period prior to the election, and is targeted to a relevant electorate.[199]

---

[194] Alliance for Better Campaigns, *Report: Lowest Unit Charge*, http://www.bettercampaigns.org/reports/display.php?ReportID=1, accessed 1 October 2005.

[195] *Ibid.*

[196] The main provisions of the Act were upheld by the Supreme Court, although a provision banning campaign donations by minors was struck down as a violation of First Amendment rights: *McConnell v Federal Election Commission* 540 US 93 (2003).

[197] 47 USC § 315(e)(B). The Act has also tightened the information that must be given to identify who is associated with, and has sponsored, the election advertisement: 2 USC § 441d(d).

[198] 2 USC § 441(b).

[199] 2 USC § 434(f)(3)(A).

Australia's regulation of access rights for political broadcasting shares similarities with the US approach, although the former offers something more minimalist, at least so far as the private broadcasting sector is concerned. With the exception of the public broadcasters, the ABC and SBS, all broadcasting services, whether free-to-air or subscription, are subject to a licence condition which is similar to the US equal opportunities rule, but which differs in one important aspect: broadcasters who broadcast election matter during election periods are required to offer political parties reasonable (not equal) opportunities.[200] The reasonable opportunities rule may be exercised only by those political parties which are already represented in the parliament (either house) for which the election is being held. The definition of 'election matter' is broad, so that it can include the broadcaster's own programming and not just campaign advertisements supplied by the political party. 'Election matter' means:

(a) matter commenting on, or soliciting votes for, a candidate at the election;
(b) matter commenting on, or advocating support of, a political party to which a candidate at the election belongs;
(c) matter commenting on, stating or indicating any of the matters being submitted to the electors at the election or any part of the policy of a candidate at the election or of the political party to which a candidate at the election belongs;
(d) matter referring to a meeting held or to be held in connection with the election.[201]

The reasonable opportunities rule does not oblige the broadcaster to broadcast election matter; the obligation arises only when election matter has been broadcast. Nor is a broadcaster required to broadcast election matter under the rule free of charge.[202] There is some constraint on the impact which paid election broadcasting might have: election advertisements are prohibited for several days prior to the polling day and until the close of the poll.[203] This blackout period is intended to provide electors with a breathing space and to make 'difficult the snatching of victory by any one party',[204] but it does not prevent broadcasters providing news and current affairs coverage of the elections or the campaigns.

Australia has been resistant to any proposals which might involve equal allocations of access time, whether on a paid or free-of-charge basis.[205] Indeed, it was an attempt in the 1990s to introduce a scheme which included the allocation of free time to political parties that led to the High Court's recognition of an implied freedom of political communication under Australian law.[206] Thus, fairness and access rights will be heavily dependent upon the interpretation of 'reasonable

---

[200] BSA (Aus), sch 2, cl 3. The rule applies to all federal, state, territory, and local government elections.

[201] *Ibid*, sch 2, cl 1.

[202] *Ibid*, sch 2, cl 3(3).

[203] *Ibid*, sch 2, cl 3A. Elections in Australia are usually held on Saturdays, so the blackout applies from midnight on the last Wednesday before the polling day until the close of the poll: *ibid*, cl 1.

[204] Gibson Committee, 60, quoted in Armstrong, above n 54, para 526.

[205] Armstrong, above n 54, para 524.

[206] See the discussion in Chapter Two, 'Valuing Media Diversity', at p 31.

opportunities'. Although it might be thought that the wording of the obligation, particularly the words 'must give reasonable opportunities', would require some positive action on the part of the broadcaster, ACMA's predecessor, the ABA, has ruled otherwise. Indeed, very little of a proactive nature is expected of the broadcaster.[207] According to the ABA, the reasonable opportunities rule did not impose upon a licensee an obligation to ensure balance or to broadcast a range of competing opinions. Nor did the licence condition amount to a requirement to promote accuracy and fairness. The requirement to give 'reasonable opportunities' simply amounted to 'an obligation not to refuse or deny access to a political party' which sought airtime.[208] Further, the rule does not require the broadcaster to solicit material or to provide equal format or equal time opportunities, or even to alert other political parties to the broadcast.[209] In these circumstances, clause 3 appears to set a low threshold for compliance, and it is difficult to envisage many situations in which a licensee would be found in breach. Clearly, a blatant refusal to broadcast the election matter of a particular political party would almost certainly constitute a breach. It might also be possible to determine that a political party has effectively been denied an opportunity to broadcast, if, for example, the licensee set airtime rates for a particular party well in excess of what might normally be expected. However, the format and timing of an election broadcast is unlikely to be a relevant consideration in determining whether reasonable opportunities have or have not been offered.

Just how difficult it will be to establish that reasonable opportunities have not been provided is well illustrated by a relatively recent matter concerning a broadcast during an election period by a commercial radio broadcasting service, 3MP.[210] The 3MP broadcast was a live broadcast from a shopping centre, situated within the electorate subject to the supplementary election.[211] The supplementary election was important because it would determine who could form government—the Liberal Party or the Labor Party. The broadcast, which took place a few days before the supplementary election, lasted for five hours, four of which were paid for by the Liberal Party. The broadcast included a standard mix of music, news, weather, and paid advertisements, but, more particularly, interviews with the candidate and various Liberal Party Members of Parliament. Although the broadcast was made to look as though the interviews were not pre-arranged (or election advertisements), the selection of interviewees, the order of the interviews, and the 'lead-ins' or discussion points for the interviews had all been arranged or provided by the Liberal Party. On learning of the broadcast, the Labor Party

---

[207] It is notable that the codes of practice developed by the broadcasting services make no reference to the reasonable opportunities rule or to election or political broadcasting generally.

[208] ABA, *Investigation Summary: Malbend Pty Ltd, Station 3MP* (Investigation No 763, 2 August 2001), 32.

[209] *Ibid*, 32–33.

[210] *Ibid.* For further discussion of this matter, see L Hitchens, 'Regulation of Election and Political Broadcasting' (2002) 21(1) *Communications Law Bulletin* 1.

[211] The supplementary state election was being held because one of the candidates, the sitting Member of Parliament, had died on the day of the main election.

requested airtime; 3MP was willing to grant time, but only if the Labor Party was willing to offer similar commercial terms.[212] In determining whether 3MP had provided 'reasonable opportunities', the question for the ABA was really whether the licensee had refused or denied access to airtime. Examining the evidence, the ABA concluded that 3MP had not breached clause 3.[213] The ABA considered several factors relevant, including the willingness of 3MP to provide airtime, subject to terms, even though, as it acknowledged, Labor would have been unlikely to have been able to broadcast in a similar format, since the Liberal Party's live broadcast had taken place just prior to the election blackout.[214] It was also influenced by the fact that the five-hour broadcast period was not exclusive to the Liberal Party, so that Labor could have broadcast election advertisements during that period, although this appears to have ignored the nature of the Liberal Party's broadcast, which was live and disguised.[215] The limited scope of the reasonable opportunities rule is illustrative of a failure to identify how political and election broadcasting might best contribute to public debate but, more generally, it illustrates also the limited role which fairness principles play in the regulatory design of Australian broadcasting.

The national broadcasting services in Australia are not subject to the reasonable opportunities obligation. Both services are free to decide the extent and manner of the broadcasting of political matter,[216] and each has developed policies in their codes of practice. In its statement of editorial policy, it is the ABC which has articulated most clearly the link between the role of broadcasting in political debate:

> For a proper functioning of representative government in a democracy, it is essential that the public should be fully informed of the issues of current debate and of the position and policies of those parties competing for political office. There are some basic assumptions underlying this view:
>
> — the airwaves are public property and the public is entitled to hear the principal points of view on all questions of importance;
> — broadcasting must not fall under the control of individuals, or organized pressure groups, who are influential either because of their wealth or because of their special position;
> — the right to hear alternative policies and points of view is inherent in the concepts of objective reporting and impartiality, which are part of the ABC's statutory duty; and
> — the full exchange of opinion is one of the safeguards of free institutions and of democracy itself.[217]

---

[212] ABA, *Investigation Summary*, above n 208, 33.

[213] *Ibid*, 34.

[214] *Ibid.*

[215] The ABA did find that 3MP was in breach of the obligation under BSA (Aus), sch 2, cl 4, to disclose the relevant particulars when broadcasting political matter. This obligation is discussed under 'Fairness', at p 177.

[216] ABC Act, s 79A, and SBS Act, s 70A. Both are subject to a requirement, similar to the private broadcasters, to provide the relevant particulars when broadcasting political matter at the request of another person.

[217] ABC, *Editorial Policies* (2002), cl 11.1.2.

Both the ABC and the SBS allocate free time to political parties for broadcasts during election periods. Each gives equal time to the political parties which comprise the government and the official opposition for that election, and may also allocate time to other political parties, whether or not represented in Parliament, on the basis of demonstrated public support.[218] In determining such allocations, each broadcaster will be guided by its general obligations of balance and fairness. Because the SBS is able to broadcast paid advertising, political parties can acquire access to more than the allotted time by payment of the appropriate advertising rates. The availability of a system of allocated time, offered free of charge, for election broadcasts compensates for some of the weaknesses of the access regime provided under the BSA (Aus), but it will not completely redress the weaknesses, because it is likely that the national broadcasters will broadcast to smaller audiences. This means that unless a party has the financial resources to pay for political advertising on the commercial services, it may not have the same reach as those parties which can afford to buy airtime on the commercial broadcasting services.

As could be seen in the earlier discussion of fairness in this chapter, the UK has a much more rigorous approach to fairness-related matters. This approach also drives the regulatory arrangements for political and election broadcasting, although another influence may also be the prohibition on paid political broadcasting.[219] The UK regime offers both generalised and specific access opportunities. The Comms Act (UK) requires Ofcom to ensure that party political and election broadcasts (and referendum campaign broadcasts) are provided by the licensed free-to-air public service television broadcasters and the national radio services.[220] Under the rules developed by Ofcom, a set of minium requirements are laid down, leaving broadcasters free to offer additional allocations, although such additional allocations would have to comply with broadcasters' general fairness obligations.[221] All of the broadcasters covered by these rules must carry general election broadcasts, but only Channels Three and Five are required to carry broadcasts for European Union parliamentary elections.[222] In general, major parties (which are defined in the rules) are to be offered a series of broadcasts before each election, whilst other parties can qualify for a broadcast by contesting a certain proportion of the seats up for election.[223] The parties are able to choose the length of their broadcasts from a range of specified lengths.[224] Television

---

[218] *Ibid*, cls 11.2.1–11.2.2, and SBS, *Codes of Practice* (2002), code 6. During state elections, the SBS only offers free airtime on its radio services.

[219] For the prohibition on political advertising, see Comms Act (UK), ss 319(2)(g) and 321(2).

[220] Comms Act (UK), s 333. The BBC sets its own rules.

[221] Ofcom, *Ofcom Rules on Party Political and Referendum Broadcasts* (14 October 2004), para 2.

[222] *Ibid*, para 5. Further provision is made for carrying broadcasts for local and regional elections, and referendums, as well as broadcasts relating to key national events, such as the Queen's Speech (which announces a government's proposed legislative measures for the forthcoming parliamentary year), the Budget, and political party conferences: *ibid*, paras 6 and 7.

[223] *Ibid*, paras 10–11.

[224] *Ibid*, para 14.

broadcasters must air the election broadcasts of the major parties, and referendum broadcasts during peak time (6 pm to 10.30 pm), and other broadcasts between 5.30 pm and 11.30 pm.[225] The BBC's Agreement now contains a provision which requires it to broadcast party political and referendum campaign broadcasts, although which services will carry these broadcasts, and the allocation and form of the broadcasts is a matter for the board of governors.[226] However, this is really only formal recognition of well-established practice. In fact, all of the broadcasters required to air these broadcasts have tended to work together, currently through the Broadcasters' Liaison Group, to reach a consensus on the allocation of broadcasts.

Although the content of a political broadcast is a matter for the political party, the broadcasts must comply with general content rules, such as taste and decency or harmful content rules, and it will be the responsibility of the licensee (or the BBC) to ensure that these broadcasts do comply.[227] This can create difficulties for broadcasters, who must balance these obligations with their fairness obligations, whilst also not infringing free speech rights. A good example of this can be seen in the refusal of the BBC to broadcast a party political broadcast on the ground that it breached taste and decency rules, because the broadcast showed images of aborted foetuses. The broadcast was made by the ProLife Alliance, a party which campaigned on an anti-abortion platform. The BBC's decision was upheld by the House of Lords, although the ruling has been criticised for its failure to give due weight to freedom of expression rights.[228] Outside of the specific arrangements for providing political parties and organisations with broadcasting access, all broadcasters will be obliged to maintain their fairness obligations.[229] Broadcasters will have to ensure that they give balanced coverage to the political parties, and this also may require them to make fine judgements about what they can and cannot broadcast. For example, a broadcaster who, during the 2005 General Election, provided extensive coverage of the Labour Party's launch of its 'Business Manifesto', followed by interviews with the Prime Minister and other senior party members, was found to have breached its fairness obligations because it failed to balance this with comparable coverage of other political parties.[230] Ofcom did not consider

---

[225] Ofcom, *Ofcom Rules on Party Political and Referendum Broadcasts* (14 October 2004), para 15. There are similar, but somewhat relaxed rules for radio: para 16.

[226] Department of National Heritage, *Agreement Dated the 25th Day of January 1996 Between Her Majesty's Secretary of State for National Heritage and the British Broadcasting Corporation*, Cm 3152 (1996), as amended by Department for Culture, Media and Sport, *Deed of Variation Dated 4th December 2003*, Cm 6075 (2003), cls 5E.1–5E.2.

[227] Ofcom, *Broadcasting Code*, section 6, and BBC, *Editorial Guidelines*, s 10.

[228] *R v BBC (ex parte ProLife Alliance)* [2003] UKHL 23. See also Chapter Two, 'Valuing Media Diversity', and, for a critique of the decision, E Barendt, 'Free Speech and Abortion' [2003] *Public Law* 580.

[229] For broadcasters other than the BBC, a special section of the Broadcasting Code, section 6, addresses impartiality obligations during elections and referendums. The BBC Editorial Guidelines also include a section (section 10) on broadcasting during elections.

[230] Ofcom, *Ofcom Content Sanctions Committee, re Bloomberg LP*, 28 April 2005. The rules under consideration were the rules in force prior to the current Broadcasting Code, but the fairness obligations have been retained.

that the broadcaster was intentionally biased, but it found that a broadcaster could not rely on the refusal of other political parties to take up similar opportunities as sufficient for compliance. In other words, a broadcaster who has offered broadcasting opportunities to other political parties and had these declined will have to rethink its coverage of the election issues. This type of obligation illustrates the marked differences in approach between the UK, on the one hand, and the US and Australia, on the other.

Apart from general fairness obligations, broadcasters have a specific obligation when including one candidate in a report about a constituency to invite all candidates of the major parties to participate.[231] However, the broadcast can still proceed, even if some of those invited have declined or are unable to participate. This is a change to previous rules whereby the refusal of one candidate to participate effectively vetoed the broadcast.[232] This meant that programmes which might have been valuable for the public could not be broadcast; on one occasion a plan to follow the progress of black candidates during an election had to be abandoned, because of concern that other candidates could veto their appearance.[233] The old rule provides a good illustration of how rules designed to ensure fairness can perversely have a chilling effect on debate. The current rules ensure that this veto cannot arise, although broadcasters will still have to keep in mind their general fairness obligations, and care will be needed in deciding whether or not a report is a report about a candidate's constituency. Ofcom has indicated that a profile about a candidate who is leader of the opposition which inquires into what type of prime minister he or she will make is unlikely to be a constituency report, but a profile of a candidate simply because the candidate, or his or her constituency, is of interest may fall within the rules.[234] In relation to constituency reports, a positive fairness obligation is also evident: if a broadcaster intends to broadcast a programme about a constituency, then candidates (where there is evidence of electoral support) must be offered an opportunity to participate, although once again the programme is not prevented from being aired by their refusal.[235]

Another form of access right can arise through the right of reply, which might be available to anyone affected by a broadcast. The right of reply which previously arose under the US Fairness Doctrine can no longer be relied upon, so that anyone seeking a right of reply will have to depend upon the willingness of a broadcaster to grant it. Likewise, no general right of reply is offered in Australia, although both the national broadcasting services, the ABC and SBS, show a willingness to consider granting one.[236] Only the UK has an explicit right of reply, which derives from an obligation under the EU Television Directive. A right of reply will

---

[231] Ofcom, *Broadcasting Code*, rule 6.9.
[232] That rule was necessitated by the Representation of the People Act 1983, s 93, which has since being repealed.
[233] *Press Gazette*, 30 August 1996, 14.
[234] Ofcom, *Guidance Notes, Section 6: Elections and Referendums* (28 September 2005), 2.
[235] Ofcom, *Broadcasting Code*, rule 6.10.
[236] ABC, *Editorial Policies* (2002), cl 10.15, and SBS, *Editorial Guidelines* (2002), code 2.5.2 (for radio).

normally be offered where a programme has alleged 'wrongdoing or incompetence or [has made] . . . other significant allegations'.[237] However, it is clear that a broadcaster does not have to reproduce a response in full, provided that the substance of the response is conveyed.[238]

Advertising

Regulation of broadcast advertising will have a number of purposes. Much of the regulation arises out of a concern to protect viewers and listeners—the audience generally, or, in some instances, specific audience categories, such as children—from, say, misleading or inappropriate advertising. But advertising regulation can also have a role in the promotion of broadcasting pluralism. Two main areas are relevant: the amount of time devoted to advertising; and the separation of programming and advertising. Imposing restrictions on the amount of advertising can be seen as essentially a consumer matter: 'minimising the impact of interruptions on consumer satisfaction (but at the same time recognising that there is some benefit from obtaining information)'.[239] This certainly comes through in the Australian code for television, which refers to the purpose of the rules: 'to ensure that . . . there is a reasonable balance between program and non-program matter broadcast by a licensee, having regard to the interests of viewers in uncluttered program presentation, and the commercial interests of advertisers and stations'.[240]

But there is also a wider public interest concern here. If advertisers were to have unlimited access, this would encroach on the rights of others, particularly viewers and listeners, to have access to programming. Rules controlling the amount of advertising mean that the interests of viewers and listeners have to be recognised and accommodated by broadcasters and advertisers who would otherwise seek access to maximum advertising time. Rules which address the relationship between programming and advertising are relevant to two aspects of broadcasting pluralism. First, they relate to the question of the advertiser's access to broadcasting space. If advertisers were able to use regular programming to advance their message, then this would amount to an inappropriate degree of access. Secondly, and, more importantly, maintaining clear separation of programming and advertising will help to ensure that editorial independence is maintained, which is essential if the programmes are to contribute to public debate and understanding. Thus, these rules are designed to ensure that listeners and viewers are not misled into believing that what is, in effect, promotional material has greater substance or credibility, just because it appears in another format. Given the audience's entitlement to information, if that information is to be of value, it is important that the

[237] Ofcom, *Broadcasting Code*, r 7.11. The BBC also provides for a right of reply: BBC, *Editorial Guidelines* (June 2005), s 5.
[238] Ofcom, *Guidance Notes, Section 7: Fairness* (28 September 2005), 2.
[239] Bureau of Transport and Communications Economics, *Economic Aspects of Broadcasting Regulation*, Report No 71 (1999), 103.
[240] Free TV Australia, *Commercial Television Industry Code of Practice* (July 2004), cl 5.1.1.

viewer or listener has knowledge about its true origins, so that he or she can properly evaluate its weight or value.[241] Rules which address the relationship between
programming and advertising, which are relevant to this discussion, are of two
types: those designed to keep programming and advertising distinct; and those
which govern the relationship between sponsorship and programming to ensure,
for example, that inappropriate influence is not being exerted on programme content and the editorial process.

Once again there are differences in the way each of the jurisdictions deals with
these issues, and, by now, along predictable lines. There is limited regulation of
advertising in the US, again a reflection of free speech principles and the preference for market or industry regulation. Australia gives more attention to regulation of advertising but, under the co-regulatory arrangements, the rules are
relatively basic, and implementation and enforcement of the rules has been found
wanting in the past few years. It is the UK which again provides the most detailed
regulation, in part as required by European Union law,[242] although the UK has
traditionally regulated closely in this area.[243] Whether this will remain so, however, has yet to be seen. In December 2005, the European Commission announced
proposals for a new directive which would amend the EU Television Directive.[244]
One of the main areas of focus is the regulation of advertising and, if the proposals become law, then there will be some significant changes to the regulation of
some of the matters considered in this section. These will be briefly noted where
relevant. Although the EU Television Directive allows Member States to impose
stricter regulation on the broadcasters under their own jurisdiction, it is reasonable to expect that the UK, like other Member States, will be under pressure to
relax rules consistent with the amendments.

Apart from restrictions on the amount of advertising which can be shown during
programming aimed at children, US regulation imposes no quantitative restrictions
on advertising. This is a matter for the marketplace, and even voluntary industry
codes have been abandoned.[245] Industry quantitative rules are in place for

---

[241] This concern is similar to the measures which require clear identification of political matter and
advertisements, reviewed in the previous sections of the chapter.

[242] EU Television Directive, above n 107.

[243] As part of the 2003 communications reform, some aspects of advertising regulation have been
contracted out to industry bodies, under the general control of the Advertising Standards Authority, a
self-regulatory body with a long history of regulating non-broadcast advertising. Ofcom retains back-
up enforcement powers, and in some areas, such as scheduling and sponsorship, retains primary regulatory responsibility.

[244] Proposal for a Directive of the European Parliament and of the Council Amending Council
Directive 89/552/EEC on the coordination of certain provisions laid down by law, regulation or administrative action in Member States concerning the pursuit of television broadcasting activities, COM
(2005) 646/final. For further information on the proposal, see also Chapter One, 'United Kingdom', at
p 12. For simplicity, the term 'broadcaster' is still used in the text to describe the EU obligations, but
under the proposed amendments the term 'media service provider' is also used, and, in some instances,
would replace 'broadcaster': again, see Chapter One.

[245] In fact, these codes were abandoned in the 1980s by the industry body, the National Association
of Broadcasters, because they were facing proceedings brought by the Department of Justice alleging
that the codes were a restraint on trade: Overbeck, above n 35, 575.

Australian commercial services, although, in practice, they affect television only. The radio rule applies where there is only one commercial radio station in a licence area and, since most licence areas have more than one commercial radio station operating, the rule has little practical importance.[246] Although there is some flexibility about how the averages are worked out in the actual scheduling, commercial television services are restricted to, on average, no more than 13 minutes per hour between 6 pm and midnight, and 15 minutes at other times.[247] There has been industry pressure for the removal of quantitative rules. In 1987, the Australian Broadcasting Tribunal removed the rules relating to length, number, and placement of advertisements but, when the amount of advertising increased substantially, the restrictions were reimposed.[248] The Productivity Commission noted that any removal or relaxation of the rules would very likely lead to an increase in the amount of advertising aired.[249] Until 1997, subscription television services were prohibited from broadcasting any advertising. These services remain subject to a licence condition which requires that subscription fees must be the predominant source of revenue.[250] This rule was designed to protect the revenue of the commercial free-to-air services and has little to do with any policy about appropriate levels of advertising for subscription television. The main focus for quantitative rules on advertising is obviously commercial television, but some other services are also subject to rules. The national broadcasting service, the SBS, is allowed to broadcast advertisements on both its television and radio services, but is limited to not more than five minutes per hour, and advertisements may only be broadcast between programmes and during natural breaks.[251] For television, the usual practice is to broadcast advertisements only between programmes. Although community broadcasting services are prohibited from broadcasting advertisements, they are allowed to broadcast sponsorship announcements, but limits apply here also and are imposed by way of licence condition. Community radio services are limited to five minutes of sponsorship announcements per hour, whilst television has a slightly more generous allowance of seven minutes to reflect the increased financial demands of television.[252] Although the Australian rules provide some limits on the ability of advertisers to access broadcasting space, the rules are rudimentary. With the exception of children's programming, no attention is given to whether different types of

---

[246] Commercial Radio Australia, *Codes of Practice and Guidelines* (September 2004), cl 3.2. Even this is quite generous: 'the licensee . . . must not broadcast more than 18 minutes of advertisements in a period of an hour'.

[247] Free TV Australia, *Commercial Television Industry Code of Practice* (July 2004), cl 5.6. Different rules apply during periods where programmes are likely to be watched by children. Sponsorship announcements are not included within these rules provided that they do not exceed a specified length, in general 10 seconds for a single sponsor: cl 5.5.4. To be exempt from the scheduling rules, the sponsorship announcement must also omit reference to the price of goods or services, and make it clear to the viewer that there is a sponsorship arrangement between the sponsor and the programme.

[248] Productivity Commission, above n 106, 137.

[249] *Ibid.*

[250] BSA (Aus), sch 2, cl 11(2).

[251] SBS Act, s 45(2).

[252] BSA (Aus), sch 2, cl 9(3).

programming might require different scheduling rules. Apart from any other considerations, this type of differentiation could be important as a means of relieving pressure on the broadcaster to use every opportunity to gain advertising revenue.

The UK also has rules controlling the amount of television advertising.[253] In addition, the UK rules provide more detailed regulation of the placing of advertisements—showing a degree of regulatory intervention which would probably not be tolerated in the US and Australian contexts. These additional rules can be seen to serve several objectives. There are some programmes during which advertising cannot be inserted. For example, a news, current affairs, or documentary programme of less than 30 minutes cannot carry any advertising. Other categories of programming included in this prohibition, either generally, or because of the length of the programme, are children's or school programmes, formal Royal events, religious programmes, and parliamentary proceedings.[254] It is clear that this prohibition is about something more than just consumer interest: there is a recognition that certain types of programmes have an importance or sensitivity which requires that there should be no commercial association.[255] This is borne out also by a provision in the rules which allows Ofcom to specify other types of programmes which should be included in the prohibition, such as 'programmes of a particularly harrowing or sensitive nature'.[256] Further provisions detail both quantitative and qualitative rules as to when advertising breaks can be broadcast. Thus, section 5 covers how many breaks relative to the duration of a programme can occur, and the expected time which should elapse before an advertising break occurs, whilst section 6 is concerned with rules which ensure that advertising occurs only during natural programme breaks, and includes rules as to what might constitute a natural break for different types of programmes. The matters addressed in sections 5 and 6 can be seen on the one hand from a consumer interest perspective (and from the perspective of the programme maker),[257] but a public interest concern is also evident. This is made explicit in the rules themselves, which refer to the necessity to avoid 'damage [to] the integrity or value of the programme'.[258] The proposed amendments to the EU Television Directive

---

[253] No such rules apply to commercial radio services. Quantitative rules on television advertising are required by the EU Television Directive: Ofcom, *Rules on the Amount and Distribution of Advertising*. The limits are much tighter than their Australian counterparts, the basic rule, applicable to the public service television channels which carry advertising, being no more than an average of seven minutes per hour, and for all other services, no more than an average of nine minutes for spot advertising and three minutes for teleshopping per hour: Ofcom, *Rules on the Amount and Distribution of Advertising*, ss 1.1.1(A) and 1.1.2(B). Different rules apply for teleshopping channels: s 8.

[254] *Ibid*, s 3.2.

[255] Of course, there is not a complete prohibition. In relation to some of these programmes, such as news, the prohibition does not apply to lengthier broadcasts. Presumably this is because there is less danger of any confusion between the programme and the advertisement; and it will be easier to determine a more appropriate advertising break for longer programmes.

[256] Ofcom, *Rules on the Amount and Distribution of Advertising*, s 3.2(ix).

[257] *RTL Television GmbH v Niedersächsische Landesmedienanstalt für Privaten Rundfunk* (ECJ, 2003), cited in European Commission, *Commission Interpretative Communication on Certain Aspects of the Provisions on Televised Advertising in the 'Television without Frontiers' Directive*, C102/02 (2004), fn 26.

[258] Ofcom, *Rules on the Amount and Distribution of Advertising*, s 5.1.

would maintain the maximum limit of 12 minutes of advertising per hour, but regulation of when advertising breaks should occur would be greatly reduced. With a few exceptions for programmes such as news, children's content, and religious services, determining advertising breaks will be a matter for the broadcaster, the only constraint being that advertising breaks should respect the integrity of the programme and not prejudice the rights of the right-holder.[259]

Another aspect of advertising regulation relevant to the concerns of this study is the separation of advertising and programming content. Whilst one purpose of such rules will be to make sure that quantitative rules are not undermined, another important purpose is to equip viewers and listeners with the means of understanding the nature of the content they are viewing or listening to, so that they will be able to evaluate the information being provided. A variety of regulatory measures are relevant, such as rules to keep separate programming and advertising, or to ensure that sponsorship information is available, or that promotional material is not surreptitiously introduced into programmes. In the UK, both licensed television and radio services are governed by rules regarding the separation of advertising from other content. A guidance note for the television rules makes clear the concerns about separation:

> Section 2 [Programmes and Advertising] has two purposes. The first is to ensure that viewers know at all times whether they are watching programming or advertising. The second relates to editorial independence and is to ensure that programmes are not distorted for commercial purposes; links between advertisers and programme properties are restricted for that purpose.[260]

The radio rules are more rudimentary, but similar concerns are evident.[261] Although the current television rules for separation of content are a somewhat scaled-down version of those which previously applied when advertising content was regulated by the Independent Television Commission, rules have been retained which amplify the requirement that 'there must be a clear distinction between programmes and advertisements'.[262] The concerns behind separation are evident in these more detailed rules, as can be seen in the following sample:

Advertisements must not:

(a) use expressions reserved for important news and public service announcements (eg 'news flash');

    . . .

---

[259] Proposal for a Directive Amending Council Directive 89/552/EEC, above n 244, Arts 11 and 18.
[260] Broadcast Committee of Advertising Practice (BCAP), *Television Advertising Standards Code* (2004), s 2(1).
[261] BCAP, *Radio Advertising Standards Code* (2004), s 2, r 1.
[262] BCAP, *Television Advertising Standards Code* (2004), r 2.1.1. In connection with television services, Ofcom also includes a requirement in its scheduling rules that television advertising must be recognisable and kept separate from other parts of the programme service: Ofcom, *Rules on the Amount and Distribution of Advertising*, s 3.1. There is also a separate code, administered by the BCAP, dealing with specific issues relating to separation of programmes and advertisements: *BCAP Rules on the Scheduling of Advertising* (2004). These rules are more concerned with consumer protection, as can be seen by the focus on particular audiences (eg children), and types of programmes and/or products.

(d) include extracts from broadcasts of parliamentary proceedings;

(e) feature, visually or orally, anyone who regularly presents news or current affairs on television.[263]

In the Australian context, there are rules governing the separation of programme content from advertising, although these are simply generalised statements of the need to ensure that it is clear that advertising is able to be distinguished from programmes.[264] With respect to radio, however, it is interesting to note that news programmes are expressly mentioned. The 'cash for comment' affair, discussed earlier in this chapter, provides a good illustration of the temptation for advertisers to try and insinuate their content into ordinary programme material. In the ABA inquiry, one of the issues was whether there had been a failure to keep separate programmes and advertisements. The ABA observed that, although the broadcasts were designed to promote the relevant organisation or commercial entity with which the presenter had a commercial arrangement, they had the characteristics and content of a current affairs programme, appearing to be concerned with matters of political, social and/or economic relevance to the community.[265] The affair provides a stark illustration of the failure to keep separate editorial independence and commercial influence. There is little detail in the rules, but they are nevertheless clear. It is likely, however, that other factors contributed to the failure in compliance, such as the design of the co-regulatory process, and the ABA's adoption of a relatively passive monitoring and enforcement role. It is suggested also that another contributory factor is the absence of anything more than a nominal acknowledgement of the public interest responsibilities of broadcasting. The inquiry showed how widespread commercial influence was on radio programming content. The position concerning commercial television is less clear, but there is reason to suspect that here, also, commercial relationships are influencing content, particularly news and current affairs content.[266] It is certainly clear that advertisers seek these types of connections, as can be seen by the revealing comments made to *Media Watch* by one advertising executive: 'Getting in-show integration [where the line between advertising and programme content is blurred] gets [advertisers] value money can't buy.'[267] *Media Watch* went on to report:

---

[263] BCAP, *Television Advertising Standards Code* (2004), r 2.1.2.

[264] Free TV Australia, *Commercial Television Industry Code of Practice* (July 2004), cl 1.15, and Commercial Radio Australia, *Codes of Practice and Guidelines* (September 2004), cl 3.1(a).

[265] See, generally, 2UE Report, above n 162, schs 13 and 14. Usually the commercial entity had provided 'talking points' for the presenter.

[266] Examples have been offered by *Media Watch*, the ABC programme which exposed the relationships which led to the radio inquiry: ABC Television, 'Advertising Gets Integrated', *Media Watch* (2 September 2002), <http://www.abc.net.au/mediawatch/transcripts/020902_s2.htm>, accessed 19 January 2003. The commercial television code of practice now also includes rules for the disclosure of commercial arrangements: Free TV Australia, *Commercial Television Industry Code of Practice* (July 2004), cls 1.18–1.22.

[267] Henry Tajer of Zenith Media, reputedly the largest media-buying agency in Australia: *Media Watch*, above n 266.

Henry says that the best examples of integration are in television entertainment and drama, but he's optimistic about pushing into News and Current Affairs. [Quoting Mr Tajer:] 'This used to be an area that was pretty tightly protected by stations, and most of the networks like to keep it sponsorship free. But gradually this is changing, and the networks are becoming more flexible than they used to be . . . This is a positive thing, because the market has been crying out for more integration.'[268]

This attitude reflects the view taken by those giving evidence at the inquiry that having an advertising message incorporated into programming content was of much greater value. There is a certain irony in this. Advertisers seek integration, particularly in news and current affairs, because, one might suggest, such programming appears to offer independence, objectivity, and an authoritative voice. Yet, the act of integration undermines the very values sought by advertisers. Thus, it can be seen that the integrity of the relationship between advertising and programming will be crucial to the integrity of information and opinion provided by broadcasting to the public.

As the Australian example shows, and the comments of the advertising executive confirm, commercial interests may be keen to increase their access to airtime, but in such a way as to avoid advertising time limits,[269] or to overcome audience impatience with excessive advertising, or scepticism about the content. Advertisers' concerns about reaching audiences are compounded by the development of technical means to bypass advertisements. Both the UK and the US have specific measures which try to control the insinuation of commercial messages into programming; these measures can be seen as an elaboration of the basic principle of separation of advertising and programme content. With the exception of the new rules put in place after the 'cash for comment' affair, this is an area about which Australian regulation, including industry regulation, has been remarkably complacent. This may change, and, ironically, not through the efforts of the broadcasting regulator, ACMA, but those of another regulator, the Australian Competition and Consumer Commission (ACCC). In 2005, the ACCC commenced proceedings against one of the commercial television services, the Seven Network, accusing the broadcaster of misleading and deceptive conduct under the Trade Practices Act 1974, section 52, in relation to items broadcast on its current affairs programme, *Today Tonight*. The programme had carried reports of a commercial mentoring programme about investment designed for women, Wildly Wealthy Women. The ACCC's concern was that the broadcast programme had made misleading statements about the results which participants in the mentoring programme could expect.[270] What was

---

[268] Henry Tajer of Zenith Media, reputedly the largest media-buying agency in Australia: *Media Watch*, above n 266.

[269] An ongoing problem in the US has been the use of what the FCC terms 'program-length commercials' as a way of avoiding the advertising time restrictions applicable to children's programming: see Zelenksy, above n 182, 408, and KC Creech, *Electronic Media Law and Regulation*, 4th edn (Burlington MA, Focal Press, 2003), 203–4.

[270] ACCC, 'ACCC Takes Federal Court Action against Seven Network, Wildly Wealthy Women over Today Tonight Broadcasts', Media Release 235/05 (28 September 2005), available from www.accc.gov.au.

interesting about these proceedings was that normally a news or information item broadcast by a broadcast licensee or other media outlet would be exempted from such action under section 65A. However, the exemption will not apply to advertisements, or where material has been broadcast pursuant to some commercial arrangement.[271] Thus, the ACCC in bringing the proceedings was alleging that the item was not a genuine news or information item.

One approach is to ensure that the audience is always provided with information which will enable it to identify when airtime has been purchased: the public is 'entitled to know who seeks to persuade them with the programming offered over broadcast stations and cable systems.'[272] This is the long-standing principle behind the US payola rules. Indeed, as one FCC Commissioner has noted, these rules have been retained, whilst many other rules, embraced within the public interest rubric, such as the fairness doctrine, have been repealed.[273] This is crucially important if broadcasting is to fulfil its proper public interest function because, as will be seen below, these rules can have a significance beyond the orthodox commercial context. One aspect of this principle is the sponsorship identification rule, which provides that whenever a station broadcasts matter for valuable consideration, it is required to announce that fact and to identify who has provided the consideration.[274] The rule applies to all paid-for airtime, including ordinary spot advertisements, but here mention of the trade name will be sufficient.[275] Clearly this is unlikely to be a problem, because the very nature of such advertising implies that the sponsor will want its identity, or the identity of its product or service, to be known. However, the sponsorship identification rules are also intended to apply to situations when programmes may be sponsored, or where any part of a programme is paid for.

Related to the sponsorship identification rule is a requirement that any employee, or person, involved with the production or preparation of programme content, who receives consideration for the provision of content to be broadcast, or any person who provides such consideration, shall disclose the same to the licensee.[276] A licensee having received such a disclosure will then have an obligation to comply with the sponsorship identification rules.[277] These rules have a long history, but equally, covert advertising and payola[278] practices appear to be well

---

[271] *Seven Network v ACCC* [2004] FCA 885, para 22. These proceedings arose out of a challenge by the Seven Network to certain preliminary steps taken by the ACCC. The challenge was dismissed, as was an appeal to the Full Federal Court: [2004] FCAFC 267.

[272] FCC, *Public Notice, Commission Reminds Broadcast Licensees, Cable Operators and Others of Requirements Applicable to Video News Releases and Seeks Comment on the Use of Video News Releases by Broadcast Licensees and Cable Operators*, FCC 05-84 (13 April 2005), 1–2.

[273] JS Adelstein, '"Fresh is Not as Fresh as Frozen": A Response to the Commercialization of American Media', Speech delivered at The Media Institute, Washington, DC (25 May 2005), 2.

[274] 47 USC § 317(a)(1). The FCC has developed rules to support § 317: 47 CFR § 73.1212 (for commercial and public broadcasting) and 47 CFR § 76.1615 (for cable systems).

[275] 47 CFR § 73.1212(f).

[276] 47 USC § 508. Under the Comms Act (US), this rule is found in § 507.

[277] 47 USC § 317(b).

[278] The term 'payola' is a contraction of 'pay-for-play', and reflects the origins of the practice within the music industry: Office of New York State Attorney General, 'Sony Settles Payola Investigation'

entrenched.[279] Payola has often arisen with regard to the promotion of music and, in 2005, a major investigation into payola practices was carried out. The investigation resulted in Sony BMG Music Entertainment agreeing to pay 10 million US dollars to non-profit-making institutions to fund music education and appreciation programmes, after the investigation revealed that payments and gifts were being made to radio stations and employees in order to secure airplay for various artists.[280] The practice was on a wide scale, and ranged from blatant bribes to payments disguised through a variety of mechanisms; for example, mock contest winners.[281] However, music payola is just one example of the type of practices which should be caught by the sponsorship identification and payola rules, and there are concerns about the growing commercialisation of US media, which one FCC Commissioner, Adelstein, sees as one of media consolidation's 'most pernicious symptoms':

> We see reports of video news releases masquerading as independent, legitimate news; PR agents pushing political and commercial agendas that squeeze out real news coverage and local community concerns; product placements turning news and entertainment shows alike into undisclosed commercials; and well-trained marketers preying on the unsuspecting minds of our young children.[282]

Concerns have been expressed that practices such as product placement are widespread, and conducted with disregard for current identification rules. And there is also concern that the current rules are not adequate to meet the degree and variety of covert advertising (or 'embedded advertising') currently being experienced.[283] Adelstein has also admitted that the FCC may have become lax in enforcing the sponsorship and payola rules.[284] It might be tempting to take the view that excessive concern about the insinuation of commercial interests into

(Press Release, 25 July 2005), http://www.oag.state.ny.us/press/2005/jul/jul25a_05.html, accessed 14 December 2005, para 5.

[279] For a comprehensive discussion of the history of these rules, see R Kielbowicz and L Lawson, 'Unmasking Hidden Commercials in Broadcasting: Origins of the Sponsorship Identification Regulations, 1927–1963' (2003–4) 56 *Federal Communications Law Journal* 329.

[280] Although the matter was completed with regard to Sony, the investigation was continued because of evidence of widespread industry payola practices: Office of New York State Attorney General, above n 278. The FCC also commenced an investigation into payola practices: FCC, 'Statement of FCC Chairman Kevin J Martin', News Release (8 August 2005), www.fcc.gov, accessed 24 September 2005. In November 2005, a settlement was reached with another major record company, Warner Music Group, with Warner agreeing to pay $US 5 million to non-profit-making institutions to fund music education and appreciation programmes. Other companies remained under investigation. The New York State Attorney-General, who conducted these investigations, was critical of the lack of progress in the FCC's investigation: J Leeds, '2nd Music Settlement by Spitzer', *New York Times* (23 November 2005), http://www.freepress.net/news/12511, accessed 15 December 2005.

[281] Office of New York State Attorney General, *Assurance of Discontinuance Pursuant to Executive Law § 63(15)* (22 July 2005), http://www.oag.state.ny.us, accessed 14 December 2005, para 27, and generally.

[282] Adelstein, above n 273, 3.

[283] Commercial Alert, *Complaint to FCC, re: Complaint, Request for Investigation, and Petition for Rulemaking to Establish Adequate Disclosure of Product Placement on Television* (30 September 2003), http://www.commercialalert.org/fcc.pdf, accessed 24 September 2005.

[284] Adelstein, above n 273, 2.

programming is unwarranted; after all, most programming is within the entertainment genre, and much of it, not particularly elevating. But there are several matters to consider here. First, to the extent that commercial interests are able to exert control over choice of programmes or content, this intrudes on the authorial and editorial freedom of the programme maker. Secondly, as discussed in Chapter Two, media freedom contemplates that the audience has a right to receive programmes of both information and entertainment value, and programmes within both genres can play a role in helping the viewer or listener to understand the world in which he or she lives. Knowing the source of the programme will be relevant to the programme's impact. Even within the personal world of the audience, the role played by commercial interests might be critical. There is evidence, in the US, of well-known celebrities and actors being paid by pharmaceutical companies to appear on television talk shows, where they discuss personal health issues and promote the use of specific branded drugs, but without disclosure of the payments being received.[285] What the audience might perceive as being an independent presentation by a journalist of a health problem and treatment is little more than an advertisement. But, without that crucial knowledge, the viewer might receive the information in quite a different way. This illustration points also to the real danger that is present when commercial messages might be influencing the production and content of news and current affairs programmes. Viewers or listeners will have a certain expectation about the journalistic processes which have produced that content, which can be used by them to assess the information, and to reach their own view of the matter. Those expectations and processes will be undermined if relevant information about the real source of the content is withheld.

The Australian 'cash for comment' affair revealed that it was not only commercial messages which were being insinuated into programming; industry groups were also using the radio presenters to advance views which were relevant to political and policy debates occurring at that time. Thus, some political groups may have an interest in also being able to promote particular views or positions under the cloak of disinterested and professional news and current affairs programmes. Such practices are also within the scope of the US rules on sponsorship identification and payola and, in 2005, there was evidence that the US government routinely engaged in this type of promotional activity. Two different practices were involved. The first concerned a government department paying a presenter to promote a specified government policy. Several instances of this came to light, but it was the first one which attracted the most attention.[286] Here, a political commentator, Armstrong Williams, was paid 240,000 US dollars by the Department of Education to promote, on national television, a key policy of the government's education programme. There was no disclosure of this payment, which specifically

[285] Commercial Alert, above n 283, 5 and 11.
[286] ABC Radio National, 'American Cash for Comment', *The Media Report* (3 February 2005), http://www.abc.net.au/rn/talks/8.30/mediarpt/stories/s1294962.htm, accessed 7 February 2005.

required him to 'regularly comment on NCLB [No Child Left Behind] during the course of his broadcasts', and to interview the Education Secretary.[287] The irony of this was that Williams was well known as a right-wing commentator, and would probably, regardless of the payment, have been willing to promote the policy and interview the Education Secretary.[288] Nevertheless, it is clear that such a payment will still serve a purpose, because for the government it provides some assurance that the specific policy will be promoted and be given priority for discussion over other issues which might be on the news agenda at the relevant time. As such, the necessity for such disclosure is still evident. The Williams example, however, shows the complexity and interdependence of content regulation that is relevant to broadcasting pluralism. Without a strong regulatory commitment to fairness, particularly balance, the role which identification of sources can play may be limited, although still necessary.

The second practice is one which is even more disquieting, not only because it appears to have been well established and widespread, but also because broadcasters appear to have been willing to tolerate it. This practice involved the supply to broadcasters of 'video news releases' (VNRs). VNRs are pre-packaged news stories, designed to be used in news programmes, without alteration, and are generally supplied with a script to be used as the introduction to the video. The VNR may use actors playing reporters. In a sense, they can be seen as the video equivalent of a press release, but clearly they are something more, given that they become the item itself, rather than just background. VNRs may be used by commercial or lobbying groups, but it has been their use by the US government that has caused most concern. It would appear that hundreds of VNRs were prepared and supplied to broadcasters by government departments and agencies.[289] Although, these were generally supplied to the broadcaster without any consideration, the sponsorship identification rules are still relevant, because identification is required if the programme is a political one, or one discussing controversial issues.[290] In early 2005, the FCC issued a reminder to broadcasters of their obligations under the sponsorship identification rules, and called for information about VNR practice.[291] An amendment to the Comms Act (US) was also under consideration by Congress, which, if passed, would require any government-sponsored VNR to identify clearly the government as its source.[292] The revelation of the VNR practice, whether relat-

---

[287] Freepress, 'Free Press Calls for an Investigation into Bush Administration's "Payola Pundits"' (13 January 2005), http://www.freepress.net/press/release.php?id=40, accessed 13 January 2005.

[288] ABC Radio National, above n 283.

[289] Letter from Senator John Kerry to [then] FCC Chairman, Michael Powell (15 March 2005), http://www.reclaimthemedia.org/print.php?story=05/03/16/7516824, accessed 15 December 2005.

[290] 47 USC § 317(a)(2) allows the FCC to make rules for political and controversial programmes. Identification is required under 47 CFR § 73.1212(d) (for broadcast) and § 76.1615(c) (for cable). There is evidence that in some cases payment was made to guarantee airing of the VNR, although this appears to be confined to commercial providers: JS Adelstein, 'Statement of Jonathan S Adelstein', US Senate Committee on Commerce, Science and Transportation (12 May 2005), 2.

[291] FCC, *Public Notice* (2005), above n 272.

[292] Truth in Broadcasting Act of 2005, s 967. The Bill was introduced into the Senate.

ing to commercial influence or political influence, as did the Australian 'cash for comment' affair, throws into doubt broadcasting's role in the presentation of news and information and, indeed, questions the very nature of news and information programming. As Adelstein, observes, as FCC Commissioner, these practices undermine the expectations the public will have about what is being broadcast:

> It is a cardinal right of every American to assume that radio and TV programs that appear to be based on authentic editorial judgments of the stations are in fact just that, unless the public is told otherwise. After all, the most fundamental responsibility of broadcast stations is to serve the public interest, and broadcasters are accountable to their communities. We have a right to know that people who present themselves to be independent, unbiased experts and reporters are not shills hired to promote a corporate—or governmental—agenda.[293]

The UK regulation addresses some of these issues more directly, and it is a measure of the importance of this area of regulation that Ofcom retains direct regulatory responsibility. Section Ten of the Ofcom Broadcasting Code deals with commercial references in relation to all licensed services. The principles behind these rules are:

> To ensure that the independence of editorial control over programme content is maintained and that programmes are not distorted for commercial purposes.

> To ensure that the advertising and programme elements of a service are clearly separated.[294]

However, it is clear that a different attitude towards commercial content applies in the UK. Whereas in the US there is a toleration of commercial content within programming, provided that there is appropriate identification, in the UK there is not. Thus, there is an explicit prohibition on programme promotion of goods and services and product placement.[295] A prohibition also applies to giving any undue prominence within a programme to a product or service, where it can not be editorially justified.[296] Any reference to a brand should not be as a result of any agreement or negotiation with a supplier.[297] It is in this area that the European Commission proposal to amend the EU Television Directive would have most impact. Whilst the proposal retains a prohibition on surreptitious advertising, it would, if enacted, allow product placement. Product placement would generally be permitted, provided that this was made clear at the commencement of the programme, but not for some programmes: news; current affairs; documentaries; and children's programming.[298] The Commission's justification for permitting product placement was to enable EU media to be competitive with the US media

---

[293] Adelstein, above n 273, 8.
[294] Ofcom, *Broadcasting Code*, s 10.
[295] *Ibid*, rr 10.3 and 10.5.
[296] *Ibid*, r 10.4.
[297] Ofcom, *Guidance Notes, Section 10: Commercial References and Other Matters* (5 December 2005).
[298] Proposal for a Directive Amending Council Directive 89/552/EEC, above n 244, Art 3h.

industry, which seems ironic in light of the recent concerns in the US about commercial (and other) intrusion into programming.[299]

Another difficult area in terms of the relationship between commercial and programme content is programme sponsorship. Programme sponsorship is often seen as a less intrusive form of advertising. It is thought not to attract the type of pressures usually associated with advertising funding, and thereby is seen as an acceptable form of revenue raising for non-commercial services. Thus, public broadcasting in the US and community broadcasting services in Australia are allowed to raise revenue through sponsorship.[300] In Australia, there is little specific regulation of programme sponsorship. In the US, the sponsorship identification rules are relevant, and additional rules are imposed on public broadcasting services to ensure that sponsorship identification is not used as a form of promotional material.[301] In Australia, there is no prohibition on community broadcasting sponsorship announcements incorporating promotion, the only practical difference between a sponsorship announcement and an advertisement will be that the former will include a statement acknowledging the sponsor's financial support.[302] Indeed, community television sponsorship announcements have the look and feel of normal spot advertisements, although of a lower professional quality. Although the UK allows its commercial services to carry programme sponsorship, this is more tightly regulated and focuses, particularly, on the maintenance of editorial independence. This reflects the ambiguous nature of sponsorship because, although generally regarded as a more benign means of attracting revenue, it might put broadcasters under greater pressure regarding programming choice. Whilst advertising of the traditional kind can influence programme diversity, programme sponsorship brings with it the risk that the sponsor may want to have some control over the editorial content.[303] Commercial interests may become more selective about the type of programming a broadcaster offers if it is to be named as the sponsor, compared with simply arranging to advertise within a certain time slot. A UK inquiry into the funding of the BBC considered that sponsorship could pose a greater threat to editorial independence than traditional advertising.[304] Although sponsorship is permitted in the UK, providing that the sponsor exercises no influence over the programme, its inherent risks are recog-

---

[299] European Commission, *The Commission Proposal for a Modernisation of the Television Without Frontiers Directive: Frequently Asked Questions*, Memo/05/475 (13 December 2005), 2. In December 2005, Ofcom announced a consultation on deregulation of product placement for both television and radio, citing specifically the potential of product placement as an additional revenue source: Ofcom, 'Product Placement—A Consultation on Issues Related to Product Placement', News Release (19 December 2005), http://www.ofcom.org.uk/consult/condocs/product_placement/, accessed 20 December 2005.

[300] Community broadcasting in the UK is allowed a limited degree of both advertising and sponsorship.

[301] 47 USC § 399a. Although given that identification announcements can include 'logograms' the line between identification and promotion might be finely drawn.

[302] BSA (Aus), sch 2, cl 2(2).

[303] Committee on Financing the BBC, above n 12, paras 406–8.

[304] *Ibid*, para 406, and, generally, paras 406–8.

nised in the prohibition on sponsorship of news and, for television, current affairs programmes.[305] Other rules address the basic principle of the separation of programme content from any direct commercial influence: thus, sponsored programmes have to be clearly identified, and sponsorship credits separated from programmes. Sponsorship credits cannot include any promotional or advertising message.[306]

Conclusion

As this study has sought to argue, crucial to the proper functioning of the public sphere will be the role played by media, and an important part of the media's role will be its ability to provide access for the public to a range of programmes, views and opinions. It was argued in Chapter Three that, although structural regulation will have an important contribution to play, structural regulation alone will not be sufficient. Structural regulation and, particularly, structural regulation in the form of ownership and control regulation, cannot be relied upon to guarantee that sufficient diversity of voice is attained. Indeed, this chapter has provided examples of the need to revisit content regulation as a consequence of the impact of consolidation in the broadcasting industry. Although structural regulation has its place in the regulatory space which serves the public sphere, it needs to operate in tandem with the type of regulatory measures reviewed in this chapter, which can provide more focused, and less ad hoc, opportunities for ensuring diversity in voice, idea, and view. Even the US, with its preference for a, seemingly, hands-off structural approach, recognises that, in certain situations, extra-regulatory intervention will be necessary: a good example of this is the access-related measures for political candidates. However, if content regulation is to play an effective role in promoting broadcasting pluralism, it needs to be comprehensive, based upon a proper appreciation of how content is influenced and shaped by its origins, production, and transmission. Although the US and Australia provide regulatory schemes to enable the public to have access to political voices, they offer weak regulatory protection of general fairness standards. The demise of the Fairness Doctrine in the US, and the sketchy fairness regulatory scheme in Australia leaves fairness guarantees largely dependent upon the willingness of individual broadcasting organisations to acknowledge professional or ethical standards. As the evidence of both jurisdictions shows, this is unlikely to be an adequate buttress against the pressures, commercial and political, that broadcasters may face in producing broadcasting content. The experience of these two jurisdictions, in

---

[305] Ofcom *Broadcasting Code*, r 9.1.
[306] Ibid, rr 9.7–9.8 and 9.13–9.14. The prohibition on advertising within the sponsorship credit is somewhat relaxed for radio: r 9.10. However, a sponsorship credit should not sound like an advertisement: Ofcom, *Guidance Notes, Section 9: Sponsorship* (28 September 2005).

particular, points also to another arm of content regulation which has been emphasised in this chapter: namely, rules which seek to maintain the integrity of what is broadcast. Although all three jurisdictions offer examples of this aspect of content regulation, such as rules which enable the audience to distinguish between programming and commercial content, it is this aspect of content regulation which illustrates starkly another important matter, and that is the need for content regulation to be embedded within an effective regulatory system which provides for compliance, monitoring, and enforcement. The Australian 'cash for comment' affair shows the dangers of a weak regulatory scheme, whilst more recent experiences in the US highlight the risks of regulatory complaisance.

Like all aspects of broadcasting regulation, content regulation is also being reappraised. It is a reappraisal that may arise on two fronts: the actual rules with which broadcasters have to comply; and the type of regulatory process for enforcing those rules. This can be seen most clearly in the UK as it relaxes many rules relevant to this discussion, and also moves away from statutory regulation to a greater emphasis on industry regulation. Therefore, it will be important to be able to make a positive case for why effective regulation of broadcasting content is appropriate and necessary. Content regulation reform needs to be considered in the light of the impact it will have on broadcasting's contribution to the public sphere, rather than on weak 'demise of spectrum scarcity' arguments. Whilst growth in the number of broadcasting outlets might provide more opportunities for greater programme diversity, there may still be limitations, for reasons discussed in Chapter Six, on what the market alone can provide. In any event, regulation to ensure the integrity of programming is hardly dependent upon issues of spectrum scarcity or non-scarcity. However, in Chapter Two, the point was made that if the media are to function properly within the public sphere, they must not be subverted by political or economic power. Some of the examples of regulatory failure provided in this chapter show that the media have indeed been suborned by commercial, even political, influences. Undeniably, some sectors of the media operate within a commercial context, but this does not mean that commercial influences, for example, should prevail at the expense of the public's right to receive information and ideas. Referring again to Chapter Two, it was stated there that 'the task must be to structure an environment which recognises media's potential to enhance public discourse, but minimises its capacity for distortion of that same discourse'.[307] Ensuring the integrity of broadcasting content would seem particularly relevant to this. Indeed, it may be one of the most important aspects of content regulation's role in protecting the public sphere, and likely to remain so, given the increasing competition for advertising revenue, and the pressure on traditional forms of advertising. Both the US and Australia demonstrate the consequences of failing to acknowledge and protect sufficiently the public interest role of broadcasting. The recent experience of these two jurisdictions should serve as a warning to the UK (and the EU). The proposal to amend the EU Television Directive also contains a

---

[307] See Chapter Two, 'Reclaiming the Public Sphere', at p 60.

provision which expressly encourages the use of co-regulatory solutions.[308] Co-regulation can have a role to play, but, here too, the weaknesses in the Australian co-regulatory design should be noted. Content regulation can be an important adjunct to structural regulation, but its value will depend upon the adequacy of the rules and the effectiveness of the regulatory process.

---

[308] Proposal for a Directive Amending Council Directive 89/552/EEC, above n 244, Art 3(3).

5

COMPETITION REGULATION

Introduction

The use of specific rules governing ownership of broadcasting does not mean that competition law will not have a role to play. Indeed, ownership rules are a form of competition regulation, designed to operate pre-emptively to prevent or minimise concentration. And, notwithstanding the use of ownership regulation, general merger law will generally still be applicable. A proposed merger or acquisition which complies with relevant media ownership rules might, nevertheless, not be allowed to proceed under merger rules. Although general competition law, designed to deal with practices which are anti-competitive or an abuse of market power, will be applicable to the media industry, it has been common also to impose media-specific regulatory measures, rather than to rely only on generic competition law enforcement and remedies. Similarly, jurisdictions may also adopt a sectoral approach to merger regulation to enable additional matters to be taken into account, having regard to the special nature of that industry. Merger regulation is concerned with the impact of a merger or acquisition on competition in particular markets; it is not primarily concerned with the impact of a merger on broadcasting pluralism, but specific tests can be incorporated to address public interest concerns. Competition law enforcement (in other words, ex post regulation) can be used where the market has failed to operate competitively, because of anti-competitive behaviour or market power abuse. However, there may be situations where ex post regulation will not be sufficient because of particular characteristics or market failures of the industry. It may be more useful to apply ex ante competition regulation by designing rules which help to shape the market, or behaviour within it, and promote competition and reduce barriers to entry.[1] Ex ante competition regulation has become increasingly important within the media industry. It may apply generally, or it may be used to regulate the behaviour of particular providers who might, for example, occupy a dominant position in the

---

[1] The distinction between ex ante and ex post competition regulation may not be as clear cut as this description suggests. Cave and Crowther examine the extent to which ex post enforcement has become regulatory through the use of undertakings: M Cave and P Crowther, 'Pre-emptive Competition Policy meets Regulatory Anti-Trust' (2005) 26(9) *European Competition Law Review* 481.

relevant market. It is with the operation of ex ante regulation that this chapter is primarily concerned.

With the development of new delivery platforms and the increased channel capacity of these platforms, competition law, particularly ex ante regulation, has become of growing importance to the broadcasting regulatory map, able to adapt to situations or practices which are outside the scope of traditional ownership regulation. The presence of natural monopolies and the importance of access to content, for example, increase the scope and pressure for industry practices which may be anti-competitive. Hence, there may be measures which address particular practices, such as the making of exclusive agreements for the rights to content. Another concern is the presence of natural monopolies or oligopolies, and gatekeeper controllers. Cable is an example of a delivery mechanism, which may be a natural monopoly or oligopoly. In other words, the economies of scale in building and operating the infrastructure are such that it is efficient for only one or a few participants to operate in the market.[2] However, this does not mean that there is not room for competition for the programme services which can be delivered by cable, and so it makes sense to provide opportunities for others to gain access to the delivery platform, in order to be able transmit their programme services.[3] Thus, regulatory measures may be in place which try to ensure that those who are in a position to control these natural monopolies or those who are gatekeepers do not abuse their position by, for example, excluding access or setting restrictive access conditions. Particular concerns will arise in situations of vertical integration—where the controller of, say, a cable network is also operating as, or is linked with, a content provider. Although these competition regulatory measures are located within a policy context which is focused on trying to ensure that markets are open to economic competition, they can also have a relevance to the goals of broadcasting pluralism. By promoting access to infrastructure, and by opening up scope for competing sources of programme production or distribution, these measures are, indirectly, providing the conditions which enable the public to have access to a wider range of services and programmes. In one sense, these mechanisms for promoting access are merely a continuation of traditional broadcasting regulatory practices. For example, licensing of the spectrum can be seen as a means of controlling who has access to a limited delivery platform, whilst measures such as the regulation of network arrangements, or measures which require the transmission of a certain proportion of independently produced content can be a way of ensuring that those who control this limited platform provide access to other programme sources. However, with the development of new technologies and delivery mechanisms, the potential for gatekeeper control has increased, necessitating more complex and more wide-ranging regulatory measures, and a greater reliance on industry-specific competition rules as a supplement to generic competition regulation.

This chapter will consider a range of regulatory measures which are illustrative of the role competition law plays in the broadcasting environment. Concerns can

---

[2] G Doyle, *Understanding Media Economics* (London, Sage Publications, 2002), 169.

arise at both the wholesale level (that is, the business-to-business dealings) and the retail level (the dealings with the end-user: that is, the viewer and listener), but, in general, the focus in this chapter will be on the regulatory measures applied at the wholesale level. Each of the three jurisdictions can provide examples of these competition regulatory measures, although, as so often seen in the previous chapters, there are differences in the extent and manner of these regulatory measures. The UK and the US have been more disposed to develop ex ante rules to address specific practices in order to promote 'fair and effective competition', whereas in Australia ex ante regulation is less well developed and less comprehensive.

Merger Regulation

Merger regulation will generally be concerned with whether a merger is likely to lessen competition substantially in the market, such that the merged firm would be able to act within the market without being constrained by its competitors.[4] In answering this question, those investigating the impact of the merger will not be concerned with its impact on the diversity of information and ideas. Determination of a merger's impact on competition will be dependent upon a decision about what market or markets are affected by the proposed merger. The boundaries of that market will usually be determined by identifying all the goods or services which are close substitutes. Whilst this approach may be appropriate for a determination of the effect of a merger on competition, it may not assist concerns about how the merger will impact upon the diversity of information, views, and opinion, in other words, the market for ideas.[5] In fact, market definitional limitations mean that mergers between a newspaper and a television or radio service would probably not breach merger regulation; without specific media ownership rules, such a merger would be likely to proceed.

One way of trying to deal with this dilemma is by requiring mergers to pass not only the competition threshold, but also some form of public interest test. UK merger regulation makes provision for a merger which involves media companies to be examined on public interest grounds as well as on the usual competition grounds.[6] The introduction of the public interest test for broadcasting and

---

[3] Productivity Commission, *Broadcasting*, Report No 11 (Canberra, AusInfo, 2000), 372–73.

[4] See, for example, Australian Competition and Consumer Commission (ACCC), *Merger Guidelines* (June 1999), para 5.12, and Office of Fair Trading (OFT), *Mergers: Substantive Assessment Guidance* (May 2003), paras 3.5–3.7.

[5] Productivity Commission, above n 3, 349–50. The limitations of competition law for broadcasting pluralism, with particular reference to market definition, are considered further in Chapter Six.

[6] There are separate public interest regimes depending upon whether the merger involves newspaper companies alone, or broadcasting, or cross-media interests. Prior to these new regimes, which are part of the reforms of merger law introduced by the Enterprise Act 2002 (and amended by the Comms Act (UK)), there had already been in place, under the Fair Trading Act 1973, a procedure whereby public interest considerations for newspaper mergers could be taken into account. The new

cross-media was directly related to the 2003 relaxation of the UK media ownership rules (detailed in Chapter Three). The public interest test was designed to provide protection against mergers resulting in a concentration of ownership which could be against the public interest, and it was an express acknowledgement that competition law could not be relied upon to protect the marketplace of ideas.[7] The intention is that the Secretary of State[8] will be able to intervene in mergers to ensure:

> a sufficient plurality of media ownership, to protect the availability of a wide range of high quality broadcasting and to ensure that those with control of media enterprises have a genuine commitment to the broadcasting standards objectives set out in the Communications Act 2003.[9]

Normally, for mergers to be investigated on competition grounds they have to be of a certain size, but the Enterprise Act 2002 allows the public interest test to be considered also in mergers which fall below the relevant threshold tests, by applying lower thresholds.[10] In this instance, only public interest grounds will be considered.[11] Not every media merger will give rise to a public interest intervention. The Secretary of State has discretion to decide whether or not the merger raises public interest concerns. If there is to be no intervention, then the merger will be investigated on competition grounds alone, in the same way as any other merger. In addition, it is necessary to be mindful of the Secretary of State's general policy on intervention. Other than in exceptional circumstances, the Secretary of State will intervene only in situations which would have been covered by ownership and control rules prior to their removal as part of the 2003 reforms.[12] This means that, in general, intervention is likely only in merger situations involving free-to-air

---

regime for newspaper mergers is more concerned with changes to the procedure, rather than with substantive changes: Department of Trade and Industry (DTI), *Enterprise Act 2002: Public Interest Intervention in Media Mergers, Guidance Document* (May 2004), para 2.5. The newspaper regime will not be considered here.

[7] *Ibid*, para 2.6.

[8] It will be the Secretary of State of Trade and Industry, not the Secretary for State for Culture, Media and Sport.

[9] DTI, *Guidance Document*, above n 6, para 2.6.

[10] The merger regime normally applies only to mergers which result in two or more enterprises ceasing to be distinct, and where the merger is of a certain economic significance (having regard to the turnover test—ie, where it exceeds £70 million), or which would create or enhance at least a 25% share of the supply of the goods or services relevant to the merger in the UK: Enterprise Act 2002, s 23. Some mergers will fall to be considered by the European Commission rather than by the OFT and the Competition Commission, but it is open to a Member State to 'take appropriate measures to protect legitimate interests': Council Regulation (EC) No 139/2004 of 20 January 2004 on the control of concentrations between undertakings [2004] OJ L 24/1, Art 21(4). This means that the public interest test can still be applied, even though the competition aspects of the merger will be considered by the European Commission: DTI, *Guidance Document*, above n 6, para 11.1. In such circumstances, the Secretary of State will issue a 'European intervention notice'.

[11] Enterprise Act 2002, as amended, s 59(1). In this instance, the Secretary of State will issue a 'special intervention notice' rather than an 'intervention notice' which would be appropriate for a merger which falls within the relevant thresholds.

[12] DTI, *Guidance Document*, above n 6, para 8.2. At the time of writing, there have been no public interest interventions in relation to media.

television and/or radio services, or broadcasting and newspapers. This seems unfortunate, because one of the concerns about the old ownership and control regime was the way in which some services, such as satellite, were omitted from the regime. Similarly, as discussed in Chapter Three, another concern about ownership regulation is that it is generally wedded to 'old media'. A media public interest test could overcome the limitations of merger law, and widen the scope for pluralism protection by incorporating also new media platforms. This seems to be entirely the sort of approach which is needed if traditional ownership and control regimes are to be relaxed or removed, and broadcasting pluralism protection measures are to remain effective. Even if current ownership regulation is retained, a public interest test could add a further dimension of protection by being made applicable to mergers involving services falling outside the mainstream media. However, the general policy will not allow intervention in situations where ownership rules never applied, nor will intervention be likely in situations which continue to be subject to ownership rules.[13] Situations likely to give rise to 'exceptional circumstances' have been indicated as follows:

— where a large number of specific genre channels, such as news or education, would come under single control;
— where there would be single control of all music channels; or
— where a new entrant to local radio had not shown a proper commitment to broadcasting standards, in connection with other media or in another jurisdiction.[14]

Once a decision has been made to intervene on public interest grounds, then the Office of Communications (Ofcom) has a responsibility to provide advice on the public interest considerations, whilst the Office of Fair Trading (OFT) gives advice on the competition matters.[15] Ultimately, having intervened, the Secretary of State can decide to clear the merger, to refer the merger to the Competition Commission (CC), or to require the OFT to seek undertakings, in lieu of a reference to the CC. If the merger is referred to the Commission, a report will be made back to the Secretary of State, who then has discretion on whether or not to make an adverse public interest finding, although the competition findings must be accepted. It might be questionable whether it is good practice, in such a sensitive area, to leave the final decision within the political sphere. The Enterprise Act specifies the public interest considerations, which apply to a broadcasting or cross-media merger. These are:

(a) the need, in relation to every different audience in the United Kingdom or in a particular area or locality of the United Kingdom, for there to be a sufficient plurality of persons with control of the media enterprises serving that audience;

---

[13] In the latter case, however, the Secretary of State may consider intervening where the media owner is from outside the European Economic Area: DTI, *Guidance Document*, above n 6, para 8.7.
[14] DTI, *Guidance Document*, above n 6, para 8.8.
[15] Enterprise Act 2002, as amended, ss 44–44A.

(b) the need for the availability throughout the United Kingdom of a wide range of broadcasting which (taken as a whole) is both of high quality and calculated to appeal to a wide variety of tastes and interests; and

(c) the need for persons carrying on media enterprises, and for those with control of such enterprises, to have a genuine commitment to the attainment in relation to broadcasting of the standards objectives set out in section 319 of the Communications Act 2003.[16]

The test will come into play when a merger is being proposed, or has been completed, between two broadcasting enterprises, or between broadcasting[17] and newspaper enterprises. For the purpose of the public interest consideration, all these enterprises will become media enterprises. One benefit of this is that it enables the inquiry to range more broadly than the traditional merger inquiry, which will be bounded by market definitions.

Guidelines indicate the type of matters which will be considered in relation to the public interest considerations. Thus, in relation to the first factor, plurality of persons, the Secretary of State may consider not just the number of persons controlling merger enterprises after the merger but also audience shares of the merged enterprise and other media enterprises.[18] Ofcom has issued its own guidance statement, although this is really only a statement of procedure, and gives little indication of how it would approach the public interest considerations. Ofcom does give details of the type of information which it would need from the media enterprises, which may indicate something of its lines of inquiry. Apart from obvious information about ownership structures, business activities, and audience share, the information sought includes, additionally for newspapers, details on readership demographics, policies on editorial independence, complaints history, and future plans; and for broadcasting, information on programming, regulatory compliance history, and future plans.[19]

Only the UK has adopted this approach whereby there is an attempt to bring into the merger evaluation a competition and public interest analysis, although as indicated, it clearly has its limitations. Neither the US nor Australia has adopted this approach, although in the US the public interest implications of a merger can be considered if the merger involves transfers of licences or authorisations.[20]

---

[16] Enterprise Act 2002, as amended, s 58(2C).

[17] 'Broadcasting' is defined to include the radio and television services licensed under the Broadcasting Act 1990 (BA 1990 (UK)) and the Broadcasting Act 1996 (BA 1996 (UK)), and the services provided by the BBC and the Welsh Authority, and any services provided by broadcasters established abroad but broadcasting into the UK under European Union licences: Enterprise Act 2002, as amended, s 44(9). This means that free-to-air and subscription services, analogue and digital, will be included. This wide definition will be relevant to the application of the public interest test.

[18] DTI, *Guidance Document*, above n 6, para 7.10.

[19] Ofcom, *Ofcom Guidance for the Public Interest Test for Media Mergers* (2004), Appendix 1.

[20] This is not the case in Australia. Transfers of commercial broadcasting licences, or changes in control, do not require the approval of the ACMA: BSA (Aus), s 48. Subscription television licences can also be transferred without approval: *ibid*, s 113(1). Consistent with their non-profit, non-commercial nature, there is no mechanism for transfers of community broadcasting licences.

Although the competition law implications of a merger will be a matter for the Anti-Trust division of the Justice Department, and the Federal Trade Commission, those mergers which require licences, and other authorisations, to be transferred will have to seek the approval of the Federal Communications Commission (FCC) and, under its mandate, the Commission will have to consider whether the transfers will serve the 'public interest, convenience, and necessity'.[21] This approval process can provide the FCC with an opportunity to look broadly at the transaction, as can be seen from the following statement of its approach:

> Our public interest evaluation under Section 310(d) necessarily encompasses the 'broad aims of the Communications Act', which includes, among other things, preserving and enhancing competition in relevant markets, ensuring that a diversity of voices is made available to the public, and accelerating private sector deployment of advanced services. To apply our public interest test, then, we must determine whether the transaction violates our rules, or would otherwise frustrate implementation or enforcement of the Communications Act and federal communication policy. That policy is shaped by Congress and deeply rooted in a preference for competitive processes and outcomes.
>
> Our determination of the competitive effects of the proposed transaction under the public interest standard is not limited by traditional antitrust principles. The Commission and the Department of Justice ('DOJ') each have independent authority to examine communications transactions involving mergers and acquisitions, but the standards governing the Commission's review differ from those of DOJ. The review conducted by DOJ is pursuant to Section 7 of the Clayton Act, which prohibits transactions that are likely to substantially lessen competition in any line of commerce. The Commission, on the other hand, is charged with determining whether the transaction serves the broader public interest.[22]

The matters raised by this investigation might result in the FCC approving a transfer, but imposing additional conditions on the licences.

Promoting Competition and Access

Access to Infrastructure

Access measures arise in a number of forms. Chapter Four gave an indication of some types of access measures, but those were more concerned with content-related access such as the provision of locally produced content or political broadcasts. Such measures still leave the licensee for that channel or service largely in control of content and programming decisions. The access measures considered

---

[21] 47 USC § 310(d).

[22] FCC, *Memorandum Opinion and Order, In the Matter of General Motors Corporation and Hughes Electronics Corporation, Transferors and The News Corporation Limited, Transferee, for Authority to Transfer Control,* FCC 03-330 (19 December 2003), paras 2–3.

in this section are more concerned with giving platform access. This is a recognition that the controller of the delivery platform may be in a monopoly position, able to act as a gatekeeper by keeping out those who do not have control of a platform. The concerns about the potential for monopoly control are competition-related, but regulatory measures opening access will also be influenced by the desirability of the public having access to a variety of programming sources. Here, the concerns are more akin to those influencing structural policy and regulation, as examined in Chapter Three, although the focus of access regulation is not about ownership, but about the exercise of ownership control.

Access to delivery mechanisms has, with the development of cable and satellite, become more of a concern for regulators. When broadcasting was usually delivered over-the-air by wireless technology, the general practice was to allow one person to control a channel, and the content delivered through that channel. Structural regulation (of the type discussed in Chapter Three) and content regulation (as discussed in Chapter Four) ensured that there was in place some competition (between channels), and that there were opportunities to access the channel, in certain circumstances. But, in general, carriage and content were linked. However, with cable and satellite delivery mechanisms able to offer many channels, and with the more recent exploitation of digital technology, separation of carriage and content has become more common. This separation might be by choice, for commercial reasons, or it might be as a consequence of regulation. One of the concerns about delivery mechanisms such as cable and satellite is that they may be natural monopolies, because the high cost of establishing these networks makes it uneconomic for more than one network to operate in an area.[23] Australia is something of an exception here, because government policy encouraged two cable networks (Telstra and Optus) to be built (or 'overbuilt') within the same areas.[24] This means that the cable networks in Australia are not in the usual monopoly position, although the situation has probably had an impact on competition for programming (see below). However, in the more typical scenario, where the network may be a monopoly, there may still be potential competition in related markets (for example, programme provision) but this means that anyone wanting to offer programme channels must try to gain access to an existing network for the carriage of those channels. Meanwhile, for those who have invested in the network there will be an incentive to achieve economies of scale, and to generate income through these related markets.[25] Difficulties of access may therefore be compounded if the network operator is also delivering programme channels. For example, in Australia, the subscription television service, Foxtel, is half-owned by the dominant telecommunications operator, Telstra, which operates the cable

---

[23] R Jones, 'Competition, Broadcasting and Pay TV', Speech delivered at the Australian Broadcasting Summit, Sydney, 20 February 2003, http://www.accc.gov.au/content/index.phtml/itemId/255876, accessed 14 December 2004, 11.

[24] Productivity Commission, *Telecommunications Competition Regulation*, Report No 16 (Canberra, AusInfo, 2001), 527.

[25] Jones, above n 23, 11.

network over which Foxtel is carried. Foxtel also controls, either through ownership or exclusive contracts, many of the channels which it broadcasts.[26] This is a
pattern which is also replicated in the UK and the US. Because of the characteristics of the subscription television market, a common regulatory response has been
rules which open up or facilitate infrastructure access. Each of the three jurisdictions considered in this study provides such a framework, although there are
variations in the regulatory approach.

In Australia, the regulation of access to networks is the responsibility, not of the
Australian Communications and Media Authority (ACMA), but of the generic
competition regulator, the Australian Competition and Consumer Commission
(ACCC). Although there is a specific telecommunications access regime set out in
Part XIC of the Trade Practices Act 1974 (TPA), the Australian approach emphasises commercial negotiation, so that the access regime only comes into play if
negotiations fail. Even within the access regime, the emphasis is still on 'promoting commercial and self-regulated outcomes'.[27] The regime operates through the
declaration of services, so that once a service is declared by the ACCC,[28] the
service provider is obliged to provide access pursuant to the standard access
obligations.[29] One of the key considerations for the ACCC in deciding to declare
a service is the promotion of the 'long-term interests of end-users'.[30] End-users are
understood to be the final consumers, not the likely access seekers.[31] The terms
and conditions governing the access can be agreed commercially between the parties, or they can be in the form of an access undertaking given by the service
provider, and approved by the ACCC. If the parties are unable to agree terms of
access, and there is no access undertaking, the ACCC can arbitrate and impose
terms and conditions for access.[32]

The ACCC declared the service for the carriage of an analogue subscription
television broadcast service in 1999.[33] The declared service included the carriage
of analogue signals, and the use of conditional access services, including set-top
unit and subscriber management services.[34] The ACCC justified its declaration by
reference to:

---

[26] Productivity Commission, above n 24, 688. Through exclusive contracts, Foxtel can usually also
control whether any of these channels can be carried over other networks: *ibid.*

[27] A Grant (ed), *Australian Telecommunications Regulation*, 3rd edn (Sydney, UNSW Press, 2004),
88.

[28] TPA, s 152AL.

[29] *Ibid*, s 152AR. The standard access obligations set out the basic obligations of access, which
include ensuring technical and operational quality, and provide a basis for access, pending more
detailed commercial negotiations: Grant, above n 27, 95.

[30] TPA, s 152AL(3)(d).

[31] Productivity Commission, above n 24, 257.

[32] TPA, s 152AY(2).

[33] There had been an earlier deemed declaration, carried over from a previous access regime. The
ACCC had considered making the 1999 declaration 'technology-neutral', but given the lack of digital
services at that stage, confined the declaration to analogue: Grant, above n 27, 107.

[34] ACCC, *A Report on the Assessment of the Analogue Pay TV Access Undertaking Proffered by Telstra
Multimedia Pty Limited on 23 December 2003* (March 2004), 4.

the distinct nature of the subscription television market (which it regards as a market separate from free to air television), substantial barriers to entry in . . . [the] industry, and the vertical integration between carriage and retail subscription television services which provides an incentive for cable operators to deny access to services that may compete with their own. Without the declaration, the ACCC . . . stated that 'a narrower range of programming would be available, and at higher prices, than would otherwise be the case'.[35]

Vertical integration in the Foxtel pay service has made it difficult for third parties to gain access to the cable networks, particularly the network owned by Telstra, which carries the Foxtel service.[36] Those who sought access to the Telstra cable network, in the light of the declaration—a sports channel, C7, owned by the Seven Network, and Television and Radio Broadcast Services Pty Limited (TARBS), a provider of foreign language channels—were initially refused access by Telstra, on the ground that it already had an exclusive agreement with Foxtel.[37] Following from the court proceedings dealing with this argument, C7 and TARBS were unable to reach commercial agreement and had to enter into arbitration.[38] Given that two of Foxtel's major shareholders, Publishing and Broadcasting Limited and News Corporation Limited, also held interests in one of Foxtel's channels, Fox Sports, it is clear that Foxtel may have had an incentive to deny access to a potential competitor.[39] The abandonment of C7 means that there is now only one main supplier of sports content, Fox Sports. Even the ACCC has commented that the access regime does not seem to have provided any impetus towards commercial negotiation and, in general, appears to have limited effect on the subscription television market.[40] In 2005, the Seven Network launched proceedings against a large number of media companies and sporting associations, including Publishing and Broadcasting Limited, News Corporation Limited, Telstra, Optus, and Foxtel in connection with the demise of C7. The proceedings claimed that a number of the defendants had colluded and engaged in predatory pricing to deny C7 the rights to certain sporting subscription television rights, and in order to force C7 out of business.[41] Although the proceedings were not directly related to the access dispute, this dispute, the dominant position of Foxtel (and its control over content), and the failure of the access regulatory scheme certainly form the backdrop to the dispute. Indeed, one of the remedies sought by the Seven Network was a restruc-

---

[35] Productivity Commission, above n 3, 374.

[36] The cable network is owned by Telstra Multimedia Pty Ltd, a wholly owned subsidiary of Telstra.

[37] Productivity Commission, above n 3, 374. Pre-existing rights can be a reason for refusing access: TPA 1974, s 152AR(4). This refusal was challenged successfully in proceedings before the Federal Court. The court decided, on the basis of the documentation, that no such right existed: *Seven Cable Television Pty Ltd v Telstra Corporation Ltd* [2000] FCA 350, and *Foxtel Management Pty Ltd v Seven Cable Television Pty Ltd* [2000] FCA 1159.

[38] The arbitration process was not completed: the Seven Network abandoned its C7 service; and TARBS went into voluntary liquidation.

[39] Productivity Commission, above n 3, 374.

[40] Jones, above n 23, 12.

[41] At the time of writing, the proceedings were still ongoing, although the claim of collusion had been dropped by the plaintiff.

turing of the subscription television industry, with orders that Publishing and Broadcasting Limited and News Corporation Limited be required to dispose of their interests in Fox Sports or Foxtel.[42]

More recently, as a result of an agreement, in 2002, between the two main subscription television providers, Foxtel and Optus, a number of undertakings have been required of Foxtel and Telstra. Primarily a content-sharing arrangement, the deal between Foxtel and Optus further illustrates the complexity of the competition concerns which can arise concerning subscription services. The agreement between Foxtel and Optus required Foxtel to supply its channels to Optus, for resale on its cable network, and to assume Optus's financial obligations under its content agreements. In return, Foxtel gained access to Optus's content and its subscriber base.[43] The ACCC took the view that the agreement would result in a substantial lessening of competition: primarily it was concerned that the agreement would allow Foxtel to prevent competition in the subscription market by blocking access to programming and/or the cable network.[44] The ACCC's conclusions were based upon an application of the generic competition provisions of the TPA, contained in Part IV, because there is no industry-specific regulatory framework governing access to content. Under TPA Part IV, there is a procedure whereby a potentially anti-competitive arrangement can proceed if the parties provide undertakings, which are judicially enforceable, pursuant to section 87B. However, in the process of obtaining section 87B undertakings, the ACCC has also secured undertakings pursuant to the Part XI access regime. In November 2002, the ACCC accepted the section 87B undertakings, provided by Telstra, Optus and Foxtel, which included undertakings that:

— Telstra would provide 10 channels for use by persons other than Foxtel or Telstra;
— Foxtel and Optus would not acquire certain channels on an exclusive basis;
— Foxtel would enable other subscription television competitors to carry the Foxtel service on terms comparable with the supply to Telstra;
— Foxtel would ensure that at least 30 per cent of channels in its basic tier comprised non-affiliated channels; and
— Optus would provide at least seven non-Foxtel channels, and two channels made up of programming created by Optus or supplied by independent third parties.[45]

[42] ABC Radio National, 'C7 Trial', *The Media Report* (22 September 2005), http://www.abc.net.au/rn/talks/8.30/mediarpt/stories/s1465901.htm, accessed 1 October 2005.
[43] This agreement had benefits for Foxtel, giving it access to content which it did not previously have, and for Optus, relieving it of heavy liabilities, incurred because of the large sums it had been forced to pay to secure this content. The arrangement means that subscribers to either Foxtel or Optus will see essentially the same content, and that, where Foxtel and Optus have the same geographic coverage, there is in effect one network, although there will still be some differences between the two networks because of the other services offered, such as telephony and broadband.
[44] ACCC, *Emerging Market Structures in the Communications Sector, A Report to Senator Alston, Minister for Communications, Information Technology and the Arts* (June 2003), http://www.accc.gov.au/content/index.phtml/itemId/356694/fromItemId/356751, accessed 19 April 2005, para 3.2.2.
[45] See *Undertaking to the Australian Competition & Consumer Commission by Foxtel Management Pty Ltd (for and on behalf of the Foxtel Partnership) and Foxtel Cable Television Pty Ltd, Public Version*

The section 87B undertakings also included a commitment by Foxtel and Telstra to provide Part XIC access undertakings to the analogue network with transition to digital, as well as a commitment to digitise the cable network.[46] Approval of the access undertakings took longer, following an initial rejection by the ACCC, but these undertakings were approved in March 2004.[47] Essentially, the undertakings now provide the terms and conditions for access to Telstra's cable network, and to Foxtel's set-top boxes. The Australian access regime, and the Foxtel/Optus content-sharing agreement illustrate how complex it can be to try to ensure a competitive environment for these subscription services, particularly when there are no ex ante rules to shape behaviour within the market.

The resolution of the anti-competitive impact of the Foxtel/Optus arrangement led to undertakings designed to provide more open access for competitors both to infrastructure and to programming. However, in the Australian regime, there are no generally applicable rules which require a cable network, or other delivery platform operator, to provide access to third parties; for example, by setting aside a number of channels. As seen, in the Australian setting, it will be a matter for commercial negotiation, unless the service has been declared, and, even then, much is likely to rest upon the ability of the parties to negotiate. This can be problematic in a small and concentrated market like Australia. In the US, a different approach applies.[48] For example, under a measure introduced by the Cable Communications Policy Act of 1984, as part of the franchising process, a local franchising authority may require a cable network operator to provide access to the network for 'public,

(November 2002); *Undertaking to the Australian Competition & Consumer Commission Given for the Purposes of Section 87B of the Trade Practices Act 1974 by Telstra Corporation Limited and Telstra Multimedia Pty Ltd* (November 2002), and *Undertaking to the Australian Competition & Consumer Commission Pursuant to Section 87B of the Trade Practices Act 1974 by Optus Vision Pty Limited and Optus Vision Media Pty Limited* (2002). Undertakings were also given by a satellite service, Austar. The undertakings can be accessed at http://www.accc.gov.au.

[46] This obligation was contingent on the ACCC accepting their application for exemption from the Standard Access Obligations in relation to a digital television carriage service. Although the ACCC approved the exemption, it was refused on a review to the Australian Competition Tribunal. However, because the undertakings by Foxtel and Telstra included a commitment to provide access to third parties if they had commenced a digital service by the end of 2007, the non-acceptance of the exemption will have no impact: ACCC, *Foxtel's Special Access Undertaking in Relation to the Digital Set Top Unit Service, Discussion Paper* (November 2005), 2.1.1–2.1.3.

[47] ACCC, *A Report on the Assessment of the Analogue Pay TV Access Undertaking Proffered by Telstra Multimedia Pty Limited on 23 December 2003* (March 2004), and *A Report on the Assessment of the Analogue Pay TV Access Undertaking Proffered by Foxtel Management Pty Ltd on 22 December 2003* (March 2004). The undertakings can be accessed at http://www.accc.gov.au.

[48] The US regulatory provisions for access might be seen to resonate with the US essential facilities doctrine. This doctrine asserts that, contrary to the general rule that a firm is not required to deal with its competitors, it may be required to give access to its competitors if it controls a facility which is essential for the conduct of that competitor's business. For a discussion of its possible application to the cable sector, see R Dibadj, 'Towards Meaningful Cable Competition: Getting Beyond the Monopoly Morass' (2002–3) 6 *New York University Journal of Legislation and Public Policy* 245 at 304–6. Interestingly, the Supreme Court has recently exhibited a somewhat lukewarm attitude towards the doctrine (although 'neither recognising or repudiating it'): *Verizon Communications Inc v Law Offices of Curtis V. Trinko* 540 US 398 (2004). The case concerned telecommunications access, and the court considered that the doctrine was irrelevant when there was effective power to compel access. Here the FCC had effective power under the Telecommunications Act of 1996: at 411.

educational, or governmental' use.[49] These channels (usually known as PEG channels) are designed to provide for distribution of community-focused information
about, for example, local meetings and activities, and local government activity,
and they are carried on the basic tier.[50] Although it would be open to a cable system to operate the PEG channels itself, the vast majority are operated by non-profit
entities. There are around 5,000 such channels, spread across 1,500 cable systems,
although there is considerable variation in the number of channels per system, with
some systems offering up to 12 channels, and others only one.[51] There is, of course,
no guarantee that the public will have access to PEG channels, since it is left to the
local authority and the franchise negotiations to determine whether any, or how
many, PEG channels will be set aside, and the funding arrangements, so that the
determination of the local authority and the commercial strength of the cable system may be important influences on the outcome. Certainly it seems that some
cable systems are keen to limit access, and franchise renewal negotiations are often
an opportunity for cable operators to try to negotiate downwards their access commitments.[52] Satellite operators are under a different access obligation: they must set
aside at least 4 per cent of their channel capacity for public interest channels
described as 'non-commercial programming of an educational or informational
nature'.[53] The difference between the obligations of cable and satellite is a reflection
of the fact that satellite was a less well-established delivery platform, compared with
cable, and was less suited for locally aimed programming. The FCC has reaffirmed
the view that it is not appropriate to impose PEG channel access obligations on
satellite operators.[54]

Cable operators, depending upon their size, are also required to provide leased
access for commercial use by non-affiliated enterprises.[55] The legislation states
that the purpose of this access obligation is 'to promote competition in the delivery of diverse sources of video programming and to assure that the widest possible
diversity of information sources are made available to the public from cable systems'.[56] The number of channels which must be set aside for such access will vary
according to the overall channel capacity of the cable operator, with the largest
cable systems (more than 100 activated channels) having to provide access to
15 per cent of all their channels, whilst cable systems with less than 36 channels are

---

[49] 47 USC § 531(a).

[50] FCC, *Eleventh Annual Report, In the Matter of Annual Assessment of the Status of Competition in the Market for the Delivery of Video Programming,* FCC 05-13 (14 January 2005), para 170.

[51] *Ibid.* Franchise authorities can draw up procedures for cable operators to use reserved, but unused PEG channels: 47 USC § 531(d)(1).

[52] For further information, see Alliance for Community Media at http://www.alliancecm.org.

[53] 47 USC § 335 & 47 CFR § 25.701(f). The channels can only be used by non-profit entities.

[54] FCC, *Report and Order, In the Matter of Implementation of Section 25 of the Cable Television Consumer Protection and Competition Act of 1992,* 13 FCC Rcd 24279 (1998), para 60, and FCC, *Second Order on Reconsideration of First Report and Order, In the Matter of Implementation of Section 25 of the Cable Television Consumer Protection and Competition Act of 1992,* 19 FCC Rcd 5647 (2004), para 43.

[55] 47 USC § 532(b).

[56] 47 USC § 532(a).

exempted from the access provisions.[57] FCC rules deal with issues such as access rates, tier and channel positions, and procedures for requests in excess of capacity.[58] Within the constraints of the rules, arranging access is a matter for commercial negotiation, although there is provision for anyone unable to obtain access to apply to the FCC.[59] There is also provision for the FCC to impose additional measures to secure 'diversity of information sources', where cable systems with 36 or more channels reach 70 per cent of households within the US, and have a subscription rate of 70 per cent of households.[60]

Another US measure, introduced by the Cable Television Consumer Protection and Competition Act of 1992, was aimed at opening up competition at the infrastructure level, although it does not directly create access opportunities. With the explicit objective of enhancing effective competition, the FCC was empowered to introduce rules to address horizontal and vertical integration of cable operators.[61] Under the horizontal rules established by the FCC, a cable operator (or group of associated operators) was prohibited from having a cable subscription reach of more than 30 per cent nationwide.[62] Pursuant to the vertical rules, a cable operator was prohibited from devoting more than 40 per cent of its channels to the carriage of programming services which the cable operator had an interest in or owned.[63] However, the rules were reversed following a legal challenge, and have been under review.[64]

The UK also relies on ex ante regulatory measures when dealing with infrastructure access, although the regulation is applied to specific operators. Currently the rules affect only Sky Subscribers Services Ltd (SSSL), which is part of the BSkyB group, and they relate to the provision of access to, what Ofcom terms 'technical platform services', namely conditional access, access control, and electronic programme guide (EPG) services for the digital satellite platform.[65] In essence,

---

[57] 47 USC § 532(b)(1)(C) and (D), respectively.

[58] See 47 CFR §§ 76.970-76.971.

[59] 47 CFR § 76.975.

[60] 47 USC §532(g). This threshold has not yet been met: FCC, *Eleventh Annual Report (2005)*, above n 50, para 20.

[61] 47 USC § 533(f)(1)(A) and (B), respectively.

[62] 47 CFR § 76.503(a).

[63] 47 CFR § 76.504(a). The rule applied only to cable systems with channel capacity of up to 70 channels: 47 CFR § 76.504(b).

[64] *Time Warner Entertainment Co v FCC* 240 F 3d 1126 (2001). The vertical limit rule was held to infringe the First Amendment. As part of the review the FCC is also considering the relationship between a horizontal rule under § 533(f)(1)(A) and § 532(g): FCC, *Second Further Notice of Rule Making, In the Matter of the Commission's Cable Horizontal and Vertical Ownership Limits,* FCC 05-96 (13 May 2005), para 163.

[65] The power to impose access-related conditions arises under Comms Act (UK), ss 45 and 73. The regulations governing SSSL were originally put in place by one of Ofcom's predecessors, Oftel, and have been carried over: *Continuation Notice to a Class of Persons Defined as the Licensee for the Purposes of the Provision of Electronic Programme Guide Services Under Paragraph 9 of Schedule 18 to the Communications Act 2003* (23 July 2003); *Continuation Notice to a Class of Persons Defined as the Licensee for the Purposes of the Provision of Access Control Services Under Paragraph 9 of Schedule 18 to the Communications Act 2003* (23 July 2003); and *Notification Pursuant to Section 48(1) of the Communications Act 2003: The Setting of Access-related Conditions Under Section 45 of the Communications Act 2003 as Authorised by Section 73(5) of the Communications Act 2003* (24 July 2003).

these services will enable a channel provider or broadcaster to access the platform operated by SSSL, and to make use of the platform's technical services, encryption systems, and so forth, which will allow the broadcaster to provide programmes, subscription and pay-per-view services, and interactive services to its customers, and through the EPG service to ensure that potential viewers are made aware of the service, scheduling changes, and so forth.[66] For those channel providers who choose to be distributed as part of the BSkyB service, such access does not need to be separately obtained, but for those who want to offer their own programme services via the digital satellite platform it will be necessary to negotiate access with SSSL. The UK regulatory approach is informed by the EU Communications Directives, which became effective in July 2003, although the current regulation of SSSL is basically a continuation of regulation which was already in place.[67] In essence, SSSL, or a regulated provider, is required to provide third parties with access to technical platform services on fair, reasonable, and non-discriminatory terms. There are also additional obligations regarding publication of charges, and separation of accounts. The position regarding regulation of EPG services should be explained. As noted above, EPG services are regulated as part of the mix of technical platform services provided by SSSL. However, there is also a separate EPG code, discussed later in this chapter under 'Electronic Programme Guides and Channel Positioning' (at p 240). This latter code has been developed by Ofcom, but under different statutory authority. The access regulation imposed upon SSSL is pursuant to Ofcom's power, under section 45 of the Communications Act 2003 (Comms Act (UK)), to impose access-related conditions on a provider. However, before imposing conditions, Ofcom must be satisfied, inter alia, that the conditions are objectively justifiable, not unduly discriminatory, and proportionate and transparent in terms of their objective.[68] Ofcom has decided that regulation of SSSL satisfies these tests because it operates an open platform (that is, open to other providers seeking independent carriage), and is linked with the main television service carried on the satellite platform.[69] However, the same cannot be said of cable or digital terrestrial services. Cable is a closed platform, and regulation would be disproportionate because cable operators should have a sufficient incentive to provide all channels they are carrying (as part of their service) with listing access.[70] Although digital terrestrial is an open platform, there is very little

---

[66] Ofcom, *Provision of Technical Platform Services, Consultation* (2 November 2005), s 3, and generally.

[67] The EU communications framework consists of five directives, of which the Access Directive (2002/19/EC, [2002] OJ L 108/7) is the most relevant for access to electronic communications networks and services. It carries over regulatory obligations, in similar terms, which were applicable under an earlier directive, the Advanced Television Standards Directive (95/47/EC, [1995] OJ L 281/51), although regulation is no longer confined to operators possessing significant market power. Ofcom has separate powers to impose conditions on persons exercising significant market power: Comms Act (UK), s 45.

[68] Comms Act (UK), s 47(2).

[69] Ofcom, *The Regulation of Electronic Programme Guides* (16 January 2004), paras 13, 15–16.

[70] *Ibid*, para 14.

spare capacity, so that effectively it is a closed platform, and the providers of digital multiplex services are already obliged to transmit programme data for services carried; hence, regulation would be disproportionate and unnecessary.[71] However, Ofcom is also required to draw up a code for licensed EPG providers under separate provisions of the Comms Act (UK), and so all such EPG providers will be governed by this code, which is discussed in the later section 'Electronic Programme Guides and Channel Positioning'.

In relation to the access rules imposed upon SSSL, there are detailed guidelines in place, originally developed by Oftel, which provide guidance regarding the interpretation of these rules, although at the time of writing, Ofcom was conducting a consultation with a view to developing a new set of guidelines.[72] The tenor of the consultation document points to a more prescriptive approach by Ofcom. However, notwithstanding the rules and the guidelines, access remains a matter of commercial negotiation between the access provider and the access seeker, although Ofcom has the power to investigate complaints and resolve disputes. Although the regulatory context of access regulation can be asserted to be competition, there would seem to be a discernible shift in Ofcom's approach compared with that of Oftel (which had been responsible for telecommunications regulation). The guidelines developed by Oftel strongly reflect a competition perspective; for example, fairness and reasonableness would be assessed on the basis of whether offered terms are those which would be expected in a competitive market; whilst differential treatment, which might point to discriminatory behaviour, would be examined as to whether it had a material adverse impact on competition.[73] However, Ofcom's approach is informed by its broad statutory duties, which, in general, require it to further 'the interests of citizens in relation to communications matters' and the interests of consumers through the promotion of competition.[74] Ofcom has stated that, in relation to access regulation of SSSL, and the interpretation of 'fair, reasonable and non-discriminatory', it will consider to what extent its duties to secure '*range* and *plurality* of high *quality* television and radio services that *appeal* to a variety of tastes and interests are fulfilled'.[75] Whether it is realistic to expect a set of rules about the terms and conditions for securing access to be able to do this is debatable, but the language, at least, is an interesting reflection of the potential impact of a converged regulator.

---

[71] Ofcom, *The Regulation of Electronic Programme Guides* (16 January 2004), para 15.

[72] Ofcom, *Provision of Technical Platform Services, Consultation* (2 November 2005), s 2.15. The Guidelines developed by Oftel are *Terms of Supply of Conditional Access: Oftel Guidelines* (October 2002), and *The Pricing of Conditional Access Services and Related Issues* (May 2002), available at http://www.ofcom.org.uk/static/archive/oftel/publications/broadcasting/index.htm.

[73] Oftel, *Terms of Supply of Conditional Access: Oftel Guidelines* (October 2002), paras 2.1 and 2.9.

[74] Comms Act (UK), s 3(1).

[75] Ofcom, *Provision of Technical Platform Services, Consultation* (2 November 2005), s 4.6 (emphasis in original).

Access to Content

One of the areas in which the changing media environment has had a noticeable impact has been that of content. In a traditional free-to-air broadcasting market, content is important because it will reflect the attractiveness of the service to advertisers, and certain types of content, such as sporting events, may be particularly attractive. However, with the growth of subscription services, whether pay-for-service or pay-for-view, control over content, and particularly certain types of content, becomes crucial, because now the viewer is directly funding the service. Thus, if a subscription service is to attract subscribers it will have to show content which the audience is willing to pay for. A subscription service provider is also constrained from using advertising as a way to 'bulk up' its income, because subscribers will be unwilling to pay for a programme service which requires them to watch a lot of advertising. Given that the viewer can also access content via free-to-air television, subscription service content will need to be particularly attractive and/or distinctive to the subscribing audience.[76] Because of the importance of content services, and the growth in the number of media outlets requiring content, demand has become highly competitive. Sport, particularly, with its ability to attract large-scale audiences, and its 'perishable' nature, has been 'a major driver of subscription to pay television'.[77] Films, particularly on their first television screening, will also be attractive content, although they lack the unique characteristics of sporting events. The demand for content, particularly valuable (or premium) content for which a higher subscription fee can be charged, gives rise to certain concerns. It may mean that some content is available only on subscription services and, hence, can be accessed only by those who can afford to subscribe to subscription television. Secondly, premium content will be scarce, and broadcasters may want to secure exclusive rights to that content. This may raise competition concerns if scarcity, high prices, and exclusive arrangements make it difficult for others to enter the market.[78]

Rupert Murdoch has been particularly proactive in using sport as a means of building up subscription television services, describing his intention 'to use sports as a battering ram and a lead offering in all our pay television operations'.[79] In the UK, Murdoch's satellite service, BSkyB, was able to use its subscription income to outbid the free-to-air services for access to film and sporting events.[80] A crucial

---

[76] Doyle, above n 2, 76.

[77] Productivity Commission, above n 3, 425. Sporting events are regarded as perishable because their particular value comes from the live coverage: M Williams, 'Sky Wars: The OFT Review of Pay-TV' [1997] 18(4) *European Competition Law Review* 214 at 218. They are also valuable because they will often be part of an ongoing competition and can therefore attract return audiences.

[78] D Geradin, 'Access to Content by New Media Platforms: A Review of the Competition Law Problems' (2005) 30 *European Law Review* 68 at 70.

[79] *Business Review Weekly* (23 July 1999), 88–92, quoted in Productivity Commission, above n 3, 425.

[80] Doyle, above n 2, 77.

advantage for operators of subscription services is that they are able to pass on the costs of the content acquisition to their subscribers, either on the basis of a charge for premium content packages, or on a pay-per-view basis—something which advertising-funded television is unable to do.[81] Doyle observes that the increased range of programming, assisted by direct viewer payments, will constitute 'a welfare gain for consumers', but this gain will be at the expense of those consumers who are unable to afford subscription services, if premium content migrates from free-to-air to subscription services.[82] Doyle points to the emergence of a '"two-tier" economy amongst television sports fans' in the UK.[83] The high costs which have resulted from the demand for premium content also have wider implications. As the proportion of programming budgets spent on premium content increases, pressure will be put on other parts of the programme budget.[84] This can have an impact on both the subscription and free-to-air sectors. The Productivity Commission in Australia reported that the value of broadcast rights to major sports events increased dramatically during the 1990s, noting that, at one stage, one commercial network, Seven, was paying 40 million Australian dollars per year for rights to broadcast Australian Football League (AFL) (previously known as the Victorian Football League) games compared with one million dollars 12 years previously.[85] However, these sums seem insignificant compared with the most recent sale of AFL rights. In early 2006, the Seven and Ten free-to-air networks, in a joint bid, agreed to pay 780 million Australian dollars for the rights, for a five-year period.[86] A similar experience can be observed in Europe: in 1992, the television rights to the English Premier League cost 430 million Euro for five seasons, but, in 2000, the cost was 2.6 billion Euro for coverage of three seasons only.[87]

Both general competition law and sector-specific measures are available for the task of providing more open access to content. The migration of content from free-to-air to subscription services raises concerns about access, and the possibility that there could be significant national, or even international, events able to be viewed only by those able or willing to subscribe. Sport may not be regarded by all as being within this category, but, nevertheless, there are certain types of sporting events that are commonly regarded as important to the general community for which access should be preserved. Indeed, the likelihood is that the more significant the event, the more attractive it will be to a subscription broadcaster. This raises the risk that events more closely related to the public and democratic life of the community could also migrate to subscription services. The link with access is

---

[81] Doyle, above n 2, 77.
[82] Doyle, above n 2, 78.
[83] *Ibid.*
[84] *Ibid.*
[85] *Business Review Weekly* (23 August 1999), 88, cited in Productivity Commission, above n 3, 425.
[86] ABC Sport, 'Seven and Ten win AFL Rights' (5 January 2006), http://www.abc.net.au/sport/content/200601/s1542491.htm, accessed 23 January 2006. The $780 million is split between $693 million in cash and $87 million in free advertising. Not long after the deal was announced, the Seven network announced that it would be cancelling some Australian-produced programmes.
[87] T Toft, 'TV Rights of Sports Events' (Brussels, 15 January 2003), cited in Geradin, above n 78, 69.

highlighted if one contemplates the type of events which could migrate: a papal funeral; a royal coronation; a presidential inauguration; or even the reporting of national election results. This might seem remote, and highly speculative, but it may also reflect the fact that subscription broadcasters have simply determined that they cannot guarantee that viewers would be willing to spend money to view such events. It might be precisely because such events are accessible via free-to-air delivery, that they are viewed by thousands, even millions, of people. However, the fact that most people might not be willing to pay for these events, does not mean that they might not be regarded as important by the public. They are probably the type of events or programmes which would come within the description of 'merit goods', or in other words, programmes which the community would consider should be available, even if they would not be prepared to pay for them directly or personally.[88]

The possibility that certain types of content could be removed from general access has led to specific measures to try to secure content for free-to-air services. Even the US has in place rules to prevent the siphoning of content. These rules developed because of concern that cable services would take content, particularly film and sporting content, away from the free-to-air services. Under current rules, cable services and satellite services are prohibited, upon request, from broadcasting local live sports events if that event is not also available on the local free-to-air service.[89] The problem of siphoning has remained a matter of concern, and the FCC was directed by Congress, in 1992, to re-examine the issue.[90] Although the FCC acknowledged that sports migration had been a concern for many years, the evidence appeared to be equivocal, with suggestions that sports were moving back to free-to-air services.[91] To some extent, the pressure on migration may have been eased by the creation of games or events specifically for subscription television.[92] The US experience has also shown that, where there has been migration, the free-to-air services have found new sports content, so that some sports which had not previously been broadcast are now being aired.[93]

The UK provisions recognise that events other than sport may require protection. This principle derives from the EU Television Directive, which refers to the right of Member States to preserve certain events for general access 'events which are regarded by that Member State as being of major importance for society'.[94]

---

[88] See, further, Chapter Six.

[89] 47 CFR § 76.111 (cable) and 47 CFR § 76.127 (satellite).

[90] KC Creech, *Electronic Media Law and Regulation*, 4th edn (Burlington MA, Focal Press, 2003), 125.

[91] *Ibid*, 126.

[92] Productivity Commission, above n 3, 439.

[93] *Ibid*, 440. In a report to Congress, the FCC recommended that there should be no change to the sports blackout rule: FCC, *Retransmission Consent and Exclusivity Rules: Report to Congress Pursuant to Section 208 of the Satellite Home Viewer Extension and Reauthorization Act of 2004* (8 September 2005), para 58.

[94] Council Directive 89/552/EEC of 3 October 1989 on the coordination of certain provisions laid down by law, regulation or administrative action in Member States concerning the pursuit of television broadcasting activities [1989] OJ L 298/23, as amended by Directive 97/36/EC of the European Parliament and of the Council of 30 June 1997 [1997] OJ L 202/60, Art 3a.

Although the UK provisions refer to protection for sporting and other events of national interest, only sporting events are currently protected. The general approach is to provide for two categories of listed events, Group A and Group B, and events must be allocated to one of these groups.[95] Group A refers to those events for which full live coverage is protected, whereas Group B protects secondary coverage only. For events falling within Group A, neither the free-to-air services nor the subscription services can acquire exclusive rights to live coverage, unless the other category of service also has such rights, or Ofcom has given its consent.[96] For the Group B events, exclusive live coverage will be allowed, provided that some other person has acquired additional alternative coverage rights.[97] Alternative (or secondary) coverage rights will include rights to delayed coverage, edited highlights, or live radio commentary.[98] With some exceptions, such as the Olympic Games, Group A events are confined to final matches in a series. This approach reflects the fact that free-to-air broadcasters will not have the channel capacity (even, probably, with digital delivery) or scheduling freedom to carry lengthy sporting events, whilst providing protection for some events which will have a 'national resonance', such as the FA Cup Final.[99] The listed events protection regime does not guarantee that key sporting events will be shown on free-to-air broadcasting, but it provides a framework for protection, and an incentive for broadcasters from one category to negotiate with broadcasters within the other category. Overall, the UK approach has tried to balance out the interests of the free-to-air and subscription broadcasters, by maintaining a reasonably narrow list of protected, but key events, recognising that subscription services, with their greater multichannel capacity, are well placed to devote time to sporting events. However, the narrow list of protected events has allowed significant migration to subscription and, as will be seen further in this section, regimes such as this one do not resolve all issues concerning access to premium content.

The type of balance sought by the UK regime has not been the approach in Australia, where an extensive list of protected events has ensured that sporting events are preserved for free-to-air broadcasting. It has been estimated that there are more than 2,000 protected events (taking into account individual matches and games).[100] It is less clear whether the purpose behind the Australian approach has been the preservation of important sporting events for the public, or the protection of free-to-air broadcasters. Both the Productivity Commission and the ACCC

---

[95] BA 1996 (UK), as amended, s 97.

[96] *Ibid*, as amended, s 101. Ofcom would give its consent, for example, if it was apparent that no broadcaster within the other category was interested in acquiring the rights: Ofcom, *Code on Sports and Other Listed and Designated Events* (2002). This code, which was originally administered by the Independent Television Commission, is still in force, and being administered now by Ofcom. Ofcom has prepared a draft code, but there are no substantive changes in approach.

[97] BA 1996 (UK), as amended, s 101(1C).

[98] Ofcom, *Code on Sports and Other Listed and Designated Events* (2002), paras 18–19.

[99] The Advisory Group on Listed Events, *Report and Recommendations* (March 1998), 2–3.

[100] D Crowe and N Shoebridge, 'Coonan Tackles TV Rights', (2005) *The Australian Financial Review* (Sydney), 5 August, 4.

have commented on the disproportionately anti-competitive nature of the scheme.[101] Under section 115 of the Broadcasting Services Act 1992 (BSA (Aus)), the Minister can nominate the events to be included in the 'anti-siphoning' list. Events which are included in this list are intended to be available free-to-air. Subscription broadcasters are also subject to a licence condition which prevents them acquiring rights to the listed events, unless either the national broadcasters or a commercial television licensee broadcasting to more than 50 per cent of the population also has a broadcast right.[102] However, if the free-to-air broadcaster acquires exclusive rights, covering free-to-air and subscription broadcasts, then it can exclude the subscription service broadcaster. Although a more tailored list came into force in January 2006 (and the Minister has directed ACMA to investigate and report on the rights protected under the list), the list remains extensive, particularly when compared with the UK.[103] Currently the list covers the expected sporting events, such as cricket, rugby union, and rugby league matches, and the perhaps less expected, such as golf, motor sports, and netball coverage. Similarly, within each sport, despite some reduction in the new list, the coverage is very broad. Thus, for example, in cricket, every test match (including every one-day cricket match) played by the Senior Australian team in Australia or the UK is protected, whilst for tennis, every match in the Australian Open tournament and every Wimbledon tournament match is included. This contrasts with the UK which protects only final Wimbledon matches (at least under Group A). The Productivity Commission was critical of the inconsistencies and lack of transparency regarding the compilation of the list.[104] Although examining an earlier list, some of the Commission's comments remain valid; for example, swimming, one of Australia's most popular sports, both in terms of spectator interest and public participation, is not included in the list.[105] However, the English Football Association Cup Final is protected, and it is difficult to envisage what national resonance this has for Australia. Participants to the Commission's inquiry also pointed out that much of the material on the list was never broadcast, and never had been broadcast on the free-to-air services, and that it would be impractical for the broadcasters to transmit much of what was protected; for example, to broadcast all the protected Wimbledon matches would require 90 hours of transmission per day.[106]

As noted, the anti-siphoning list does not prevent subscription broadcasters from showing these events, but they will be dependent upon the free-to-air

---

[101] Productivity Commission, above n 3, 444, and ACCC, *Submission to the Productivity Commission, Inquiry into Broadcasting* (August 1999), 21.

[102] BSA (Aus), sch 2, cl 10(1)(e).

[103] Broadcasting Services (Anti-Siphoning Monitoring) Direction (No 1) 2005. Although ACMA has to report at six-monthly intervals, its final report is not due until July 2011. The current Anti-Siphoning list is available at http://www.acma.gov.au/ACMAINTER.65668:STANDARD:936618985:pc=PC_91822.

[104] Productivity Commission, above n 3, 432–33.

[105] *Ibid*, 432.

[106] *Ibid*, 431.

broadcaster acquiring rights also, and even then the subscription service may be prevented from showing the event if the free-to-air broadcaster has acquired exclusive rights. There is now, however, a provision whereby events are automatically delisted 12 weeks prior to the start of the event—this will mean that a subscription broadcaster will then be free to acquire rights, as they will no longer be protected sporting events.[107] This automatic delisting provision was introduced in 2001 to replace a procedure whereby delisting could occur only by application to the Minister. That procedure was heavily criticised by the Productivity Commission for its cumbersome and impractical nature, which often made it difficult to release events in time for the rights to be acquired.[108] When originally introduced, the automatic delisting procedure provided for a period of six weeks only, but this was not successful, because it did not allow broadcasters sufficient time to acquire rights, and arrange marketing and scheduling. The delisting period was extended in 2005 to 12 weeks, which appears to have industry support as offering a more realistic period.[109] Despite the automatic delisting provision, the overall design of the Australian scheme seems to raise the likelihood that audiences will have even less opportunity to access sporting events than might otherwise be the case.[110] Even when the free-to-air services do acquire the rights, they often provide only limited or delayed coverage because, for example, they do not want the sporting event to interfere with other prime-time programming.[111] One notorious example of this was where the commercial broadcaster Channel Nine had acquired the rights to broadcast 'The Ashes' cricket test (which was being played in England), but chose not to broadcast the first session, because it did not want to interrupt its prime-time programme schedule.[112] As a result of this type of practice, anti-hoarding provisions were introduced in 1999 to circumvent the free-to-air broadcasters obtaining the rights to, but not televising, sporting events.[113] Under the anti-hoarding provisions, a free-to-air broadcaster who has acquired rights to a designated listed event must, if it does not intend to broadcast the event live, offer the rights to one of the national broadcasters (that is, the ABC or SBS), for a nominal sum.[114] A national broadcaster in the same situation must offer the

---

[107] BSA (Aus), s 115(1AA). The Minister has discretion to prevent the automatic removal if he or she believes that a free-to-air broadcaster has not had a reasonable opportunity to acquire the rights: s 115(1AB).

[108] Productivity Commission, above n 3, 431.

[109] Environment, Communications, Information Technology and the Arts Legislation Committee, The Senate, *Inquiry into the Provisions of the Broadcasting Services Amendment (Anti-Siphoning) Bill 2004: Report* (March 2005), paras 2.3–2.9.

[110] Productivity Commission, above n 3, 443.

[111] *Ibid*, 433.

[112] Australian Broadcasting Authority (ABA), *Investigation into the Implementation of the Anti-Hoarding Rules: Issues Paper* (June 2000), 8.

[113] The Productivity Commission observed that the need to introduce such rules confirmed its view that the anti-siphoning provisions were more extensive than necessary: Productivity Commission, above n 3, 434.

[114] BSA (Aus), s 146E. Not all listed events will fall within the anti-hoarding list, only those designated by the Minister. Currently, and curiously, the only designated events are the Federation of International Football Associations World Cup Soccer Tournament held in 2002 and 2006, including

rights to the other national broadcaster.[115] However, these provisions do not guar-antee that events will be broadcast, because it may be difficult for the broadcasters to adjust their schedules within the available time or to meet the costs which might be involved in the transmission. It might also be that the original contractual arrangements for the broadcast will include obligations regarding the promotion on-air of sponsors to the sporting event with which a national broadcaster would be unable to comply.[116] The anti-siphoning regime has probably contributed to the slow growth of subscription television in Australia. This seems paradoxical, because at a time when scarcity should be less of a constraint, a form of mandated scarcity is being encouraged in Australia. The Australian approach to preserving access to content for the public demonstrates that care needs to be taken to balance out the need to preserve access with the desirability of encouraging the growth, and economic health, of new services.

The regulatory measures looked at so far in this section aim to ensure that there is access to certain types of content for viewers, even for those who may not be able to afford subscription services. However, the importance of content for subscrip-tion services has led to the providers of such services seeking exclusive control over content which is outside the special protection regimes, as well as pursuing other methods of gaining access to content; for example, through vertical integration of content and distribution. If competition in the content market is limited, particu-larly for premium content, then this may lead to foreclosure of competition in the subscription market, restricting other competitors and deterring new entrants. The practices of exclusive contracts and vertical integration have been experienced by each of the three jurisdictions. Once again, it is sports content which illustrates these risks particularly starkly. As a general matter, the pressure for premium sports content has also led broadcasters to explore other ways to secure privileged access to such content. Apart from trying to create sporting competitions specifi-cally for subscription services, broadcasters have also sought commercial links with sporting events or teams as a basis for securing broadcasting rights. This has been a strategy particularly used by corporate interests associated with Rupert Murdoch. For example, until 2004, News Corporation, in the US, owned a base-ball team, the Los Angeles Dodgers; whilst in Australia, it owns one-half of the National Rugby League competition.[117] Another approach can be seen in the investment by the Australian free-to-air network Seven in one of the main football stadiums in Australia, which could give it a say in who should have access to the

---

the opening and closing of these events: Broadcasting Services (Designated Series of Events) Declaration No 1 of 2000. The choice of soccer seems surprising because, although increasingly popu-lar in Australia, it could not be classified as a sport of traditional national significance, and, therefore, one in relation to which there might be a particular concern about anti-hoarding practices. However, the explanation may have more to do with the timing of the event: if it is likely, because of time zone differences, to clash with prime-time schedules, then the temptation will be to delay the broadcast or not to air it at all: see ABA, above n 112, 21.

[115] BSA (Aus), s 146L.
[116] ABA, above n 112, 15–16.
[117] Productivity Commission, above n 3, 426.

stadium for the purpose of broadcasting matches.[118] Primarily matters of concern for general competition law, one can nevertheless see that such practices may also impact upon the public's access to these events, whether they are broadcast free-to-air, or on a subscription basis.

The UK provides a good example of the multifarious issues associated with sought-after content and the application of general competition law—once again involving Murdoch-related interests. In 1998, BSkyB sought to acquire a soccer club, Manchester United plc, a leading club in the Premier League competition. BSkyB's strategy was based on the belief that control of the soccer club would give it access to information, and a stake in the decisions made by the Premier League about broadcasting rights. In effect, it would sit 'on both sides of the negotiating table'.[119] Following a report by the Monopolies and Mergers Commission (now the Competition Commission) concluding that the acquisition would be against the public interest, the Secretary of State for Trade and Industry prohibited it.[120] One of the particular concerns was BSkyB's dominance as a provider of premium sports content, which could close off the market for sports premium channels to new entrants.[121] It was also relevant that BSkyB had chosen for its acquisition 'the Premier League's most prized asset'.[122] Despite the failure of this acquisition, broadcasters' demand for premium content remains, and various strategies have been used to gain influence over rights to content.[123] The position of BSkyB in the UK subscription television market has been especially concerning, and there have been several investigations. In 1996, a review was conducted regarding BSkyB's position in relation to the supply of programming at the wholesale level of the subscription broadcasting market.[124] Although BSkyB was regarded as having a dominant position in the supply of premium programming to cable operators, it was not found to be acting anti-competitively. Following an investigation which began at the end of 2000, after a review begun earlier in the year, the Director General of Fair Trading found that, although BSkyB was dominant in the market for wholesale provision of television channels which carried premium sports content and in the market for premium pay television film channels, it had not abused its position by behaving anti-competitively either by imposing a margin squeeze on distributors or through its bundling practices. As a result of these reviews, BSkyB has provided a series of undertakings to ameliorate the constrained competitive

---

[118] Productivity Commission, above n 3, 426.

[119] D Geey, 'Where Broadcasting and Football Collide: Conflicting Approaches to Football Club Ownership' (2004) 15(2) *Entertainment Law Review* 42 at 42.

[120] Monopolies and Mergers Commission, *British Sky Broadcasting Group plc and Manchester United plc: A Report on the Proposed Merger*, Cm 4305 (1999).

[121] *Ibid*, para 1.5.

[122] Geey, above n 119, 42.

[123] For a discussion of these strategies, see, generally, Geey, above n 119, and Geradin, above n 78.

[124] Office of Fair Trading (OFT), *The Director General's Review of BSkyB's Position in the Wholesale Pay TV Market* (December 1996). In fact, this was the second review; an earlier review had led to BSkyB providing informal undertakings: para 2.1.

market which arises out of the company's dominant position.[125] But the example of these investigations into BSkyB's role in the subscription television sector highlights some of the limitations of relying on ex post competition law enforcement, which will usually require lengthy and complex investigations. Although the outcome, through, for example, the provision of undertakings, may help to regulate future conduct in the market, irreparable damage to competitors might already have occurred.

BSkyB's exclusive rights to broadcast the Premier League competition have been particularly problematic. BSkyB has had, since 1992, an exclusive right to broadcast live Premier League matches; in fact, these rights have been viewed as instrumental in securing its leading position in the subscription television market.[126] A particular feature of these rights is that they are negotiated with a broadcaster as a joint package on behalf of all clubs in the League; it is not possible for individual Premier League clubs to negotiate rights, including rights to matches which might not be part of the package.[127] In practice, this has had the advantage of securing a premium price for the Premier League, but it has made it difficult for all but the largest media groups to enter the market. The joint selling arrangements have also meant that only about 25 per cent of matches were broadcast live, because unless a match was included in the package, the rights to it could not be negotiated.[128] The joint selling of rights to premium sports content has been a matter of concern for the European Commission for some time and, in 2001, it commenced an investigation into the Premier League with regard to whether the arrangements were a breach of Article 81 of the EC Treaty which prohibits anticompetitive (restrictive) agreements.[129] There is no blanket proscription on joint

---

[125] OFT, *Decision of the Director General of Fair Trading, BSkyB investigation: alleged infringement of the Chapter II prohibition* (CA98/20/2002, 17 December 2002), para 647. The Chapter II (specifically s 18(1)) prohibition under the Competition Act 1998, which is the equivalent of Art 82 of the EC Treaty, prohibits conduct which amounts to an abuse of a dominant position. Some of the undertakings provided by BSkyB were later overtaken by more general regulation imposed by the Independent Television Commission regarding practices concerning, inter alia, the packaging of channels and use of minimum carriage requirements. The guidance issued by the Independent Television Commission (*Guidance on ITC's Bundling Remedies*, June 1998) remains Ofcom policy.

[126] See OFT, *The Director General's Review of BSkyB's Position in the Wholesale Pay TV Market* (December 1996), paras 2.19, 4.57–4.62, H Ungerer, 'Competition in the media sector—how long can the future be delayed?' (2005) 7(5) *Info* 52 at 55–56, and BBC News, 'Football deal ends BSkyB Monopoly' (17 November 2005), http://news.bbc.co.uk/go/pr/fr/-/1/hi/business/4444684.stm, accessed 12 January 2006. BSkyB's current rights commenced in 2003 and continue until 2007.

[127] European Commission, 'Commission opens proceedings into joint selling of media rights to the English Premier League', Press Release IP/02/1951 (20 December 2002). See, also, European Commission, 'Commission reaches provisional agreement with FA Premier League and BSkyB over football rights', Press Release IP/03/1748 (16 December 2003) for transitional arrangements.

[128] European Commission, 'Commission opens proceedings into joint selling of media rights to the English Premier League', *ibid.*

[129] There have been several high-profile investigations in this area. Early in 2005, the Commission reached agreement with Deutsche Bundesliga regarding the sale of German football media rights (EurActiv, 'German Broadcasting Deal—EU template for future agreements?' (26 January 2005), http://www.euractiv.com/Article?_lang=EN&tcmuri=tcm:29-134541-16&type=News, accessed 22 February 2005), and, in 2003, the Commission cleared joint selling arrangements organised by UEFA (the Union of European Football Associations) after UEFA made various concessions: Ungerer, above

selling rights, and the Commission recognises that, in limited form, they can bring benefits to the development of a sport. However, in the case of the Premier League, the Commission's preliminary view was that the arrangements were detrimental to consumers, stalled innovation in new media platforms, and shut out competitors.[130] It is a measure of how difficult the resolution of this matter was that agreement between the Commission and the Premier League was reached only in late 2005. As a result of the Commission's acceptance of the League's commitments, rights to the 2007 season, and onwards, will be structured into six balanced packages (in terms of, for example, quality of teams), with no one bidder being entitled to acquire all six. However, it will be possible for one bidder to acquire five of the six packages, provided that bids are made for single packages only, thereby excluding any premium being paid for multiple packages. The rights sales will be under the conduct of a trustee appointed by the Commission.[131] Although this resolution means that BSkyB will no longer be able to control all broadcasting rights to the Premier League matches, the outcome has been viewed as a win for the broadcaster, because it had been hoped by other media groups that the Commission would require any single broadcaster to be limited to no more than 50 per cent of the rights.[132] Notwithstanding the outcome, the Premier League matter illustrates once again the delays and uncertainties which can be occasioned by reliance on ex post competition law enforcement.

In Australia, the Foxtel/Optus content-sharing agreement (discussed in the previous section) led to undertakings being given which have opened up access to some content but, as noted, there are no ex ante rules able to address these concerns. Exclusive arrangements and vertical integration having anti-competitive effects can be dealt with only under the generic competition rules, found in Part IV of the Trade Practices Act 1974.[133] Although, the Foxtel/Optus matter shows that there is some scope for the competition regulator to extract undertakings

n 126, 55–56. The Commission will be involved where trade between Member States is affected. However, since May 2004, Member States can also apply and enforce Arts 81 and 82 of the EC Treaty. In the UK, pursuant to Competition Act 1998, as amended, s 54, Ofcom has concurrent powers with the OFT to deal with matters falling under Arts 81 and 82, as well as Chapter I and Chapter II (the equivalent, respectively of Arts 81 and 82) prohibitions under the Competition Act 1998: see OFT, *Concurrent Application to Regulated Industries* (December 2004), and the Competition Act 1998 (Concurrency) Regulations 2004, SI 2004, No 1077.

[130] European Commission, 'Commission opens proceedings into joint selling of media rights to the English Premier League', above n 127.

[131] European Commission, 'Commission receives improved commitments from FAPL over sale of media rights', Press Release IP/05/1441 (17 November 2005).

[132] D Sabbagh, 'Analysis: winners and losers from new TV football deal', *Times Online* (17 November 2005), http://www.timesonline.co.uk/printFriendly/0,,1-27-1876524-27,00.html, accessed 12 January 2006, and 'A chance to challenge Murdoch for the Premier League' *The Observer* (11 December 2005) http://observer.guardian.co.uk/business/story/0,6903,1664403,00.html, accessed 12 January 2006. It appears also that Ofcom, which gave advice to the Commission, would have also preferred a 50–50 split: M Bose, 'Key role for Ofcom in Premier League deal', *Sport Telegraph* (1 September 2005), http://www.telegraph.co.uk/sport/main.jhtml?xml=/sport/2005/09/01/sfnbos01. xml, accessed 11 September 2005.

[133] Part IV includes provisions dealing with anti-competitive agreements and practices and abuse of market power.

which can address market foreclosure, the lack of ex ante rules means that damage may already have been inflicted before investigations can be completed, and remedies imposed. As such, potential competitors may already have been deterred from entering the market, or may have left it. Reliance on ex post competition law will require a case-by-case response which, apart from being resource-intensive, may lead to commercial uncertainty, and is unlikely to provide general guidance and certainty for the market.[134] Even with the undertakings, the ACCC has expressed the view that problems of accessing premium content remain, because of the highly concentrated subscription television market in Australia, and the dominance of the vertically integrated Foxtel service.[135] The ACCC is also of the view that Part IV may not always be sufficient to address exclusive content arrangements, because the ACCC may not be able to establish sufficiently all the required elements necessary to enforce the specific provisions.[136] It has suggested that a specific access regime for content should be introduced, with provision for access to individual premium sports and film content.[137]

It was concerns about exclusivity arrangements and the difficulties of new entrants to the market gaining content access, which led the US to develop specific rules, as part of the Cable Consumer Protection and Competition Act of 1992, to open up access to content.[138] Congress was concerned specifically about the monopoly which most cable operators enjoyed in relation to programme distribution, and the incentive this gave them to favour their affiliated cable operators.[139] At that time, cable operators served more than 95 per cent of all subscribers to multichannel services.[140] Congress wanted to encourage the development of rival delivery technologies which could compete with the cable systems, and satellite broadcasting was particularly in mind.[141] There are three aspects to the access provisions, and they are intended, inter alia, to increase 'competition and diversity in the multichannel video programming market' and 'to spur the development of communications technologies'.[142] There is a general prohibition on cable operators or affiliated programming vendors engaging in unfair competition or practices, 'the purpose or effect of which is to hinder significantly or to prevent any multichannel video programming distributor from providing satellite cable programming or satellite broadcast programming to subscribers or consumers'.[143]

---

[134] ACCC, *Emerging Market Structures*, above n 44, para 6.3.1.

[135] *Ibid*, ch 6.

[136] *Ibid*, para 6.3.1. For a more detailed discussion of the limits of the specific Part IV provisions (Trade Practices Act 1974, ss 45–47) relevant to exclusive agreements, see Productivity Commission, above n 23, 539–42.

[137] ACCC, *Emerging Market Structures*, above n 44, para 6.5.

[138] *Ibid*, para 6.2.2.

[139] HR Conf Rep No 102-862, 93 (1992), cited in FCC, *Memorandum Opinion and Order* (2003), above n 22, para 41.

[140] FCC, *Report and Order, In the Matter of the Cable Television Consumer Protection and Competition Act of 1992*, FCC 02-176 (13 June 2002), para 20.

[141] HR Rep No 102-628, 165–66 (1992), cited in FCC, *Memorandum Opinion and Order* (2003), above n 22, para 41.

[142] 47 USC § 548(a).

[143] 47 USC § 548(b).

Under the statutory provisions, the FCC was required to draw up rules to deal with the three aspects of the prohibition. First, there is an outright prohibition on exclusive agreements between cable operators and affiliated programming vendors in areas not served by a cable operator (as at October 1992).[144] Secondly, there is a similar prohibition on exclusive agreements for areas already served by a cable operator, unless the FCC decides that the agreement is in the public interest.[145] This second prohibition was also subject to a sunset clause: unless the FCC decided, upon review, that it was necessary, for the protection of competition and diversity, to maintain the provision, the prohibition was due to expire in 2002.[146] Thirdly, the FCC was required to draft rules which would protect against unfair practices and discrimination in relation to the sale of programming, its price, terms, and conditions.[147] The FCC can deal with complaints, and impose terms and conditions and prices.[148]

The FCC conducted a review of the sunset clause in 2002, and concluded that, although the competitive landscape for distribution of programming had improved, the prohibition was still necessary given the degree of dominance still enjoyed by cable, and the degree of vertical integration. The Commission found that cable operators still served the great majority (78 per cent) of all multichannel subscribers.[149] The prohibition was extended for another five years, until October 2007.[150] The extension is recognition of the extent to which an advantageous position with regard to access to content can influence strongly the development of competitive markets. One aspect of the prohibition, however, has been troublesome because the rules apply only to programming which is transmitted via satellite. This has been an ongoing irritation for cable's competitors, because it is argued that cable operators have delivered sought-after content via terrestrial delivery in order to escape the provisions.[151] However, the FCC has taken the view that terrestrially delivered programming is outside the legislative provisions.[152] Two other rules can be mentioned in this section which, although not directly about opening up access to content, aim to ensure that broadcasters' rights to content, once acquired, are not undermined by the ability of cable and satellite delivery to import distant signals. The network non-duplication rule, as it is known, allows a broadcaster, commercial or non-commercial, which holds the

---

[144] 47 USC § 548(c)(2)(C).
[145] 47 USC § 548(c)(2)(D). § 548(c)(4) sets out the public interest matters to be considered, which include (in broad terms) examining the effect of the contract on the development of competition in the relevant markets, and the impact on the attraction of new investment in programming.
[146] 47 USC § 548(c)(5).
[147] 47 USC § 548(c)(2)(A) and (B). The FCC rules are found at 47 CFR §§ 76.1000–4.
[148] 47 CFR § 76.1003.
[149] FCC, *Report and Order* (2002), above n 140, para 65. As noted in Chapter One, satellite broadcasting, after a slow start, has been growing in popularity; by June 2004, the reach for cable had decreased to 72%: FCC, *Eleventh Annual Report* (2005), above n 48, para 4.
[150] 47 CFR § 76.1002(c)(6).
[151] FCC, *Report and Order* (2002), above n 140, paras 71–72. See, also, FCC, *Eleventh Annual Report* (2005), above n 50, para 155.
[152] FCC, *Report and Order* (2002), above n 140, para 73.

exclusive rights to a networked programme for the local area to request the cable or satellite operator to remove the programme from an imported signal.[153] The syndicated exclusivity rule, referred to, usually, as the 'syndex' rule, has a similar operation, but applies in relation to syndicated programmes and only for the benefit of commercial stations.[154]

Must-Carry Requirements

A different kind of access-related measure is provided by 'must-carry' requirements. Must-carry provisions are a recognition that some services or channels may be so important that they should be available over all delivery platforms, and the providers of those services should not be dependent upon being able to negotiate terms of access. Unlike the UK and the US, Australia stipulates no must-carry obligations, so that it is a matter for commercial negotiation. It may be, of course, that a subscription service will want to carry certain channels, such as, for example, the public broadcasting channels, as a way of encouraging subscribers, and Foxtel, the dominant subscription television provider, does carry the ABC and SBS. However, the only other free-to-air service which Foxtel carries is the commercial service the Nine Network. If it is recalled that the Nine Network is controlled by Publishing and Broadcasting Limited, which has a 25 per cent interest in Foxtel, then the lack of any must-carry requirements appears hazardous. The ACCC noted, in 2003, that Foxtel intended to reach agreements with the other free-to-air broadcasters for carriage on Foxtel's digital platforms, although at the time of writing it is not apparent that such agreements have been reached.[155] Even the public broadcaster, the ABC, which is being carried by Foxtel has argued for mandatory must-carry provisions, citing the uncertainty of relying on commercial arrangements which are in place for defined periods only. The ABC has also noted that not all of its services are available, and that commercial arrangements do not provide 'a guarantee that the ABC's services will always be available to all Australians on all platforms'.[156]

In the UK, the Comms Act (UK) makes provision for the carriage of the digital version of the public service channels.[157] Currently, the channels specified for carriage are the BBC television services, Channels Three, Four/S4C, and Five, and a public teletext service.[158] The government's commitment to a must-carry requirement was influenced by eventual total switch-over to digital. Without a must-carry

---

[153] 47 CFR § 76.92 and 47 CFR § 76.122.

[154] 47 CFR § 76.101 and 47 CFR § 76.123. Both the network non-duplication rule and the syndex rule restrict satellite operators only in relation to nationally distributed superstations, which are carried on satellite only.

[155] ACCC, *Emerging Market Structures*, above n 44, para 7.4.1.

[156] ABC, *ABC Comments on the ACCC Report on Emerging Market Structures in the Communications Sector*, 2.

[157] Comms Act (UK), s 64.

[158] *Ibid*, s 64(3). The Secretary of State is required to review the list from time to time, and the legislation specifies matters to be taken into account in deciding to amend the list: s 64(7)–(10).

requirement, it might have been necessary for viewers to possess more than one set-top box to access both the public service channels and subscription services.[159] Ofcom, however, has set the must-carry requirements more firmly in the public interest context, which requires 'diversity of programming for citizen-consumers'.[160] It is a matter for Ofcom, pursuant to section 64(1), through the imposition of conditions, to decide which 'electronic communications networks' should be subject to the must-carry obligation, although under section 64(2)(b) only those networks which 'are used by a significant number of end-users as their principal means of receiving television programmes' can be made subject to the must-carry requirement. The implementation of these provisions had an unexpected outcome, for Ofcom chose not to impose must-carry obligations on cable or satellite transmission, but indicated its intention to impose a must-carry condition on the providers of the terrestrial transmission network, on the grounds that there were no other networks for terrestrial transmission, and the presence of high barriers of entry.[161] Ofcom considered that there were sufficient commercial and regulatory guarantees to ensure that satellite and cable services carried the public service broadcasting channels.[162] In the case of satellite, the conditional access obligations, reviewed earlier in this chapter, were considered to provide sufficient protection, whilst cable operators voluntarily provided carriage of the channels, and free of charge.[163] However, in the former situation, this overlooks the difference in nature between access and must-carry obligations, whilst in the second situation, carriage is only guaranteed whilst it is commercially attractive, and the concerns of the ABC in Australia should be recalled. In fact, the must-carry regime represents something of a back-track for the government, because in the lead-up to the 2003 reforms, it seemed to be intended that cable and satellite delivery platforms would be subject to a must-carry obligation.[164] Nevertheless, the public broadcasting channels, particularly the BBC, will be desirable content, and other developments such as Freesat (referred to in Chapter One) provide evidence of the attractiveness of the public service channels for cable and satellite platforms. However, the requirement that the public broadcasters must offer their services may weaken their bargaining position.[165]

More controversial have been the US must-carry provisions. First instituted in 1965, the rules, which required cable networks to carry local television services,

---

[159] Department of Trade and Industry (DTI) and Department for Culture, Media and Sport (DCMS), *A New Future for Communications*, Cm 5010 (2000) ('White Paper'), para 3.4.3.

[160] Ofcom, *Provision of Managed Transmission Services to Public Service Broadcasters, Consultation Document* (28 February 2005), para 2.1, and, generally, paras 2.1–2.7.

[161] *Ibid*, paras 2.17 and 3.1. See also Ofcom, *Broadcasting Transmission Services: A Review of the Market, Explanatory Statement and Notification* (11 November 2004). The must-carry obligation will be on the basis of fair and reasonable terms and conditions, and charges.

[162] Ofcom, *Provision of Managed Transmission Services to Public Service Broadcasters, Consultation Document* (28 February 2005), para 1.13.

[163] Ofcom, *Broadcasting Transmission Services: A Review of the Market, Explanatory Statement and Notification* (11 November 2004), paras 3.23–3.24.

[164] DTI and DCMS, White Paper, above n 159, para 3.4.

[165] Comms Act (UK), ss 272–73.

were designed to protect the local free-to-air television stations, and their markets.[166] This was to ensure that broadcasting services would still be available for those members of the public who did not have access to cable. In the early days, the rules were more of a benefit to the cable systems than a burden, because the free-to-air stations provided them with a good source of programming, but, by the 1980s, this position had changed as more sources of programming became available, and the scope for carrying more lucrative channels had widened.[167] The must-carry rules went through a series of changes and challenges which led to their demise in the late 1980s. However, they were revived by the Cable Television Consumer Protection and Competition Act of 1992, save for very small cable systems. The impetus for the revival was recognition of both the importance of local over-the-air stations in providing local news and public affairs programming, and a need to protect the viability of the over-the-air services.[168] Under the new rules, broadcasters, although not public broadcasters, were able to elect between must-carry rights or retransmission consent. Under the must-carry rules, a broadcaster's signal has to be carried by all cable systems operating in that area, but without compensation.[169] If a commercial station elects the retransmission option, the station's signal may only be transmitted with consent and, inevitably, payment or some other form of compensation.[170] In general, most broadcasters opted for the retransmission consent path, although few broadcasters received cash compensation for the retransmission rights. However, many were able to secure some form of compensation such as free promotional time, or the opportunity to broadcast short local news segments.[171]

The 1992 must-carry obligation was challenged under First Amendment principles by cable operator the Turner Broadcasting System, which resulted in two Supreme Court decisions.[172] In the first decision, a majority of the court held that the must-carry rules were content-neutral, and thereby should be subject to an intermediate level of scrutiny only. In the majority's view, the requirement

---

[166] Creech, above n 90, 98.

[167] *Ibid.*

[168] House Committee on Energy and Commerce, HR Conf Rep No 102-862, 102d Cong., 2d Sess. (1992), reprinted at 138 *Cong Rec* H8308 (14 September 1992), 2–3, cited in FCC, *Memorandum Opinion and Order* (2003), above n 22, para 46.

[169] 47 CFR § 76.56(a) for public broadcasting services, and 47 CFR § 76.56(b) for commercial services. A cable operator is only obliged to use up to one-third of its channel capacity for the carriage of commercial broadcasting services: § 76.56(b)(2).

[170] 47 CFR § 76.64. Broadcasters are under an obligation to negotiate in good faith: §76.65. Satellite (DBS) operators are bound by slightly different must-carry arrangements: a must-carry obligation does not arise until a DBS operator elects to carry one local service (to the local market), in which case the DBS must carry all such services: 47 CFR § 76.66. Retransmission rights also apply: § 76.66(c).

[171] Creech, above n 90, 103–4, and W Overbeck, *Major Principles of Media Law*, 15th edn (Belmont CA, Thomson Wadsworth, 2004), 487. See, also, FCC, *Retransmission Consent and Exclusivity Rules: Report to Congress* (2005), above n 93, paras 36–45, where the FCC has noted concerns that some broadcasters try to tie in carriage of their stations with carriage of affiliated non-broadcast networks or content.

[172] *Turner Broadcasting System, Inc v Federal Communications Commission* 512 US 622 (1994), and *Turner Broadcasting System, Inc v Federal Communications Commission* 520 US 180 (1997).

imposed upon cable operators to carry local broadcast stations did not arise because of any particular views or content conveyed by the cable operators, nor did carriage depend upon views or content conveyed by the broadcast stations. The obligations applied to all cable systems (at least of a certain size), and distinguished between speakers, not on the basis of their speech but on the basis of the manner in which it was transmitted.[173] In holding that the must-carry rules furthered important governmental interests, the majority noted the reasons for the rules given by Congress: the preservation of free-to-air, over-the-air television broadcasting; the availability of sources from a multiplicity of sources; and the promotion of fair competition.[174] The court also referred to evidence about the likelihood that, without the must-carry obligation, many broadcast stations would not be carried by cable, but it did not consider that there was sufficient evidence to support a finding that local broadcasting would be in jeopardy without the obligation, or to determine whether there were any less burdensome means available to protect the recognised governmental interests.[175] The matter was remanded to the District Court, and it was that court's judgment which was challenged again by Turner. However, in the 1997 decision, the Supreme Court, again by a majority, held that there was sufficient evidence to show that the rules addressed real harm, and that the rules were not more burdensome than was necessary to protect the identified governmental interests. It is worth noting that the must-carry rules were recognised as serving more than just competition goals; they were seen also as promoting diversity by ensuring the existence and availability of a range of commercial and non-commercial broadcasting services. However, there was a strong dissent from Justice O'Connor, particularly in relation to the finding that the rules were content-neutral, and her judgment points again to the rather strained assumption that structural regulation sits more comfortably with First Amendment principles, compared with the type of content regulatory measures reviewed in Chapter Four. In her judgment, the references in the legislation to the promotion of diversity, localism, educational programming, and other types of programming, and the distinction made between commercial and non-commercial stations, all pointed to a direct connection with 'the content of what the speakers will likely say,' and as such, required strict scrutiny.[176] It was irrelevant that the motivations for the regulation were benign.[177]

The implications of the development of digital for the must-carry rules have been another issue. Cable operators have resisted the extension of the must-carry rules to digital, because of the likelihood that this could mean an obligation to

---

[173] *Turner v FCC* (1994), *Ibid,* 644–47.

[174] *Ibid,* 662–63.

[175] *Ibid,* 667–68.

[176] *Ibid,* 676–68.

[177] *Ibid,* 676. See, also, E Barendt, 'Structural and Content Regulation of the Media: United Kingdom Law and Some American Comparisons' in E Barendt (ed), *The Yearbook of Media and Entertainment Law 1997/98* (Oxford, Clarendon Press, 1997), 75 at 80–82.

carry four or five digital programming streams for each local station.[178] In 2005, the FCC ruled that it was necessary for a cable operator to carry only one digital programming stream—the 'primary video', and that a broadcaster would have to elect which stream would be the 'primary video'. In reaching this decision, the FCC was influenced by the need to justify the imposition of additional burdens in the light of the *Turner* decisions.[179] In fact, one might have expected that the increased costs for the free-to-air broadcasting stations of digital and multi-channelling would have strengthened the viability justification for the must-carry obligation, but the FCC rejected this: there was no evidence that the viability of a free, over-the-air service was jeopardised, nor was there evidence that it was necessary for the dissemination of a multiplicity of sources. The FCC decided that diversity was promoted by having one programming stream of the broadcaster carried, but that (source) diversity would not be promoted by having more than one stream carried.[180] The focus on source diversity was consistent with the *Turner* decisions, but is a narrow interpretation of diversity.

Electronic Programme Guides and Channel Positioning

In a multichannel viewing environment, viewers will increasingly rely on an electronic programme guide (EPG), an on-screen guide to assist them in finding out what is available to view. Inevitably, the guide will only be able to display a certain amount of information at any one time, and so it may be necessary for the viewer to 'click' through once, or more, to obtain full information about what is available. As such, EPGs, through their design and modes of presentation and categorisation, can influence audiences in their choice of services.[181] This poses a risk if the controller of the EPG is also a provider of programme services, or associated with others who are, because the information available through the EPG may be presented in a way which promotes certain services, whilst 'hiding' competitive services. The impact of such discriminatory behaviour will be felt the more, given that there will usually only be one EPG service for each delivery platform. In Australia, EPG services represent another area where regulatory attention has been rudimentary. There is no specific regulation of EPG services, and so it will be a matter for competition law to act in situations where control of an EPG may be being used in an anti-competitive manner. An obvious concern is the position of Foxtel, which will have an incentive—and, because of its dominance, scope—to promote

---

[178] FCC, *Second Report and Order and First Order on Reconsideration, In the Matter of Carriage of Digital Television Broadcast Signals: Amendments to Part 76 of the Commission's Rules,* FCC 05-27 (10 February 2005), para 32.

[179] *Ibid,* especially paras 37–41. The FCC also reaffirmed an earlier decision that cable operators are not required, during the transition period, to carry, simultaneously, the analogue and digital signals of the broadcaster (referred to as 'dual carriage'): para 27.

[180] *Ibid,* paras 38–39.

[181] See Ofcom, *Statement on Code on Electronic Programme Guides* (26 July 2004), Annex 2 for an indication of the type of concerns listing practices can raise.

the programme services with which it is associated. However, as part of the under-taking process, which was the outcome of the Foxtel/Optus content-sharing arrangements, the ACCC obtained undertakings from Foxtel, which require it to negotiate in good faith to supply EPG services upon request by an access seeker, although this may not address all the concerns about presentation of services on the EPG. Certainly the draft digital access undertaking which Foxtel has lodged with the ACCC provides little coverage of those issues which might typically be of concern in the provision of EPG services.[182]

A different approach can be seen in the UK, where Ofcom is required by section 310 of the Comms Act (UK) to draw up a code which deals with access for persons with visual and hearing impairments, and with the listing and promotion of the public service channels. Ofcom is also permitted to require EPG providers to com-ply with a code to secure fair and effective competition.[183] Ofcom has drawn up a code which applies to all providers of EPGs, licensed under the Broadcasting Act 1990 (BA 1990 (UK)), as amended, and deals with how EPGs will list and promote services.[184] With regard to the provision of 'appropriate prominence' to the listing and promotion of the public service channels, the code sets down general prin-ciples which the providers must take into account. Thus, they should ensure that their approach for listing organisation and display is objectively justifiable and transparent, having regard to the interests of citizens and consumers. Access for regional services has also to be catered for.[185] Some degree of discrimination in favour of public service channels in deciding methods of listing and display is acceptable.[186] Discriminatory use of an EPG service could undermine the purpose of the must-carry requirements, previously considered. Clauses 14–15 set out requirements in relation to fair, reasonable, and non-discriminatory treatment. The code is not prescriptive as to how EPG providers design their listings, but in so doing they must, inter alia: publish an objectively justifiable method of allocat-ing listings; refrain from giving undue prominence to channels with which they are connected; ensure viewers are able to access all radio and television services on the same basis; and, ensure that free-to-air services are at least as accessible as pay services.

The US does not appear to provide any general regulation of EPGs, although this would presumably form part of the negotiations for leased access, discussed

---

[182] ACCC, *A Report on the assessment of the Analogue Pay TV Access Undertaking Proffered by Foxtel Management Pty Ltd on 22 December 2003* (March 2004), 16. See, also, Foxtel Management Pty Limited for and on behalf of the Foxtel Partnership and Foxtel Cable Television Pty Ltd, *Special Access Undertaking to the Australian Competition & Consumer Commission* (October 2005), and ACCC, *Foxtel's Special Access Undertaking in Relation to the Digital Set Top Unit Service, Discussion Paper* (November 2005).

[183] Under Comms Act (UK), s 316, licensees have an obligation to secure fair and effective competition. See also s 317. Reference should also be made to the section 'Access to Infrastructure' (at p 213) which deals with a separate regime regulating EPG services.

[184] Ofcom, *Code of Practice on Electronic Programme Guides* (July 2004). Ofcom's predecessor, the Independent Television Commission, had also supervised a code.

[185] *Ibid*, cls 2-3.

[186] *Ibid*, cl. 3.

earlier in this chapter. However, there are provisions designed to prevent the must-carry provisions being undermined. For example, a broadcaster which has elected to have a cable operator carry its signal will be allocated the same channel position as applies to its over-the-air service.[187] This at least ensures that viewers will be able to find the channel simply by recall of the channel number. Although a commercial broadcaster electing the retransmission consent procedure will not have the same guarantee, if it is a sought-after broadcaster, then this would be something which it could negotiate. Local television over-the-air services also have to be carried on the cable operator's basic tier.[188]

Networks

All three jurisdictions have licensed free-to-air broadcasting services on a regional basis, although ownership rules might not prevent common ownership of these regional companies. In the UK, for example, the Channel Three television service is made up of 15 regional licences, but, as previously noted, the English and Welsh licences (11 in total) are now held under common control. One reason for licensing on a regional basis will be to ensure that programming is able to serve the local population of that licensed service. Localism has been a key policy driver for US broadcasting, both radio and television, regulation.[189] However, an emphasis on local or regional broadcasting services, whilst serving one objective, might also undermine the goal of providing a wide range of programming, something which a larger broadcasting company might be better able to provide. The content production costs for a broadcasting company serving a small community will be greater per viewer or listener, limiting the scope for certain types of programming to be produced.[190] Similarly, a broadcasting company is likely to be attracted by the possibility of achieving economies of scale for programme costs, by being able to distribute programme costs across the largest possible audience. The broadcasting industry is particularly vulnerable to economies of scale, for reasons discussed in Chapter Six, and networking or syndication has been a common practice in both the radio and television sectors, for each of the jurisdictions. These factors will be particularly relevant to television broadcasting, because of the high costs of programme production, and explains why regulatory attention has focused more on television networking practices than radio. In the changing broadcasting environment, there is no reason to expect that the advantages of networking will change. Networking enables economies of scale to be enjoyed, but it can also provide regional, local, and small broadcasters with the opportunity to provide a

---

[187] 47 CFR § 76.57. The same obligation does not apply to satellite, although the channels should be contiguous: 47 CFR § 76.66(i).

[188] 47 CFR § 76.901.

[189] FCC, *Report and Order and Notice of Proposed Rulemaking, In the Matter of 2002 Biennial Regulatory Review—Review of the Commission's Broadcast Ownership Rules and Other Rules Adopted Pursuant to Section 202 of the Telecommunications Act of 1996,* FCC 03-127 (2 June 2003), paras 73–76.

[190] Doyle, above n 2, 70.

much greater range of programming, much of which they would be unable to afford to produce themselves. Typically, broadcasting networks will be made up of commonly owned broadcasting companies, or companies linked through contractual arrangements, or, frequently, a mix of both. However, the advantages of networking have to be tempered by the risks inherent in such arrangements. Whilst networking can provide audiences with access to a greater range of programming, there is also a risk that, in the longer term, networking arrangements could restrict choice. If a network becomes too large, having achieved significant economies of scale, it may be difficult for other programme producers to enter the market.[191] A lack of competition and competitive incentive may jeopardise diversity in programming, and commitment to new and different types of programming. Networking arrangements might also mean that the regional and smaller broadcasters have reduced control over their broadcasting schedules and programme offerings. Another reason for concern over networking arrangements is that they may be used as a means of circumventing ownership restrictions. Certainly, the Australian legislation contemplates this possibility, and includes within the interpretation of 'being in a position to exercise control' the possibility that control could arise through selection of programming.[192]

It is Australia, again, which shows the greatest regulatory complacence to networking practices, paradoxically so, because early Australian broadcasting policy, first for radio, and later television, developed out of a desire to avoid the US pattern of network dominance.[193] To avoid this, Australia emphasised localism: localism in ownership, and in programme production.[194] Whilst the ABC would be a national broadcaster, the commercial service would serve local needs. Yet, in practice, and as seen in Chapter Three, the commercial networks established their influence very early in the development of broadcasting and, through both ownership and affiliate arrangements, have ensured virtually a national commercial broadcasting system.[195] This is despite an ownership and control rule which prohibits a person controlling licences with a combined national reach of more than 75 per cent of the population.[196] In fact, part of the rationale for the national reach rule (which effectively prevented the main commercial networks being able to expand into the non-metropolitan markets) was the expectation that it would allow regional companies to develop their own networks and support local production.[197] However, each of the regional networks has an affiliation with one of the three main networks, and even the larger regional operators have not produced local content to any significant degree. Evidence to the Productivity

---

[191] Doyle, above n 2, 72.

[192] BSA (Aus), sch 1, cl 2(1)(b)(ii).

[193] P Chadwick, *Media Mates: Carving Up Australia's Media* (Melbourne, Macmillan, 1989), 125.

[194] *Ibid,* 124. It is particularly ironic that this should have been the Australian attitude, given the US emphasis on localism.

[195] *Ibid,* 125ff, and Productivity Commission, above n 3, 367.

[196] See Chapter Three, 'Australia: Current Rules', at p 130. This rule, in any event, enables control of a licence in each of the mainland capital city markets.

[197] Productivity Commission, above n 3, 367.

Commission indicated that the strong bargaining position of the major networks left little option to the regional networks but to take networked programming, when compared with the costs of local production.[198] The virtual monopoly created by the major commercial networks through ownership and networking arrangements effectively undermines the national reach rule, and serves as a reminder of the need to look at broadcasting pluralism regulatory measures holistically. Radio has no national ownership limits, and is dominated also by networks and programme-sharing arrangements. Thus, despite commercial radio being structured around a local radio model, even local talk-back radio programmes can have a national audience reach: one of the local talk-back programmes, presented by John Laws, which was part of the 'cash for comment' matter (see Chapter Four), was broadcast over 77 stations across Australia.[199]

Although there were repeatedly expressed concerns about the impact of networking on localism, no specific regulation of networking practices developed, in contrast to the US, even though proposals modelled on the US rules were suggested.[200] It was probably never realistic to expect that, in Australia, with its small population thinly spread outside the metropolitan areas, local broadcasters could viably produce their own programming across the whole range of programming needs. Other Australian broadcasting policies, such as aggregation of licence areas, have also increased the dependence of the regional broadcasters on the networks, and new regulation has had to be imposed to preserve local news content.[201] In a broadcasting market, like that found in Australia, networking might be a sensible means of increasing the incentives for investment in programme production, to provide a greater range of programming. However, in the Australian context, networking practices will be a matter for general law, and in the absence of specific regulation, there are no safeguards to minimise the impact of the dominance of the major networks, or to ensure that networking arrangements will lead to greater investment in content.

Like Australia, the US networks developed organically through ownership of broadcasting stations, and the establishment of affiliate arrangements with other broadcasters. As discussed in Chapter Three, the development of the networks, their practices, and ability to dominate programme schedules were matters of early concern for the FCC, and led it to develop rules governing networking practices (or 'chain broadcasting', as it is sometimes known in the US).[202] The National Broadcasting Company (NBC) was also required to divest itself of one of its networks, which became the American Broadcasting Company (ABC) network. The rules, which developed out of the 1941 inquiry into chain broadcasting,[203] are still in place, although there have been modifications over time. Although the FCC has

[198] *Ibid*, 368–69.
[199] Australian Broadcasting Authority, *Commercial Radio Inquiry: Report of the Australian Broadcasting Authority Hearing into Radio 2UE Sydney Pty Ltd* (February 2000), 9.
[200] Chadwick, above n 193, 131–33.
[201] See Chapter Four, 'Regulatory Measures: Programme Diversity', at p 160.
[202] See Chapter Three, 'United States: Early Regulatory Steps', at p 103.
[203] FCC, *Report on Chain Broadcasting*, Commission Order No 37 (Docket 5060, May 1941).

no direct power to regulate the networks, it has used its powers over licensees to impose rules. Radio licensees are prohibited from any arrangement with a network organisation which prevents another station broadcasting in the same area being able to broadcast network programmes not taken by the licensee, or which prevent a station broadcasting in a different area being able to broadcast any network programme.[204] For television broadcasting networks, there is a more extensive set of rules which prohibit certain arrangements with a network organisation, including: preventing a licensee from obtaining programmes from other networks; granting time option rights, which prevent a licensee scheduling that time period until the network has vacated it, or which requires the time to be cleared for the network; preventing a station rejecting a network programme which the station believes unsatisfactory, or contrary to the public interest, or replacing it with one of greater local or national importance; and a prohibition on territorial exclusivity, similar to the radio rule.[205] These rules reflect many of the practices which concerned the FCC during its 1941 inquiry.

Two rules, no longer extant, are worth mentioning; developed in conjunction in 1970, they were both important rules in shaping network behaviour. Both rules applied only to the original networks: ABC, NBC, and CBC. The prime-time access rule, which was repealed by the FCC in 1995 (effective 1996), applied only to the largest markets, and restricted the number of hours which could be given to networked programmes during evening prime-time periods by network-affiliated television broadcasters. It had developed out of concerns that the networks' domination of prime-time viewing periods strengthened their domination of the programme production market, and control over much of the television content received by the public. It was anticipated that the rule would increase competition in programme production.[206] The FCC's repeal of the rule was based on its conclusion that the networks no longer dominated the programme markets, as well as evidence of the growth of new broadcasting networks and independent stations, and the increase in the number of competing sources of television programming available to the public.[207] With purposes similar to the prime-time rule, the second rule, known as the financial interest and syndication rule (finsyn), restricted severely the ability of the networks to own and syndicate television programming.[208] It was, in effect, an early recognition of the problems of vertical integration. The rule meant that the networks had to rely on independent programming sources and, being precluded from domestic syndication rights, the production

---

[204] 47 CFR § 73.132 (for AM), and 47 CFR § 73.232 (for FM). The rule does not apply to arrangements with stations under common ownership.

[205] 47 CFR § 73.658.

[206] FCC, *Report and Order, In re Review of the Prime Time Access Rule, Section 73.658(k) of the Commission's Rules*, FCC 95-314 (28 July 1995), para 1.

[207] *Ibid*, paras 113–15, and generally.

[208] FCC, *Report and Order, In re Review of the Syndication and Financial Interest Rules, Sections 73.659-73.663 of the Commission's Rules*, 10 FCC Rcd 12165 (1995). There was a series of orders, commencing in 1991, which led to the phasing-out of the finsyn rules: paras 3–4.

companies were able to benefit from the syndication right profits.[209] As with the prime-time rules, the repeal of finsyn rule was motivated by increased competition faced by the networks and increased competition for programming.[210] Since the demise of the fynsyn rule, it is apparent that programming offered by the networks has been dominated by network-owned content, and there has been lobbying for a return to the rule.[211]

The UK provides a different perspective on networking practices, at least in relation to television, because networking has been actively fostered as a way to provide a national service capable of competing with the BBC but, at the same time, serving regional needs. Initially, too, it was seen as a means of promoting competition, and enabling regional broadcasters to sell programmes to the network and reach a national audience. In practice, however, the larger licensee companies tended to dominate.[212] The BA 1990 (UK) provided a mechanism for restructuring the networking arrangements to ensure more effective competition, but it was left to the licensees themselves to devise the arrangements, although they had to be approved by the Independent Television Commission, and the Director General of Fair Trading, the predecessor to the OFT.[213] Since that restructuring process, the networking arrangements have remained substantially the same. ITV Network Ltd is established as a company limited by guarantee, its members being each of the licensees. In brief, overall strategy and budgets (to which each licensee makes a contribution) are set by the ITV Network Council (the equivalent to a board of directors), on which each licensee is represented. There is a separate management body, the Network Centre, which commissions and acquires programmes, and organises the national schedule. A code of practice requires the Network Centre to consider programme proposals fairly and impartially.[214] One problem of the Carlton–Granada merger, now ITV plc, which brought under single control 11 of the regional licences, is the dominance that it now has in the networking arrangements.[215] ITV plc now commands 90 per cent of the voting rights in the Network Council.[216] However, it has provided undertakings, as a

---

[209] Overbeck, above n 171, 525–26.

[210] FCC, *Report and Order (1995)*, above n 208, para 29.

[211] Overbeck, above n 171, 526.

[212] T Gibbons, *Regulating the Media*, 2nd edn (London, Sweet & Maxwell, 1998), 230. Networking in radio is permitted, subject to licensees meeting their obligations to broadcast locally made content, as set out in the format for the licence: see Ofcom, *Radio—Preparing for the Future, Phase 2: Implementing the Framework, Consultation* (19 October 2005), paras 7.39–7.45.

[213] BA 1990 (UK), s 39 and sch 4. For the history of these arrangements, see Gibbons, above n 210, 230–2, and Ofcom, *Review of ITV Networking Arrangements, Consultation Document* (28 February 2005) ('Networking Review'). For current statutory arrangements, see Comms Act (UK), ss 290–94 and sch 11.

[214] Ofcom, Networking Review, above n 213, para 3.18. This code of practice applies to dealings with licensees and independent producers. However, as required by the Comms Act (UK), s 285, a separate and additional code also covers dealings with independent producers: paras 3.25–3.31.

[215] Despite appearances, ITV plc and ITV Network Ltd are separate entities. The former is the commercial entity which, inter alia, controls and operates the Channel Three licensees; the latter is the entity which is responsible for the networking arrangements with the Channel Three licensees.

[216] Ofcom, Networking Review, above n 213, para 3.14.

condition of the merger's approval, which are designed to preserve a balance within the network, and to protect some of the smaller members.[217]

Under section 293 of the Comms Act (UK), Ofcom is required to review the networking arrangements at various intervals, or under certain circumstances. The impact of the arrangements on competition is an important element of these reviews, but there are broader considerations to be taken into account also. The networking arrangements are exempt from the Competition Act 1998 prohibition on restrictive or anti-competitive agreements, provided that they satisfy the competition test provided in schedule 11 of the Comms Act (UK).[218] Under the schedule 11 competition test, the networking arrangements will be satisfactory if they do not have as their object or effect, the prevention, restriction, or distortion of competition or, if they do, they contribute to improving production or distribution, or promoting technical or economic progress, subject also to various balancing tests.[219] However, the legislation also requires Ofcom to consider broader public policy objectives. The first is identified by Ofcom as the 'Effectiveness' test which examines whether the networking arrangements will enable the establishment of a nationwide service which can compete effectively with other television programme services. Secondly, the 'Regional Programming' test requires an examination of whether the networking arrangements will enable the licensees to maintain the quality and range of regional programmes and other programmes contributing to the provision of a regional service.[220] Finally, Ofcom is enjoined to consider whether the networking arrangements would be likely to impede fulfilment of the licensees' public service remits, and other statutory obligations, such as regional programme-making and broadcasting.[221]

The networking arrangements in the UK provide a sharp contrast with those of the US and Australia. First, they are the product of a specific policy, rather than the result of the expansion of certain broadcasting companies. As such, the existence of a separate entity, to which all the licensees belong, can provide, even for the smaller companies, a transparent and controlled means of accessing the market. Of course, the dominance now of ITV plc raises new concerns about the effective working of the network, although this is precisely the type of concern which the merger undertakings sought to address. Further, the review process required of Ofcom provides an opportunity for the arrangements to be modified to address such issues.[222] Secondly, compared with the US and, particularly, Australia, the UK television networking arrangements are, as noted above, subject to close regulatory supervision. UK networking practices must also be considered keeping in mind other regulatory obligations, imposed upon Channel Three licensees, such

---

[217] Ofcom, Networking Review, above n 213, paras 3.19–3.24.

[218] Competition Act 1998, sch 2, para 5.

[219] Comms Act (UK), sch 11, para 6(3)–(4).

[220] Comms Act (UK), sch 11, para 7(3)–(4). See also Ofcom, Networking Review, above n 213, paras 4.7–4.9.

[221] Comms Act (UK), sch 11, para 8.

[222] See Ofcom, Networking Review, above n 213, section 6, which examined, inter alia, the position of ITV plc.

as requirements to produce and broadcast regional programmes, and to broadcast a certain percentage of independently produced programmes. Indeed, any assessment of the effectiveness of networking in the UK probably has to be seen in the context of the broader regulatory obligations imposed upon Channel Three licensees, such as those just mentioned, European production quotas, and, especially, the public service remits of the broadcasters. Networking practices offer a mix of public benefits and risks. Curiously, although operating in a manner which would seem counter-productive to this outcome, networking can help to increase programme diversity by providing greater scope for programme investment. At the same time, however, networking, particularly where there are ownership connections between broadcasters and networks, can operate anti-competitively, and restrict opportunities for independent programme production. The UK networking arrangements restricts the network to primary rights only, which prevents independent producers being pressured into giving up valuable secondary rights as part of a commissioning or programme acquisition deal.[223] Until its repeal, the US finsyn rule also gave independent producers the chance to exploit the rights to a programme. As such, it seems likely that networking practices, if they are to operate positively, will need also some regulatory supervision. Networking may well help to ensure the wider availability of programmes but, in isolation, it does not necessarily offer a guarantee that the resulting content will provide greater diversity or a wider range of programming: commercial constraints and the dictates of an advertising-funded market are also likely to influence programming production decisions. Other regulatory measures, such as those reviewed in Chapter Four, may be necessary to secure true diversity and range. Perhaps all that networking—and the UK model may be most relevant here—can offer is the opportunity to provide beneficial economic conditions, which will make the fulfilment of requirements such as the public service mandates more feasible.

Conclusion

Through the examples provided in this chapter, it can be seen that competition law is an increasingly essential tool for disciplining a complex media environment. The presence of natural monopolies, common ties between those who control distribution and content, and the importance of content in a channel-rich media environment can lead to situations and practices which, aside from their effect on competition, may undermine the pursuit of broadcasting pluralism. Competition law has always been applicable to media, but reliance on ex post competition law enforcement has its weaknesses: it is cumbersome and lengthy, and more importantly it can deal with only positions already established, and behaviour which may

---

[223] Independent Television Commission, *A Review of the UK Programme Supply Market* (November 2002), para 24.

already have occurred. Ex ante competition regulation, however, can help, to a degree, to shape the market and lay the conditions for behaviour in the market, whether applied generally or to specific operators. Its flexibility can address situations, relationships, and practices, which are beyond the ambit of media ownership regulation. Both the UK and the US provide examples of the use of ex ante regulation, whereas in Australia this has been less well developed. One of the advantages of ex ante regulation is that it may be able to deal with specific operators who have a dominant position in a market—BSkyB is the obvious example here. Ex post competition law enforcement can only act if there has been an abuse of that position but, of course, a provider who holds a dominant position may not find it necessary to engage in behaviour which is an abuse of that position, but competition may nevertheless be inhibited, and new entrants deterred. Ex ante regulation can assist here. It is ironic that many of the situations being dealt with now by ex ante competition rules, such as monopoly control of delivery platforms or content, and vertical integration of distribution and content, have arisen because media ownership rules did not address these scenarios, and governments were unwilling to extend the scope of such rules.

However, ex ante competition regulation also has its limitations, particularly as a guarantee of broadcasting pluralism and diversity. Its effectiveness may be circumscribed by market definitions, and it is being used in situations where it is not possible for the market alone to establish effective competition, and where dominant positions may be already entrenched. As Ungerer has noted, '[competition policy] is formulated against a background of existing power relationships set by ownership, markets, and gatekeeper positions'.[224] In addition, as seen in many of the examples given in this chapter, successful application of the rules will often be dependent upon the resolution of commercial negotiations. The example of Foxtel, in Australia, shows the difficulties which can arise pursuing these commercial negotiations, and the importance also of strong regulatory powers which can be used if negotiations fail or are abused. Nevertheless, it remains an important regulatory tool within the communications industry, and one which can contribute to the protection of broadcasting pluralism and diversity. As discussed more fully in the next chapter, it is likely that there will be ongoing features of the communications sector which will make it doubtful that the market alone can be relied upon for effective competition, and so competition regulation—whether through ex ante rules or ex post enforcement—will remain necessary, albeit that it is unlikely to be a sufficient regulatory tool for the maintenance of the public sphere.

---

[224] Ungerer, above n 126, 54.

Part III

Regulatory Futures

6

BROADCASTING AND ECONOMIC ISSUES

Introduction

Earlier chapters have referred to spectrum scarcity as one of the rationales for broadcasting regulation, but the economics of broadcasting have also influenced the regulatory choices, and can help to explain why broadcasting has not been regulated like other industries (including other parts of the media industry).[1] It has generally been understood that broadcasting does not operate like other markets and, therefore, regulation has been necessary to compensate for its propensity to market failure. The decline of spectrum scarcity and the scope for paying directly for broadcasting, such as subscription television, require a reconsideration of the case for regulation of broadcasting on economic grounds. A related issue is whether general competition law is an appropriate regulatory response to ensure broadcasting pluralism. This chapter will examine these two issues.[2]

The Economics of Broadcasting

Certain characteristics associated with the nature of broadcasting mean that broadcasting does not conform to the requirements of a normally functioning market, which can be seen in the following description:

---

[1] Department of Trade and Industry (DTI) and Department for Culture, Media and Sport (DCMS), *A New Future for Communications*, Cm 5010 (2000) (White Paper), paras 5.3.4–5.3.5. Other aspects of the media industry may share with broadcasting some of these economic characteristics, but the focus here will be on broadcasting.

[2] As the references will show, this chapter (being written by a non-media economist, indeed a non-economist of any description) has relied heavily on a number of other authors, in particular: G Doyle, *Understanding Media Economics* (London, Sage Publications, 2002) (a very clear introduction to media industry economics); A Brown, *Commercial Media in Australia: Economics, Ownership, Technology, and Regulation* (St Lucia, University of Queensland Press, 1985); and G Withers, 'Broadcasting' in R Towse (ed), *A Handbook of Cultural Economics* (Cheltenham, Edward Elgar, 2003), 102.

Economically efficient outcomes are generally produced by competitive markets. In a competitive market, the price of a good and the quantity of a good supplied are set by equating supply and demand. At this point, there are no potential customers who would be willing to pay more for the product than it would cost to produce additional units of the good. In addition, the value to society of consuming an additional unit of the good is equal to the value to the individual who purchases the good, and the social and individual values of producing the good are also equal. That is, in an efficient market, the interests of the firm and society exactly coincide.[3]

This non-conformity manifests itself in several ways, directly affecting the nature of broadcasting's output. For the most part, the market failure features of broadcasting are confined to free-to-air broadcasting delivered over the radio spectrum, but as will be seen, market failure problems are not completely resolved by other mechanisms for delivering radio and television.

One of the difficulties associated with over-the-air broadcasting is the lack of an effective mechanism for obtaining payment from those receiving the programme services.[4] Viewers and listeners have no incentive to pay for the programmes they are receiving, because, provided they have the receiving equipment, they would receive the programmes anyway. This means that there is no mechanism for excluding those who have not paid for the programmes.[5] It follows that, without more, there is little incentive for producers to provide broadcasting services.[6] One solution to this has been to fund broadcasting through advertising revenue, which provides an incentive for the production and transmission of content. But this also compounds some of the market inefficiencies of broadcasting, because the broadcasters will choose to be responsive to the advertiser, rather than the audience, in order to 'maximise advertising revenue and profits'.[7] This is usually achieved by providing programmes which will attract large audiences even though they may be less highly valued by the audience, whilst programmes which are regarded as more desirable by the audience will not be provided if they attract smaller audiences.[8] What matters is how the advertiser values the audience, not the value a programme has for the audience.[9] This will have an impact on the diversity and range of programming which a broadcasting system will offer, and it may be difficult for minority or niche programming to be aired, either at all or during peak programming periods. It might be thought that, where broadcasters are competing for advertising revenue and audiences, they would have an incentive to provide programmes which are different from those being broadcast by competing

---

[3] Independent Review Panel, *Report: The Future Funding of the BBC* (July 1999), 202

[4] Doyle, above n 2, 60.

[5] Early arrangements for radio broadcasting in Australia experimented with the idea of a 'sealed receiver set' whereby the sets could receive only the stations licensed to that set. However, the scheme was abandoned because it was not possible to prevent unauthorised receivers listening in to the stations: M Armstrong, *Broadcasting Law and Policy in Australia* (Sydney, Butterworths, 1982), para 302.

[6] Productivity Commission, *Broadcasting*, Report No 11 (Canberra, AusInfo, 2000), 93.

[7] Independent Review Panel, above n 3, 206.

[8] *Ibid*, and Productivity Commission, above n 6, 94.

[9] Brown, above n 2, 62.

broadcasters, and that this would naturally produce a more diverse range of programming, but this is not so, as Withers explains:

> [S]tations based on advertising revenue will seek to maximize their audience (and thereby their revenue). Stations will therefore duplicate programme types as long as the audience share obtained is greater than that from other programmes. Hence a number of stations may compete by sharing a market for one type of programme (such as crime dramas) and still do better in audience numbers than by providing programmes of other types (such as arts and culture).[10]

Thus, competition for audience actually produces a form of 'competitive duplication' or 'copycat programming'.[11] Programme choice theory suggests that differentiation in programming will come about only when the number of channels in the market means that duplicating programming (and sharing the audience between all these channels) is no longer more profitable than providing a programme which caters for a different interest.[12] Thus, diversity in programming requires an unrestricted number of channels to be available, although there may be practical reasons as to why this is not feasible.[13] Curiously, particularly in light of the emphasis on structural regulation, a monopoly owner of, say, three channels in the market would have a greater incentive to provide differentiated programming.[14] However, for other reasons, this might not be seen as desirable. Another aspect of the competitive duplication practice is that the programming provided will not necessarily be programming which represents the first preference of the audience. First preferences might be too distinctive and not appreciated by a sufficiently large audience size, hence the programming will be more likely to be 'common denominator programming', or in other words programming which is 'middling', which is 'neither especially interesting nor uninteresting', programming with which the audience 'will make do'.[15]

One way of dealing with the limitations presented by an advertising-funded broadcasting market is to supplement it with publicly funded broadcasting services. The Australian Competition and Consumer Commission (ACCC) has noted that virtually every OECD country has a form of public broadcaster, even where there are many free-to-air channels available.[16] Public broadcasters using over-the-air delivery systems will also be associated with the dilemma that the audience is unable to express its preferences directly, but they can at least

---

[10] Withers, above n 2

[11] Doyle, above n 2, 73–74.

[12] *Ibid*, 73–75, and Brown, above n 2, 65–67 and ff.

[13] Brown, above n 2, 67.

[14] Doyle, above n 2, 74.

[15] Brown, above n 2, 67. An audience will be willing to make do because there is no direct cost for the programme. Another model which is frequently referred to in describing these duplication practices is the 'hotelling effect': Doyle, above n 2, 74–75.

[16] Australian Competition and Consumer Commission (ACCC), *Emerging Market Structures in the Communications Sector, A Report to Senator Alston, Minister for Communications, Information Technology and the Arts* (June 2003), http://www.accc.gov.au/content/index.phtml/itemId/356694/fromItemId/356751, accessed 19 April 2005, para 5.2.1.

compensate for the commercial sector market failures by broadcasting a more diverse range of programming, including programming which serves minority interests. Freed from the need to maximise audience size to attract advertising revenue, public broadcasters will be able to provide some programming which might actually be more highly desired by the audience. Those public, or 'public-like', broadcasters, such as the US public broadcasting system and the Australian community broadcasting sector, can also provide a counterbalance to these market failures, although their contribution, because of more limited funding sources, will be smaller. One way that these services will raise funds will be by subscriptions to the service, but of course they will have no mechanism for excluding those who do not subscribe or become members. Those willing to subscribe to the service will be those who are strongly committed to its continuing existence, so that they are willing to pay knowing that others can receive the service without having to subscribe or become a member. However, the subscription fee will probably be set at a level which reflects this, and the more general dilemma that there is still no mechanism for direct expression of preferences. The free rider problem is probably most equitably addressed through public funding of broadcasting, which can use a licence fee or taxation system to raise funds for the broadcasting service.

Free-to-air broadcasting has the characteristics of a 'public good', and this may also impact on the market's efficiency in the provision of broadcasting services. Brown suggests that broadcasting is almost a pure public good.[17] A public good is one

> for which: (a) the provision for one person means provision is available for all people at no additional cost; (b) consumption or use by one person does not deprive others of any of the benefits; and (c) it is not feasible to exclude people from the benefits of provision.[18]

These characteristics are also described as 'non-exclusivity' and 'non-rivalry'. 'Non-exclusivity' refers to the problem already discussed, namely that consumers of broadcasting will not wish to pay for the service if others are able to consume it for free.[19] As discussed, this has led to different mechanisms for funding broadcasting. 'Non-rivalry' refers to the inexhaustible nature of the good. Consumption of the good by one person does not affect the good or diminish the good's availability to others.[20] This means that the marginal costs of producing and supplying the good to another person is zero or virtually zero.[21] The low marginal cost of broadcasting means that broadcasting is characterised also by significant economies of scale.[22] The non-rivalrous nature of broadcasting means also that, even where it is possible to restrict supply, it is difficult to justify this given that everyone could have access to the programme at no additional cost:

---

[17] Brown, above n 2, 60.
[18] Productivity Commission, above n 6, 93, fn 4.
[19] Independent Review Panel, above n 3, 202.
[20] *Ibid,* and Doyle, above n 2, 65. Doyle refers to it as the 'non-exhaustible' characteristic.
[21] Doyle, above n 2, 65.
[22] Brown, above n 2, 60.

restricting the viewing of programmes that, once produced, could be made available to everyone at no extra cost, leads to inefficiency and welfare losses.[23]

Thus, the costs of production, acquisition, and supply of a public good will not bear any relationship with the number of people who consume the good.[24] Funding broadcasting by advertising is at least efficient, because it gives an incentive to provide a service which would otherwise have a zero price, whilst it does not inefficiently exclude viewers or listeners from programming which has a zero marginal cost.[25] However, for the reasons already discussed, advertising will not be completely satisfactory. On the other hand, requiring consumers to pay for programming will still be inefficient because it will exclude some potential viewers or listeners, so that the welfare loss is greater than the costs of allowing these persons to be included in the audience.[26]

Another aspect of the market failure associated with broadcasting relates to the nature of the information which a viewer or listener will possess. A market is assumed to work efficiently because consumers will be 'fully, indeed "perfectly", informed'.[27] What is being 'sold' through broadcasting is an experience, whether for educational or entertainment purposes, but the audience will not know how to value the experience being offered by a particular programme until they have actually consumed it. But having consumed it, they will have no further incentive to pay for the good.[28] This information problem is likely to have an impact also on the programming provided by broadcasting, because it will encourage programmes which fall into familiar or recognisable categories, so that the audience can use its experience of an earlier programme as information to assess, to some extent, the new offering. One can see that this is likely to affect both advertising-funded and subscription broadcasting services.

Some types of broadcasting content can also be viewed as having the qualities of a 'merit good'. Merit goods can also provide a reason for intervention in the broadcasting market, although this might be viewed by some as controversial, and, possibly, paternalistic.[29] A merit good is recognised as having a value beyond its value to an individual, even though the individual may benefit from its provision—in other words, it has a value for society as a whole. Thus, education, health care, and cultural activities may be treated as merit goods because they are seen to confer benefits on the wider community. If left to the market, however, they might not be provided in sufficient quantities, because individuals may not be willing to consume and pay for these goods to the extent needed to ensure that they are

---

[23] Independent Review Panel, above n 3, 203.
[24] Organisation for Economic Co-operation and Development (OECD), *Competition Policy and a Changing Broadcast Industry* (Paris, OECD, 1993), 79.
[25] *Ibid*, 80.
[26] *Ibid*, 85.
[27] Independent Review Panel, above n 3, 203.
[28] Doyle, above n 2, 65.
[29] I Nitsche, *Broadcasting in the European Union: The Role of Public Interest in Competition Analysis* (The Hague, TMC Asser Press, 2001), 17–18.

adequately provided.[30] Certain types of programming, such as news and current affairs, documentaries, and cultural programmes will fall into this category. The community may consider that it is desirable that these programmes be available, even if as individuals they do not want to watch them extensively: '[j]ust as with education or training, consumers tend to buy less "good" programming than is in their own long-term interests. So, under free market circumstances, programming that is intrinsically "good" will be under-supplied.'[31] The difficulties of ensuring such programming is available may be exacerbated under a system funded by advertising, since the broadcaster will have no interest in acquiring or producing programming simply because of its intrinsic value, or because it may be beneficial to the wider community. Similarly, the very nature of a merit good means that subscription broadcasting will not overcome this problem. Solutions such as public broadcasting or content regulation can be seen as ways to address the merit good problem, to ensure that the market provides such programming on an adequate basis. Another example of the merit goods problem might be seen with programming produced domestically. For most countries, domestically produced content will be more expensive compared with the cost of importing content produced in the US. Although audiences may prefer locally produced content,[32] they, or advertisers in an advertising-funded system, may not be willing to pay the extra amount that is required for its production. In a report prepared for the BBC, it was suggested that the entry of subscription television into the UK market had not resulted in any improvement on the classic commercial mix of imported programming combined with 'a home-grown programme mix of cheaper entertainment, reality programmes and soap operas'.[33]

Another type of market failure is the externalities produced by broadcasting, whereby certain effects or costs will fall upon third parties, and not on those who have contracted to supply or receive the product.[34] An obvious example, from another context, is where a manufacturing process results in the pollution of a local area. The costs of that pollution may not be borne by the manufacturer, but by the local inhabitants who may not receive the benefits of the production process. Broadcasting can throw up similar types of externalities. For example, programming which incorporates explicit sexual content or violence might be beneficial to those producing and choosing to receive the programme, but there may be external costs such as the impact of sexual and violent material on society in general, or on children if they are exposed to it.[35] The likelihood that a broadcasting system may not produce a full range of programmes might also be seen as an externality, whereby the cost—such as lack of access to local content or

[30] Independent Review Panel, above n 3, 203, and Doyle, above n 2, 66.

[31] Doyle, above n 2, 66.

[32] BBC, *UK Television Content in the Digital Age, Sustaining the UK's TV Content Creation in the Globalised 21st Century—The Role and Importance of the BBC* (2003), 4.

[33] *Ibid.* In 2001, subscription television generated £3.4 billion but only £100 million (less than 3%) went to developing new UK content: *ibid.*

[34] Withers, above n 2, 107.

[35] Doyle, above n 2, 65.

children's programmes—is borne by the community, not those producing or broadcasting the programmes. A particular problem of relevance to broadcasting pluralism which was examined in Chapter Four is the commercial influence on news and current affairs programming. This can also be understood through the externalities analysis. Although commercially influenced programming may confer benefits on the commercial interests associated with the programme, those commercial interests will not have to bear the full costs of such content. Some of the costs of commercially influenced content, in the form of loss of access to independent and balanced debate and information, will be borne instead by the community.

This review of the market failure aspects of broadcasting can be seen to have a direct relevance to the policy concerns underlying this study: namely, the importance of broadcasting's role in the public sphere. These market failure aspects of broadcasting can also be associated with certain features of the broadcasting environment, particularly spectrum scarcity, and the delivery of radio and television over-the-air, with its inability to charge the audience directly for the programmes being received. As the broadcasting environment changes to enable an increased number of broadcasting outlets to operate, and the practice of paying for broadcasting received becomes feasible and more pervasive, it is necessary to consider whether a more efficiently functioning broadcasting market can emerge. As noted earlier, increasing the number of channels available is likely to ensure that a greater range of programming is provided, because a point will be reached whereby it is no longer profitable to duplicate what is offered. Clearly, the use of digital technology is able to alleviate the traditional spectrum limits. However, to the extent that some of these new channels are still part of an advertising-funded market, multichannelling will not erase all of the market failure limitations. For example, there is still the problem that viewers and listeners have no direct way to express their preferences, and that the broadcaster's primary concern will be the advertiser.[36] More importantly, however, programme production costs create difficulties which are likely to continue even where there is an abundance of channels. For example, increasing the number of channels is not likely to result in viewers spending longer watching television, and there is no reason to expect a different outcome for radio.[37] Instead, an increased number of channels is more likely to fragment the available audience, which will have an impact on advertising income and production costs.[38] Although, a multichannelled environment opens up the scope for more targeted audiences and increased advertising opportunities, it may not provide sufficient funding to replace the revenue levels associated with the old mass-audience programming.[39]

---

[36] Withers, above n 2, 109.

[37] Independent Review Panel, above n 3, 205.

[38] *Ibid.*

[39] Doyle, above n 2, 76. Paradoxically, advertising costs rise in this new market, because an advertiser will now require so many more advertising 'slots' to reach the required audience level: *ibid.*

Another problem, which is not resolved by an increased number of channels, is that the costs of programme production are very high compared with the marginal costs. In other words, once made, it costs, within the same transmission area, the same to distribute the programme to one person or to a million people.[40] These economies of scale tend to favour a concentrated market.[41] Although digital technology has the potential to reduce entry costs, as well as some production and duplication costs, it is unlikely that it will change the basic cost structure of audio-visual programming, particularly the traditional high-cost genres, such as drama, comedy, and documentaries, because of their fixed costs and labour intensity.[42] Indeed, digital technology could increase production costs, because audiences may have increased expectations about what can be provided technically.[43] Economies of scale and cost pressures may even be exacerbated in the digital environment, because even more programming will be required, and the competition for content will intensify.[44] Thus, digital technology can vastly increase the number of broadcasting channels available to viewers and listeners, and address some of the particular economic features associated with broadcasting, but not all of the market failure aspects of broadcasting will be removed. Further, broadcasting may experience new pressures, which will affect its capacity to provide certain types of programming, so that the case for market intervention may not be diminished in a multichannelled environment. Some other factors need also to be taken into account here. Digitally produced material has much greater flexibility in how it can be used and reformatted, making it much more feasible to repackage programmes, or even parts of programmes, or to deliver them via a different platform. This means that economies of scope, in addition to economies of scale, are more readily available. In other words, there are benefits to be gained by diversifying the firm's output. Costs can be saved if the firm can produce two related products rather than one.[45] The potential for economies of scope can be seen in the trend towards multimedia mergers over the last decade, as firms try to position themselves to exploit these economies of scope across a number of delivery platforms.[46] This can have an impact on media concentration, and broadcasting pluralism.

Some of the instances of market failure reviewed here relate to the difficulties of making the viewer or listener pay for receipt of the broadcasting service. However, each of the jurisdictions being considered now has available the means to charge for the receipt of broadcasting services, providing scope for overcoming some of these barriers to a properly functioning broadcasting market. Clearly some of the main limitations of the advertising-funded market can be addressed by subscription broadcasting: consumers can now express their preferences directly, and so

---

[40] N Garnham, 'The Broadcasting Market and the Future of the BBC' (1994) 65(1) *The Political Quarterly* 11 at 13.

[41] *Ibid*, and Independent Review Panel, above n 3, 205.

[42] BBC, above n 32, 28.

[43] *Ibid.*

[44] Independent Review Panel, above n 3, 205.

[45] Doyle, above n 2, 14–15.

[46] Withers, above n 2, 111.

producers can respond by providing programmes which some viewers may value highly, and for which they are willing to pay. Thus, subscription broadcasting can help to ensure that programmes which would not be provided in an unregulated advertising-funded market can now be available.[47] The broadcasting market can begin to look more like an ordinary market. However, difficulties still arise. The problem remains that whilst programmes are still expensive to produce, the marginal cost of adding a new subscriber will be zero or almost zero. This means that potential viewers who cannot afford to pay the subscription fee are excluded even though they may still value the programme highly.[48] Thus, 'pay television will exclude viewers to an extent not justified by the marginal costs that would be involved in allowing them to have the service'.[49] Subscription broadcasting raises equity concerns, therefore, which are directly relevant to the protection of broadcasting pluralism. Whilst subscription services may mean that programming is provided which would not otherwise be provided in a free or advertising-funded market, it may also mean that the provision of such programmes is at a cost which excludes those who are unable to afford the service.[50] Doyle points to the migration of key sporting events to subscription services, and the development of something like a two-tier market.[51] The potential for other types of programming which might be considered important to the public sphere to migrate should raise concerns about the ability of the community to access information and opinions.

Despite the potential for subscription services to overcome some of the limitations of an advertising-funded market, it is unlikely that subscription broadcasting will be able to compensate fully for the market failures. Whilst subscription services will be less biased against high-value, small-audience programming compared with an advertising-funded system, it will not eliminate that bias completely.[52] The high fixed costs of programme production will be faced by providers of subscription services, just as they are by the providers of advertising-funded services. Another characteristic of programme production, which was mentioned earlier, is also relevant here. Broadcasting is selling information and experience, and it is not possible to try out these goods before consuming them. This problem, which still arises with subscription services, may limit the willingness of audiences to subscribe for unfamiliar services or programming. This obviously presents a problem for providers of subscription services seeking to find a market for programmes, and it helps to explain why subscription broadcasting often focuses on familiar programme categories such as sport, film, and news.[53] A service with a high proportion of content from these categories will ensure that subscribers are able to have a good idea of what they will receive for the cost of their subscription.

[47] Brown, above n 2, 71.
[48] Withers, above n 2, 111.
[49] Doyle, above n 2, 78.
[50] Productivity Commission, above n 6, 94–95.
[51] Doyle, above n 2, 78.
[52] Brown, above n 2, 71–72.
[53] White Paper, above n 1, para 5.3.6.

Content will be crucial for the providers of subscription services, which means that subscription television markets tend to move towards vertical integration of distribution and programming, because, aside from any tendencies towards natural monopoly, occupying a monopoly or dominant position will ensure 'the non-contestability of the market for premium sports and film rights'.[54] This was no doubt one of the incentives for Foxtel in making a content-sharing agreement with Optus (see Chapter Five). A monopoly or dominant position does not appear to guarantee greater expenditure on original content:

> If having a large installed base of subscribers, a lower-cost delivery method and exclusive access to key sports and film rights is sufficient to protect the position of a pay TV platform, then domestic content investment levels are likely to be very low in the thematic channel sector, as the platform puts downward pressure on thematic channel carriage fees.[55]

The US subscription network, HBO, is often cited as an example of a subscription service which has been able to achieve quality original programming. However, its main content is still film and sport; its programming budget benefits from being in a very large market and a high monthly subscription fee. Therein lays the dilemma: by charging a high fee, it is able to fund original programming, but it must exclude some viewers from receiving that content.[56] Although subscription broadcasting's increased channel capacity and direct payment can alleviate some of broadcasting's traditional tendencies towards market failures, it is apparent that some market failure features will continue, and might even be exacerbated. These continuing failures have a direct impact for the protection of broadcasting pluralism, because it is clear that the market alone will be unable to provide a broadcasting service which can properly serve the demands of the public sphere. In considering the arguments for reform of broadcasting, it is important to have regard to the ongoing characteristics of the broadcasting market.

Competition Law as a Regulatory Mechanism

With the focus on structural regulation of media, particularly ownership and control rules, there has been less focus on competition law, but it has always had a role to play in media regulation, and it is becoming increasingly important in a media environment where control over networks and content is regarded as crucial to maintaining a viable position in the broadcasting sector. Of course, regulation of media ownership and control is itself an application of competition regulation, even though its policy motivations stem from different concerns. As Doyle explains:

[54] BBC, above n 32, 14.
[55] *Ibid.*
[56] *Ibid*, 15, fn 12.

Competition policy has traditionally worked on the assumption that the efficiency of markets depends directly on their competitive structure and, especially, on the extent of seller concentration. So competition policy may sometimes involve 'structural' interventions—i.e. attempts to bring about market structures which are less concentrated—on the assumption that this will ensure good behaviour by competing firms and promote improved industrial performance . . ..

Upper restrictions on levels of media ownership represent a means of structural intervention through which competition amongst media can be promoted and seller concentration can be avoided. Special restrictions on media ownership are a common feature in most European countries and elsewhere, but they usually owe their existence to concerns about pluralism and not competition. Media ownership restrictions are generally intended to protect political and cultural pluralism which, as a policy objective, is quite different from promoting competition. None the less, ownership limits intended to preserve pluralism may also serve to prevent the development and subsequent possible abuses of excessive market power by dominant media firms.

The use of ownership rules to alter the structure of a market represents what some economists would consider to be a fairly extreme form of intervention.[57]

Competition law will be particularly concerned with regulating the behaviour of firms to ensure that they do not seek to abuse their position, or engage in practices which would restrict competition, or entry into the market. Chapter Five examined the current role of competition law, and provided examples of some types of sectoral competition regulation.

The growth in the number of channels available or potentially available, the decline of spectrum as a constraint, and the ability to download content over a variety of platforms have, in each of the three jurisdictions, led to calls for the removal or relaxation of specific rules constraining media ownership and control. It is argued that these changes to the communications environment have made such a form of regulation redundant, and that general competition law can be relied upon to discipline the market where necessary. This argument has played a role in the moves to reform ownership and control rules in the UK, the US, and Australia. It is important to be aware that this change is not simply a change from one form of regulation to another; it changes also the policy focus. Whilst the policy concerns of ownership and control regulation have a public interest focus—the interests of citizens—the policy focus and language of general competition law is about 'opening up markets, ensuring free and fair competition between producers and promoting the interests of consumers'.[58] This is not to say that a market which is open to fair competition, and allows new entrants, will not be beneficial for broadcasting pluralism.[59] The converse, of course, may not be true: some forms of broadcasting pluralism regulation will, in pursuit of public interest goals, restrict

---

[57] Doyle, above n 2, 168–69.

[58] P Lowe, 'Media Concentration & Convergence: Competition in Communications', Speech delivered at the Oxford Media Convention 2004, Oxford, 13 January 2004, 1, available at http://www.ippr.org.uk/uploadedFiles/events/Philip%20Lowe%20speech.doc.

[59] *Ibid*, 8, and M Ariño, 'Competition Law and Pluralism in European Digital Broadcasting: Addressing the Gaps' (2004) 54(2) *Communications and Strategies* 97 at 101.

behaviour which could otherwise be seen as pro-competitive, and impose additional costs on the community.[60] Although the instrument of competition law may work to the benefit, rather than the detriment, of broadcasting pluralism, there are features of competition law which make it insufficient for the proper protection of pluralism.[61] As the previous section has described, despite the developments in the communications sector, not all of the market failure tendencies of broadcasting will be removed. Competition law, itself, is a response to a market failure—namely that it is rare for a market to be in a state of 'perfect competition'. 'Perfect competition' is understood as a market in which there are no barriers to entry or exit, and where there are many suppliers who offer homogeneous products to buyers with perfect knowledge of the available substitutes.[62] In a perfectly competitive market there would be an efficient allocation of resources.[63] However, perfect markets are rare, and the more likely market scenario is a market with a small number of suppliers, with a degree of market power that they may seek to extend or abuse.[64] Hence, competition law will have a role in trying to ensure that the market is kept open to other entrants, and that market power is not abused. It has already been noted that, in relation to broadcasting, the sector is characterised by a predisposition towards concentration, a tendency which is exacerbated by the economies of scale and scope which are a feature of the industry.[65]

One difficulty, therefore, of relying on competition law to discipline the market is that it might not adequately serve the public interest objectives of broadcasting pluralism. This risk is underlined by another feature of competition law, which is crucial to the operation of competition law, namely the definition of a market: 'market definition is a tool to identify and define the boundaries of competition between firms'.[66] In asking whether a potential merger is likely to lead to a lessening of competition, or whether a firm is engaging in some anti-competitive practice, competition law is only interested in what impact that merger or behaviour will have on the particular market or markets which it has identified as relevant to the economic activity. Defining the market enables one to identify which firms are in competition.[67] It is within the defined market that a determination will take place as to whether or not there is adequate competition. The expectation that the promotion of competition, through the application of competition law, could have positive outcomes for pluralism and diversity is challenged by the process of defining a market within the media industry. The process of determining a mar-

---

[60] ACCC, above n 16, para 5.2.2.

[61] Ariño, above n 59, 101–2.

[62] Doyle, above n 2, 168, and Nitsche, above n 29, 20.

[63] Doyle, above n 2, 168.

[64] *Ibid.*

[65] R Jones, 'Competition, Broadcasting and Pay TV', Speech delivered at the Australian Broadcasting Summit, Sydney, 20 February 2003, http://www.accc.gov.au/content/index.phtml/itemId/255876, accessed 14 December 2004, 4.

[66] Commission Notice on the definition of the relevant market for the purposes of Community competition law, OJ C 372 (9 December 1997), quoted in Nitsche, above n 29, 24.

[67] Nitsche, above n 29, 24.

ket will involve a consideration of the relevant products or services and geographic scope.[68] Most crucial will be the delineation of the product market. Under competition policy, markets are defined by determining all the products or services which are close substitutes. One product will constitute a close substitute for another, if a rise in the price of one will lead consumers to increase substantially their consumption of the other product.[69] In general, the more a product is heterogeneous, the greater the likelihood that the product market will be small.[70] Thus, setting the price of a fashion magazine may be quite sensitive, because there may be a number of other such magazines to which consumers could turn in the event of a price rise. However, a rise in the price of a fashion magazine is unlikely to have an impact on automobile magazines, because the nature of the product is quite different, having regard to the subject matter and the audiences targeted by the two magazine categories. Similarly, a rise in the price of a magazine is unlikely to have an impact upon the consumption of newspapers, and therefore magazines and newspapers might be said to represent different markets.[71] As the example of the fashion magazine shows, there may also be submarkets within the markets for newspapers and magazines. The ACCC considers that, for the purposes of applying competition law, the relevant product market for media is advertising and, on this basis, that newspapers, radio, and television constitute different markets.[72] This is because the evidence of the advertising industry, gathered by the ACCC, has indicated that competition for advertising between the print and the electronic media has been limited.[73] Apart from the possibility that advertising in the different media may be targeting different audiences, there will also be some types of advertising which will be more suitable to different forms of media: classified advertising is an obvious example.[74]

In fact, identifying the relevant product markets for media is a complex process, and there may be a number of relevant markets,[75] but, nevertheless, one can begin to see the difficulty which this process might present from a pluralism perspective. Whilst competition law might be concerned about the anti-competitive impact of a merger within the newspaper industry, it may not consider that an issue arises between a merger of a newspaper company and a television or radio broadcasting company. In the former situation, the application of competition law could

[68] Another dimension of the market may be temporal: *ibid.*

[69] Productivity Commission, above n 6, 349. This is a reference to the 'demand cross-elasticity' of the goods: Nitsche, above n 29, 25.

[70] *Ibid*, 25.

[71] Productivity Commission, above n 6, 349.

[72] *Ibid*, 350.

[73] *Ibid.*

[74] R Albon and F Papandrea, *Media Regulation in Australia and the Public Interest* (Melbourne, Institute of Public Affairs, 1998), 22.

[75] See OECD, above n 24, 102–12, Ariño, above n 59, 118–19, and D Geradin, 'Access to Content by New Media Platforms: A Review of the Competition Law Problems' (2005) 30 *European Law Review* 68 at 72–74. For an analysis of market definition as applied in the EU and across several Member States, and its complexities, see Bird and Bird, *Market Definition in the Media Sector: Comparative Legal Analysis, Report for the European Commission, DG Competition* (2002).

incidentally benefit the goals of pluralism and diversity, but in the latter situation, competition law will not be able to have an impact on these concerns, even though the merger might lead to a 'concentration in diversity of information and opinion'.[76] Even the focus on substitutability may be difficult to encapsulate in the media context:

> what is valued in the media is diversity, both of content and of sources. Thus, two economically non equivalent products (radio and newspapers, broadcasting and publishing) would still be part of the same wider marketplace of ideas.[77]

Competition law may not then be well suited to address the wider public interest concerns of cross-media concentration. As the Australian Productivity Commission noted, whilst the identification of advertising as a means of identifying the product market and testing market power might make economic sense, it is also somewhat artificial, having regard to the broader public interest concerns, because it is the public which actually consumes the print and electronic media.[78] Regardless of the substitution possibilities, each of these different types of media will be a source of information and ideas, but competition law will only incidentally provide protection for this 'market for ideas'.[79] Even within television broadcasting, free-to-air television and subscription television have generally been regarded as different markets.[80] Although the ACCC has noted some degree of substitutability between these services, and some degree of competition for content, it considers that they remain as separate markets having regard to differences in funding and range of programming.[81] In Australia, the separation of these markets is highlighted by regulatory factors, which constrain the ability of these two sectors to compete with each other.[82] However, even in more mature pay-television markets, a similar view has been adopted; for example, by the Federal Trade Commission and the Federal Communications Commission in the US, and the European Commission.[83] More recently, the UK Competition Commission decided that free-to-air services and subscription services were part of the one television advertising market, although they were seen as differentiated products.[84]

Market definition processes may mean that competition law will not be a sufficient means of ensuring broadcasting pluralism. However, a move in the other direction—that is by defining market boundaries very broadly; for example, the media market encompassing 'all forms of media [which] are a source of information, entertainment and opinion'[85]—does not offer an adequate solution. Whilst

---

[76] Productivity Commission, above n 6, 350.
[77] Ariño, above n 59, 119.
[78] Productivity Commission, above n 6, 350.
[79] *Ibid.*
[80] ACCC, above n 16, para 5.3.
[81] *Ibid.*
[82] *Ibid.*
[83] ACCC, *Submission to the Productivity Commission, Inquiry into Broadcasting,* Attachment C, 3-4.
[84] Competition Commission, *Carlton Communications plc and Granada plc: A Report on the Proposed Merger* (October 2003), para 5.33.
[85] Jones, above n 65, 10.

superficially attractive, because it could encompass both traditional and new media, a broadly defined market, because of its size, would be much less likely to give rise to any market power concerns and, in turn, would leave exposed the public interest implications of a merger within such a market.[86] As the communications market changes, it is likely that there will also be a revision of media market definitions. The Australian competition regulator, the ACCC, has suggested that as digital technology becomes more pervasive, and begins to have an impact upon the free-to-air television market, free-to-air and subscription television may become closer substitutes.[87] More recently, the ACCC chairman has noted that changing business practices within the media industry, and the delivery of content across a variety of platforms, may also be changing the market for advertising.[88] Advertising which might traditionally have found its home in one media sector may now be able to be distributed across other platforms. Once again, classified advertising provides a good example: where it might have been assumed that newspapers were the only suitable platform for this type of advertising, it is now clear that the internet is a suitable vehicle for traditional classified advertisements. Indeed, some forms of classified advertising could be even more suitable for the internet. Recent evidence seems to bear out the growing attraction of the internet for advertising: it has been estimated that the online advertising (global) market will have doubled in the six years from 2004, but at the expense of the traditional media.[89]

Implications for Regulation

This chapter has attempted to provide a brief description of some of the economic and competition policy issues which might have implications for broadcasting policy and regulatory design. The calls for a move away from traditional broadcasting regulatory approaches are frequently influenced by the changes being wrought within the industry: the end of channel scarcity and proliferation of different ways in which to receive content are seen as justifying the removal or relaxation of much of the old regulatory apparatus, particularly rules limiting media ownership and control. However, it is clear that the broadcasting sector will still be shaped by certain attributes which will impede its functioning as an ordinary market. These characteristics will also mean that the industry's tendency towards concentration will continue. Whilst competition law will have an important role to play in the increasingly complex communications market, particularly through

---

[86] *Ibid.*

[87] ACCC, above n 83, 4.

[88] G Samuel, 'Media Ownership and Convergence', Speech delivered at the Melbourne Press Club Journalism 2005 Conference, Melbourne, 26 August 2005, 10.

[89] D Teather and J Martinson, 'Á bruised Murdoch has another go at mastering the Internet', *Sydney Morning Herald* (Sydney), 13 September 2005, 21.

regulatory measures aimed at opening up access to markets, it is also clear that it will not serve all of the policy objectives which are seen as important for the effective functioning of broadcasting. In re-examining the regulatory environment, these are matters which should not be over-looked.

7

REFORMING BROADCASTING PLURALISM REGULATION

Introduction

Common to each of the jurisdictions considered in this study has been an attempt, in recent times, to reform media ownership and control regulation. At the time of writing, only the UK has been successful in bringing such reform to fruition, although it remains likely, if not inevitable, that both the US and Australia will renew their attempts. In each case, the reforms, implemented or under consideration, constitute a substantial relaxation, and, in some respects, abandonment of ownership rules.[1] Although this study has examined a range of measures which it is argued contribute to the promotion of pluralism and diversity, the focus in this chapter will be on media ownership, because it is this area which has galvanised policy and regulatory attention. Although there has been some discussion of the possibility of wider reforms in Australia, the political reality means that this is probably unlikely. Even in the UK, where ownership reform was only part of a major communications regulatory reform process, media ownership dominated the policy and legislative debates. There is another reason that it is relevant to focus closely on this area and the policy drivers influencing it. Policy attitudes about broadcasting and the media generally and the role they play, or should play, in democratic debate tend to be brought into sharpest focus when media ownership regulation is under discussion.

Central to these jurisdictions' reform, or attempted reform, processes have been claims that, in light of a dynamic communications environment, media ownership regulation has a diminishing role. Yet, none of the three jurisdictions has been willing to abandon such regulation completely. The result seems to be a somewhat emasculated form of media ownership regulation, which will leave broadcasting pluralism increasingly reliant upon the discipline of the market and general

---

[1] For brevity, 'ownership' rather than 'ownership and control' will generally be used, but it should be understood to encompass the concepts of ownership and control: see, further, Chapter Three, 'Structural Regulation of Ownership and Control', at p 86. As a reminder, the term 'broadcasting pluralism' is also used to refer collectively to the concepts of pluralism and diversity: see, further, Chapter One, 'Terminology', at p 8.

competition law enforcement. Those who would advocate liberalisation of media ownership regulation would argue that this is entirely appropriate in a communications environment which promises diversity through the abundance being created by technological changes. In this chapter, the legitimacy of these claims and the case being made for media ownership reform will be considered. Finally, the chapter will consider what impact the changing media environment is likely to have on pluralism and diversity regulation, if the media are to play their part in an active public sphere.

Reforming Broadcasting Pluralism

Throughout this study, it has been apparent that despite significant differences between the jurisdictions in regulatory approach, there have also been many points of commonality. The policy objectives driving media ownership reform also demonstrate this. Certain themes, such as the desirability of promoting competition and the benefits of exploiting economic efficiencies, emerge strongly across the three jurisdictions. Similarly, each of the three jurisdictions appears to share common assumptions about the factors driving the case for reform. Thus, the demise of spectrum scarcity, the development of digital technology, and the availability of content across a variety of delivery platforms, traditional and non-traditional, are all seen as both justifying and requiring liberalisation of media ownership. There are differences in emphasis in these policy debates, and different regulatory solutions have been selected, but there remains much common ground.

United Kingdom

Reference has been made elsewhere in this study to various aspects of the UK reform which, based on the Communications Act 2003 (Comms Act (UK)), constituted a major overhaul of the communications sector, both broadcasting and telecommunications, together with the establishment of a single regulatory authority, the Office of Communications (Ofcom). These changes to the regulatory environment formed the backdrop to the reform of the media ownership regime which was also a part of the 2003 reforms.[2] In this section, the focus will be on the policy reform process relating to the regulation of media ownership, but it is useful, first, to note briefly some of the policy values driving the 2003 reforms generally. In contrast to the US regulatory rule-making process, considered below,

---

[2] Details of the media and ownership rules introduced by the Comms Act (UK) can be found in Chapter Three, 'United Kingdom: Current Rules', at p 100, and further information about the public interest test used with media mergers is given in Chapter Five, 'Merger Regulation', at p 209.

the UK process was centred on government initiative and parliamentary process. In addition to its White Paper, the government also published several other documents, either to state policy, or to enable further consultation, as well as a draft Communications Bill. Apart from the parliamentary debates in the course of the legislative process, parliamentary committees also considered and reported on the reform proposals.[3] The most significant of these was a joint committee of the House of Lords and the House of Commons, under the chairmanship of Lord Puttnam (the 'Puttnam Committee'). Many of the recommendations of the joint committee's report (the 'Puttnam Report') were accepted by the government, either wholly or in part, and incorporated into the legislation.[4]

The initial policy discussion, the government's White Paper, set forth the government's key objectives. The government wanted to make the UK market 'the most dynamic and competitive communications and media market in the world.' Secondly, there was to be universal access to a range of diverse and high-quality services; and, thirdly, the interests of citizens and consumers were to be safeguarded.[5] It was consistent with the government's intention, to regulate for both a changing and converging communications environment, that the three objectives did not distinguish between different communications sectors. Thus, the elaboration of each of these three objectives made reference to both infrastructure and content. It may be noted also that the objectives addressed both industry and end-user (citizen/consumer) levels. Each of the objectives, even the first objective with its concern about building up a competitive market, is also viewed as contributing to democratic process or debate. Indeed, in general, the language used in the statement of these objectives, and their elaboration, provides the cue to policy values or concepts which have informed the communications reforms generally, and the media ownership reforms specifically. Thus, terms such as competition, investment, consumers and citizens, democracy, democratic debate, access, and, economic interests all form part of the jumble of concepts referred to in the statement of objectives and their elaboration. Perhaps, this miscellany of concepts should not be unexpected, given that the White Paper and the 2003 reforms are the product of two government ministries, the Department for Culture, Media and Sport and the Department of Trade and Industry.

---

[3] Culture, Media and Sport Committee (CMS Committee), *Second Report, The Communications White Paper*, HC 161 (15 March 2001) ('Second Report'), and CMS Committee, *Fourth Report, Communications*, HC 539 (1 May 2002) ('Fourth Report'). See also Department of Trade and Industry (DTI) and Department for Culture, Media and Sport (DCMS), *Government Response to the Second Report from the Culture, Media and Sport Select Committee, Session 2000–2001*, Cm 5316 (2001), and DCMS and DTI, *Government Response to the Fourth Report of the Culture, Media and Sport Select Committee, Session 2001–2002*, Cm 5554 (2002).

[4] Joint Committee on the Draft Communications Bill, *Report, Draft Communications Bill*, HL 169-I and HC 876-1 (25 July 2002) ('Puttnam Report'). See, also, DTI and DCMS, *Government's Response to the Report of the Joint Committee on the Draft Communications Bill*, Cm 5646 (2002) ('Response to Puttnam Report').

[5] DTI and DCMS, *A New Future for Communications*, Cm 5010 (2000) ('White Paper'), paras 1.2.1—1.2.12.

An important underlying feature of the 2003 reforms was the government's approach to regulation. In its White Paper, and early consultation documents, it made clear its preference was for 'light touch' regulation, and that Ofcom should be 'required to ensure that regulation is kept to the minimum necessary'.[6] Associated with this was also a preference for self-regulation and co-regulation.[7] The preference for 'light touch' regulation was not just a direction for Ofcom; the government saw its legislative package as manifesting a 'light touch' regulatory approach, and cited its proposed media ownership rules as an example of this.[8] This seems a curious application, but it is more easily understood when the government's attitude towards, or understanding of, regulation is noted also; for it is clear that it operated from the assumption, discussed in Chapter Two, that the market was the norm, not another regulatory instrument.[9] This preference for 'light touch' regulation was to cut across the whole of the communications environment. The 'light touch' regulatory approach, or deregulatory thrust,[10] noting the government's own assessment, caused the Puttnam Committee some concern.[11] It considered that a duty to exercise 'light touch' regulation could make it difficult for Ofcom to exercise tough regulatory action when needed. The Committee also referred specifically to the government's preference for general law, rather than sector-specific regulation, as part of its 'light touch' requirement, but, as the Committee noted, general law, such as competition law enforcement, did not necessarily mean 'light touch': competition law powers could be 'extensive, and potentially intrusive.'.[12] The Puttnam Report recommended that, instead of 'light touch' regulation, Ofcom should be directed to have regard to the principle that regulation should be 'proportionate, consistent and targeted only at cases in which action is needed', and the government adopted this approach.[13] Nevertheless, the government's deregulatory preference remained a strong influence on the legislation.

As noted, above, one of the key regulatory objectives of the government was the promotion of competitive communications markets, and it is clear too from the government's promotion of 'light touch' regulation, that this was influenced by a preference for competition and market solutions.[14] Even whilst media's special situation is being acknowledged, there appears an implicit acceptance that the market is the starting point:

> But as we create a much improved business environment we must also recognise the special nature of the media and its role in our lives as citizens as well as consumers.

---

[6] DTI and DCMS, *The Draft Communications Bill—The Policy*, Cm 5508-III (2002) ('Policy Statement'), para 5.2.1. See, also, White Paper, above n 5, paras 8.11.1–8.11.4.

[7] White Paper, above n 5.

[8] Policy Statement, above n 6, para 5.2.1.

[9] *Ibid*, para 5.2.2.

[10] Puttnam Report, above n 4, para 63.

[11] *Ibid*, paras 64–68.

[12] *Ibid*, para 65.

[13] *Ibid*, para 67. See Comms Act (UK), s.3(a).

[14] For an interesting discussion of the influence of competition rhetoric on the workings of Ofcom, see T Gibbons, 'Competition Policy and Regulatory Style—Issues for Ofcom' (2005) 7(5) *Info* 42.

Governments all over the world, across Europe and America, recognise that relying on competition policy alone may jeopardise the effective operation of modern democracy. It remains essential to retain sufficient safeguards to secure a plurality of voice and a diversity of services across our media. In the emerging digital world, these safeguards can be set at lower thresholds than in the past, enabling a significant relaxation of regulation.[15]

A preference for a competition-based approach in relation to media ownership is even more evident in the government's second reading speech, the speech introducing the Communications Bill into Parliament. Referring to the consultation on media ownership rules, the Secretary of State observed: '[w]e consulted in a framework on ways of promoting competition through deregulation while recognising that competition alone is not enough to safeguard the nature of the media in the UK'.[16] This approach is reflected also in the policy and legislative references to the public as citizens and consumers. Section 3(1) of the Comms Act (UK) describes the principal duty of Ofcom in the following terms:

(a) to further the interests of citizens in relation to communications matters; and
(b) to further the interests of consumers in relevant markets, where appropriate by promoting competition.

The White Paper had promoted strongly the idea of the reforms serving the public both as consumer and citizen, where the interests of the consumer were relevant to matters such as the availability and price of services, whilst the interests of the citizen were to be found in ensuring access to communications systems, and information and ideas. However, it is harder to see the translation of these policy ideas into section 3(1), which is so broad as to be almost meaningless. 'Communications matters' and 'relevant markets' are broad terms: the former is defined as meaning the matters in relation to which Ofcom has responsibilities, and the latter, as the markets for any of the services, facilities, apparatus, or directories for which Ofcom has responsibilities.[17] In the first of its reports, the Culture, Media and Sport Committee commented that the White Paper had emphasised the interests of the public as consumers at the expense of citizens' interests, even in relation to matters such as access to new technologies.[18] This was even more apparent in the draft Communications Bill, which referred only to Ofcom's duty 'to further the interests of the persons who are customers for the services and facilities' related to Ofcom's responsibilities.[19] It is noticeable that even the term 'consumer' has been replaced, and the reference to 'customer' was defined to include customers in either a personal or business capacity.[20] Concerns about this

---

[15] Policy Statement, above n 6, 2.
[16] T Jowell (Secretary of State for Culture, Media and Sport), HC Deb, 3 December 2002, vol 395, cols 783–84.
[17] Comms Act (UK), s 3(14).
[18] Second Report, above n 3, paras 14–17.
[19] Draft Communications Bill, Cm 5508-I (2002), cl 3(1)(a).
[20] *Ibid*, cl 3(7).

change of terminology were expressed to and by the Puttnam Committee, because it was felt that the term 'customer' connoted only a commercial relationship, whereas 'consumer' implied something broader than merely commercial dealings.[21] The Puttnam Report recommended that the term 'consumer' should be used, except where the context was about a specific commercial relationship. But, even with this change, the Puttnam Committee was not satisfied that 'consumer' terminology would capture all of the interests for which Ofcom would have responsibility—particularly those matters which related to the interests of citizens.

The Comms Act (UK) now makes reference to both citizen and consumer interests, although the government did not adopt a Puttnam Report recommendation which would have been more specific about the nature of these interests, and the priority to be accorded to them. This is perhaps to labour a seemingly minor point, but the government's language at various points of this process illustrates once again the way in which commercial and economic language and concepts permeate the policy and reforms. In the Policy Statement which accompanied the draft Communications Bill, it is notable that the discussion of the broadcasting and media ownership proposals appears to make no reference to citizens' interests. Even the references in these sections to public service broadcasting and broadcasting pluralism, and their importance to democratic process, are couched in terms of the interest of the public as consumers.[22] During parliamentary consideration of the Bill, it was noted that the policies of economic regulation and protection of citizens' interests did not represent balanced objectives, given the powerful commercial interests which stood behind the promotion of economic regulation.[23] There is clearly an underlying preference for characterising much of communications, including broadcasting, in transactional terms. Although there is recognition that sector-specific regulation may be necessary, it is tolerated only to the extent that the market might not yet be able to function fully. It might be argued that in practical terms this has no great significance, since it seems likely that the market will not be able, or at least for some time, to provide certain of the objectives sought by broadcasting policy, such as, for example, a sufficient quantity of specific types of programming, such as children's or local interest programmes. However, the preference for seeing the market as the ideal, in respect of which any regulatory intrusions must be justified, is likely to skew consideration of what should be appropriate regulatory responses for broadcasting. This pressure is exacerbated if the basis for broadcasting regulation rests on negative reasoning, related to matters of spectrum scarcity and differential treatment of media, instead of a strong normative basis which begins with the inquiry as to what it necessary to ensure that the media fulfil their role within the public sphere.

---

[21] Puttnam Report, above n 4, para 20.

[22] Policy Statement, above n 6, eg, paras 8.1 and 9.1.3. In the section on media ownership, there is a reference to the interests of citizens, but this is in the context of reporting on earlier consultation responses, and does not seem to receive any particular government affirmation: para 9.1.8.

[23] S Thomas, HC Standing Committee E, 10 December 2002, col 12.

Although the 2003 reforms covered the whole spectrum of the communications environment, it was ownership and control which attracted the most media attention.[24] This is not surprising. Any consideration of media ownership regulation, across the three jurisdictions, tends to be high profile, and in the UK, the attention given to the 2003 ownership reforms is consistent with the experience of the legislative reforms of 1990 and 1996. The ownership provisions went through significant alteration during the legislative process from when they were first announced in a relatively tentative form in the White Paper. The White Paper set out the government's policy attitude towards media ownership, which predictably made reference to the democratic importance of the media and the need for a diversity of opinion and expression to be available. But the discussion of the regulatory solution is revealing. There is no immediate connection or assumption that a policy goal of plurality translates into regulation of ownership and control. Rather, promoting a competitive market is seen as the foundation for promoting plurality, although there is a recognition that 'backstop powers' might be needed given the important public interest concern that is involved here.[25] This presumably refers to having a specific ownership regime. Ownership regulation appears to be legitimate only to the extent to which it does not impede competitive developments. Thus, the White Paper refers to the need to build in flexibility to allow for further liberalisation of the rules. To be fair, all this is stated with the proviso that pluralism objectives must not be compromised, but it is clear that a balancing assessment will constantly be required.[26] This might be difficult when dealing with something as intangible as pluralism, and such differently constituted objectives as pluralism and competition. This policy approach, as later exemplified in the Communications Bill, was the subject of a strong critique from Lord Puttnam who played an influential role in securing amendments to the Bill:

> The second fundamental flaw in the Bill results from a confusion of aims and means. The achievement of 'plurality and diversity' is not just the stated aim of this particular government; it must be a core ambition of any plural democracy. It tends not to happen by accident and, when it does occur, it can, and to my mind should, be supported by intelligent and sensitive regulation.
>
> What is absolutely certain is that plurality and diversity are not a natural by-product of unregulated market forces. That is particularly true of a market in which the 'cost of entry' has become all but entirely prohibitive. . . .
>
> The very notion that you stimulate plurality and diversity through the encouragement of market dominance is, frankly, risible. Recent history points only one way—towards the inevitable consolidation of conformity and power.[27]

At the White Paper stage, the media ownership regime reforms were not fully spelt out, although some commitments were clear. For example, an early intention was

---

[24] House of Commons Library, *Broadcasting and the Communications Bill* (29 November 2002, Research Paper 02/69), 15.

[25] White Paper, above n 5, para 4.2.6

[26] *Ibid*, paras 4.2.7–4.2.8.

[27] Lord Puttnam, HL Deb, 25 March 2003, vol 646, cols 673–74.

the elimination of rules which limited ownership of Channel Three licences. This would, and did, open the way for consolidation of the regional licences, subject to merger law. The reasoning used was indicative: consolidation of Channel Three licences would enable a more efficient 'strategic decision making process,' and would promote Channel Three's international standing. Protection of pluralism could be achieved by retaining a prohibition on the joint ownership of a national Channel Three service and Channel Five. In contrast to the US approach, discussed below, the White Paper does not explore an approach for measuring plurality, although there is some indication of this, although not well developed, because it is expected that such a prohibition would ensure a minimum of at least four free-to-air broadcasters, including the BBC and Channel Four.[28] The approach is fairly makeshift. There is no explanation as to why four in the market should be the relevant indicator of plurality but, more pertinently, it does not take account of broadcaster size, which is relevant if one compares Channel Three and the BBC with Channels Four and Five, which have a much smaller audience share. Although, the availability and abundance of new media forms a backdrop, justifying media ownership reform and liberalisation, there is no investigation of the nature and impact of this new media abundance. The White Paper did not contain any specific proposals concerning radio and cross-media ownership, although there remained a commitment to providing regulation of these areas. Continuing cross-media regulation was justified on the ground that, for the present, most people remained dependent upon terrestrial broadcasting and newspapers, although the internet was cited as providing access to an increased number of media services.[29]

The White Paper was followed by a further consultation, specifically on media ownership. The Consultation Document did not contain much in the way of specific proposals. Apart from a continuing commitment to relaxation of the Channel Three rules, it was very much about exploring possible approaches.[30] The early policy discussion in the document about the need for ownership rules shares some of the same territory that will be seen in the policy arguments raised by the other jurisdictions, particularly the US. Hence, the desire to encourage competition and economic growth, and deregulation was expressed. The key question was how to balance the need to 'safeguard democracy and encourage an open and competitive market'.[31] But there is a difference also, because the importance of content regulation, as a means of securing diversity, was also emphasised, and used to legitimise the liberalisation of media ownership rules. Compared with the US, there seemed also to be a more sceptical attitude about the extent to which corporate con-

---

[28] White Paper, above n 5, para 4.6.2

[29] *Ibid*, paras 4.8.4–4.8.5. The White Paper also addressed other issues such as foreign ownership, and control of licences by advertising agencies and religious organisations. These matters will not be addressed in this section, but have been referred to in Chapter Three.

[30] DCMS and DTI, *Consultation on Media Ownership Rules* (November 2001) ('Consultation Document'). The government later published a summary of responses to the Consultation Document; in the main, the responses fell along predictable lines.

[31] *Ibid*, paras 1.1–1.2.

solidation and the realisation of economies of scale could contribute to greater diversity of programming. Whilst acknowledging the 'hotelling effect' which can arise in a market with a number of small competitors, who will target a middle ground of programming in order to attract the largest audience, the Consultation Document doubted whether larger companies would target much more than ' an expanded centre-ground.'.[32] As such, content regulation was considered essential to support a full range of programming. However, there was a much greater willingness to relax ownership rules on the basis of economic arguments. Thus, it was asserted, liberalisation would enable greater consolidation and efficiency, promote investment, and contribute to a greater international influence. These arguments are familiar but, in the light of the Consultation Document's acknowledged doubt about the ability of consolidation to deliver diversity, the statement which the Document seems to adopt, that '[p]roponents of a freer market suggest that only through deregulation can choice and diversity really flourish,' seems at odds with the earlier reasoning.[33] Indeed, the Consultation Document's conclusion to this section on plurality and diversity seems to confirm that, rather than being the primary focus, broadcasting pluralism will have to compete with other policy goals for regulatory protection, with a safety net provided by content regulation:

> The Government's task is to find a middle ground that safeguards both competition and democracy, re-aligning ownership rules to adapt to the new market that is emerging. In other words, we should act to encourage a dynamic market whilst at the same time guaranteeing plurality, diversity and quality for the consumer.[34]

Also justifying the changes to ownership rules was the influence of a changing media environment, described with reference to convergence, new media, and abundance.[35]

In relation to cross-media ownership, the Consultation Document presented a wide range of possibilities, from no regulation of cross-media to retention of the then current regime, but many of these options were not discussed at all. It briefly examined a couple of models. One was to retain the existing regime but to relax thresholds. This had the virtue of simplicity and certainty, but at the cost of flexibility. An alternative to meet the need for flexibility in a changing market was to have permeable limits which could be exceeded subject to a plurality test. However, this was seen as costly in terms of the regulatory and commercial uncertainty which it would produce.[36] The Consultation Document also considered a 'share of voice' approach, which was an idea that the government had floated prior to its 1996 reforms. In its previous examination of the model, the government had eventually decided it was likely to be too complex and controversial to work, particularly because of the difficult, but central, task of determining the degree of

---

[32] *Ibid*, para 1.5.
[33] *Ibid*, para 1.8.
[34] *Ibid*, para 1.11.
[35] *Ibid*, paras 3.1-3.10.
[36] *Ibid*, paras 6.5.3–6.5.4.

influence of each type of media. The Consultation Document did not appear any more optimistic that these difficulties could be overcome, and, indeed, considered that the presence of the internet made the idea even more problematic. A more arbitrary approach was also canvassed, whereby a company would be limited to 40 per cent of a single market, 30 per cent of two markets, and so forth. This had the advantage of avoiding the difficult 'media influence' determination, but came at the cost of arbitrariness, because it would have to be assumed that all media had the same degree of influence and made the same contribution to plurality and diversity. This, of course, was not the case when one compared the different types of media, and especially when one took into account the fairness obligations imposed on broadcasting.[37] The Culture, Media and Sport Committee encapsulated succinctly the difficulties of 'share of voice' type approaches:

> Proposals for such an approach fail to take account of the fundamentally different regulatory environments of different media. Such proposals either involve a whole range of unproven assumptions about the relative impact of different media or rely on economic indicators that may bear little relation to actual influence. Even more fundamentally, all arguments for 'share of voice' regulation that we have heard take no account of the impact of the Internet. The new media have had the effect of ensuring that newspapers compete in a more diverse market, for example, regardless of circulation, readership, turnover and profit.[38]

The next stage of the process was the announcement of the government's proposals for media ownership reform; this came with the publication of the draft Communications Bill. Although the Policy Statement set out the government's intention, the actual clauses were not issued until some time later. As for cross-media ownership, the government's intention was to deregulate because 'UK companies have to be allowed to grow'.[39] It intended therefore to reduce cross-media to three core rules, which would regulate cross-media interests between national newspapers and Channel Three, and regional newspapers and comparable regional Channel Three services, and provide protection at the local level. Newspapers were considered to be the most influential media, editorially, whilst Channel Three had the most significant mass reach.[40] The government rejected the idea of a discretionary public interest test which had been disliked by media companies and regulators because it created uncertainty and was costly.[41] The same deregulatory theme could be seen in its other proposals. It remained consistent with its early intention to abolish all restrictions which prevented a single Channel Three emerging, but it dropped the earlier suggestion of retaining a prohibition on common control of Channels Three and Five. All restrictions on national radio licence ownership would be removed. Here again the role of

---

[37] *Ibid,* paras 6.5.6–6.5.11.
[38] Second Report, above n 3, para 42.
[39] Policy Statement, above n 6, para 9.4.1.
[40] *Ibid,* paras 9.4.3–9.3.4.
[41] *Ibid,* para 9.4.7.

content regulation can be seen to come into play. In the case of national licences, prescribed programme formats could be relied upon for the protection of diversity.[42]

The Puttnam Committee had the best opportunity, prior to the actual parliamentary legislative process, of considering the media ownership proposals, although it received only some of the new draft legislative provisions during its deliberations, and it did not receive any final proposals for local radio ownership regulation.[43] One of the main recommendations of the Puttnam Committee which would ultimately have a significant impact on the eventual media reforms was intended to 'facilitate a significant reduction of direct legislative limitations on media ownership'.[44] The Puttnam Committee proposed that the Competition Commission and the Office of Fair Trading (OFT), which would have responsibility for assessing the competition implications of media mergers, should be required also to consider the impact of the merger on plurality. The Committee suggested a series of matters which could be considered, such as: the maintenance of a range of broadcast owners and voices; the promotion and maintenance of a plurality of broadcast owners, each of whom demonstrates a commitment to the impartial presentation of news and factual programming; and the promotion and maintenance, across all types of media, of a balanced and accurate presentation of news, and the free expression of opinion.[45] Whilst the suggestion of a plurality test, to address the weaknesses of a competition law-only regime seems reasonable, the matters chosen by the Committee to test plurality could have been troublesome, given the fairness rules imposed upon broadcasting. The reference to newspapers and balanced representation might also be seen as problematic, even though it might accord with common expectations of professional journalistic standards. In any event, the government rejected this proposal, citing again the dislike of these discretionary tests, and asserting that the specific ownership rules offered sufficient plurality protection.[46] This seemed to miss the point because it was clearly to the removal of so many ownership rules that the Committee was responding. Nor is it clear why uncertainty should be a disqualifying factor. The degree of uncertainty, and whether it is of an unacceptable level, will obviously be important but, as Lord Borrie, during the House of Lords debate on the draft legislation, pointed out:

> The Government claim . . . that a Competition Commission involvement in such cross-media mergers would lead to uncertainty. Indeed it would. One can not deny that during a period of a reference there must be uncertainty as to the outcome—otherwise

---

[42] *Ibid*, para 9.6.1.1.

[43] Puttnam Report, above n 4, paras 261–62 and 390–91.

[44] *Ibid*, para 224.

[45] *Ibid*.

[46] Response to Puttnam Report, above n 4, para 79. The government accepted the need for a plurality test in relation to newspaper mergers, because newspapers were largely outside a specific regime, although this presumably undermines the arguments used about the undesirability of such public interest discretionary tests.

what is the point of the reference? However, I would suggest that that is a small price to pay for ensuring a free and diverse media. Once ownership is changed, it is exceedingly difficult to revert to square one; the damage may have been done.[47]

The idea of a plurality test was pushed again during the House of Lords' consideration of the draft legislation, and in the committee stage, Lord Puttnam put forward an amendment which would incorporate into the Enterprise Act 2002 a media plurality public interest test. In making the case for the amendment, Lord Puttnam was conscious of the need for ownership regulation to be flexible, but it is his use of the troublesome consumer/citizen dichotomy which is interesting:

> In a period of rapid economic, technological and ownership change, the one thing we cannot do is even begin to guess at who might or might not attempt to control this or that element of the media. What we can do, however, is refuse to contemplate any broadly unacceptable level of media concentration where each of the component parts is of significant size and reach in its own right.
>
> What we need, therefore, is the ability to identify these concentrations as and when they occur, examine them in an analytical, fact-based way and ask whether they fit our definition of 'unacceptable'. The drawback of relying on cross-media ownership rules is that they can all too easily be overtaken by changes in market circumstances . . .. We must also dispel the current fantasy that should unacceptable levels of ownership emerge, regulators can move swiftly to put the genie back in the bottle.
>
> There are two ways of accomplishing what we propose, and we need both of them. One looks from the viewpoint of the consumer, the other from the viewpoint of the citizen. For the consumer, we have competition policy, and that is already built into the Bill. For the citizen, we have the public interest plurality test. Together they represent a formidable duo, and they are both flexible and future-proof.[48]

There was strong debate on, and support for, the amendment. Indeed, in general, the House of Lords appeared to consider the communications legislation with much greater care and attention than the Commons. The government accepted the idea of the plurality test although, as discussed in Chapter Five, the circumstances in which it will be used are more limited than might be thought desirable.

Another issue with which the Puttnam Committee dealt was the lack of symmetry between cross-media rules in relation to Channels Three and Five, which would mean that there would no longer be restrictions on cross-media interests between newspapers and Channel Five. This was a rather opaque discussion (although it would be less opaque in the later parliamentary debates) since, without being explicit, many of the concerns were really about the possibility that Rupert Murdoch's press and satellite interests would now be able to acquire a free-to-air broadcaster, Channel Five, subject to general merger law.[49] BSkyB and News International, not surprisingly, were critical of the differential treatment of the two channels, questioning why Channel Three should remain subject to cross-media

[47] Lord Borrie, HL Deb, 5 June 2003, vol 648, col 1437.
[48] Lord Puttnam, HL Deb, 5 June 2003, vol 648, cols 1432–33.
[49] See, also, House of Commons Library, *Media Ownership and the Communications Bill*, Research Paper 02/68 (28 November 2002), 30–31.

restrictions, but other submissions suggested that the cross-media restriction should be applicable to both channels, citing concerns such as the scope for exploitation of newspaper control to critique the broadcasting regulatory process, and the opportunities for cross-promotion and control of programming rights. The Secretary of State's response was that the protection was needed for Channel Three as a major free-to-air broadcaster, whereas Channel Five, as a smaller broadcaster, could benefit from the investment.[50] The possibility of Channel Five being given the opportunity to grow in size was seen as beneficial to viewers and the market, because it would provide greater competition with Channel Three.[51] The Puttnam Committee was not convinced about the government's reasoning, and recommended that Channel Five should also be subject to the cross-media regime.[52] During the passage of the Bill through Parliament, these concerns about cross-media were also caught up with the possibility that there could be common ownership of Channels Three and Five. Some members of Parliament considered that the two channels, with their distinctive public service missions, should be kept independent.[53] The House of Lords also tried to amend the draft legislation to apply cross-media restrictions to Channel Five, although it was clear that those proposing this were willing to trade this provision for the plurality test.[54]

The intention for local radio ownership had been to revise the radio points scheme to ensure that in each local market (at least those with five or more stations) there would be three commercial radio owners plus the BBC ('three plus one'). However, the draft Communications Bill did not make this explicit, and it seemed that the rules would be left to statutory instrument.[55] The matter was further complicated because the commercial radio industry body, the Commercial Radio Companies Association, which had initially proposed the three plus one scheme was now critical of it, arguing that, in the light of consolidation being permitted in the television market, the radio industry was now carrying the burden of plurality, although these arguments were generally rejected.[56] The government had tried to argue that the failure to have the proposals ready was because the scheme was complex and technical, but the Puttnam Committee was sceptical, since the scheme had been supported by the then regulator, the Radio Authority, on the grounds of its simplicity.[57] The Committee recommended adoption of the three plus one rule, subject to a sunset clause which could disapply the rules if Ofcom determined them to be no longer necessary. The government's response to the Puttnam Report showed that it still had no clear proposal, although it stated that it was now considering a two plus one rule. This was the formula which was

[50] Puttnam Report, above n 4, para 257, and Response to Puttnam Report, above n 4, para 89.

[51] K Howells (Minister for Tourism, Film and Broadcasting), HC Standing Committee E, 30 January 2003, col 867.

[52] Puttnam Report, above n 4, para 258. The government did not accept this recommendation.

[53] R Allan, HC Standing Committee E, 30 January 2003, col 869.

[54] Lord Puttnam, HL Deb, 5 June 2003, vol 648, col 1525.

[55] Puttnam Report, above n 4, paras 260–62.

[56] *Ibid*, paras 263–64.

[57] *Ibid*, para 262.

eventually adopted, by means of statutory instrument. The three plus one rule would have been sufficiently liberalising in itself, a two plus one rule obviously even more so. Under the former rules, a minimum of seven owners could be guaranteed. Substantial consolidation in the radio industry would follow the introduction of these rules.

The intention of the government to introduce the rules by secondary legislation raised a more general issue which the Committee picked up on.[58] It noted that the draft Bill gave the Secretary of State extensive powers to amend the media owner-ship laws by secondary legislation; the rationalisation for this being the need for flexibility. However, the Puttnam Report noted also the concerns expressed to the Committee, as well as by the Media, Culture and Sport Committee, and, previ-ously, the government itself, that media ownership was too important an area to be left to secondary legislation, with the lesser scrutiny which this would entail. The Committee also questioned the justification of flexibility, which it saw as an economic tool, not relevant to the protection of plurality, which was the primary concern of media ownership rules. A point which has often be made throughout these chapters is the sensitivity of media ownership regulation, with the risk that governments will be vulnerable to pressure from media interests, upon which they, in turn, depend for their access to the public. The obvious risks which this entails makes it essential that there is as much transparency as possible built into the media regulatory process, but especially in relation to media ownership rules. This is particularly so when the public interest consideration of media ownership policy and rules tends to be so readily subordinated by economic and industrial dictates.

United States

The 2003 reform process had its origins in the Telecommunications Act of 1996 (TA 1996 (US)), which directed the Federal Communications Commission (FCC), pursuant to section 202(h), to review media ownership rules on a biennial basis, with a view to determining whether, in the light of competition, any of the rules were required in the public interest.[59] Congress directed the FCC to modify or repeal any rules which were no longer required in the public interest. As noted in Chapter Three, the TA 1996 (US) brought with it a deregulatory and liberalis-ing agenda, and this agenda formed the backdrop for the third biennial review, which was launched in 2002.[60] This review was a comprehensive review of existing ownership rules. It launched a review of four rules: national television

---

[58] Puttnam Report, above n 4, paras 281–83.

[59] Congress has since amended this to require a quadrennial review: Consolidated Appropriations Act 2004, § 629(3).

[60] FCC, *Notice of Proposed Rule Making, In the Matter of 2002 Biennial Regulatory Review—Review of the Commission's Broadcast Ownership Rules and Other Rules Adopted Pursuant to Section 202 of the Telecommunications Act of 1996*, 17 FCC Rcd 18503 (2002).

ownership; local television; radio–television cross-ownership; and dual networks; and it folded into the review two further rules, already under review: local radio ownership; and broadcasting–newspaper cross-ownership. The influence of the TA 1996 (US) is obviously evident throughout the FCC's formal notice launching the review, and there seems also to be an implicit assumption that the broadcasting environment is characterised by increased diversity, although there is also an acknowledgement of increased consolidation.[61] The conduct of this review was also influenced by an interpretation which had been given to section 202(h) following the decision in *Fox* that the section required a presumption in favour of modification or repeal.[62] Although this interpretation would later be rejected by the US Court of Appeals reviewing the 2003 reform proposals, it no doubt influenced the FCC's approach.[63]

As a result of the review, the FCC released, in June 2003, its report ('the Report'), announcing changes to all six rules, save for the dual network rule, which was left unchanged.[64] The FCC decided that a merger of two of the largest networks would give rise to a degree of economic power, having regard also to the degree of vertical integration of each of the networks, which would threaten both localism and competition.[65] The proposed changes were as follows:[66]

— The national television rule was relaxed by increasing the audience reach limit of 35 per cent to 45 per cent.
— The local television rule which had allowed ownership of two stations in a market, subject to certain conditions, was relaxed to allow control of three stations in markets of 18 or more stations (counting both commercial and non-commercial), provided that not more than one of the three was one of the four highest rating stations. The limit on two stations (with not more than one from the top four rated stations) remained for smaller markets with five or more stations. The previous requirement of eight independently owned stations remaining in the market after the merger was removed.
— The FCC proposed new cross-media rules, which would bring together the two strands of cross-ownership restrictions: newspaper and broadcasting combinations, and radio and television combinations. The proposed rules would represent a significant relaxation of the former regime. In the smallest markets, with three or less television stations, there would be a prohibition on cross-ownership, although waivers would be possible. However, in larger markets,

---

[61] See, for example, *ibid*, paras 4 and 10.
[62] *Fox Television Stations* v *Federal Communications Commission* 280 F 3d 1027 (2002).
[63] FCC, *Notice of Proposed Rule Making (2002)*, above n 60, para 3. See, also, Chapter Three, 'United States: Telecommunications Act of 1996 and Current Rules' for further information.
[64] FCC, *Report and Order and Notice of Proposed Rulemaking, In the Matter of 2002 Biennial Regulatory Review—Review of the Commission's Broadcast Ownership Rules and Other Rules Adopted Pursuant to Section 202 of the Telecommunications Act of 1996*, FCC 03-127 (2 June 2003).
[65] *Ibid*, para 621.
[66] See Chapter Three, United States, at p 115 for details of the ownership rules as they stood at the time of the review.

with nine or more television stations, there would be no restrictions on cross-ownership, whilst in markets of between four and eight television stations, cross-ownership would be permitted, but the type of combination would determine precisely the permitted limits. Thus, control of one of the following combinations was permissible:

— a daily newspaper, one television station, and up to half the number of radio stations permitted in that market;
— a daily newspaper and all of the permissible number of radio stations for that market; or,
— two television stations (subject to local television rule), and all of the permissible number of radio stations for that market.

— In relation to local radio, the FCC retained the existing rules, but changed the method of defining radio markets, from one based on signal contour to a geographic market, as defined by a recognised ratings organisation. Not all areas were covered by this system, and the FCC also announced a new rule-making procedure to develop a new approach for these areas. This change would have the effect of tightening the existing rules, because the old system contained some anomalies which meant that some markets appeared to be larger than they actually were. However, the FCC also decided that non-commercial radio stations should be included in the market count, which would have alleviated the impact of the change. A move to geographic markets, however, was not favoured by the broadcasting industry, because it would limit expansion for some in the industry.

The extensive report accompanying the FCC's order was a lengthy assessment of policy and justification for the rule changes, and it is helpful to look at some aspects in order to appreciate the FCC's policy and regulatory approach. An early statement provides a good indication of the policy attitude and rule changes:

[W]hile the march of technology has brought to our homes, schools, and places of employment unprecedented access to information and programming, our broadcast ownership rules, like a distant echo from the past, continue to restrict who may hold radio and television licenses as if broadcasters were America's information gatekeepers. Our current rules inadequately account for the competitive presence of cable, ignore the diversity-enhancing value of the Internet, and lack any sound basis for a national audience reach cap. Neither from a policy perspective nor a legal perspective can rules premised on such a flawed foundation be defended as necessary in the public interest. . . . Our current rules are, in short, a patchwork of unenforceable and indefensible restrictions that, while laudable in principle, do not serve the interests they purport to serve.

Inaction on our part and the market uncertainty that would result from a perpetuation of the open-ended policy limbo that exists today would ill serve our nation. The adoption of this *Order* is critical, therefore, to the realization of our public interest goals in that it puts an end to any uncertainty regarding the scope and effect of our structural broadcast ownership rules. Most importantly, the rules . . . serve our competition, diver-

sity and localism goals in highly targeted ways and, working together, form a comprehensive framework that is responsive to today's media environment.[67]

The FCC's comment rejecting the idea of broadcasters—here, in the sense of over-
the-air broadcasters—as information gatekeepers points correctly to the reality
that over-the-air broadcasting is no longer the only means through which
information is conveyed, but it also underplays the reality. Broadcasters continue
to act as information gatekeepers: they broadcast using a still-limited resource,
spectrum; there is no expectation of separation of content and distribution; a
significant proportion of the population is still dependent upon over-the-air
broadcasting; and, through networking, the influence of some broadcasting
organisations can be extensive. As such, and although they might operate in different ways, broadcasters can continue to be seen as gatekeepers, alongside cable
and satellite operators. The problem is not as the FCC appears to characterise it;
the problem is that regulation of the broadcasting sector (in its widest sense) has
not been adapted consistently to meet changes in the media environment, and this
is a problem common to each jurisdiction. Structural regulation, as a regulatory
tool, in the form of ownership rules, has not been deployed coherently, and has
created pressures for relaxation.

Apart from these general statements, the more specific approach of the FCC was
to review each of the policy goals which it saw as relevant—diversity, competition,
and localism—with a view to evaluating the ownership rules. There are some
interesting aspects to the FCC's policy discussion. With regard to diversity, the
FCC identified five types of diversity as relevant to ownership policy: viewpoint,
outlet, programme, source, and minority and female ownership.[68] Viewpoint
diversity[69] was sought because it was regarded as beneficial to the public interest
to have the widest range of views available, and media ownership policy had rested
on the assumption that there was a correlation between the views expressed and
ownership of a media outlet. The FCC tried to test this assumption empirically,
but the results were mixed, and the main study disputing this assumption was
methodologically flawed. There was some, although no conclusive, evidence
which supported the assumption, and the FCC was more inclined to accept this,
although it was clear also that the absence of evidence was not a major stumbling-
block. The FCC seemed willing simply to reassert its belief in the connection. It
might be questioned whether the assumption could ever have been reliably tested,
and, even, whether this is the real issue about ownership diversity. As suggested in
the conclusion to Chapter Three, there might be a number of factors which contribute to content decisions, and which might make it undesirable for monopoly
ownership to be tolerated. The influence of a particular ownership voice might not
be the most central concern, although the FCC seems to acknowledge this when it
refers to the possibility that there could be a variety of financial factors and other

---

[67] FCC, *Report and Order and Notice of Proposed Rulemaking* (2003), above n 64, paras 4–5.
[68] See *ibid*, paras 18–52 for the discussion of diversity policy.
[69] Discussed at *ibid*, paras 19–35.

matters influencing news coverage decisions.[70] However, the point is surely, also, not whether diversity of ownership leads to viewpoint diversity, but that monopoly of ownership of something as important as media is not appropriate in a democratic culture, and this the FCC does recognise: it is the potential power that media outlets possess which rules against monopoly ownership.[71]

The FCC's treatment of programme diversity, in the sense of variety of formats and content, was cursory.[72] Although it acknowledged it as a policy objective, it appeared to take the view that programme diversity could best be achieved through competition between delivery systems, rather than regulation, although, in the light of the economic issues discussed in Chapter Six, this might be questionable. Outlet diversity,[73] which is understood by the FCC to be the presence of multiple independently-owned outlets within a specific market, was viewed as a contributing factor to the attainment of viewpoint diversity. Outlet diversity was seen as most relevant for radio broadcasting, which was regarded as a viable entry point for new participants in the media industry. Public safety provided a further reason for promoting outlet diversity: the FCC considered that there was less likelihood that, in an emergency, vital public information would not be communicated if there was independent control within the market. The origin of this concern lies possibly in an incident which occurred in 2002. Clear Channel, one of the largest media companies in the US, largely as a result of the 1996 radio ownership rule relaxation, owned all six of the commercial radio stations in Minot, North Dakota. When police in the area tried to have emergency information broadcast about a toxic ammonia cloud caused by a train derailment, they were unable to contact anyone at the radio stations, which were broadcasting automated programming, produced and distributed remotely.[74]

Source diversity was understood to be the availability of content from a variety of producers, something which the FCC also saw as contributing to viewpoint and programme diversity.[75] However, the FCC rejected source diversity as an objective for ownership policies; the number of television channels available in the US market was considered sufficient. The question of source diversity highlights one of the difficulties of examining ownership rules in isolation. Submissions made to the FCC in the course of this review highlighted the absence of source diversity during prime-time broadcast programming, and called for new rules requiring broadcasters to transmit a certain proportion of independent programming during

---

[70] *Ibid*, para 29.

[71] *Ibid*, para 28. See, also, CE Baker, 'Media Structure, Ownership Policy, and the First Amendment' (2005) 78 *Southern California Law Review* 733 at 735.

[72] Discussed at FCC, *Report and Order and Notice of Proposed Rulemaking* (2003), above n 64, paras 36–37.

[73] Discussed at *ibid*, paras 38–41.

[74] 'Media Ownership Rules: Too Little, Too Late', (2003) *The Economist* (London), 17 May, 56–57. The details of this incident have been disputed, particularly as to whether there were any staff present at the radio stations and whether the incident was in fact a failure of the emergency system in place.

[75] Discussed at FCC, *Report and Order and Notice of Proposed Rulemaking* (2003), above n 64, paras 42–45.

prime time. This, as the FCC was aware, was a direct reference to the now-repealed network rules, the prime-time access rule and the financial interest and syndication rule, and it points to the absence of proactive measures in the US regulatory scheme, and the failure to consider the extent to which structural regulation might be undercut by other commercial factors, such as, for example, networking arrangements. The FCC appeared to reject the claims that there had been a decline in independent programming, but, in any event, did not see it as an issue for regulation.[76] Despite the past controversies, as mentioned in Chapter Three, concerning policies fostering minority and female ownership,[77] the FCC continued to see this as an important objective. However, it merely noted the suggestions made by submissions to the review, and left the matter for a further rule-making. Nor is it likely that any regulatory solutions devised by the FCC will have a direct impact on ownership rules; more likely would be rules to promote transparency and investment.

One of the concerns of the FCC in discussing the policy objective of competition[78] was to determine whether competition was an objective which the FCC should pursue as part of its public interest mandate, particularly in light of the TA 1996 (US) reforms, the alternative being to leave all competition issues to the competition regulatory authorities. However, the FCC decided that there was a strong connection between a commitment to promote competition and the Commission's public interest responsibilities. Further, ownership regulation, whilst promoting economic competition, also promoted viewpoint diversity, and it saw antitrust theory aligned with the values underlying viewpoint diversity, namely, 'that the aggregation of inordinate market share by a small number of firms will tend to harm public welfare'.[79] Yet, the FCC's attempt to justify its ownership and control regulatory approach as one 'grounded in economic competition analysis', and to assert that its rules are based on 'standard antitrust principles' appears strained when it is recalled that general competition law market definition does not generally assist in the protection of certain types of combinations, such as cross-media.[80] However, the FCC did acknowledge that antitrust, or competition, approaches will not always meet the needs of viewpoint diversity, at least in smaller markets. The FCC also sought to separate its regulatory task from that of orthodox antitrust theory when considering how to evaluate the degree of competition in the market; hence, a focus, for example, on price competition might not be appropriate for its public interest inquiry.[81] Nevertheless, the FCC's consideration of the competition objective, and, indeed, the Report generally, is imbued with a desire on the part of the Commission to legitimise its regulation by its use of antitrust reference. Yet, it is not clear why this should be necessary.

---

[76] These rules are discussed in Chapter Five, 'Networks', at p 241.
[77] FCC, *Report and Order and Notice of Proposed Rulemaking* (2003), above n 64, paras 46–52.
[78] Discussed at *ibid*, paras 53–72.
[79] *Ibid*, para 58.
[80] *Ibid*, para 59.
[81] *Ibid*, see paras 65, 67–68.

Whilst ownership regulation can be seen as an extreme form of ex ante competition regulation, it is fundamentally concerned about different issues, and should not have to seek legitimacy through the use of competition rhetoric. On localism, the FCC affirmed that this remained an important policy objective for ownership regulation.[82] Effective localism would be evidenced by the provision of programming which served local needs and interests, and the provision, both quantitatively and qualitatively, of local news. And, of course, it was consistent with the US preference for structural regulation that the FCC would see the promotion of localism policies through market structures.[83]

The examination of whether any of the rules should be repealed or modified, having regard to these policy objectives was lengthy, and there is not the space here to consider this in detail, but it is worth noting some aspects of the FCC's application of the policy to the rules, and the development of a diversity index for the determination of new cross-media rules. The FCC considered the necessity for each of the rules in the light of the three policy objectives. Yet, despite the detailed analysis, the reference to empirical studies, and the identification of relevant markets, the conclusions seemed to be along broad and familiar lines.[84] Thus, assessments of the rules in relation to the protection of competition invariably referred to the abundance of media now available in the market. Rather than promoting localism, the rules were viewed as undermining that policy, because they inhibited investment, whilst diversity too was achieved by the availability of a variety of media in the marketplace. When considering the local television and national television rules in connection with the promotion of competition policy objective, the FCC was persuaded that there was much greater competition in the relevant markets because of the growth in other media, and that the current rules constrained competition and inhibited investment, because they prevented mergers which could increase efficiency and make smaller operators more competitive.[85] This argument that consolidation and growth in the television industry, at both local and national level, could actually serve the public interest was also an important influence on the consideration of the impact of the rules on localism. In fact, paradoxical as it might seem, the local ownership rules were viewed as counterproductive to the promotion of localism. Indeed, the FCC, when considering localism and the local radio review, stated firmly that localism was more likely to be affected by national size of radio groups rather than local limits.[86] This seemed an incon-

---

[82] Discussed at *ibid*, paras 73–79.

[83] *Ibid*, para 77.

[84] For a review of the studies cited in the Report, see AL Plamondon, 'Proposed Changes in Media Ownership Rules: A Study in Ventriloquism?' [2003] *Communication and the Law* 47, and see, also, M Cooper, 'Reclaiming the First Amendment: Legal, Factual, and Analytic Support for Limits on Media Ownership' in RW McChesney, R Newman, and B Scott (eds), *The Future of Media* (New York, Seven Stories Press, 2005), 163, for a critique of the evidence and an analysis of the likely effects if the ownership rules had come into force.

[85] See, eg, FCC, *Report and Order and Notice of Proposed Rulemaking* (2003), above n 64, paras 148 and 154 (local), and 509 (national).

[86] *Ibid*, para 304

sistent position, given that national radio ownership limits were removed in 1996, and, indeed, some of the submissions received by the FCC referred to consolidation in the radio industry and the impact this had had on local markets. As one submission put it: 'large group owners downsize local staff so that "they can run stations all over the country more cheaply"', and another: 'consolidation has resulted in "nearly identical programming" in *different* local markets'.[87] The FCC seemed to dismiss these comments as being irrelevant to the review. Yet, these very points seemed to undermine their argument that localism would be served by allowing growth because the cost cuttings would contribute to greater investment in programming.

Thus, rules which prevented consolidation (at least to a certain degree) would be harmful to the goal of localism, whereas the opportunity to realise efficiencies through mergers would lead to greater investment in programming.[88] This, of course, is a familiar line, but in the absence of content regulation, it is difficult to see that economic efficiencies, cost savings, and so forth will inexorably lead to greater investment in local programming—the FCC was persuaded that consolidation could lead to improvements in both quantity and quality of local programming.[89] It should be noted that the FCC did refer to empirical evidence (and anecdotal evidence) which suggested that stations which were part of a commonly owned group were more likely to provide more local news, and of increased quality (measured by awards), than independently owned stations.[90] The fact that this empirical evidence was provided by the Fox Network did not seem to trouble the FCC. Structural regulation can shape the market, but it cannot direct or guarantee that efficiencies realised will be utilised in investment in programming. Programming is a cost of business, and unless this translates clearly into a commercial benefit, then broadcasters will have no incentive to invest in more expensive programming, if commercial benefits can be achieved with less. Nevertheless, this approach justified a relaxation of the local television rule, as well as the increase in the national television audience reach cap from 35 per cent to 45 per cent. The FCC accepted that a national ownership rule for television was necessary to preserve localism, because the non-networked broadcasters would have an incentive to provide greater local programming,[91] but the recognition that network-owned stations will be less likely to be responsive to local communities seems also to undercut its reasoning.

Viewpoint diversity would also require the relaxation of television rules. In relation to the local television rule, the FCC dispensed with the requirement for at least eight other independent stations (commercial or non-commercial) in the market, because it considered that viewpoint diversity should be measured by reference to all of the other media available in the market, and should not be confined

---

[87] Idaho Wireless and UCC, respectively, quoted in *ibid* (emphasis in original).
[88] *Ibid*, para 155, discussing localism and local television rules.
[89] *Ibid*, para 164.
[90] *Ibid*, paras 159 ff.
[91] *Ibid*, paras 546–52.

to television. An earlier FCC decision to consider only television had been the subject of a successful legal challenge, and so the FCC was responding to the court's view that the FCC had not properly explained why only television was relevant in measuring diversity.[92] Whereas, in its 1999 review, the FCC had not been persuaded that other media were substitutes for television, which it saw as the primary source of news and information, it now accepted, albeit with relatively little explanation, that the public did have access to many other sources of news and information.[93] There is obviously a sort of logic about this, but this approach draws no distinction between the different ways in which different media sources might be used by the public—something which was a matter of concern to the FCC in its 1999 consideration of this rule. Nor did it seem to be concerned about the proportion of the public which only had access to over-the-air services; this was raised by some submissions, but is noted by the FCC in a footnote only.[94] The FCC saw viewpoint diversity as a matter more relevant to the local rules than to a national ownership rule.[95] However, this seems again to portray a rather simplistic view of the manner in which ownership might affect viewpoint diversity. National consolidation, through group organisational and commercial policies, could have an impact on diversity in local markets. The radio industry is evidence of this with its practices of centrally compiled automated programming.

The consideration of the two cross-media ownership rules, newspaper–broadcast combinations and radio–television combinations, in the light of the policy objectives was consistent with the assessment of the other rules, although the cross-ownership rules were not regarded as necessary for the protection of competition, since radio, television, and newspapers were considered separate markets.[96] However, the same arguments about expansion conferring public benefits for localism and diversity policies were used, even in relation to newspaper–broadcasting combinations, where it was accepted that there was scope for the exploitation of cross-efficiencies and synergies.[97] Probably the most important influence on the FCC's redesign of the cross-media rules was its assessment of the diversity which was present in local media markets, aided by its development of a diversity index, and its willingness to assess diversity on the basis of the availability of other types of media in the market: '[t]he record in this proceeding provides ample evidence that competing media outlets abound in markets of all sizes—each providing a platform for civic discourse.'[98] Thus, in assessing whether the cross-media rules were necessary to achieve diversity, the FCC considered that it was now appropriate to take into

---

[92] See Chapter Three, 'United States: Telecommunications Act of 1996 and Current Rules', p 115 for the decision in *Sinclair Broadcast Group v Federal Communications Commission*, and the FCC's justification of its position.

[93] FCC, *Report and Order and Notice of Proposed Rulemaking* (2003), above n 64, para 178.

[94] *Ibid*, para 179, fn 386.

[95] *Ibid*, para 535.

[96] *Ibid*, paras 341 and 381.

[97] *Ibid*, paras 347 and 383 (localism), and 356 (diversity).

[98] *Ibid*, para 365. For the FCC's analysis of the impact of other media on diversity, see *ibid*, paras 365–67 (newspaper–broadcast cross-media), and 386–89 (radio–television cross-media).

account not just over-the-air broadcasting and newspapers, but also cable and satellite services, and the internet:

> In short, the magnitude of the growth in local media voices shows that there will be a plethora of voices in most or all markets absent the rule. . . . Our rules should account for these changes and promote, rather than inhibit, the ability of media outlets to survive and thrive in this evolving media landscape.[99]

The diversity index was used as a means of informing the FCC about the degree of concentration and diversity in markets; using the diversity index would enable the FCC to make a judgement about which markets needed protection from cross-media concentration.[100]

Essentially, there were two parts to the construction of the index. The first was to decide the media to be included in the index, and to assign weights to them; and the second was to determine the share of each media owner in the local market. The result of this process would be a diversity index count for each market, enabling an assessment of the degree of concentration of that market. Based on the findings of a consumer survey inquiring into consumers' use and perception of different types of media as sources of news and information, the FCC chose to include in the index newspapers, over-the-air television and radio, and the internet, which it saw as viable substitutes for each other in the provision of news, information, and opinion, but it excluded other media such as magazines, cable, and satellite, mainly because they were more likely to have a national rather than a local news and information focus.[101] Although the FCC considered that the various media were substitutes, it acknowledged that they were not each of equal importance, and accordingly assigned weights based on frequency of use, by the consumers surveyed, as a source of local news and current affairs. This inquiry led the FCC to assign weights as follows: television, 33.8 per cent; daily newspapers, 20.2 per cent; weekly newspapers, 8.6 per cent; radio, 24.9 per cent; and the internet, 12.5 per cent. The second part of the exercise was to determine the share of each media owner within the market. The general approach here was simply to count the number of, say, radio outlets operating within the radio market, which would provide a percentage share for each outlet. Cross-ownership was separately counted. This could be translated into a figure for the owner's share of the total viewpoint market, taking into account all the media for that market, and the weighting given to that type of media. Each owner's share of the viewpoint market would be squared to arrive at a points total, which would be combined with the points for all outlets in the viewpoint market. The overall total would be the diversity index for that local market.[102]

---

[99] *Ibid*, para 367. This was referring to newspaper–broadcast cross-media, but the same arguments were used for radio–television cross-media.

[100] The diversity index is discussed at *ibid*, paras 391–431. The index was based on the Herfindahl-Hirschmann Index (usually referred to as 'the HHI index'), an index used in competition analysis to measure concentration: paras 394–97.

[101] *Ibid*, paras 405–8, and para 413 for satellite.

[102] *Ibid*, para 431.

The FCC chose to assume that all outlets in the market had equal weight, on the basis that all outlets at least had similar technical reach, although it acknowledged that this was not an entirely accurate assumption.[103] Thus, regardless of each station's commercial size and the owner's reach into other markets, an owner with two stations would be treated as having exactly double the influence of an owner with only one station. Based on the diversity index, the FCC identified which markets were at risk from high levels of viewpoint concentration. It calculated that a fully competitive market was one with 10 or more equally sized firms, and a market with 10 such firms would be the equivalent of 1,000 points on the diversity index. A market with six firms would have a diversity index of 1,800 points, which the FCC viewed as moderately concentrated. The higher the diversity index, the more concentrated the market.[104] Application of the diversity index, and sampling the effects of hypothetical mergers on the index, led the FCC to conclude that it was markets of three or less television stations which were most vulnerable to viewpoint concentration, and which should be most fully protected by cross-media regulation.

On the face of it, the FCC's development of the diversity index is a reasonable means of trying to assess something as difficult to measure as diversity, taking into account also the impact of a changing media environment. The FCC acknowledged that it was a blunt tool, which could measure only large effects in what it termed 'typical' markets.[105] However, there are some aspects of the FCC's approach in devising the index which seemed to ensure that it was likely to be blunter than necessary or desirable. Whilst it might have been reasonable to include the internet as one of the media in the index, the method used to determine the weightings for each type of media was problematic. As noted above, the FCC relied upon consumers' responses to questions about how often they used the different type of media, over a specified period, to access local news and information. This resulted in a weighting for the internet, which was only half of radio's weighting, and slightly less than half of that for newspapers. It might not be surprising that frequency of access to the internet is high, but it might be questionable whether this really means that the internet forms another media voice in the market. One of the difficulties with the FCC's approach is that it makes no allowance for the nature of that use. This might be particularly relevant when one is assessing the internet's voice, because a significant proportion of the internet's content is likely to be content which has been produced for another forum; the obvious example here is newspapers. To assess the internet as another voice existing alongside broadcasting and the press is to confuse mode of delivery with content. Some submissions to the review questioned the extent to which the internet added to diversity, but the FCC seemed to discount these comments quite

---

[103] FCC, *Report and Order and Notice of Proposed Rulemaking* (2003), above n 64, para 421. It took a different approach for the internet because of the significant differences between a service delivered by cable and one delivered by telephone: para 426. For the internet, subscription shares were used.

[104] *Ibid*, para 448.

[105] *Ibid*, paras 391 and 398.

readily.[106] Indeed, the Commission's arguments for excluding cable and satellite could well be applied to the internet. It had concluded that cable and satellite did not broadcast sufficient local material (save in the form of broadcast station carriage), and where it did carry local material such as the PEGs channels, these were of little impact.[107] Yet, this is a characterisation which could apply also to the internet, but here the FCC seemed much less concerned about these types of distinctions.[108]

The FCC also saw the diversity index as a more comprehensive means of measuring diversity compared with previous approaches based on counting the number of outlets. The diversity index could give a clearer picture of what the loss of a voice in the market meant, because it would indicate also the 'diversity importance' of that particular voice.[109] Yet it is questionable whether the FCC achieves this, given that it assigned equal value to each outlet within each media category, including for broadcasting both commercial and non-commercial services. Although each voice or outlet is still measured for its diversity importance, given the heavy weighting assigned to the internet, the likelihood is that the diversity importance of the traditional media is being significantly under-measured. It should, of course, be recalled that the diversity index is only applicable to a determination of which markets the rules governing cross-ownership between broadcasting and newspapers will apply to; it does not seek to incorporate the internet into its rules. One can understand the FCC's inclination for incorporating the internet into the index, even if, when compared with its approach to cable and satellite, its reasoning looks a little strained, but it could be argued that the end result only serves to show that the internet, despite all its flexibility and abundance, is a form of media (and/or media delivery) which cannot be ranked and measured alongside the traditional media, without further attention to what exactly the internet is delivering.

The new rules proposed by the FCC provoked considerable criticism, both from within the Commission and more broadly. Aside from numerous submissions to the review, about two million people communicated with the FCC, by letters, email, and petitions, to express opposition to any further relaxation of the media ownership rules.[110] A legal challenge to the Order was brought by a number of public interest groups.[111] One of the key issues addressed by the court was whether the FCC's diversity index provided a reasoned basis for its redesigned rules. The court

---

[106] *Ibid*, para 427.

[107] See *ibid*, paras 408 and 413. The FCC was also concerned that there was some confusion in the consumer responses as to whether what was being watched via cable was in fact broadcast-originated material. Nevertheless, this was a distinction which the FCC seemed less bothered by in relation to the internet.

[108] *Ibid*, para 427.

[109] *Ibid*, para 396.

[110] *Prometheus Radio Project v Federal Communications Commission* 373 F 3d 372, 386 (2004).

[111] *Ibid*. All of the new rule changes were challenged, with the exception of the dual network rule. However, the challenge to the national television rule was rendered moot by Congress's amendment to the rule. There was a partial dissent from Scirica CJ.

held that it did not, and referred to the weaknesses discussed above.[112] In relation to the inclusion of the internet, there was 'a critical distinction between websites that are independent sources of local news and websites of local newspapers and broadcast stations that merely republish the information already being reported'.[113] The website which merely republished should have been excluded. The court also considered that the FCC's decision to assign equal weight to each media outlet undermined its rationale for using the index.[114] The role of other media in measuring diversity was also a matter for the court when considering the local television rule. The court accepted that other media, in addition to broadcast media, could contribute to diversity, although it noted that the evidence provided by the FCC was weak.[115] Indeed, the FCC's assumption that outlets of the same type of media could be treated equally was a common factor in the court's ruling that the cross-media rules, and the local television and radio rules had not been sufficiently reasoned.[116] Although the court found that the FCC had erred in the reasoning used to justify the revised rules, it did not question the policy approach used by the FCC, and its interpretation of the relationship of the policy objectives of competition, localism, and diversity to ownership regulation. Thus, a reconsideration of the rules will be likely to focus more on being able to justify the rules and, especially, the construction of the diversity index, but it is unlikely that there will be any substantive policy reconsideration. As noted in Chapter One, at the time of writing, a new rule-making procedure had not been announced, so that, in the meantime, the 2003 rule revision remains stayed, pending this reconsideration.

Two FCC Commissioners, Copps and Adelstein issued strong dissents, the tone of which is reflected in Copps's introductory words:

> This morning we are at a crossroads—for the Federal Communications Commission, for television, radio, and newspapers, and for the American people. The decision we five make today will recast our entire media landscape for years to come. At issue is whether a few corporations will be ceded gatekeeper control over the civil dialogue of our country; content control over our music, entertainment and information; and veto power over the majority of what we and our families watch, hear and read.[117]

Both Commissioners were critical of the review's process and lack of consultation, particularly the failure to take into account the general public's views. Adelstein and Copps held a series of public forums across the country, funded out of the resources of Copp's own office, to discuss the changes.[118] Both were critical also of

---

[112] *Prometheus Radio Project v Federal Communications Commission* 373 F 3d 372, 386 (2004), 403 and 405–9.

[113] *Ibid,* 405–6.

[114] *Ibid,* 408.

[115] *Ibid,* 414–5.

[116] *Ibid,* 435.

[117] FCC, *Report and Order and Notice of Proposed Rulemaking* (2003), above n 64, 'Statement of Commissioner Michael J Copps, Dissenting', 1.

[118] *Ibid,* 5–8, and 'Statement of Commissioner Jonathan S Adelstein, Dissenting', 4–5. The then Chairman of the FCC, Michael Powell, had consented to only one public hearing: G Beckerman, 'Tripping Up Big Media' (2003) *Columbia Journalism Review,* November–December, 1 at 5.

the arbitrary conclusions drawn from the evidence, both generally and in relation to the diversity index. But the dissenting Commissioners were also at odds with the majority over the policy objectives and the nature of these policy objectives, and it is these differences which perhaps best explain their dissent from the Order and its reasoning. Adelstein, like Copps, referred to the public interest as the foundation for the ownership rules, although Copps thought that the ownership rules, even prior to the reform, could barely sustain the public interest responsibilities, because so much of traditional public interest regulation had been dismantled.[119] Unlike the majority Report, both Commissioners cited problems of extensive ongoing industry consolidation and vertical integration, and viewed the impact of the 1996 deregulation of radio ownership rules as indicative of the adverse consequences of rule relaxation.[120] Implicitly rejecting the majority line that localism and diversity could actually be enhanced by allowing more scope for industry consolidation, Copps argued that the policies, and understanding, of localism and diversity had become subordinated to the competition discourse.[121] This was echoed by Adelstein, who rejected the equation of localism with efficiency. Indeed, Adelstein argued that the promotion of localism and diversity, and even competition, might actually require the tolerance of a degree of inefficiency. This, he argued, was implicit in the very regulatory framework established for broadcasting by Congress, which was structured along local lines rather than a more efficient national or regional framework.[122] Adelstein's point is an important one, because it is a reminder that the public interest aspect of media—its role within the public sphere—cannot be driven simply by ordinary industry economic or commercial imperatives. These may have to be subordinated, in the light of the public-regarding role of the media industry.

Australia

Whatever the weaknesses of the UK and US reforms, they were the product of open debate and consideration: through the parliamentary process in the UK; and the FCC's rule-making procedures in the US. Although criticisms can be made of the conduct of these processes, and there were criticisms in the UK Parliament, and, indeed, by some of the US FCC commissioners, about aspects of the processes, these jurisdictions nevertheless provide a sharp contrast to the Australian approach to media reform, and media policy making in general. In Australia, the likely areas for reform are cross-media ownership and foreign ownership, and these are the only rules being given any consideration. At the time of writing, the government's proposals had not been announced, although it is expected that legislation will be brought forward in 2006, but the broad thrust of

---

[119] Adelstein, above n 118, 3, and Copps, above n 117, 4.
[120] Copps, above n 117, 2 and 9, and Adelstein, above n 118, 10–11.
[121] Copps, above n 117, 16.
[122] Adelstein, above n 118, 11–12.

the changes can be anticipated. Almost certainly foreign ownership restrictions, currently applicable to free-to-air and subscription television only, will be removed and cross-media rules will be considerably relaxed.[123] There seems to be no interest in examining mono-media ownership rules but, as seen in Chapter Three, these are already quite generous. It is the cross-media rules which have caused most aggravation to the media industry. Achieving media ownership reforms will be the realisation of a long-held desire of the current government, dating back to the late 1990s. However, as explained in Chapter One, the government's earlier attempts were thwarted. Now it seems unlikely that hindrance to the liberalisation of the media ownership rules remains.[124]

To gain a sense of the government's thinking, one can look to an earlier reform attempt but, before doing that, it is worth looking briefly at the Productivity Commission's conclusions on cross-media ownership, because they point to one of the difficulties of looking at media ownership reform in isolation, in the Australian context. The Commission noted that cross-media rules represented a radical intervention in the market, but acknowledged that the pursuit of diversity in ideas might not be easily met if one was to rely on general competition law alone.[125] It also observed that it was difficult to measure what impact the rules had had on diversity and on industry, since there was very little clear evidence about the economies of scale and scope which might be achieved in the absence of such rules.[126] Nevertheless, it considered that cross-media rules had to be reconsidered because the development of subscription television, digital broadcasting, and the internet challenged the traditional basis for cross-media rules, although it recognised the continuing need for some form of specific regulation.[127] It was disinclined simply to retain or modify the existing rules because of their arbitrariness.[128] The Commission's preferred approach was to substitute the cross-media rules with a public interest test which would be applied by the competition authority, the Australian Competition and Consumer Commission (ACCC).[129] It saw this approach as a way of addressing the weaknesses of both sector-specific cross-media regulation and the application of general competition law. The Productivity Commission envisaged that the public interest test approach could be used for mergers covering a much wider net of media types, including subscription services, the internet, and telecommunications firms. Mergers above a certain size would have to satisfy a public interest test before being considered under normal

---

[123] The discussion here will not address the likely repeal of foreign ownership rules. A brief discussion of foreign ownership rules and policy is provided in Chapter Three, 'Structural Control over who can Broadcast', at p 83.

[124] The government could face some opposition from its coalition partner, the National Party, which represents regional interests, but it is unlikely that this would threaten the reform completely, provided that the government could show that regional interests would be protected or benefited.

[125] Productivity Commission, *Broadcasting*, Report No 11 (Canberra, AusInfo, 2000), 343 and 349–50.

[126] *Ibid*, 344–49.

[127] *Ibid*, 351 and 355.

[128] *Ibid*, 356–57.

[129] *Ibid*, 358–64.

competition merger principles. The Commission did not specify what would be incorporated into the public interest test, but it referred to such tests as were then administered by the UK Independent Television Commission and Radio Authority as guidance, and suggested also that advice on the public interest matters could be obtained from the communications regulator (at that time, the Australian Broadcasting Authority (ABA)).

However, there was an important reservation to the Commission's recommendation.[130] One of the overall concerns of the Commission's inquiry had been the way in which in Australia potential diversity and competition had been artificially constrained: for example, the development of subscription television was constrained by rules limiting its ability to raise advertising revenue, and by rules which provided extensive protection of sporting events for the benefit of free-to-air broadcasting; whilst regulatory decisions about digital broadcasting had meant that there was virtually no opportunity for multichannelling possibilities to be exploited, or for new services to develop. Many of these decisions had been made to protect free-to-air broadcasters, and they precluded new entrants to the market. It recommended that there should be no repeal of the cross-media rules unless, in addition to the public interest test, the government set about making other structural changes to the broadcasting environment which would enable new entrants to the market, and better exploitation of spectrum and technology. The Commission also recommended that foreign ownership restrictions should be repealed before cross-media rules were removed. Thus, media ownership reform should only be as part of a package of reforms. This is an important point, because in Australia, where the subscription and digital television markets are still so underdeveloped, the argument of media abundance is particularly inapplicable. Despite the extensive inquiry conducted by the Commission (instigated by the government), and its comprehensive report, the government made no response to the Productivity Commission's report, save for a comment, some months later, by the then Minister for Communications, during a 'door stop' press conference, when he referred to the Commission's view that the foreign and cross-media ownership rules were anachronistic. This was cited as support for government plans to reform these rules. No reference was made to the Commission's caution on reforming these rules in isolation.[131] The only substantive comment on the Commission's public interest test proposal came when Parliament was considering a government proposal to reform media ownership rules in 2002. However, the government's allusions to media ownership reform during 2005 did acknowledge the Commission's concern that media ownership reform should take place only as part of a holistic package of reform.

To gain a sense of the government's policy thinking, one can look to its attempts to introduce changes in 2002 and 2003. The government introduced legislation,

---

[130] *Ibid*, 364–66.
[131] Senator R Alston, 'Media Ownership', Door Stop Press Conference, 29 August 2001, http://www.dcita.gov.au/Article/0,,0_4-2_4008-4_16012,00.html, accessed 11 January 2002.

the Broadcasting Services Amendment (Media Ownership) Bill 2002 ('the 2002 Bill'), into Parliament in March 2002. However, when it became apparent that the Bill, even after amendments, was not going to be able to proceed through Parliament, it was laid aside in June 2003. A second Bill, the Broadcasting Services Amendment (Media Ownership) Bill 2002 [No 2] ('the No 2 Bill'), was introduced in November 2003, incorporating the previously agreed amendments, but debate on this Bill was adjourned and eventually lapsed when parliamentary elections were called. Apart from the odd ministerial reference, there was no policy process leading up to the introduction of the 2002 Bill. In fact, the Bill itself might be viewed as something of a Green Paper, because it was apparent that this draft legislation was to be used as a sort of testing of the waters. The government did not have control of the senate, the parliamentary Upper House, and so the Bill was useful as a means of ascertaining what might be acceptable, and what compromises might be necessary. That this was intended was clear from the government's decision that the Bill should proceed immediately to a senate committee (before debate in either House) in order to allow consultation.[132] The 2002 Bill did not remove the cross-media rules, but allowed instead offending mergers to be exempted from the rules if the parties obtained an exemption certificate from, now, the Australian Communications and Media Authority (ACMA).[133] The draft legislation provided that ACMA had to issue an exemption certificate if it was satisfied that the objective of editorial separation would be met, that is, each media operation would maintain 'separate editorial decision-making responsibilities'.[134] Editorial separation would be established by three tests which would require evidence of:

— separate editorial policies;
— appropriate organisational charts; and,
— separate editorial news management, news compilation processes, and news gathering and interpretation capabilities.[135]

Editorial separation did not prevent the sharing of resources or other forms of cooperation, so long as editorial separation was maintained.[136] The sharing of resources provision was to assist media proprietors to realise efficiencies from jointly owned organisations,[137] but one can envisage that it might also provide scope for undermining the editorial separation policy. If the same source materials are being used, the scope for diverse editorial and interpretative influences obviously becomes limited. In recognition of concerns about the provision of local and regional news and information programmes, regional radio and television

---

[132] P McGauran, House of Representatives, 21 March 2002, 1924.
[133] The references in the 2002 Bill and the No 2 Bill were, of course, to the regulator at that time, the Australian Broadcasting Authority, but to avoid confusion all references in this discussion will be to the ACMA.
[134] The 2002 Bill, sch 2, cl 4, to insert s 61F(1) into the BSA (Aus).
[135] P McGauran, House of Representatives, 21 March 2002, 1926.
[136] The 2002 Bill, sch 2, cl 4, to insert s 61F(3) into the BSA (Aus).
[137] P McGauran, House of Representatives, 21 March 2002, 1926.

licensees were to be required also to meet certain minimum levels for local news, weather, community service announcements, and emergency warnings.[138]

The second reading speech for the 2002 Bill set out the government's rationalisation for these reforms, which were essentially, and not surprisingly, that the rapidly changing communications environment provided much greater choice to the public, and that the current rules were anachronistic and impeded media operators taking advantage of investment opportunities.[139] Matters of pluralism and diversity were dealt with briefly: the government acknowledged that diversity of opinion was important, but did not consider that diversity of ownership was necessary to achieve this. The editorial separation test was seen as a means of ensuring that media proprietors did not exploit their position.[140] The government referred to this as a public interest test but, as public interest tests go, the editorial separation test did not bode well for the maintenance of diversity. It was clearly designed to minimise discretionary judgements, and was held up as providing certainty for industry.[141] Whilst certainty might be a desirable objective, the test risks promoting a checklist attitude towards compliance. Although the government emphasised the importance of monitoring, the record of the ACMA, or more precisely its predecessor, the ABA, was not likely to encourage confidence that there would be active and rigorous monitoring. This concern is heightened by the potential lack of transparency in the process for granting the exemption certificates, since commercial in confidence protection could be claimed for the information provided to obtain the certificate.[142]

The rejection of a wider public interest test, on the basis that this would provide too much discretion and uncertainty, limited the scope for more comprehensive protection against the effects of media concentration, which could be diffuse, and not easily categorised in pre-set rules or easy definitions. This is precisely why the area in need of protection might be best served by a more open, discretionary test. It should not automatically be assumed that a discretionary test is a less desirable form of regulation—it is rather a question of what is the appropriate tool for the matter to be regulated. The issue here is to protect the public interest, and thus the choice of regulatory tool should not be overly subservient to the demands of business. In any event, a discretionary test will still have appropriate administrative law protection built around it. The editorial separation test was seen as a more objective test which would avoid these perceived deficiencies.[143] It is also one which 'focuses on diversity of sources of information and opinion rather than plurality

---

[138] *Ibid*, 1926. The 2002 Bill, sch 2, cl 4, to insert s. 61R into the BSA (Aus).

[139] P McGauran, House of Representatives, 21 March 2002, 1924–77.

[140] *Ibid*, 1925.

[141] *Ibid*, 1926.

[142] Senate Environment, Communications, Information Technology and the Arts Legislation Committee, *Report on the Broadcasting Services Amendment (Media Ownership) Bill 2002* (June 2002), para 4.35, referring to submissions made by the Communications Law Centre.

[143] Explanatory Memorandum, Broadcasting Services Amendment (Media Ownership) Bill 2002, para 98.

of ownership'.[144] This is an interesting change of emphasis, particularly since content regulation has not been a strong element of the regulatory framework, and much would have to rest on the effectiveness of the editorial separation test. The Explanatory Memorandum to the 2002 Bill incorporated a regulatory impact statement, which also asserted that there was a need for change because existing cross-media regulation was inflexible, failing to take into account, or to allow for, changes in industry structure and differing levels of media influence.[145] Yet, it is not clear that the proposed reforms met this challenge. Only the traditional media would remain subject to the regime, and there was nothing in the proposed reforms which recognised different degrees of influence. The new rules would not, for example, have prevented a media company with extensive cross-media interests under the protection of an exemption certificate also acquiring interests in subscription television. In fact, it is reasonable to suspect, given the somewhat complacent attitude to broadcasting regulation in Australia, that the reforms, if they had succeeded, would have provided more or less a blank cheque for cross-media mergers, subject only to the restraints of competition law, which itself would be limited by the problems of market definition.

The Senate Committee made some recommendations to amend the 2002 Bill, mainly to provide further support for regional media, which the government accepted. In the main, the Senate Committee accepted readily the arguments used to support liberalisation of media ownership.[146] It seemed to acknowledge the argument put forward, mostly by the media industry, that consolidation could ensure greater diversity and quality, because obtaining a more optimum critical mass would enable media companies to be able to spend more on programming.[147] The Committee also asserted that, unlike other jurisdictions, the cross-media regulation was not being repealed; rather it was being varied by the exemption process. This seemed a weak argument, given that any media organisation which could satisfy the exemption process could hold cross-media interests. And, as noted, the effectiveness of the exemption process was dependent upon a robust regulatory system, an attribute not readily associated with the Australian broadcasting regulatory framework. In order to try and secure the Bill's passage through the senate, the government agreed to a variety of amendments, but the most significant was to add a further layer onto the application of the exemption certificate, with the use of a minimum number of voices test. Thus, the exemption certificate could only be granted if, after the merger, there would remain in the relevant licence area at least five separately controlled media groups in metropolitan markets and four in regional areas, although there were exemptions for remote areas. There was a further layer which prohibited a person controlling

---

[144] Explanatory Memorandum, Broadcasting Services Amendment (Media Ownership) Bill 2002, para 98.

[145] *Ibid*, paras 82–83.

[146] Senate Environment, Communications, Information Technology and the Arts Legislation Committee, above n 142, paras 2.2–2.10.

[147] *Ibid*, eg, paras 4.7–4.8.

more than two types of media (of the type covered by the cross-media rules) in the market. These provisions, although providing an additional layer of protection to the originally proposed exemption certificate process, are still relatively arbitrary, since they do not address differences in size of the media operations. Despite these concessions, the government was unable to push the Bill through, as opposition parties in the senate pushed for further amendments.

Although it is widely anticipated that the government will introduce legislation in 2006 to remove foreign ownership rules and cross-media rules, there has been no public policy-making process. Instead, likely directions have, on the whole, to be gleaned from newspaper articles and leaks. In the description of Australian ownership and control history in Chapter Three, the point was made that policy decisions were crudely arrived at, with media interests not shy to press their case with governments, and governments eager to appease powerful media proprietors. The picture does not seem to have changed greatly, and it says something about media policy in Australia that when Kerry Packer, head of one of the major, family-controlled, media groups, Publishing and Broadcasting Limited, died late in 2005, there was speculation that this could impact on the direction of the government's reforms. In late August 2005, the Minister for Communications, Senator Coonan, gave a major address in which she set out her thinking on media reform.[148] In one sense, the speech was typical fare, as she described the media revolution apparently taking place, with the predictable consequences for liberalisation of media regulation. However, her address was also important for two reasons. The first was that, in reviewing a variety of aspects of the media environment, she made it clear that she saw media ownership reform as part of a package of broader reforms. In this respect, she identified digital broadcasting, multichannelling, and the anti-siphoning provisions as areas which needed to be addressed if competition and new entrants were to be encouraged into the market, and new technologies to be properly exploited.[149] This, of course, was a recognition of the Productivity Commission's position. Secondly, the Minister gave some indication of her thinking on media ownership reform. As expected, foreign ownership rules would be removed. With regard to cross-media rules, the Minister suggested that new rules would allow cross-media mergers within a licence area, subject to a minimum number of voices, or media groups: four in regional markets, and five in mainland capital markets. This represents an adoption of one aspect of the 2002 Bill. The Minister made it clear that the reforms would apply only to the traditional media. Some form of the exemption certificate idea seemed likely to be retained, although no details were given.

To the extent that the Minister appeared willing to address some of the shibboleths of the Australian broadcasting environment, her approach was quite radical,

---

[148] Senator H Coonan, 'The New Multimedia World', Speech delivered to the National Press Club, Canberra, 31 August 2005, http://www.minister.dcita.gov.au/media/speeches/the_new_multimedia_world_-_address_to_the_national_press_club_-_canberra_-_31_august_2005, accessed 1 September 2005.

[149] *Ibid*, 3.

yet, soon after her speech, there were signs that the old ways of media policy-making were still to the fore with newspaper articles suggesting that the Prime Minister favoured 'plain vanilla' reforms—that is reforms just to media owner-ship—and that plans to reform digital broadcasting, anti-siphoning, and so forth, had been dropped.[150] Commenting on the reports, former Prime Minister, Paul Keating, the person who originally developed the cross-media reforms, wrote:

> The Government's apparent decision to close down any option for new free-to-air tele-vision outlets or multiple channels while removing the existing cross-media laws and foreign ownership restrictions is a recipe for massive media concentration and further abuses of power by the existing network owners.
>
> In effect, what the Government is proposing is to abandon everything the Productivity Commission said when it recommended that a change to the cross-media regulations could only be contemplated in the context of the wholesale issuance of new licences which would render any changed system more diverse.
>
> The fallback position for the Prime Minister and the Communications Minister, Senator Helen Coonan—to change the cross-media laws while opening the television spectrum to foreign ownership—is simply a policy designed to suit, principally, two operators only: the Packer-controlled Publishing and Broadcasting Limited and the Murdoch-controlled News Limited.
>
> Such a change would see the potential for the greatest and most unseemly concentra-tion of media in Australia's history. And if people think they have seen exercises in media power already, it will be as nothing like it may be should these two corporations have their way unfettered.[151]

If these reforms to media ownership proceed, then it is likely that there will be a significant increase in concentration throughout the Australian media environ-ment. In relation to broadcasting, this has to be assessed in the light also of a sec-tor where competition and development of new technologies has been artificially restricted, and where effective content regulation cannot be relied upon to ensure diversity in content or the maintenance of ethical standards in news and informa-tion services. It has been estimated that these reforms, if implemented, would halve the number of media operators in most markets.[152]

Reform Rhetoric

As can be seen from the discussion in the previous section, a strong driver for the reform process has been the growth in the availability of content which can be

---

[150] S Lewis, 'Howard reins in media reforms', *The Australian* (Sydney, 28 September 2005), http://www.theaustralian.news.com.au/printpage/0,5942,16745680,00.html, accessed 1 October 2005.

[151] P Keating, 'A crude end to cross-media laws signals a dangerous power trip', *Sydney Morning Herald* (Sydney, 29 September 2005), http://www.smh.com.au/news/opinion, accessed 1 October 2005.

[152] R Aedy, Interview with F Papandrea, ABC Radio National, *The Media Report* (17 November 2005), http://www.abc.net.au/rn/talks/8.30/mediarpt/stories/s1507658.htm, accessed 1 December 2005.

delivered across a variety of platforms, from the traditional over-the-air broad-casting, cable, and satellite delivery platforms to the new forms of content delivery such as the internet and mobile telephones. For those supporting change, or, more particularly, liberalisation of the media ownership rules, these developments have provided the case for radical change. Although industry might argue for complete removal of ownership regulation, governments and regulatory bodies have been reluctant to take this full step. It is questionable just how substantial this abundance of content and outlet is, and the impact of the so-called 'new media' will be considered in the next section.

Nevertheless, whatever the validity of the abundance claims for new media, they have had a substantial influence on the reform processes for all three jurisdictions. A further theme to rationalise reform is the idea that structural regulation—in the form of media ownership—no longer fits with the contemporary media environment, because it embraces only a limited set of the types of media now available. As such it is seen as lacking flexibility and not reflecting the true state of media availability, competition, and diversity. The regulatory response to this is intriguing, but similar across the three jurisdictions. None of the jurisdictions is prepared to remove ownership rules completely, and to rely solely upon general competition and merger law. The result has been, instead, the retention of rules, but substantially relaxed. However, it is not clear how relaxing the rules, and removing some of them, actually addresses the cited defects of the rules. If, it is the case as, for example, the UK government and the FCC asserted, that that the rules are outmoded but, at the same time, a necessary adjunct to general competition law, then it does not follow why liberalisation is the appropriate regulatory response. One of the limitations on the effectiveness of ownership rules has been the unwillingness of rule-makers to extend their reach, and to address issues of vertical integration. The result has been that despite the rules, powerful media groups have been able to develop through acquisition of other media operations which fall outside the rules. The debate in the UK on cross-media rules and on common ownership of Channels Three and Five was clearly influenced by the position occupied by Murdoch's News Corporation, with its control of satellite broadcasting and newspaper interests, and the prospect that the group might be able to gain control of a free-to-air service. In the US, 90 per cent of the top 50 cable networks are controlled by the same groups which own the broadcasting networks.[153] Relaxing or removing ownership rules does not address any of these situations, situations which have been allowed to arise through conscious regulatory choice.

Although the US and the UK adopted new approaches to ownership regulation, neither of these really addressed the arguments raised about the limitations of ownership regulation. In the US, the general approach to ownership reform was to relax thresholds. There was no attempt to adapt the rules to reflect the media environment beyond the traditional broadcasting media. Although the diversity

---

[153] T Turner, 'My Beef with Big Media: How government protects big media—and shuts out upstarts like me' (2005) 57 *Federal Communications Law Journal* 223 at 228.

index was an acknowledgement of new media, its approach to measurement of media influence was flawed. The UK tried to build in more flexibility—lack of flexibility being one of the criticisms—with the introduction of a public interest test, but this too was limited because it was limited in the type of media to which it could be applied. In effect, ownership rules are being forced into redundancy. There is a reluctant toleration for these rules, but it is clear that the space for this form of structural regulation is being narrowed. The problem relates back to the tendency to see the norm as the market. The lack of a normative approach means that structural regulation is viewed as something of an anomaly, and without a strong normative case, brings pressure for liberalisation.

A strong and common theme in the policy justifications was also the need to allow industry to take advantage of the efficiencies which this new media environment could provide. With such abundance of media and increased competition, it was asserted that allowing media operators to grow in size would enable economic efficiencies to be realised. This would ensure that the realised efficiencies would lead to increased spending on programming. Each of the jurisdictions seemed willing to make this claim, and, indeed, if one looks back to the history of media ownership reform in the US, it has been a long-standing basis for rule relaxation. Yet, the evidence to support this appears weak, and perhaps it would be surprising if the situation were otherwise. It is true that relaxing ownership rules usually leads to consolidation. The reforms initiated by the TA 1996 (US) led to a massive degree of consolidation. In the UK, the 2003 liberalisation of radio ownership rules has seen a similar pattern of consolidation. For the reasons discussed in Chapter Six, it is not surprising that consolidation does tend to result. However, what is less clear is why it should be expected that this consolidation will translate into increased expenditure and improved programming. Consolidation may well allow greater efficiencies to be realised, but there is no reason to expect that this will lead to something more than a return to investors. Indeed, the impact of consolidation may well have the opposite effect. One of the consequences of radio consolidation in the US has been the increasing use of automated programming which is distributed to the local channels, a practice also developing elsewhere. Although there has been an increase in format diversity (within geographic markets), many of these differentiated formats have playlists which overlap by around 76 per cent.[154] Consolidation clearly has implications for freedom of expression. In the US, one of the major radio companies, Clear Channel, which has grown massively as a result of relaxation of media rules, and owns around 1,200 channels, banned a rock group which criticised President Bush's policy on Iraq.[155] In fact, Clear Channel has come to represent to radio what Murdoch is to newspapers and satellite, and warnings about Clear Channel—'channelisation'—because of its

---

[154] Future of Music Coalition, 'Executive Summary, Radio Deregulation: Has it served its citizens and Musicians?', at http://www.futureofmusic.com/images//FMCradioexecsum.pdf (2002), cited in K Smith, 'The FCC Under Attack' (2003) *Duke Law and Technology Review* 19 at para 15.

[155] C Leanza and H Feld, 'More than a "Toaster with Pictures": Defending Media Ownership Limits' (2003) 21(3) *Communications Lawyer* 12 at 20.

operations in the US and in Australia, were often voiced during the parliamentary consideration of the 2003 UK reforms. In the absence of content regulation, which can have an impact on investment decisions in programming, there is little evidence of how consolidation will lead to better programming. Certainly, the evidence before the FCC seemed weak. It is noticeable also that the UK government used content regulation as a kind of surety against the impact of ownership liberalisation and industry consolidation.

Finally, the role of competition was seen as an important justification in the policy debates. Thus, it was argued that the growth in the ways to access media content and the increased need for content opened up the scope for new entrants to the market and greater competition. This competition would create its own diversity. Yet, this argument too seems vulnerable. It appears to contradict the previous rationalisation which encourages consolidation in order to generate economies of scale and scope. Further, as discussed in Chapter Six, the particular economic aspects of broadcasting and programme production exacerbate the tendency towards consolidation, with the result that the market will tend to try to close off new entrants. However, the promotion of competition to justify the relaxation of ownership rules has a different level of significance, because what it actually signals is that there has been a change in priority of regulatory measures. Media concentration is no longer constrained through a set of specific rules defining ownership limits; instead it is to be controlled through the operation of markets and the discipline of competition law. Of course, as is perfectly apparent in this study, none of the jurisdictions has removed ownership regulation completely, and, at least in the medium term, would probably find an attempt to do so politically unacceptable. However, as the balance between pre-emptive ownership regulation and competition law enforcement changes, ownership regulation is increasingly a regulatory option which has to be carved out, grudgingly, from what is perceived as the standard approach to regulation. With this comes also a shift in the policy language: as seen in this discussion, terms such as competition and efficiency must be fitted within the policy space, to sit alongside (or even to dominate) traditional public interest values used to justify specific regulation of media. The incorporation of the media public interest test into UK merger law might seem to argue against this, but too much should not be presumed. As Prosser has commented, there is no sense in which competition law incorporates a balancing exercise between competition issues and public interest issues (as he argues it once did, in the UK and even the US); instead, it is concerned with 'minimizing impediments to competition', whilst public interest considerations such as the media public interest test operate as ' limited exceptions to the general law'.[156]

---

[156] T Prosser, *The Limits of Competition Law: Markets and Public Services* (Oxford, Oxford University Press, 2005), 27. Prosser's book, which examines the relationship between competition law and public services, including broadcasting, is relevant to some of the issues raised in this study. For another relevant study, see, also, M Feintuck, *'The Public Interest' in Regulation* (Oxford, Oxford University Press, 2004).

Impact of a Changing Media Environment

In addressing the background to its decision to relax US media ownership rules, the FCC made the following statement:

> Today's media marketplace is characterized by abundance. The public is better informed, better connected, and better entertained than they were just a decade ago. Traditional modes of media (e.g., newspapers, television, radio) have greatly evolved since the Commission first adopted media ownership rules in 1941, and new modes of media have transformed the landscape, providing more choice, greater flexibility, and more control than at any other time in history. Today we can access news, information, and entertainment in many enhanced and non-traditional ways via: cable and satellite television, digital transmission, personal and portable recording and playback devices, handheld wireless devices, and perhaps the most extraordinary communications development, the Internet. In short, the number of outlets for national and local news, information, and entertainment is large and growing.[157]

This has been a common catch-cry, used by rule-makers across the three jurisdictions as a basis for questioning the justification for continued regulation of media ownership, even broadcasting regulation more generally. This can be seen in the policy deliberations and regulatory choices examined earlier in this chapter. And it is true that the public (although to a lesser extent in Australia) is no longer locked into the offerings of traditionally delivered media, but has a larger choice both of content and how content, whether information, opinion, or entertainment, is accessed. There are several, interconnected ways in which the impact of this new media abundance can be understood. First is the obvious fact that the public is not dependent upon buying a newspaper or sitting down before a television or radio to receive content. Much of this 'traditional' content can be accessed through other mechanisms, such as the internet, iPod-like devices, and mobile phones. Secondly, there is another sense in which content is now accessed differently. Because content can be accessed from a range of different platforms, there is no longer the same dependence upon a broadcasting schedule. Content and programmes can be 'pulled' from the internet, for example, when it is convenient. Even for those who may still make use of television as their primary access point, the prevalence of more sophisticated recording devices, such as personal video recorders (or digital video recorders), like TiVo, offers much greater flexibility in the way in which programmes are selected and received. Finally, there are differences in the structure and type of content which is being received. For example, whereas television programmes would be presented in regular time packages, such as a half-hour or one-hour programme, or newspapers would be purchased in complete editions, content which is being accessed via the internet, for example, might be single news items, or parts only of a programme, delivered in discrete

---

[157] FCC, *Report and Order and Notice of Proposed Rulemaking* (2003), above n 64, para 86.

components. New content is also being produced for these new delivery platforms: podcasting; mobicontent; and internet-originated content are certainly adding to the amount of content which is available, as well as the way in which content is being produced. Internet content, particularly, has generated a range of content which is outside the traditional professional production processes.

This changing environment has provided the impetus for the reforms which have been examined in this chapter, and elsewhere in this study. It has provided the rule-makers with a basis for rationalising their preference, express or implied, for less centralised regulation, a preference which is apparent in the deliberations of each of the three jurisdictions. For the UK and Australia, this changing environment has been, or will be, used as the backdrop to liberalisation of regulation, although there has been very little real investigation into the impact of this new media abundance, whilst the US attempt to do this, with its diversity index, relied on simplistic assumptions. If regulation is to promote and protect pluralism and diversity, then it is necessary to consider what effect these types of changes are likely to have on regulatory design. To some extent this is an unknown. Despite this changing media environment, there is still a heavy reliance on mainstream media, and the growing dimensions of the television screen may indicate that the public still views television as a primary source of content. Whilst the internet is now a well-established content source, it is still early days for the development of mainstream rivals, such as internet television and mobile content, and so it is difficult to envisage precisely what the media environment might be like in the medium to long term. Nevertheless, it is clear that there is change, and even the long-established, over-the-air broadcasting is undergoing change as digital technology increases its channel capacity and opens up interactive possibilities. Despite these uncertainties, there are some pointers which, confusingly, indicate on the one hand the necessity for change in regulatory approaches, and on the other hand the need for caution before too readily jettisoning existing regulation.

The UK, the US, and Australia have all cited the internet as a new source of content and a contributor to diversity, with the prospect of some of these other alternative platforms not far behind, which has diminished the need for regulation of the traditional media. However, this needs to be looked at more closely. First, there is the issue of the extent to which this content is new material. One of the weaknesses of the US diversity index was that it did not take into account the extensive degree of duplication, because the internet is another way to access material which is already available in newspapers or on radio, and to a degree, television. Podcasting can be seen in the same light, with mainstream over-the-air broadcasters quick to expand their audience reach by providing podcasts of their over-the-air content. As one advertising executive in Australia put it, 'It's just a giant recycling exercise. Yes, you can get the *Herald* [an Australian newspaper] via the website, SMS or iPod, but so what? That's not increasing diversity of information.'[158] If this seems

---

[158] J Porter and L Murray, 'New Media, Old Story', *Sydney Morning Herald* (Sydney), 28 January 2006, 27.

too cynical, it could be noted that the internet enables international content to be accessed, even though it might be duplicated. Thus, a person in Australia can access *The New York Times* or *The Guardian* via the internet much more easily than the paper versions. In this sense there can be said to be an increased diversity of content, although accessing international content may be less important than the ability to access a variety of sources of information and opinion on local matters. But when it is recalled that in the US the top 20 internet news sites are owned by the same corporate groups which control the broadcasting networks, cable networks, and major newspaper chains, it will be clear that duplication of content is likely to be a persistent feature of the internet.[159]

Thus, before liberalising broadcasting regulation, it is important to look closely at exactly how diversity is affected by the internet. It is true that the internet, and to an extent the facility for podcasting, has generated new content. This can range from the homespun blog and interest group websites to the more sophisticated forums or virtual magazines. Many of these may become important reference sites, or sources of additional comment, but in many cases, these sites, particularly the blogs, the amateur podcasts, and such like, will remain niche sites, lacking professional resources and news-gathering facilities.[160] Many of these sites may reflect a dissatisfaction with mainstream media, and certainly references have been made in this study to situations which would justify this discontent, but it has also been said, that

> the Internet is the 'ultimate vanity press' and it is afflicted with some of the same problems as the non-virtual version: the quality of editorial control, its capture by personal preferences and agendas, the ethics which guide publishing practices, and the issue of authenticating the status of the evidence it presents. The open access the Internet provides is both its benefit and its curse.[161]

Perhaps what is remarkable, given the rapid expansion and the ubiquity of the internet, is how few professional independent news and information sites there are. This might suggest that entry costs act as a barrier for the internet, just as much as they do for the traditional media. Although production of an online site may be relatively inexpensive, generation and production of news and current affairs content is likely to be comparable in cost to other media, and here also the established mainstream content providers will have an important advantage, because they will be able to exploit the extensive content resources already available to them.

---

[159] N Hickey, 'Power Shift' (2003) *Columbia Journalism Review*, March–April, 26–31, cited in AL Plamondon, 'Proposed Changes in Media Ownership Rules: A Study in Ventriloquism?' [2003] *Communication and the Law* 47 at 78.

[160] Comments reported from panel discussions at the ACMA Broadcasting Conference 2005 (2005–6) 4 *ACMASphere* 16.

[161] G Turner, *Ending the Affair: The Decline of Television Current Affairs in Australia* (Sydney, UNSW Press, 2005), 137, and citing T Flew, *New Media: An Introduction* (Melbourne, Oxford University Press, 2002), 99.

Similar issues arise with mobile content, which is a more recent development. Mobile content can be a repackaging of content already available through other media. Hence, in the UK, mobile phone users can download Sky Channels, and in Australia, sports coverage from one of the free-to-air broadcasters is available as well as channels from free-to-air or subscription television. Programmes, which have originated on television, are also being adapted for mobile phone viewing: *Big Brother* has been adapted for mobile delivery and, in other cases, mini-versions of programmes, often only a few minutes long, are being developed. New content is also being developed. In Australia, a comedy/drama which consisted of three, three-minute episodes weekly was available; the series was also interactive, so that viewer feedback determined the direction of the next episode.[162] Also being tri-alled is a new technology, digital video broadcasting—handheld (DVB-H), which allows more efficient broadcast of television signals over mobiles (and other hand-held devices), given the limitations of screen size and battery life.[163] However, although, at least in Australia, there appears to be a real demand for mobile con-tent, the extent to which it creates a new and substantial opportunity for content diversity seems again limited. It has been recognised that mobile content is seen as a 'filler', something to be used whilst people are away from home, but not as a substitute for mainstream media.[164] Apart from the incentives for established media to exploit repackaging opportunities, the 'filler' role of mobile content might discourage significant investment in content.

The growth in uptake of broadband has made more feasible delivery of video programming via the internet. Internet television, known as Internet Protocol TV (IPTV) is likely to become more established over the next few years, although there remain technical issues about its delivery.[165] Delivered as it is via broadband, it is of particular interest to telecommunications operators keen to bundle telephony, the internet, and video.[166] This bundling, known as 'triple play', highlights again the problems of limited media ownership rules, and the dependency upon com-petition regulation to address the gatekeeper problems which might arise. Australia's major telecommunications company, Telstra, which has a 50 per cent stake in the main Australian subscription television service, Foxtel, has been an earlier purchaser of content for an IPTV project. Another Australian telecommun-ications operator and internet provider, Primus, has tried to negotiate content

---

[162] R Yiacoumi, 'TV to go', *Sydney Morning Herald* (Sydney), 22–23 October 2005, Icon, 3.

[163] BBC News, 'Major UK mobile TV trial starts' (22 September 2005), http://news.bbc.co.uk/go/pr/fr/-/1/hi/technology/4271474.stm, accessed 1 October 2005.

[164] Comments reported from panel discussions at the ACMA Broadcasting Conference 2005, above n 160, 10. A survey in the UK, however, reported that British mobile phone users were not interested in mobile phone content: C Marriner, 'TV on mobiles proves a turn-off', *Guardian* (London), 7 November 2005, http://technology.guardian.co.uk/print/0,3858,5327275-117802,00.html, accessed 20 December 2005.

[165] Comments reported from panel discussions at the ACMA Broadcasting Conference 2005, above n 160, 10.

[166] P McIntyre, 'Tension Grows as telecom's take up Internet TV', *Sydney Morning Herald* (Sydney), 21 April 2005, 29.

agreements with the free-to-air networks.[167] However, it has been suggested that IPTV is unlikely to 'drive a market'; instead, it will be more likely to be an alternative delivery mechanism.[168] Its attractions will be interactivity, and the capacity for viewers to access content in their own time, but its content may also be mostly duplication of content available on other platforms.

This brief review of 'new media modes' is a reminder of the need to exercise caution when speaking of the changing media environment. First, it is important not to confuse diversity of access with diversity of content. Secondly, it is important to look closely at the extent to which the content being delivered over these new delivery platforms represents new content, or merely the repackaging of content available elsewhere. Of course, it might be argued that having a variety of delivery platforms available will open up opportunities for new entrants keen to access platforms for content delivery. But, again, caution is needed, and it is necessary to be mindful of past practices of media and communications companies, which have shown a voracious appetite for gaining control over as many points of the content and distribution chain as possible. As Ted Turner, the founder of CNN, has commented:

> Today, the only way for media companies to survive is to own everything up and down the media chain—from broadcast and cable networks to the sitcoms, movies, and news broadcasts you see on those stations; to the production studios that make them; to the cable, satellite, and broadcast systems that bring the programs to your television set; to the Web sites you visit to read about those programs; to the way you log onto the Internet to view those pages. Big media today wants to own the faucet, pipeline, water, and the reservoir.[169]

The failure of media ownership regulation to adapt to changes in the media environment, the limitations of competition law, and the natural tendencies of the industry to seek economies of scale and scope mean that a degree of scepticism must be maintained about the extent to which the market will provide the appropriate protection for the goals of pluralism and diversity.

Although it has been suggested that the new media environment, whatever its true impact, does not remove the case for regulation, it does require a rethinking of how broadcasting is regulated, and a consideration of the connection between regulation and the electronic media, in its broader sense.[170] If regulation is about ensuring that the media are able to serve the public sphere then, as new ways of accessing and using content develop and become established, it is important that regulation remains appropriate to the policy objectives. A couple of illustrations

---

[167] *Ibid*, 29.

[168] Comments reported from panel discussions at the ACMA Broadcasting Conference 2005, above n 160, 10.

[169] T Turner, above n 158, 227.

[170] For a consideration of this area in the US context, see EP Goodman, 'Media Policy Out of the Box: Content Abundance, Attention Scarcity, and the Failures of Digital Markets' (2004) 19 *Berkeley Technology Law Journal* 1389.

can be given here. One issue which arises, as new ways of delivering content develop, is what content should be regulated. IPTV is a good example to use here, because it may become the most television-like outlet, although the same difficulties arise in relation to content distributed by other means. The likelihood is that services like IPTV will not fall under the established regimes for regulating content, and yet the content and format being transmitted could be very similar to the content being delivered over traditional broadcasting. If, for example, it is expected that news programmes broadcast via television and radio should comply with certain obligations—for example, in relation to disclosure of commercial relationships—it is difficult to see why a news programme delivered via a mobile phone or via IPTV should be able to bypass such regulatory obligations. As examples from Australia and the US discussed in Chapter Four showed, commercial influences on content production are clearly present, and can distort the information and opinion being provided to the public. As the media ownership reforms have also shown, there are those who would argue that the content available via new delivery platforms will ensure that the public has access to a new diversity of content, views, and opinions, thereby removing the need for traditional forms of broadcasting regulation. Yet, if this 'new' content is to have such an important role to play, then it must surely be equally important that the integrity of that content can be assured. Yet, the three jurisdictions face difficulties under current regulatory frameworks in asserting jurisdiction over such content. In Australia, for example, the merging of regulators to form the ACMA has not solved this problem, because there remain two separate regulatory frameworks governing broadcasting and telecommunications. Thus, something like IPTV is unlikely to fall within the definition of a 'broadcasting service' under the Broadcasting Services Act 1992 (BSA (Aus)), which, although intended to be technology-neutral, excludes, inter alia, services which make programmes available 'on demand on a point-to-point basis, including a dial-up service'.[171] It may be that the Telecommunications Act 1997 would have jurisdiction, but there is very little specific regulation of content under that regime.[172] Similarly, there appear to be doubts as to whether the Comms Act (UK) could claim jurisdiction over content delivered via these other means.[173]

The European Commission has proposed that the EU Television Directive should be extended to include what it describes as non-linear content. The Commission distinguishes between linear and non-linear content, the former being regularly scheduled television content, whether delivered via traditional

---

[171] BSA (Aus), s 6(1). There is also a ministerial determination which states that a service providing radio and television programmes delivered over the internet is not a broadcasting service: Determination under paragraph (c) of the definition of 'broadcasting service' (No 1 of 2000).

[172] For a fuller discussion of these issues, see N Abrahams and G Stubbs, 'Legal Issues Arising from IPTV' (2005) 24(3) *Communications Law Bulletin* 14.

[173] R Hooper, 'Content Regulation in the Multiplatform Multichannel Digital Age', Speech delivered at the 'Regulation in a Convergent Environment' Hong Kong Broadcasting Authority and Office of Telecommunications Authority Seminar, Hong Kong, 29 August 2005, http://www.ofcom.org.uk/media/speeches/2005/08/hk, accessed 11 September 2005.

television platforms or over the internet or mobile phones, whilst the latter will be content which the viewer can 'pull' on demand. Thus, the linear/non-linear distinction can be seen to reflect the push/pull characterisation which is often drawn to distinguish between traditional broadcasting, which is 'pushed' to audiences, and online services, which are 'pulled' by the user.[174] The Commission's intention is not that all aspects of the Television Directive should extend to non-linear services, but that there should be certain minimum standards. Under the proposal, non-linear services would be subject to a basic set of rules, such as those aimed at protecting minors and preventing incitement to racial hatred. It is not intended to cover 'blog-like' content; but is designed for commercial services which provide visual content to the general public, in order to inform, entertain, or educate. Nor is it intended to cover radio or newspaper content which appears online.[175] The proposed rules, except in relation to a requirement to promote the production of and access to European works, do not cover the type of regulatory concerns affecting content addressed in this study, but do raise the question of whether some of the regulatory measures examined in Chapter Four, particularly, perhaps, those which relate to the integrity of news and information content, should be considered for non-linear services. There might be differences in the degree of regulation, which could take into account the different ways in which linear and non-linear content is used; for example, the fact that the user has greater control over whether or not to view non-linear content—when, how much, and so forth. In other words, there could be tiers of regulation in the manner of content regulation under the Comms Act (UK).

Of course there are difficulties which are likely to beset the European Commission's proposal too. An obvious challenge will be jurisdictional, given the potential for the internet especially to move beyond jurisdictional boundaries. Definitional problems, and changing technologies and modes of exploitation of these technologies, could also make it difficult to ensure that the regulation 'bites' as intended. However, this is the sort of problem which is not new to the communications sector. Perhaps the biggest difficulty facing a proposal to extend regulation to non-linear content would be resistance. Just as there has been resistance to extending media ownership regulation beyond the traditional mainstream media, so it is likely that an extension of content regulation would be similarly resisted. The inclination, as the discussion in this chapter has shown, is for removing regulation, not extending it. Resistance is, of course, to be expected from industry, but it can be found in other quarters. The UK government has already expressed the view that the European Commission's proposals are unnec-

---

[174] The terms 'lean-back' and 'lean-forward' are also used to draw this type of distinction.

[175] Proposal for a Directive of the European Parliament and of the Council Amending Council Directive 89/552/EEC on the coordination of certain provisions laid down by law, regulation or administrative action in Member States concerning the pursuit of television broadcasting activities, COM (2005) 646/final, Art 1(a). See, also, European Commission, *The Commission Proposal for a Modernisation of the Television Without Frontiers Directive: Frequently Asked Questions*, Memo/05/475 (13 December 2005).

essary and unworkable.[176] It is noticeable also that the opposition from the UK government is one which is rationalised, in part, on the need not to impede competition and market growth, and on the basis that the reduction in spectrum scarcity lessens the need for regulation.[177] The UK government's reaction to this proposal is one which would probably be found also in the US and in Australia. The reluctance of these jurisdictions to engage fully with the regulatory implications of pluralism and diversity, and the UK government's conversion to deregulatory endeavours make it unlikely that there will be any serious consideration of the role providers of new forms of content and/or means of delivery will play in the public sphere, and the responsibilities which should be assumed, beyond the mantra-like assumption that abundance equals diversity. Here, again, the poverty of a normative case for the role of media is apparent.

Another illustration points to a different kind of tension affecting established policy and regulation, and it relates also to the different ways in which the changing media are having an impact. As discussed elsewhere in this study, the ability of the public to access a wide range of programming has been seen as an important component of diversity. This objective has been sought through a variety of regulatory means, and across the jurisdictions, with differing degrees of intervention. The UK, with its long tradition of public service broadcasting, has been the most interventionist, whilst Australia and, especially, the US have focused on structural solutions. Yet, this objective has relied on certain assumptions about the way in which media, particularly television, operates; for example, scheduled programmes have meant that there were predictable patterns of viewing, with regard to times and programmes, and identifiable categories of audiences. Content obligations of broadcasters depended partly for their effectiveness on such assumptions. The US Prime Time Access Rule, discussed in Chapter Five, was an example of a rule which could work because of these assumptions. However, these assumptions have broken down as channel capacity increases, and the public develops increasing control over what content is accessed, and when and how. Even if much of this content is merely duplication of content available through another source, the relationship between content provider, content, and recipient has clearly changed. Another pressure on programming arises from the increased competition for advertising (and, indeed, subscription) revenue. UK public service broadcasting was formerly able to rely upon a relatively stable and controlled advertising fund, alongside a predictable audience size and pattern, which could enable investment in programming. However, this has broken down, and expectations of UK public service obligations are steadily diminishing.

Thus, the pressures occasioned by the changing relationship with the media environment, also have to be factored into any consideration as to how regulatory measures, structural or content-based, can help to achieve programme and

---

[176] J Purnell (Creative Industries Minister), 'Lessons for EU Regulation: How Does the Revised TVWF Directive Affect Competitiveness?', Speech delivered at the Foreign Policy Centre Seminar, London, 26 January 2006.

[177] *Ibid*, paras 36–37, 61, 65–67, and generally.

content diversity. In the longer term, it may become necessary to reconsider the idea that certain broadcasters can be simply identified as the public service broadcasters who will provide the desired programming range across an identified set of channels. In fact, the BBC could be said to have already moved beyond this: although its core public service 'business' remains its free-to-air television and radio services, it has extended its public service responsibilities to online content. Nevertheless, there is a larger challenge than this if it is thought to be important, as this study has argued, to ensure that there is available programming which can meet a wide range of interests and needs beyond those which might be easily able to attract the largest audience. Whether it is entertainment or news or current affairs programming, the maintenance of such programming will remain important. Under the traditional media model, and with secure funding, it was important that a range of broadcast services were obliged to provide diversity of programming. To confine such obligations to one or two channels—for example, the public broadcasters—risked ghettoisation of content, which could itself impede the quality of the diversity offered, and provide only minimal exposure. There could also be access concerns if certain types of content were available only by subscription. However, as the traditional model breaks down, it may be necessary to rethink the way in which diversity of programming is achieved, and investment in programming encouraged.

One model which has been suggested is a type of obligation-trading model. This was considered by the US Advisory Committee on Public Interest Obligations of Digital Television Broadcasters.[178] The Committee recognised that despite an expansion in the number of broadcasting stations, which would expand even further with digital technology, market forces could not be relied upon to generate some programmes which would meet public interest expectations, and children's educational programming and local content were cited as examples.[179] It suggested that a 'play-or-pay' model could be adopted, whereby broadcasters could be given the choice of maintaining public interest obligations or paying a share of revenue to bypass these obligations. The funds paid could be used to subsidise the provision of such programming by the non-commercial broadcasters.[180] The model was not unanimously recommended by the Committee: some members saw it as undermining 'the ethos of public trusteeship on which broadcasting had been built', whilst others raised the issue of ghettoisation if public interest programming was to be confined to the non-commercial services.[181] The model suggested by the Advisory Committee is still concentrated on traditional broadcasters, but there is no reason why it has to be confined to them. It might have had more potential if it had developed the model across a broader sector of the media environment and provided the opportunity for other broadcasters, commercial

---

[178] Advisory Committee on Public Interest Obligations of Digital Television Broadcasters, *Final Report: Charting the Digital Broadcasting Future* (Washington, 18 December 1998).

[179] *Ibid*, 24 and 27–30.

[180] *Ibid*, 65.

[181] *Ibid*.

and non-commercial, or other content providers, to assume these responsibilities. Nevertheless, there is something unattractive about the idea of broadcasters being able to trade in their obligations, particularly when such obligations are seen to have a strong public interest role, even taking into account the more limited US public interest responsibilities. There is also the likelihood that off-loading obligations would be the privilege of the wealthy broadcasters; ironically so, perhaps, because it might be these broadcasters who could most afford to invest in public interest programming.

A different approach has been suggested by Ofcom, one which moves beyond the traditional media, and tries to deal with what it considers to be the non-sustainability of the traditional public service broadcasting model and the vulnerability of certain types of programming. Ofcom has proposed the establishment of a Public Service Publisher (PSP), which would commission content from independent producers, and then act as a publisher by arranging the content's distribution across a range of distribution systems, including broadband and mobile telephony, but also terrestrial television, cable, and satellite.[182] A particular role for the PSP would be to exploit the opportunities for interactivity and on-demand access to content, and the scope for content to be adapted across different platforms.[183] Ofcom's intention is that the PSP would be operated as a non-profit body, and that it would receive public funding for its operations. The concept is an interesting one because it represents an attempt to preserve the values of public service broadcasting, and to extend them to the new media opportunities, in circumstances where it would not be feasible or, probably, acceptable, simply to expect that the traditional public service regulatory model could somehow be extended. The establishment of the PSP could also lessen the ghettoisation risk that public service programming would be increasingly confined to the public broadcasters, particularly the BBC. It ensures another source for diversity, and lessens the danger that certain content could be effectively under monopoly control. Ofcom's motivation for proposing that the PSP's activities be funded from public funds, rather than advertising revenue, was designed to provide greater revenue certainty, as well to avoid the problems associated with advertising-funded content.[184] However, reliance on public funding brings with it the risk of a constant squeeze on funding levels, and might also bring greater pressure on BBC funding. In the responses to Ofcom's proposal, there was some scepticism about whether public funding would be forthcoming.[185] Some responses, particularly from existing broadcasters, also suggested that the idea of the PSP was unnecessary and could damage existing public service broadcasters, and that instead a fund

---

[182] The proposal is discussed in Ofcom, *Ofcom Review of Public Service Television Broadcasting: Phase Two—Meeting the Digital Challenge* (2004) ('Phase Two Report'), paras 6.33–6.55, and Ofcom, *Ofcom Review of Public Service Television Broadcasting: Phase Three—Competition for Quality* (2005) ('Phase Three Report'), ch 5.

[183] Phase Three Report, above n 182, paras 5.2 and 5.4.

[184] Phase Two Report, above n 182, para 6.41.

[185] Phase Three Report, above n 182, para 5.14.

could be used to support existing public service broadcasters.[186] However, the problem with this is that it is likely to entrench public service content within the mainstream media culture, whereas the PSP model from the outset need have no such loyalties. On the other hand, there is a risk that, if the PSP has to spread its content fund across all delivery platforms, public service content will be diluted, particularly if the obligations of the traditional public service broadcasters are being rolled back at the same time. This is a real risk, particularly given changed public attitudes about the role of public funding generally, but it has to be assessed in the light of another risk, namely that the public service broadcasting model is eventually dismantled. There are already signs of this, as broadcasters renegotiate their obligations with Ofcom. In such a scenario, some remnants of the public service model might remain, but they would probably be confined to a weakened BBC. Whilst public policy preferences are for competition and market solutions, the pressures on the continued existence of the public service model will be strong. The PSP model at least offers a way to respond to these pressures, as well as taking into account the reality of a changing media environment.

Closing Comments

This study has argued that the media has an important public interest role to play in the community. Such an assertion is not new; the examination of policy debates in this chapter has shown that a public interest role for the media is cited in public discussions about the basis for regulation of broadcasting. However, as Chapter Two argued, the public interest case usually made for broadcasting has been essentially a negative one, which has made the case for regulation vulnerable. This case, caught up with trying to explain the differential treatment of broadcasting and the press, has focused on spectrum scarcity, mainly as a means of justifying regulation of broadcasting. As spectrum scarcity declines in importance, making a case for the continued regulation of broadcasting has become increasingly difficult, especially in the light of the clear preference displayed by the three jurisdictions for market solutions and less government regulation. As the examination, in this chapter, of the policy debates has shown, the absence of a distinctive voice for the public interest means that it is more likely to be subsumed by other policy agendas. Instead, this study has argued that it is possible to make a normative case for the regulation of the media based on the importance of the media's—commercial and public—role within the public sphere. The media's role in facilitating public debate is a crucial one; the media might be seen as a trustee of the public sphere, of public debate. Such trusteeship arises not because of access to spectrum or public airwaves, but because the media seek to have a public voice. However, for the media's contribution to the public sphere to be a positive one, for it to fulfil its

---

[186] Phase Three Report, above n 182, para 5.13.

obligations as trustee, it will be essential that attention is given to the way in which the media are structured and operate. Recognition of media's contribution to the public sphere provides, therefore, a foundation for determining an appropriate regulatory design. Although it was suggested in Chapter Two that this is an approach which should inform thinking about the press and broadcasting, this study has concentrated on broadcasting, because this is the area where most regulatory attention has been, and is, focused. A separate debate might be had about current approaches to the press, but it is one which is outside this examination.

This study has argued that if the media are to contribute to the public sphere, pluralism and diversity need to be both promoted and protected, and three main types of broadcasting regulatory activity have been examined: structural; content; and, competition regulation. Each of these regulatory categories is necessary and complementary, both in design and operation. It might be thought that this study has been backward-looking, too focused on old regulation and old media, too focused on describing an environment which no longer exists. Putting aside whether it is right to make these characterisations—old media, old regulation— this focus has been deliberate. The difficulties which have attended the justification for broadcasting regulation, the lack of a positive case for regulation, and the sensitive nature of such regulation, have often skewed the understanding and analysis of the role played by broadcasting regulation, and the role it should play. This is certainly the case now as reform is pushed within the three jurisdictions; it is a process which is ongoing, even in the UK, where Ofcom will have an influential role in shaping the regulatory environment. The media environment is certainly changing, from a rapid increase in the number of channels available to new ways to access and use content, and these changes are driving, conveniently perhaps, reform of broadcasting regulation. The nature of this reform appears to be about dismantling; in other words, the media environment has rendered broadcasting regulation redundant, or increasingly so, and the only regulatory question which needs to be asked is how soon this regulatory apparatus can be dismantled. This is, no doubt, to put the issue too simplistically, for it is clear that the three jurisdictions are likely to retain aspects of traditional broadcasting regulation for some time. Nevertheless, the current policy environments are such that the implicit question is one about dismantlement, even if, for practical or political reasons, such a process might not occur. In the context of a changing media environment, it is suggested that there are two important questions for policy-makers: what impact should the changes to the media environment have on the broadcasting regulatory framework, and how should that framework be reshaped to incorporate the new. What the discussion in this chapter seems to show is that this second question is not really being asked at all, whilst answers to the first question seem shaped by a presumption that change means removal or relaxation of rules. To answer the questions, several steps are required: an understanding of how broadcasting regulation has been designed and operated; an understanding of what impact this changing media environment is actually having; and when that is clear, a consideration of the regulatory changes which may need to be made to accommodate these changes in a way which will reflect old and new media, and enable the media environment as a whole (or, at least, the electronic media) to serve the public sphere.

In relation to the first step, Chapters Three, Four, and Five examined a range of broadcasting pluralism regulatory measures. Chapter Three examined structural regulation, with a focus on ownership and control regulation. As discussed, structural regulation is a sensitive area, whether the focus is sectoral pluralism or ownership and control regulation. Sectoral pluralism is a good example of why a positive case for broadcasting regulation is important. As discussed in this chapter, governments have an uneasy relationship with public broadcasters; even the more marginal public broadcasting sector in the US has not been free of political pressure. The demise of spectrum scarcity becomes a convenient hook for questioning the continuing role of public broadcasting: with so much abundance, the market can now provide. However, having differently constituted and funded media outlets can bring diversity to the media environment which may not be possible if all media outlets are commercial ventures, funded by advertising or even subscription. The review of economic factors in Chapter Six suggests that the demise of spectrum scarcity will not remove completely some of the difficulties of broadcasting and programme production. It was argued in Chapter Two that the media could play a more effective role within the public sphere if they were structured in a way which ensured that their activities were not completely dependent upon either state or economic power. The illustrations provided in Chapter Four about commercial influence on broadcasting should act as a warning to those who would advocate that public broadcasting is no longer necessary.

The examination of ownership and control regulation in Chapter Three, with its account of each jurisdiction's regulatory history, may have sorely tested the reader's forbearance, but given the political and industry focus on this area, it is important to understand the arguments and decisions which have shaped this area in order to evaluate properly the case now being made for reform. For example, one of the key arguments used by each of the jurisdictions to justify reform has been that ownership and control rules are not suited to the new media environment, because they apply only to the traditional mainstream media. Rather than using this as the basis for considering how they might be adapted, this seems instead to provide the excuse for relaxation or removal. Yet, an examination of the regulatory history shows that the weaknesses of current ownership and control regulation are the product of earlier decisions. This might seem self-evident, but what is important is that very often those decisions were not based on well-reasoned grounds, but were the result of choices made to accommodate particular interest groups. The resulting regulatory choices often created pressures for further change, as is likely to be the case in the current round of reforms. Thus, before condemning ownership rules as inadequate, it is important to be able to determine whether those weaknesses are inherent or contrived. It is true, as Chapter Three examined, that ownership rules are problematic. They can be difficult to design in a way which provides a reasonable degree of certainty, but also manages to cover a range of varying control situations. The link often made between ownership and voice is also tenuous but, as also asserted in Chapter Three, there is a place for such rules, because it is important that the media as participants in, and facilitators of, public discourse should not have monopoly control over that space. In the current policy climate, it would be unrealistic to expect that ownership regulation is likely to be revised in a way which might strengthen or broaden the scope of the rules, but a better case needs to be made than the ones reviewed in this chapter for the dismantling of such rules.

Content regulation has had less focus in the recent regulatory debates, with the exception of the UK but, as examined in Chapter Four, it can also have an important role in helping to shape an environment so that the public is able to have access to a range of content, information, and views. That chapter also emphasised the role which content regulation can play in ensuring that the public is able to trust the information and content which is provided. Although all aspects of the communications regulatory regime were up for discussion, the UK reforms have left in place most of the key rules considered in Chapter Four, although there are signs—for example, with the proposal to reform the EU Television Directive—that some of the areas considered in that chapter might be relaxed. However, there has been a change in the style of regulation; for example, in relation to the way in which public service obligations are monitored, and the move towards greater use of self- or co-regulation. This study has not sought to argue that the only model for broadcasting regulation is one based on centralised government or regulatory agency action; it is clear that a range of regulatory models might be appropriate. However, Chapter Four does illustrate the need to ensure that the regulatory tool chosen is effective. This can be seen in relation to the use of a co-regulatory model in Australia for much of content regulation, and its lack of effective monitoring and enforcement, and the US shows the need, when responsibility is in the hands of a statutory regulatory authority, for active monitoring of rule compliance. It is significant that the weaknesses of both of these jurisdictions have been most prominent in the area of commercial influence on broadcasting: this should serve as a warning to the UK as it contemplates further content reform.

An increasingly important area for regulation was seen in Chapter Five, which examined the use of competition law to regulate a complex and multi-dimensioned media environment. Measures which ensure that the market is not distorted by anti-competitive behaviour or subject to monopoly power abuse can be beneficial for pluralism and diversity. The use of a public interest test in merger situations offers a useful way forward. It can overcome some of the limitations of ownership regulation and merger law, and offer flexibility as new and unanticipated media combinations arise. However, in this respect, the UK's public interest test is not a satisfactory model, because it has failed to take up this opportunity given that, save in exceptional circumstances, it is applicable only to situations which were previously covered by the ownership regime. The application of general competition law will also have its limitations, because enforcement will usually require lengthy and complex investigations, by which time the market may have been damaged and competitors deterred. However, as Chapter Five showed, the use of ex ante competition rules is an important tool for the media sector. They can address situations which structural regulation has not, and they avoid some of the problems associated with general law enforcement. However, here, too, the effectiveness of the regulatory process and enforcement powers will be crucial. Ex ante rules will often depend heavily upon commercial negotiations for their realisation, and it will be essential that there are appropriate back-up powers.

Each of these regulatory approaches—structural, content, and competition—can have a role to play in promoting pluralism and diversity. They each have weaknesses, but to an extent the weaknesses in one approach can be compensated by other regulatory areas. These approaches are under pressure; the preference for market solutions and 'light regulation' make each regulatory approach vulnerable. This has been seen with structural regulation, and it can be seen too with content regulation, even though recent media practices, particularly in the US and Australia, might indicate that content regulation has a growing importance. Even within competition regulation, the use of ex ante measures is tolerated only to the extent that the market and general competition law enforcement cannot provide. These pressures and the traditionally weak case for regulation of broadcasting mean that it is difficult to guarantee that regulatory approaches to broadcasting are given the depth of consideration they require. Of course, as seen in this chapter, another pressure for change comes from the conviction that traditional regulation is increasingly unnecessary, because the changing media environment has brought with it an abundance of media. Thus, the regulation-we-had-to-have, because of spectrum scarcity, is no longer necessary. This, of course, is the negative case for regulation being brought into play. A positive case would argue that the abundance does not remove the case for regulation; instead, as suggested above, the question must be what regulatory response is necessary to ensure that the current media environment is able to contribute to the public sphere. For the reasons discussed in Chapter Six, reliance on the market may not be the appropriate regulatory response. Although the advocates for change, including the rule-makers considered in this study, have eagerly embraced this new media abundance, it would be wise to be cautious, before using this as the basis for unravelling regulation. As this chapter has discussed, this apparent abundance, both of content and delivery, may not, as yet, be providing the public with significant new content or new outlet providers.

To urge caution is not to deny that the media environment is changing, and that the public's use of media is also changing. However, this does not make the traditional media or regulation irrelevant, what it means is that the current regulatory framework must be constantly reassessed and adapted. As this study would argue, that process of reassessment should be premised on the role the media play within the public sphere. Thus, the discussion would no longer be about broadcasting regulation or broadcasting pluralism (as that term has been used in this study), it would be about media pluralism (although, unfortunately, without reference to the press). It may be that structural regulation, at least in the form of ownership and control rules, will have a diminishing role, especially because the form it takes has been so greatly influenced by previous regulatory choices. For this reason, the development of a public interest test, alhough not one confined to 'old' media, could be valuable. Content regulation will also have to be re-examined. Old ways of ensuring programming range and diversity may not be effective in the future. This chapter has briefly looked at some other approaches. The Ofcom PSP model has the advantage of targeting content whether delivered traditionally or by new technologies, although there may be issues of funding and marginalisation. The integrity of content is an issue which will remain of importance regardless of how content is accessed. The European Commission has begun to think about this in relation to other content matters, but finding ways to ensure the integrity of linear and non-linear content may be one of the most important future policy and regulatory tasks. Finally, competition regulation is likely to have an ongoing and growing role, given the degree of concentration and vertical integration. Assessing the future role for regulation of media is a complex process, not one likely to be attractive to governments keen to keep media onside. Faced with media which seem, often, to offer little more than the trivial and the trashy, it is easy to lose sight of the seriousness of the role which the media is called upon to play. However, it was suggested in Chapter One that there is a renewed need for the media's role as a provider of trusted and independent information. Assessing the role for regulation of media is an important task, however undesired, but so too is the role of the media—old and new.

SELECT BIBLIOGRAPHY

Media Policy and Regulation

General (including comparative)

E M Barendt, *Broadcasting Law: A Comparative Study* (Oxford, Clarendon Press, 1995)

R Craufurd Smith, *Broadcasting Law and Fundamental Rights* (Oxford, Clarendon Press, 1997)

J Curran, *Media and Power* (London, Routledge, 2002)

D Goldberg, T Prosser & S Verhulst (eds), *Regulating the Changing Media: A Comparative Study* (Oxford, Clarendon Press, 1998)

W Hoffmann-Riem, *Regulating Media: The Licensing and Supervision of Broadcasting in Six Countries* (New York, The Guilford Press, 1996)

P Humphreys, *Mass Media and Media Policy in Western Europe* (Manchester, Manchester University Press, 1996)

United Kingdom

E Barendt & L Hitchens, *Media Law: Cases and Materials* (Harlow, Longman, 2000)

R H Coase, *British Broadcasting: A Study in Monopoly* (London, Longmans, Green and Co, 1950)

J Curran & J Seaton, *Power without Responsibility: The Press, Broadcasting, and New Media in Britain* (London, Routledge, 6th ed., 2003)

M Feintuck, *Media Regulation, Public Interest and the Law* (Edinburgh, Edinburgh University Press, 1999)

T Gibbons, *Regulating the Media* (London, Sweet & Maxwell, 2nd ed., 1998)

United States

K C Creech, *Electronic Media Law and Regulation* (Burlington, MA, Focal Press, 4th ed., 2003)

J Lichtenberg (ed.), *Democracy and the Mass Media* (Cambridge, Cambridge University Press, 1990)

R McChesney, R Newman & B Scott (eds), *The Future of Media: Resistance and Reform in the 21st Century* (New York, Seven Stories Press, 2005)

W Overbeck, *Major Principles of Media Law* (Belmont, CA, Thomson Wadsworth, 15th ed., 2004)

J D Zelezny, *Communications Law: Liberties, Restraints, and the Modern Media* (Belmont, CA, Thomson Wadsworth, 4th ed., 2004)

Australia

T Barr, *Newmedia.com.au: The Changing Face of Australia's Media and Communications* (St Leonards, Allen & Unwin, 2000)

A Brown, *Commercial Media in Australia: Economics, Ownership, Technology, and Regulation* (St Lucia, University of Queensland Press, 1986)

J Given, *Turning off the Television: Broadcasting's uncertain future* (Sydney, UNSW Press, 2003)

P Leonard & A Henderson, *Communications Law and Policy in Australia* (Sydney, LexisNexis, 1987, looseleaf)

R Manne (ed.), *Do Not Disturb: Is the Media Failing Australia* (Melbourne, Black Inc, 2005)

Productivity Commission, *Broadcasting,* Report No. 11 (Canberra, AusInfo, 2000)

G Turner, *Ending the Affair: The Decline of Television Current Affairs in Australia* (Sydney, UNSW Press, 2005)

Specific Topics

Freedom of Expression

E Barendt, *Freedom of Speech* (Oxford, Oxford University Press, 2nd ed., 2005)

D Feldman, *Civil Liberties and Human Rights in England and Wales* (Oxford, Oxford University Press, 2nd ed., 2002)

J S Mill, *On Liberty and Other Essays* (Oxford, Oxford University Press, 1991)

F Schauer, *Free Speech: A Philosophical Enquiry* (Cambridge, Cambridge University Press, 1982)

G Williams, *Human Rights Under the Australian Constitution* (Melbourne, Oxford University Press, 1999).

Habermas and the Public Sphere

C Barnett, *Culture and Democracy: Media, Space and Representation* (Edinburgh, Edinburgh University Press, 2003)

C Calhoun (ed.), *Habermas and the Public Sphere* (Cambridge, Massachusetts, MIT Press, 1992)

P Dahlgren, *Television and the Public Sphere* (London, Sage Publications, 1995)

P Dahlgren & C Sparks (eds), *Communications and Citizenship: Journalism and the Public Sphere in the New Media Age* (London, Routledge, 1991)

N Garnham, *Capitalism and Communication: Global Culture and the Economics of Information* (London, Sage Publications, 1990)

N Garnham, *Emancipation, the Media and Modernity: Arguments about the Media and Social Theory* (Oxford, Oxford University Press, 2000)

J Habermas, *Between Facts and Norms* (Cambridge, Polity Press, 1996)

J Habermas, *The Structural Transformation of the Public Sphere* (Cambridge, Polity Press, 1989)

M E Price, *Television, the Public Sphere, and National Identity* (Oxford, Clarendon Press, 1995)

S Venturelli, *Liberalizing the European Media: Politics, Regulation, and the Public Sphere* (Oxford, Clarendon Press, 1998)

D Ward, *The European Union Democratic Deficit and the Public Sphere: An Evaluation of EU Media Policy* (Amsterdam, IOS Press, 2004)

Ownership and Control

T Congdon, A Graham, D Green & B Robinson, *The Cross Media Revolution: Ownership and Control* (London, John Libbey, 1995)

T Dwyer, D Wilding, H Wilson & S Curtis, *Content, Consolidation and Clout: How will Regional Australia be Affected by Media Ownership Changes?* (Melbourne, Communications Law Centre, 2006)

G Doyle, *Media Ownership* (London, Sage, 2002)

Competition Policy and Regulation

L Garzaniti, *Telecommunications, Broadcasting and the Internet: EU Competition Law and Regulation* (London, Sweet & Maxwell, 2nd ed., 2003)

D Geradin (ed.), *Remedies in Network Industries: EC Competition Law vs Sector-specific Regulation* (Antwerp-Oxford, Intersentia, 2004)

I Nitsche, *Broadcasting in the European Union: The Role of Public Interest in Competition Analysis* (The Hague, TMC Asser Press, 2001)

P Nihoul & P Rodford, *EU Electronic Communications Law: Competition and Regulation in the European Telecommunications Market* (Oxford, Oxford University Press, 2004)

Organisation for Economic Co-operation and Development, *Competition Policy and a Changing Broadcast Industry* (Paris, OECD, 1993)

T Prosser, *The Limits of Competition Law: Markets and Public Services* (Oxford, Oxford University Press, 2005)

Media Economics

Bureau of Transport and Communications Economics, *Economic Aspects of Broadcasting Regulation*, Report 71 (Canberra, Bureau of Transport and Communications Economics, 1991)

R Collins, N Garnharm, G Locksley, *The Economics of Television: The UK Case* (London, Sage Publications, 1988)

G Doyle, *Understanding Media Economics* (London, Sage, 2002)

R Towse (ed.), *A Handbook of Cultural Economics* (Cheltenham, Edward Elgar, 2003)

Regulation

R Baldwin, *Rules and Government* (Oxford, Clarendon Press, 1995)

R Baldwin & M Cave, *Understanding Regulation: Theory, Strategy, and Practice* (Oxford, Oxford University Press, 1999)

R Baldwin, C Scott & C Hood (eds), *A Reader on Regulation* (Oxford, Oxford University Press, 1998)

M Feintuck, *'The Public Interest' in Regulation* (Oxford, Oxford University Press, 2004)

A Ogus, *Regulation: Legal Form and Economic Theory* (Oxford, Clarendon Press, 1994)

C Parker, C Scott, N Lacey & J Braithwaite (eds), *Regulating Law* (Oxford, Oxford University Press, 2004)

INDEX

342 *Index*